W9-BYO-393

FRONTLINE SOUTHERN AFRICA

FRONTLINE

SOUTHERN

AFRICA

Destructive

Engagement

Edited by
Phyllis Johnson and David Martin

Four Walls Eight Windows
New York

Copyright © 1988 by Phyllis Johnson and David Martin.
Illustrations copyright © 1988 by Kim Berman.
Rights to individual chapters reserved by their respective authors.

All Rights Reserved.

First printing November, 1988.

No part of this book may be reproduced, stored in a retrieval system, or transmitted in any form, by any means, including mechanical, electric, photocopying, recording, or otherwise, without the prior written permission of the publisher.

Library of Congress Cataloging-in-Publication Data

Frontline Southern Africa.

   Bibliography: p.
   Includes index.
   1. Africa, Southern—Military relations—South Africa. 2. South Africa—Military relations—Africa, Southern. 3. Apartheid—South Africa. I. Johnson, Phyllis. II. Martin, David, 1956-
DT747.S6F76   1988   322'.5'0968   57-37530
ISBN 0-941423-08-5

Four Walls Eight Windows
P.O. Box 548
Village Station
New York, N.Y. 10014

Designed by Hannah Lerner.
Printed in the U.S.A.

For Fernando

May all possible pressures
be exerted
to end apartheid
so that his children
and the others of the region
can grow in peace

CONTENTS

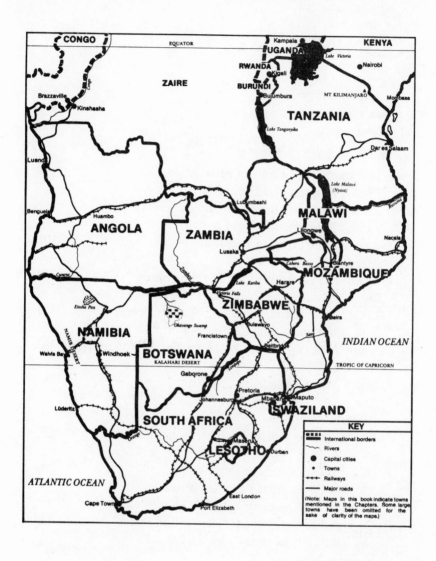

FOREWORD

When is war not a war? Apparently when it is waged by the stronger against the weaker as a 'pre-emptive strike.' When is terrorism not terrorism? Apparently when it is committed by a more powerful government against those at home and abroad who are weaker than itself and whom it regards as a potential threat or even as insufficiently supportive of its own objectives.

Those are the only conclusions one can draw in the light of the current widespread condemnation of aggression and terrorism, side by side with the ability of certain nations to attack others with impunity, and to organise murder, kidnapping and massive destruction with the support of some permanent members of the United Nations Security Council. South Africa is such a country.

The people of South Africa have been fighting against racial oppression for most of this century. Their petitions, peaceful processions and demonstrations, and even their campaigns of civil disobedience, have been met with ever increasing repression and violence. But their humanity will not be denied. While the organized nationalist movements have in recent years succeeded—at tremendous human cost to themselves—in carrying out some sabotage of military targets, the mass of the people are spontaneously rejecting the laws and instruments of apartheid by the sheer force of their will and their numbers. The daily death toll does not stop them. Nor does the torture from which they suffer when detained or imprisoned. They are challenging the guns of apartheid with their own blood and with stones picked up from the streets.

At the same time, the people of Namibia are also fighting for freedom from domination by the apartheid government of South Africa. In legal terms they at least have won the whole world to their side. But their nation continues to be occupied illegally, and the most powerful states of the world prevent any serious external action from being taken against the occupier—or even side with the oppressor. So the Namibian people's freedom struggle, and the armed struggle, continue under the leadership of SWAPO.

The intensification of the freedom struggle within South Africa during recent years does owe something to the advance of African liberation to the borders of that country. For Mozambique, Angola and Zimbabwe had to win political freedom by an armed struggle against racist administrations; their success renewed the hope and self-confidence of the South African people. Tied to South Africa by inherited economic and communication links as these countries were—and are—they are a beacon of freedom clearly visible from the towns of the apartheid state, and even from the Bantustans to which millions of South Africans have been banished.

It is that beacon of freedom which the apartheid state seeks to put out by its direct aggression, or by organizing, arming and unleashing dissidents and mercenaries, and by using its undoubted strength to exert economic pressures on its neighbours. Its objective in all cases is so to destabilise those young nations that their leaders are forced to become puppets of the South African government, and to act on its behalf in the suppression of the African liberation movement. And in the process of trying to achieve this, South Africa is happy if it is able to cause such misery and suffering among the people of the free states that their governments get a reputation of incompetence and incapacity which dims the clear light of freedom shining across their borders.

All the neighboring states—and some further away—have fallen victim to this aggressive South African policy. Botswana, Lesotho and Swaziland have not been exempted because of their geographically determined inability to do more than speak against apartheid and give a first haven for refugees from South Africa. Zambia has not been left alone on the grounds that it does not have a border with the apartheid state. Zimbabwe, which has from the beginning of its independence declared its inability to allow the South African liberation movements to operate from its territory, has still been subjected to South African sabotage of its economic and military facilities and to systematic murder campaigns against its citizens—both white and black. Mozambique and Angola, however, have been the foci of very special and sustained attack. They have been subjected to all the miseries of continuing aggressive war since the moment of their birth as independent states—or in the case of Angola, before that. Their declared philosophy of Marxism-Leninism, and their border on the Atlantic or Indian Ocean, caused them to be of special interest both to South Africa itself and to those who believe they have a right to control those oceans.

This book, *Frontline Southern Africa*, indicates something of the nature and the meaning of the aggression to which the victim states have been subjected. It provides in each case what I believe to be incontrovertible evidence of South African responsibility for the forms of this attack. And thirdly, it shows the involvement of the United States of America, both in the aggression against Angola, and in support of what President Reagan once described as 'our ally,' South Africa.

The cost to the Front Line States has been immense. In financial terms, one estimate is 30 billion US dollars worth of damage done to the infrastructure and the economies of SADCC members. All are poor countries whose resources are in any case inadequate to provide the minimum of essential services to their people and to invest in future development.

Further, this estimate takes no account of the peoples of the border states. The total number killed is not known; the larger number who have been wounded in South African-inspired attacks is uncounted—especially as many of these have no ready access to medical facilities despite the efforts of their governments. The people who have lost their homes, who have been terrorised against working in their fields, who have been bereaved or left to care for disabled family members, whose food has been destroyed—all this suffering is uncounted. And when widespread drought was added to the problems of the Mozambique government, the food convoys were attacked so that relief could not get through although sufficient food had been mobilized. Very many thousands of people died as a result.

The victim countries have received no compensation or special assistance in the light of these attacks. They have been left to carry the burden virtually unassisted. Sometimes even verbal support is denied them, as the United States of America and some European powers respond to a direct South African attack by mealy-mouthed condemnation of violence 'on both sides.' And when the victims of aggression seek military assistance from the only countries which will supply it—Cuba and the USSR and its allies—they are accused of falling into the 'Soviet sphere of influence.'

Despite all this, the beacon of freedom is kept alight in southern Africa. The struggle goes on. The condemnation of apartheid continues to be expressed with commitment by the free nations bordering South Africa even as they bury their dead from the latest raid.

Of course there have been set-backs in the struggle. The Nkomati Accord was forced on the government of Mozambique by the overwhelming pressure of innumerable murderous attacks from South African forces and the South African surrogates, combined with 'mediation' and 'assurances' from American and British diplomats and conditional promises from the South Africans. So the ceremony took place, the Mozambicans breathed a sigh of relief in the expectation of an end to the attacks on them, and P. W. Botha went off on a tour of Europe as 'a reasonable man.'

But the South African support for MNR continued unabated. The attacks on the people of Mozambique intensified and spread more widely; so did the attacks on SADCC communications facilities within Mozambique. And those Western countries which urged the need for peace on Mozambique—which had never wanted war—have done nothing and said nothing. A car bomb outside civilian residences in Maputo, where South Africa's responsibility is undisputable, is met by silence from the same powers which call upon the Third World to condemn terrorism.

Mozambique is non-aligned, poor, weak, and after 24 years of war is held together only by the commitment and will-power of its government and people; for the West, South Africa is 'our ally.' So terrorism stops being terrorism; aggression stops being aggression; solemn and signed commitments undertaken by the strong and 'mediated' by the stronger, stop being international commitments.

Lesotho, too, can with impunity be economically strangled to death by South Africa until its defiant prime minister is overthrown and a new military government accedes to South Africa's political demands. The Western world does nothing and says nothing. Even after that, a South African refugee, qualified in Lesotho and working in the legal system of Lesotho, is subjected to 15 minutes armed attack on his house and property (which he and his wife fortunately survived). Nothing will be said by the great campaigners against terrorism; the government from which the attacks emanate will not even be subjected to an orchestrated media campaign of abuse.

And on Swaziland what can be said? At a time of great national trauma arising from the death of King Sobhuza it was in the way of South African ambitions. But there are still people, including some in prominent positions, who struggle to make a reality of Swaziland's independence.

Yet despite all this suffering, and some set-backs, the struggle against apartheid continues. For it is pre-eminently an internal struggle, supported morally, politically and diplomatically by South Africa's neighbours to the utmost of their capacity—severally and jointly. But these countries are incapable of supporting a military attack against their southern neighbour even if they wished to do so—as South Africa knows.

The greatest upsurge of internal opposition to apartheid began *after* Nkomati. It finds expression in all the major urban areas of South Africa and even in the Bantustans; incidents of sabotage take place as far south as Cape Town. Yet there are no guerrilla invasions across the borders of South Africa. The few freedom fighters who do return home sneak across the long borders despite all the attempts of the South African guards to patrol thousands of miles of bush land: and if the highly equipped South Africans cannot stop these valiant people how could their poorer and weaker neighbours be expected to do so? Those naturally concentrate such limited border defence power as they possess on trying to stop incursions from South Africa—and even on that the record shows little success.

The real offence of Angola, Botswana, Lesotho, Mozambique, Swaziland, Zambia and Zimbabwe—and any other countries within reach of South African power—is their existence as proudly independent African states. As such they have the temerity to back up the demand of the Organisation of African Unity for an end to apartheid. They dare to demand world action against the cancer of apartheid and to succor those who flee from its persecutions. Through SADCC they try to loosen the economic and communications bonds which tie them to South Africa, and to increase their self-reliance through regional co-operation.

In addition, these countries proclaim that, being no longer colonies of Western Bloc nations, they intend to follow a policy of non-alignment. In so doing they compound the offence of their existence. For the West is accustomed to regarding Africa as its 'sphere of influence,' and regards with suspicion any African country which looks at the world and determines its policies without the prism of Western-slanted spectacles.

An American diplomat once urged upon me the threat to African independence constituted by Cuban troops in Angola. When I asked why Cuban troops were more of a danger to Africa's freedom than French troops elsewhere in the continent, he replied, "France is a Western country and we are the leaders of the Western world." South Africa too is regarded as part of the "Western world."

So genuine non-alignment (in the case of Angola even the prospect of it), and especially the acceptance of help against South African attacks, condemns South Africa's external victims to being just that—victims. And on occasion, particularly in the case of Angola, there is irrefutable evidence—some of it quoted in this book—of active US involvement in the attacks on independent African nations. Instead of being restrained by those whom they regard as their friends and who themselves claim to be upholders of the integrity of nations, the South African aggressors are encouraged, or even joined in making the attacks.

In the light of so much hypocrisy, so much duplicity, and so much indifference to the sufferings of southern Africa, why write and publish this book?

There are those who are ignorant because they are wilfully blind, and those who are ignorant because they have lacked an opportunity to know. It surely is not possible that the administration of the United States of America, and the governments of major European powers, do not know the facts and the effects of the economic and military attacks against the free states which share a border with South Africa or Namibia. Apart from everything else, the Great Powers have satellites covering the whole of southern Africa. In some instances our infrastructure is so poor that it is likely that these external powers know about the event and the problem before the home government. Nor is it possible for the Superpowers to be unaware that South Africa is the instigator, the organizer, the financier and supplier for virtually all the attacks which purport to be made by rebels—apart, that is, from the ones initiated by South Africa directly or by the US itself. The major Western powers are there, in South Africa, and they have a privileged position in that racist state.

Yet perhaps we do an injustice to presidents and prime ministers; for they cannot know everything which is done, or not done, in their names. Perhaps the evidence does need to be set out so that those who know the real sincerity of these leaders' opposition to terrorism and to aggression can draw to their attention what is happening in southern Africa? If so, this book should help.

But in any case it is quite certain that millions of people, including many in leading or responsible positions in democratic Western countries, are unaware of what has been happening—and what is still happening—in southern Africa. Some of them may genuinely not know that the apartheid regime they abhor is threatening the very existence of the states whose independence they welcomed so short a time ago. Some may not realize that the identification of South Africa with anticommunism is the most powerful propaganda for communism which exists in southern Africa. They may not understand the pressures in favor of an anti-Western alignment which are being exerted on the non-aligned states by the attacks from the West's friend and ally, albeit one which is acknowledged to have an unpleasant racist domestic philosophy. And other genuine people may have come to believe that the South African president's talk of 'reform' really means a change of heart on the part of apartheid's leaders.

For such people this book is intended. The evidence is collected and summarized; the major themes are extensively documented. The reality behind the "nationalist" and "democratic" claims of Unita and MNR is made clear. So are the facts about the sequence of events in Angola which has led to Cuban troops serving in that African country for more than 12 years. And so on. The economic aspects of the struggle are not forgotten, and the argument about sanctions is re-examined.

This book will be equally valuable and is equally intended for all those who, in numerous official and unofficial fora, have tried for years to draw attention to the dangers to world peace which exist in southern Africa. Its approach is openly and unapologetically political; it states the case for those independent nations and people under attack because of their opposition to apartheid. But the book is factual; it can therefore be an instrument for freedom. For Knowledge is Power; in particular it can be power for those who fight for justice, for human dignity and for human equality.

I congratulate all those who have contributed to this book. But most of all I offer, with great humility, my congratulations and my good wishes to all the people and governments of the victim states. They have kept the beacon of freedom alight by their endurance, their courage, and their absolute commitment to Africa's liberation. I salute them.

JULIUS K. NYERERE

ACKNOWLEDGMENTS

Although comparatively little space in the international media has been devoted to accurate information on South Africa's war against its neighbors, there is a growing awareness of the war's brutality and its economic and social impact on the people of the region. It is necessary to acknowledge everyone who has worked to expose these conditions. But, tragically, some people visiting the region for the first time still say, "I didn't know." This book is an attempt to redress this lack of international awareness.

We wish to thank Mwalimu Nyerere for the eloquent Foreword to this book which brings regional terrorism into focus and places it within its international context.

During the course of this study, many people have given much time to enhance our understanding. We hope they will regard their time as well spent. Our coauthors have shared their knowledge, their commitment, and their patience; and we believe that together we have contributed in some small way to a greater understanding of the circumstance of southern Africa.

We are grateful to Diana Cammack for expertly coordinating our research and documentation, to Masimba Tafirenyika and Joanne Ambridge for bringing order to our mounting archive, to Joan Thompson for typing and organizing, and to Kephas Kuipa for rearranging his workload to accommodate ours.

Finally, this book would not exist without the material support of the Swedish International Development Agency (SIDA) and the moral support of two Swedish friends, Dag Ehrenpreis and Anders Bjurner, whose determination and faith made the study possible.

THE EDITORS

INTRODUCTION

South Africa, at war with its own people, at the same time is waging an undeclared war against its neighbors—the independent black-ruled states which have the geographical misfortune to share its borders. This war is part of South Africa's "total strategy" policy which involves the mobilization of all forces—political, economic, diplomatic, and military—in defense of apartheid. The regional objective is to create and maintain a dependence that will be economically lucrative and politically submissive—and will serve as a bulwark against the imposition of international sanctions.

The combination of tactics used against neighboring countries has varied from state to state depending on its political, economic, and military vulnerabilities. Some countries have been subjected to direct attacks, or even occupation, by the South African Defence Force (SADF). Surrogates are trained and armed by the SADF to enter some countries to murder, maim, rape, and destroy on its behalf. These military tactics mask economic and political goals, but the primary targets are invariably economic. At the heart of the "total strategy" policy is the regional system of transportation and communications which has been regularly sabotaged to ensure that trade flows through South Africa.

Pretoria has threatened retaliatory sanctions against the independent states of the region in the event that international sanctions are imposed against South Africa. But what has emerged clearly from our study is that Pretoria is already imposing sanctions against the other states in southern Africa.

Sanctions are defined as "economic or military action to coerce a state to conform." The immediate objective of sanctions is to restrict or prevent access and increase costs. There is ample evidence that South Africa has already adopted both economic and military means to coerce its neighbors, restricting their access to trade routes and vastly increasing their transportation costs.

The cost to neighboring countries of South Africa's destabilization and sanctions against them is estimated at US $30 billion since 1980.[1] Given other circumstances, this money would have been used for development.

The death toll from South Africa's regional wars is approaching one million, either caused directly by the war or war related through the destruction of rural medical clinics and emergency food supplies. Most of the dead are children,[2] a disaster United Nations Children's Fund (Unicef) representatives describe as a "holocaust."[3]

The South African authorities have effectively censored international access to information about the escalating violence within the country, thereby reducing the horror of the international community and, to some extent, the pressure to end apartheid. They cannot directly stifle news of the devastation they have wrought elsewhere in the region, but some elements in the media and certain international organizations ignore South Africa's role, preferring to present it as an internal matter, what the International Committee of the Red Cross delicately calls "civil strife."

This attitude prevails among government officials in some Western countries despite the hard historical evidence of South Africa's deliberate creation of a force of destruction in

Mozambique and Pretoria's admission of its involvement prior to 1984.[4] Since 1984 there has been documentary and other evidence of its orders to surrogates to destroy communications routes and other economic targets in Mozambique.[5] The same attitude applies to acts of sabotage, invasion, and destruction in Angola, Botswana, Lesotho, Swaziland, Zambia, and Zimbabwe.

South Africa further escalated its wars against neighboring states in 1987; and the patterns that emerged have serious and long-term consequences for the region. This aggression against its neighbors proves beyond doubt that South Africa is a "threat to international peace and security," the prerequisite for sanctions in the terminology of the United Nations (UN). Yet this action remains elusive.

Pretoria's regional policy until the middle 1970s concerned itself with attempts to thwart activities by liberation movements which were growing in strength in neighboring countries, as well as at home. South Africa was shielded in this by a ring of buffer states that included the Portuguese colonies of Mozambique and Angola, as well as the British rebel colony of Southern Rhodesia, and by its own occupation of Namibia. Regional policy was directed toward reinforcing this barrier of states through various economic, political, and military alliances.

After the coup d'état in Portugal in 1974, the face of southern Africa altered dramatically, with the independence of Mozambique and Angola the following year, and of Zimbabwe in 1980. This was not achieved without considerable bloodshed; and many of the defeated colonizers retreated into apartheid's laager.

During these liberation wars, the Portuguese and the Rhodesians created or co-opted groups to use as surrogates against the nationalist parties. In Angola, there were three such groups, of which one remains relevant today: the National Union for the

Total Independence of Angola (Unita) led by Jonas Savimbi. Letters and documents that have been published elsewhere reveal that when Unita was supposedly fighting against Portuguese colonialism, it was in reality an adjunct of the Portuguese armed forces.[6]

During the course of this study, the editors visited Portugal on three occasions to interview the commanders of the Portuguese army who were in Angola in the early 1970s. None of them could be described as radicals seeking to belittle Unita. Yet, they have confirmed that the documents are authentic. They say that there was a "gentleman's agreement" to provide ammunition, medical and other assistance to Unita, a movement that purported to be anti-Portuguese when presenting itself to international forums. One of Unita's main tactics, which it uses to this day, was the disruption of the Benguela Railway, a main artery not only for the Angolan interior but for trade from Zambia and Zaire.

On the other side of the continent, the Mozambique National Resistance (MNR or Renamo) is fighting against the Mozambican government and disrupting the main trade routes to the sea for the landlocked African hinterland. The MNR was created by the Rhodesian Central Intelligence Organization (CIO) in Rhodesia in 1976. The authors have spent many hours interviewing the men who trained, armed, administered, and paid the MNR on behalf of Rhodesia and then handed these forces over to South Africa in 1980.

After the fall of the Portuguese colonial empire and then Rhodesia, both the MNR and Unita were inherited by South Africa. They are now used as proxies, not only in the "destabilization" of the region but also in the sanctions that South Africa is imposing on its neighbors.

The collapse of Portuguese colonialism gave rise to a hasty reformulation of South Africa's regional strategy. Military capacity was expanded, while then Prime Minister B. J. Vorster launched his diplomatic detente initiative, vaguely defined as a "constellation" of independent states presenting a united front against common enemies. This was coupled with minor internal changes such as the removal of some forms of "petty apartheid." However, the detente initiative began to crumble with the invasion of Angola in 1975 and the eventual expulsion of South African forces by Angolan and Cuban troops in March 1976. Any impetus to maintain dialogue was crushed by the brutal repression of the Soweto uprising a few months later.

By the end of 1976, South Africa's regional policy had collapsed, and the regime faced a growing internal crisis. Top military strategists, including the defense minister, P. W. Botha, began to flesh out the "total strategy" which they had proposed as early as 1973. This was laid out in the 1977 Defence White Paper which identified the need to "maintain a solid military balance relative to neighbouring states," while advocating economic and other "action in relation to transport services, distribution and telecommunications," with the purpose of promoting "political and economic collaboration" in the region.

After P. W. Botha became prime minister in 1978, he adopted "total strategy" as the official policy.[7] He reorganized the security structures, reflecting a desire for long-term planning to replace the kind of ad hoc decision making that had caused the embarrassing withdrawal from Angola in 1976, and a reaction to the kind of power wielded by individuals in the Vorster administration. Botha also resurrected the proposal for a "constellation of southern African states" dominated by South Africa. Rhodesia, commanding access to the regional hinterland, was seen as a vital component if a malleable government could be put in power when it became Zimbabwe.

Pretoria's hopes for implementation of this plan were shattered by two related events in the space of 27 days in early 1980. The first was the 4 March announcement of the results of the Zimbabwean independence election in which Robert Mugabe's party won an outright majority. The second occurred on 1 April when leaders from nine countries in the region—including Malawi but excluding South Africa—formed the Southern African Development Coordination Conference (SADCC) with the stated aim of reducing the region's dependence on the apartheid regime.

Central to SADCC's creation was the development of the regional transportation system to reduce dependence on South Africa, a new option for the contiguous states that Pretoria set out to destroy. The savagery of the attacks unleashed on Mozambique, Zimbabwe, Botswana, and Lesotho, and the escalation of the war in Angola and Namibia using military, economic and political weapons are documented in the first half of this book.

South Africa has sought to divert attention from the root cause of the growing conflagration within its borders by presenting it as a "total onslaught" organized outside the country by the Soviet Union and by representing itself as the last line of defense in protecting Western interests in the region. This argument, used previously by Rhodesia and Portugal in defense of the indefensible, has been appropriated by Pretoria to justify violation of neighboring territories as "hot pursuit" against "terrorists" of the African National Congress (ANC).

This representation found favor in Washington after Ronald Reagan took office in 1981. The Reagan administration's inability to distinguish between its hostility toward the Soviet Union and the real issue in southern Africa firmly allied it with apartheid and admirably suited Pretoria's intentions.

Historically, southern Africa is a British sphere of influence, not an American or Soviet one. Most of South Africa's neighbors are members of the Commonwealth, an informal grouping of former British colonies, and have good relations, military and otherwise, with Britain. The "red" peril is a red herring. But created in whose interests?

The hypocrisy of the US position in condemning apartheid while supporting South Africa's regional terrorism is most evident in the US military support of South Africa's surrogates bent on overthrowing the Angolan government. In Washington, it is convenient to ignore the well-documented fact that South Africa invaded Angola in 1975 from Namibia, which it occupies illegally. In contrast, the Cuban presence in Angola—which was a response to the South African invasion at the request of the sovereign government—is legal in international law. Angola, a State Department official candidly admitted, offered Washington an opportunity to give the Soviets a "bloody nose." To this end, the United States actively encourages, or certainly does not discourage, South African aggression and has resumed arming its African "contras" to try to overthrow the Angolan government. US policy allies Washington firmly with apartheid, a system it publicly opposes.

The US diplomatic response during the massive destruction of the region has been a policy called "constructive engagement" which has sought, through an unending shuttle by State Department negotiators, to give the appearance of positive motion where there was none, and, in reality, while gaining time.

The US engagement in southern Africa has been anything but "constructive": its "linkage" policy offers South Africa excuses for delaying Namibia's independence; it is now directly involved in trying to overthrow the Angolan government; its "mediation" in Mozambique did not prevent the escalation of the war; and it has introduced the specter of superpower conflict and nuclear war into a region that craves nothing more than peace and development. The US administration backed a World Bank loan to South Africa; yet it gives no bilateral aid to Mozambique and has suspended aid to Zimbabwe.

Analysis of South Africa's military and nuclear power, the state of its economy and that of the region, and the role of the

Reagan administration's "destructive engagement," make up the second half of this study.

As the protective colonial barrier around South Africa's borders was collapsing from 1974 through 1980, a new set of Afrikaner administrators with military experience was taking power in Pretoria. Using the new array of circumstances that have appeared since 1980, they have begun to construct a different kind of laager which has grown out of the dynamics of conflict within different sectors of their administration. This new laager is based, like the old one, on regional economic cooperation, mutual security, and a resistance to external pressure, but it uses military force beyond its borders to achieve political and economic objectives.

Since that time, different sectors of the leadership have drawn conflicting conclusions from their experiences of international and regional contacts. Diplomats involved in negotiations in Europe, the United States, and closer to home have learned that South Africa cannot rely totally on Western governments for support—and that delays can be used to build up economic and military strength to dominate the region. They have a better understanding of economic pressures used by and against South Africa, and more knowledge about their immediate neighbors. Military leaders have learned from their regional wars and acts of sabotage that although South Africa is the military power in the region, the enemy hits back, and financial and human losses may be heavier than expected.

There is also a hardline security sector which, reinforced by its experience in Namibia, still believes that suppression of black opposition remains the most effective tactic on South Africa's borders, as well as at home, and that preparation must be made for a conventional military attack from the north.

South African policy in the region is an amalgam derived from these points of view. Although still evolving, it is based on the belief that although in the long run economic control is cheaper and more effective than military domination, the latter must be used to achieve the former. In 1985, the then SADF chief General Constand Viljoen predicted that this dependence on the efficacy of the security forces would last for the "next few years, maybe even the next decade."

The weakness of this integrated approach is that any "failure"—in the Namibian war, in regional diplomacy, in the South African economy, or in coping with urban black unrest—might bring about perceptible basic divergences among the system's power brokers. "Failures," therefore, must be balanced by "successes," which are most easily achieved through high-profile cross-border attacks. Thus, in May 1986, when there was intense pressure on South Africa to concede to the initiative of the Commonwealth Eminent Persons Group, the predictable response was the attack on three Commonwealth capitals in the region.

Another pillar of South Africa's regional policy is the belief that economic and security cooperation with neighboring states will rebuild the lost colonial buffer in a neocolonial form. In addition, Pretoria wishes to destroy any belief in socialism as a development strategy for the continent and to try to show that chaos is the result of majority rule. Another major goal is to limit the role and political influence of outside powers—including the West—in the region. In Namibia, for example, Pretoria has tried with some success to minimize UN involvement and limit the US role as broker, while creating an infrastructure for long-term military and economic control.

Throughout their history, the Afrikaners have shown a strong instinct for survival. The Dutch forebears of today's Afrikaners, the Voortrekkers, were first to appreciate the geopolitical and strategic importance of Mozambique to the hinterland. On 1 July 1891, the first train to enter Mozambique steamed across the border from the northern Transvaal at Ressano Garcia heading for the Mozambican port of Maputo, then called Delagoa Bay. The Voortrekkers had been driven into the landlocked north of today's South Africa by the British. If they were to secure their independence, they needed the alternative routes to the sea. Today, the routes through Mozambique hold the same strategic importance for the independent states of the region, but this time Britain is helping to keep them open, and South Africa is trying to close them.

The last few years have reminded Pretoria of the vulnerability of its own economic dependences: internationally, on overseas financial markets for the price of gold and the exchange rate of the rand; regionally, on its neighbors for security, trade, and mutually lucrative business arrangements; internally, on the majority of its population to whom it has denied basic human rights, whom it has forced to live in appalling social conditions, and on whom it is ultimately most reliant for prosperity and security.

The reaction of most European political and financial leaders to P. W. Botha's tour in the middle of 1984, during which he sought investment and development assistance, confirmed that destabilization is bad for business and that South Africa is an embarrassing ally for capitalism because in restricting the majority of its population on the basis of color, it cannot claim to have a "free market" system. Botha did, however, on that trip secure agreement to purchase sophisticated German submarine plans despite the international arms embargo.

The Afrikaners have also had the opportunity to scrutinize the power of the United States, their closest ally. This power, which was used both to support and pressure them, is a power they would like to emulate—as a regional superpower. In late 1983, when Soviet officials summoned their South African counterparts at the UN to an unprecedented meeting to warn them that "aggression cannot be left unpunished," South Africa took it as recognition of this role as regional superpower. International acceptance of such status would prolong the survival of the apartheid system through military and economic domination, and would enhance South Africa's future ability to resist pressure, even from its allies. South Africa's view of its role as regional power broker has been further reinforced by contacts with the Soviet Union in late 1987 and early 1988.

In this period, Pretoria has become more brazen in its actions against the Frontline states and the ANC. A massive SADF exercise on the Botswana border in May 1987, described by the British publication *Jane's Defence Weekly* as the largest South African airborne exercise to date, demonstrated its ability to strike deep into the heart of neighboring states. The Iron Eagle exercise, in which 14 transport planes dropped five hundred men and 50 tons of equipment, suggested short- or long-term plans to occupy neighboring countries if necessary, coinciding as it did with the infiltration of large groups of armed men into southern Mozambique, the offensive in southern Angola, infiltrations across Zimbabwe's eastern border and, to a lesser extent, across Zambia's.

In addition to rapidly escalating the war in Angola and conducting proxy wars in Mozambique and Zimbabwe, South Africa has carried out attacks in several cities in neighboring states and initiated a campaign of political assassinations, in most cases against "soft" targets.

In early 1988, South African terror tactics against cities in the region included a blast caused by a vehicle loaded with explosives in Bulawayo, Zimbabwe's second largest city; a commando attack on a house in Gaborone, capital of Botswana; the fatal shooting of a wounded ANC member in his hospital bed in Maseru, capital of Lesotho; and a car bomb in Maputo, capital of Mozambique, that maimed the South African writer and lawyer Albie Sachs.

These strikes followed similar actions in 1987: A heli-borne commando raid into Livingstone, Zambia; a bomb in a television set that exploded in the Harare home of a senior ANC exile killing his Zimbabwean wife; a commando raid in Maputo in which a Mozambican couple were shot dead in front of their two-year-old child; a predawn rocket attack on an ANC house in Harare; the murder of a member of ANC's national executive committee, in Swaziland; and a car bomb explosion in a suburban Harare shopping center. There were fatal casualties in almost all of these attacks, and almost all of those killed were nationals of the country where the attacks occurred.

The campaign of political assassination has been stepped up inside and outside South Africa in a terror campaign extending as far away as Europe. The assassination of the ANC representative Dulcie September in France, the defused bomb at ANC offices in Belgium, and the exposure of a plot to kidnap ANC officials in Britain are part of this campaign, as is the murder of Sicelo Dlomo in a South African township, a few weeks after the teen-ager was interviewed on a CBS television program about his torture in detention at the hands of the South African police. There are many other cases that have received less publicity because the victims are less well known internationally or because South Africa's comprehensive censorship laws have suppressed them.

Conventional military strikes as far afield as Tanzania on the east African coast no longer seem implausible in an atmosphere where external attack is the response to electoral backlash at home and where growing support for a neo-Nazi party further polarizes opinion. The entire escalation of violence across southern Africa can be seen as a South African "signal" demonstrating their capacity to destroy, or at least dominate, the region.

The specter of a hostile nuclear neighbor haunts the region as South Africa improves its capability in that field. Since purchasing its first nuclear research reactor almost 30 years ago, South Africa has constructed its own fuel enrichment plant and now fits the profile of a state likely to use nuclear weapons.[8]

The Reagan administration authorized the sale of several major pieces of nuclear-related equipment with dual end uses, including a computer powerful enough to design a nuclear explosion and other testing devices. By 1981, at the latest, South Africa had all the necessary components to produce nuclear weapons and may have been stockpiling enriched uranium.

Creeping sanctions passed by the US Congress and Commonwealth countries have so far only given the South Africans a taste of what to expect and time to prepare alternatives, in Africa and elsewhere. By opposing most forms of sanctions, the British prime minister Margaret Thatcher in some ways usurped the policy of "constructive engagement," sending as ambassador to Pretoria a skilled negotiator who had played a key role in the Zimbabwe negotiations. Although the South African finance minister has admitted that sanctions hurt, and oil is costing well above market price, the international arms embargo needs tighter monitoring and adherence, particularly in the sphere of military technology.

The financial daily newspaper in Britain the *Financial Times* carried an article recently concluding that the West must get serious about arming the Frontline states. The article, titled "Constructing a Cage for South Africa," says: "While it may not be possible to browbeat President Botha into changing his domestic policies, it surely would be possible to deter his incursions into neighboring countries if he knew that they could count on Western military aid."[9]

There are not many alternatives. Despite the contacts and maneuvers of an outgoing US administration, there seems little hope for successful implementation of any new accords, given South Africa's past record. The Lusaka Accord with Angola and the Nkomati Accord with Mozambique were solemnly signed in early 1984, during another US presidential election year, but for South Africa these accords merely allowed breathing space. The Commonwealth Eminent Persons Group report confirmed that "South Africa violated both these Accords from the very outset, giving the region further proof that it could not be trusted to honour even solemn Treaty obligations."[10]

There are two spurious arguments which must finally be addressed. The first is that some elements in South Africa, particularly the military, are out of line with government policy. Given the authoritarian nature of the South African regime, such an argument is ill-informed. At another level, it may be disinformation. While the politicians may not be aware of all details of military operations, the military officers are certainly aware of the details of government policy. They sit on the highest councils of state and formulate that policy. Furthermore, as occurred in the case of Mozambique in 1985, when they were caught breaching publicly enunciated policy, they were not disciplined—they were promoted. Such promotion can only suggest that they followed official policy to the letter. Although there may be some disagreements over tactics to employ in specific situations, the policy of "total strategy"— which originated from the military—is accepted by all institutions of the regime, right down to the grassroots vigilantes operating through local committees of the regional Joint Management Centers (JMC).

The second misconception is that the sovereign governments of the contiguous states must politically accommodate South Africa's surrogates to end the wars in their countries. Although none of the contiguous states have attacked South Africa, nor do any of them pose such a threat, South Africa has attacked its neighbors, both directly and through surrogates. Thus, in recognition that Pretoria—and not its surrogates— makes both the policies and the wars, those states have talked to South Africa.

The international excuse that sanctions will harm South Africa's neighbors is rejected by all of them. The harsh reality is that destabilization and economic sanctions are already a fact of life in the region and will be as long as apartheid exists. Botswana's Vice-President Peter Mmusi has said, "The abolition of apartheid could be the greatest single contribution which could be made to the economic development of the region."

PHYLLIS JOHNSON and DAVID MARTIN
18 April 1988

FRONTLINE SOUTHERN AFRICA

1

MOZAMBIQUE
Victims
of Apartheid

In the early evening of 24 April 1974, in an office on Rua António Maria Cardoso insulated from the hubbub of Lisbon's traffic, two men sat quietly talking over glasses of vintage port. The office belonged to Major Silva Pais, head of Portugal's feared secret police, commonly known as the International Police for the Defense of the State (PIDE).

Silva Pais, his visitor later recalled, seemed depressed and distracted as if preoccupied by a major problem. The visitor's mood was exactly the opposite. In the few days he had been in Lisbon he had concluded the details of an agreement he had been trying to reach for almost five years. It was an agreement which would profoundly affect events in southern Africa well beyond the next decade.

The visitor left for Lisbon's Portela Airport to board a Portuguese Air Transport Boeing 707 bound for the Rhodesian capital, Salisbury. It was the last flight allowed to take off from Lisbon that night.

During a transit stop in the Angolan capital, Luanda, he thought it a little odd that passengers were told to remain on

1

board. The explanation for this—and for Silva Pais's preoccupation—came on arrival at Salisbury airport: there had been a military *coup d'état* in Lisbon during the night, and the civilian dictatorship of Marcello Caetano had been overthrown.

The following day a squad of Portuguese marines, led by Lieutenant Commander Martins Cavalheiro, broke into Silva Pais's office. The partially empty port bottle and two glasses on the ornate central table were of no significance to them. But they were to an organization several thousand miles away. On 4 May a photograph of the room showing the bottle and glasses appeared in the Portuguese magazine *O Seculo Illustrado*.[1]

The visitor's deputy had the picture rephotographed from the magazine and drew a bold arrow pointing to one of the glasses, adding a new caption in English: "'X' Marks Exhibit 'A'—Port glasses with K. F.'s fingerprints!"

The visitor, K. F., was Ken Flower, the director general of Rhodesia's Central Intelligence Organization (CIO).[2]

The deal Flower had put together had its origins in the colonial war that Portugal had been fighting since 1964 in Mozambique on Rhodesia's eastern border. Flower was concerned about the ability of the largely conscript Portuguese army to contain the guerrillas of the Mozambique Liberation Front (Frelimo), and he was convinced that it was necessary to operate a clandestine intelligence movement inside Mozambique to monitor infiltration by Zimbabwean nationalist guerrillas.[3]

In September 1971, and again in August 1972, Flower had travelled to Lisbon to meet Caetano, under instructions from his own prime minister, Ian Smith, to discuss "co-operation in dissident sponsorship. We offered to develop an internal resistance movement in Mozambique." In late April 1974, he travelled to Lisbon to finalize the logistical details with Silva Pais and the Portuguese military commanders.

Flower's initial reaction to the *coup d'état* in Lisbon, and the ensuing confusion, was that his plan would not get off the

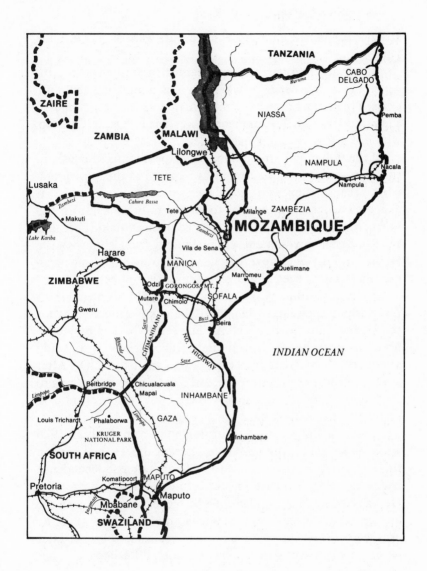

ground. But, on the contrary, these events were to play into his hands.

On 2 June, the first group of disgruntled Portuguese intelligence and military men, black and white, numbering about 40, crossed the border from Mozambique into Rhodesia and offered their services. Their commander was Major Oscar Cardoso, who had also served in Angola.

Of the individuals and groups who crossed into Rhodesia in that period, the Cardoso group was regarded as the most promising because they were largely ex-servicemen with combat experience. They were taken to an old military camp in the northern part of Rhodesia. "We located them at Makuti because the Rhodesian government was pretending friendship with the Frelimo [transitional] government and we wanted Frelimo opponents well out of the public eye," a senior CIO officer said later.[4]

However, within a year Cardoso and most of his men left for Zaire where they joined Holden Roberto's National Front for the Liberation of Angola (FNLA). The FNLA, backed by plentiful funds from the US Central Intelligence Agency (CIA), could afford to pay mercenaries better wages than the CIO.[5] After several of these early failures, the CIO decided to stop trying to use white Portuguese opponents of Frelimo and concentrate on recruiting black Africans.

Former CIO officers say a turning point came in June 1976 with the arrival of André Matade Matsangaiza. He had been in the Frelimo forces from 1972 to 1974 and after independence had worked in the quartermaster's stores at Dondo, near Beira. He was convicted of the theft of a Mercedes car and sent to the Sacuze "reeducation center" in Sofala province.[6] From there he escaped to Rhodesia to become the first leader of what later became known as the Mozambique National Resistance (MNR or Renamo).[7]

After Matsangaiza's arrival, the CIO decided to establish a permanent training camp. The site chosen was a tobacco farm just outside the small farming settlement of Odzi in eastern

Rhodesia near the city of Umtali (now Mutare). The trainees came under the control of the CIO operations desk headed by Eric "Ricky" May and were looked after by a senior instructor, three other instructors and a paymaster-administrator.[8] They equipped their groups of saboteurs with captured weapons and supplied all basic requirements, such as food. Ordinary recruits were paid $20 per month. Matsangaiza received $75 per month and his deputy, Afonso Dhlakama, who had served in the Portuguese colonial army, was paid $65. "I always consulted André on everything," the senior instructor said, "and if I didn't agree with him I'd say, 'No, we don't do that.'"

Senior officers involved in early training subsequently described their strategy in this period: "To start off with, it was sabotage, to disrupt the population and disrupt the economy ... The objectives were essentially to perpetuate or create instability in areas of Mozambique ... The MNR gave a cover for Rhodesian operations and, from initial intelligence-gathering, moved on to getting recruits and then on to the offensive, disrupting road and rail links."

Such a cover was provided for an attack on the Beira oil storage tanks in March 1979, when a Rhodesian sabotage unit was landed from a South African submarine. This was claimed as an MNR operation, but Flower and the CIO instructors confirm it was carried out by regular Rhodesian forces. This attack cost Mozambique $2 million. A simultaneous joint Rhodesian–South African attempt to blow up the Maputo refinery failed because dinghies taking the sabotage unit ashore were swamped in rough seas and the mission had to be aborted.[9]

It is noteworthy that they can recall only one major incident in that period involving the MNR: the sabotage of a generator supplying electricity to Beira, an operation commanded by Rhodesian Special Air Service (SAS) men which did not halt Beira's supply.

Evo Fernandes, a Portuguese national who became the voice of the MNR in Europe and then, briefly, its secretary-general before his murder in Lisbon in early 1988, admitted that in Matsangaiza the Rhodesians at last had a tool they could use: "He went back and recruited his family. But mostly the Rhodesians wanted information. It was an organization without a name. It was a fifth column among Rhodesian forces."[10]

Although Fernandes admitted that the MNR was no more than a Rhodesian fifth column, he claimed that six people who met at the suburban Salisbury home of a former PIDE agent, Orlando Cristina, on 1 May 1977 were responsible for choosing the name. He said the six were Cristina, Matsangaiza, Dhlakama, Armando Khembo dos Santos, Leo Milas and himself. The CIO instructors insist that Matsangaiza and Dhlakama could not have been present without their knowledge, but concede the possibility that the other four attended a meeting where the name MNR was proposed.

The backgrounds of these four provide some insight into those who came together in the MNR, if not in the CIO phase, then certainly after March 1980. Cristina, like Fernandes, had worked for Jorge Jardim, who had extensive business interests in Mozambique, where he was Malawi's consul general in Beira, and who was a godson of the Portuguese fascist dictator António Salazar. After the Portuguese *coup d'état*, Cristina moved to Malawi and then to Rhodesia, where he worked behind the scenes on the CIO-MNR radio station, Voz da Africa Livre, which first broadcast on 5 July 1976 to beam propaganda into Mozambique.

Fernandes, of Goan parentage and a lawyer by training, had worked for the Portuguese judicial police in Beira during the colonial era. He fled to Portugal on 23 September 1976 and briefly joined the Mozambique United Front (Fumo) led by Domingos Arouca, a Mozambican lawyer who had been detained in the Portuguese colonial period. "In the beginning our idea was to have a political wing led by Arouca and a military wing led by André," Fernandes said. "But we soon realized that it was not possible to work with Arouca."

Arouca tells the story differently. Cristina and Fernandes, he said, tried to use his name, well known in Mozambique, to gain political respectability. "I declined . . . They only wanted me to be a puppet outside to gain international acceptance. I decided not to be used."[11]

Armando Khembo dos Santos is the least known of the group. Briefly a member of Frelimo around the time of its formation in 1962, he disappeared for a lengthy period before resurfacing in Fumo. Fernandes claimed dos Santos is the MNR representative for Africa based in the Kenyan capital, Nairobi.

The final member of the group is the most intriguing. Variously known as Leo Clinton Aldridge, Jr., Leo-Aldridge Milas and Leo Milas, he had been elected the Frelimo secretary for information in 1962. When Frelimo's first leader, Eduardo Mondlane, was away for some months, Milas was effectively head of the movement. He expelled a number of senior officials and became secretary for defense and security. Milas excused the fact that he spoke no Mozambican language and poor Portuguese by saying he had left the country as a child and had been educated in the United States.

When Mondlane was told that Milas was not a Mozambican at all but a black American, he went to the United States to investigate personally, where he met Milas's parents. He learned that the name Milas was using in Frelimo was an amalgam of his father's name, Leo Clinton Aldridge, Sr., and his mother's maiden name, Catherine Bell Miles; and that Milas had been born in Pittsburg, a small town in northeast Texas. The Frelimo central committee expelled Milas on 25 August 1964.[12]

The Rhodesian MNR suffered two serious blows in the last quarter of 1979. Matsangaiza was killed on 17 October in a foolhardy attack on a well-fortified Mozambican army position. The radio message received at the Odzi base said, "Your Sunray got it." "Sunray" is a military code name for commander.[13]

Command was transferred to Matsangaiza's deputy, Dhlakama, although the CIO instructors had little respect for him. "I thought he was a weak character," the senior instructor said. "I don't think he liked going across. He was a chap who on 'ops' I wouldn't trust, someone who would come back and say he had done things he hadn't done. It was automatic that he should take over. But all the men realized he was by no means the same calibre as André. He had not got leadership qualities really."

Even by Dhlakama's own subsequent admission he was far from accepted. In documents captured when Mozambican forces overran the MNR Garagua base in eastern Manica province on 5 December 1981, he is recorded as saying in a report given on 9 November 1980, "Many fighters died this year including commanders and other heads, and others were maimed and crippled—all because of a power struggle." There are several unexplained assassinations, such as that of Cristina in South Africa, the subsequent disappearance of the Bomba brothers, the death of two senior MNR officials in a "car accident" in Malawi and the murder of Fernandes in Lisbon.[14]

The second, and potentially most damaging, blow to the MNR came on 21 December 1979. At Lancaster House in London the Zimbabwean nationalists and the Rhodesian rebels were forced to accept a constitution and cease-fire paving the way to elections and Zimbabwe's independence on 18 April 1980. The announcement on 4 March that Robert Mugabe's party, the Zimbabwe African National Union-Patriotic Front (Zanu-PF), had won the election came as a shock to white Rhodesia and the MNR.

The senior instructor recalled that Flower gave us "72 hours to get out of the country. . . . I was told to get as many blokes across the border into Mozambique as I could. So I shoved across everybody except for about 250. I must have put across 300 to 400, bringing the total inside to about 2,000." Two other instructors felt the figure was "getting up to 1,800," but Flower put the MNR strength at this point at less than 1,000. Whichever of these figures is true the MNR was then comparatively small and stripped of its Rhodesian rear base and support should have been relatively easy for the Mozambican army to eliminate.

Soon after the announcement of Zanu-PF's victory at the polls, Flower began to put long-range contingency plans into operation. He had been trying since 1976 to persuade his South African colleagues to support his clandestine movement in Mozambique. His overtures were through General Hendrick van den Bergh, head of the Bureau of State Security (BOSS), to South Africa's then Prime Minister B.J. Vorster. But Vorster refused to get involved, saying this would be contrary to his policy of detente with the independent black-ruled states of Africa.

However, late in 1978, first van den Bergh and then Vorster fell from office in the wake of the "Muldergate" information scandal. Vorster was replaced as prime minister by the minister of defense, P. W. Botha, and the army commander, General Magnus Malan, became minister of defense. The power of BOSS was dramatically reduced, and the vacuum was filled to a large extent by the Military Intelligence Directorate (MID), headed by General Pieter van der Westhuizen. In his move from defense minister to prime minister, Botha had taken the military men with him into key positions of civilian power. In effect, there had been a constitutional military *coup d'état*.

Flower pressed the new South African government to support the MNR. The response was immediate and positive, although initially limited. The South Africans began to supply some weapons and vehicles. Colonel Charles van Niekerk, whose name becomes much more prominent later in the MNR story, became the MID liaison officer and visited the Odzi base on a number of occasions during 1979. According to the senior instructor, the South African government committed R1 million (then worth more than US $1 million) in 1980.[15]

The South African connection, therefore, had been firmly established in the 12 months or so preceding Zimbabwe's independence. And, with the Rhodesian military openly admitting they could not defeat the Zimbabwean nationalist guerrillas, Malan and his Rhodesian counterpart, General Peter Walls, had reached an agreement. In the event of the collapse of "white" Rhodesia, "compromised" units and individuals, such as the Selous Scouts and the MNR, whom the Rhodesians feared would be subject to reprisals for the atrocities they had committed, would be transferred to South Africa. This was the contingency plan now implemented for the remnants of the MNR still in Rhodesia.

Dealing through Malan, van der Westhuizen and van Niekerk, Flower arranged the transfer of the MNR, their equipment and vehicles, and the personnel of Voz da Africa Livre, to South Africa. Van den Bergh, he said, had told him that the South African Defense Force (SADF) "might be stupid enough" to take over the MNR. The transfer was "solely my responsibility," Flower said later. But, in fact, Flower was not solely responsible. When the transfer occurred, Rhodesia had reverted from its former illegal status to that of a legal British colony, with a British governor supposedly in charge. Furthermore, the transfer occurred at a historic watershed in relations between Britain and Mozambique. Machel had played the most significant role of any outsider in the Lancaster House agreement the previous December. He had pressured Zanu's leadership into accepting the agreement despite their strong opposition to certain clauses, threatening that if they did not they might lose their rear base in Mozambique. British Prime Minister Margaret Thatcher had acknowledged her considerable debt to Machel, and relations between the two governments had reached an unprecedented high level.

In the period between the Lancaster agreement and the announcement of election results, Mozambique had pressed Britain to stop the activities of the MNR. Flower said that Sir

Anthony Duff—deputy to the governor, Lord Soames, and later head of British internal intelligence, MI5—raised the issue with him on a number of occasions. Flower says that after he made arrangements for the transfer of the MNR to South Africa, he informed Duff or another of Lord Soames's staff, Robin Renwick, then head of the Rhodesia desk in the Foreign Office and now British ambassador to South Africa. Thus, the British knew about the impending transfer of the MNR to South Africa and acquiesced. Had Flower not informed them, they would have known anyway. Members of the Commonwealth military monitoring force, which came under Soames's command, were present at all main Rhodesian army and air force bases. Their task was to monitor and report to the governor's office. They could not have missed the shuttle of South African air force C-130s landing at a Rhodesian base to airlift the MNR personnel.

It would appear that Britain's repayment of its debt to Machel was churlish in the extreme. But, debts notwithstanding, there are other considerations to bear in mind. In the first place, as one of Soames's staff frankly put it, "we had responsibility without power." Although Soames was nominally in charge, the reality of power in the dangerous weeks of the transition lay with the old Rhodesian structures: the army, air force, police, civil service and so on. A wrong move—such as trying to detain the MNR personnel and, as Mozambique wanted, handing them over—could have ignited a very unstable powder keg. Furthermore, given the daily crisis management involved in guiding the country to elections, the MNR was "a very minor issue meriting only passing attention," according to one of Soames's staff who said he had known of the transfer. Finally, it was a problem that the British authorities were glad to leave to someone else to resolve. If the MNR members were handed over to Mozambique, the British were uncertain of their fate; and if they remained in Zimbabwe after independence, the Mugabe government would certainly hand them over. Flower's formula offered the best solution to a potentially thorny problem—and at this point no one foresaw the consequences.

The transfer to South Africa was carried out in three phases. The first group to be moved were the staff of Voz da Africa Livre who, unconvincingly, announced they would be off the air for some time while they transferred their "mobile transmitter to a new location in Mozambique." A South African air force C-130 landed at the Fylde air base in central Rhodesia to fly them out with their equipment. They landed at the Waterkloof military based on the outskirts of Pretoria.

The CIO officer who had accompanied them returned to Rhodesia to take charge of the next stage of the transfer. This consisted of a team of SAS personnel driving the seven MNR vehicles from the Odzi base to the Voortrekkerhoogte military barracks in Pretoria.[16]

The third phase of the transfer was the largest and most important. Over a period of one day and one night a shuttle of South African air force C-130s landed at the Grand Reef air base in eastern Rhodesia near Odzi. They airlifted out about 250 MNR personnel and their armaments, accompanied by two CIO officers. They landed at Phalaborwa in the eastern Transvaal where they were met by a lieutenant commander. From there they were moved in a convoy of trucks to the edge of the Lutabo River, about one kilometer from the Kruger National Park. On the way to what was to become their new base, they passed through a large camp under construction for the Fifth Reconnaissance Regiment, a new SADF "special forces" unit initially set up for former SAS, Selous Scouts and members of other Rhodesian units who had fled south.

The new MNR base on the banks of the Lutabo had been a hunting camp and consisted of only a few broken-down huts. Within 10 days the South Africans began supplying equipment, ammunition, mortars and webbing; and it was immediately apparent that Pretoria intended to continue using the MNR. Next, the senior instructor was called to a meeting at the SADF headquarters in Pretoria and asked to outline his plans for future operations. He told them there were only two ways to get into Mozambique: by foot through the Kruger park or by air. Infiltration through Kruger was ruled out on the grounds that uniformed men might attract the attention of the tourists who frequent the park. Flights into Mozambique, at this juncture, were adjudged too risky. The South Africans said infiltration must be through Mapai and the bottom of Kruger near Komatipoort. "They wanted me to carry on reinforcing the MNR and take out certain targets, opportunity targets. Basically we were to proceed with my plan of cutting Mozambique in three," the senior instructor said.

The MNR was to come under the three South African intelligence services from the army, navy and special forces, a command situation which the senior instructor protested was unworkable. But it was clear, he said, that van Niekerk was really in charge of the operation. After about a month, dissatisfied with conditions and having learned that there was little likelihood of their being victimized by the Mugabe government for their role in the MNR, the CIO instructors returned to Zimbabwe.[17]

Mozambican officials now frankly admit that Zimbabwe's independence brought two distinct responses from the Frelimo leadership. There was a heady feeling of victory and that they could take on and defeat anyone. Frelimo, normally a movement that carefully considers all major matters of policy and strategy, neglected on this occasion to discuss and decide a most obviously fundamental issue: what support, if any, it could afford to give the African National Congress (ANC) of South Africa. What it did was to turn a blind eye to the activities of the ANC infiltrating through Mozambique into South Africa. For Mozambique in 1980, this omission was ill considered given the price it had already paid for supporting Zimbabwe and the level at that time of the South African struggle within the context of the changes in Pretoria that had brought the militarists to power. If criticism is to be made of Frelimo's actions, then it must begin over the failure to weigh the inherent risks of indecision at that point rather than the ugly decisions it was subsequently forced to make.

The second point to be borne in mind about Mozambique's response to Zimbabwe's independence is economic. In the colonial period the Portuguese had developed Mozambique as a service country for the landlocked African hinterland and for the northern Transvaal of South Africa. The Mozambican government's decision, on 3 March 1976, to close its border with Rhodesia had deprived it of about one-third of its foreign currency revenue earned through rail and port charges. Mozambique had been subjected to continual Rhodesian attacks, and many of the targets had been economic, not military. South Africa had reduced its usage of Maputo's port, stopped the agreement under which a percentage of mineworkers' salaries was paid in gold at preferential rates, and reduced the number of Mozambican migrant workers in the country. The total cost to Mozambique in the four years preceding Zimbabwe's independence is put at US $556 million, but the price was certainly much higher.[18] Mozambique's economy in April 1980 was on the verge of bankruptcy, and its government could not afford to take anyone on.

The headiness of this period was increased by the dramatic upturn in the Mozambican economy in 1980 and 1981. After two wars—its own national liberation struggle from 1964 to 1974 and then Zimbabwe's until 1980—Frelimo at last felt in a position to offer its people the rewards of sacrifice and struggle. The 1980 and 1981 economic statistics show the first signs of Mozambique's recovery following the devastation of the Rhodesian war. Production figures for some of Mozambique's most important exports reveal what occurred in this period. Cashew nut production in 1981 was 90,100 tons, the highest figure since 1977. (By 1984 it had fallen to 25,300 tons.) Cotton production in 1981 was 73,700 tons, the highest figure since independence in 1975. (In 1984, production was only 19,700 tons. Sugar production fell from 177,200 tons to 39,300 tons in the same period, coking coal from 167,000 tons to 23,500 tons.) In 1981, exports reached almost 10 billion meticais ($250 million), the highest level since independence. (In 1984 exports were down by 60 percent to just over four billion meticais [$100 million]. In 1985 and again in 1986, exports totalled only $80 million and the anticipated total for 1987 was $86 million.[19])

Two other developments in the region in this period had an important bearing on the actions the South Africans began to take. The first was the creation of the Southern African Development Coordination Conference (SADCC) on 1 April 1980. This brought together nine countries in a loose regional economic grouping: Angola, Botswana, Lesotho, Malawi, Mozambique, Swaziland, Tanzania, Zambia, and Zimbabwe.

The second development arose from the efforts of the Mugabe government to reduce dependence on South Africa by resuming use of traditional trade routes through Mozambique. Zimbabwe's trade through these routes was virtually nonexistent at independence in 1980 because the border had been closed for four years. But by 1983 trade through Mozambique had increased to just over half of Zimbabwe's total traffic.[20]

P. W. Botha, in one of his first speeches after becoming South Africa's prime minister, had emphasized his wish to see the creation of a southern African "constellation of states," which would be dominated by Pretoria. SADCC was such a grouping without Pretoria, although its leaders in turn emphasized that the creation of their organization was not a declaration of war on South Africa. It was rather an attempt to coordinate their development and make themselves less dependent on their powerful neighbor. That was exactly what the South African government did not want. The reopening of the Mozambican trade routes to Zaire, Zambia, and Zimbabwe meant those countries could become increasingly independent of South Africa.

Thus, while the activities of the ANC infiltrating across the border from Mozambique gave South Africa's militarists the excuse to pull the trigger, this was not the sole reason for what followed. Pretoria was determined to enforce continued dependence, and the significance of this factor is borne out by the strategic economic havoc it began to wreak in Mozambique.

The military situation in 1980 began on a positive note for Frelimo. Not only had the Rhodesian raids been ended by the Lancaster agreement but government forces carried out a successful offensive against the MNR and in late February reestablished control in the Gorongosa area. Sitatonga became the temporary MNR stronghold until it was also overrun in Operation Leopard at the end of June 1980. Evidence that the South Africans were already supplying the MNR was found at Sitatonga in the form of ammunition boxes, equipment, and parachutes.

An officer in Zimbabwe military intelligence reported that strong South African backing for the MNR began in 1980. Until mid-1979, he said, the MNR "had little other than nuisance value." In a report dated 26 June 1981, Captain Arthur Eastwood said, "By December 1980 MNR had between 6,000 and 7,000 fully armed men with an estimated 2,000 recruits in the pipeline. Trained reinforcements were airlifted in from South Africa and by February 1981 total strength was in the region of 10,000."[21] It was in this period that farmers in southeastern Zimbabwe reported seeing what they described as "an armada of helicopters passing overhead" from South Africa heading toward Mozambique. One airlift alone, it was estimated, could have ferried as many as one thousand MNR members and their equipment. On the night of 21–22 October 1980, eight helicopters heading into Mozambique were seen between Mabalauta and the Save-Rhunde confluence in southeastern Zimbabwe; an official protest was made to Pretoria about the violation of Zimbabwe's air space.

On 5 December 1981, when government forces overran the large MNR base at Garagua in Manica province, important documents were captured which revealed South Africa's strategy.[22] One aspect was the new way they planned to use the MNR.

Whereas the CIO had used the MNR as a clandestine movement with a low profile, Pretoria planned a much more public profile. At a meeting between the South Africans and the MNR, apparently in September or October 1980, it was decided to send Dhlakama on a European tour. The objectives were to make him and the MNR internationally known and to establish contacts with would-be supporters among right-wing European governments, political parties, and business circles. He left South Africa, referred to in the documents as "Africa External," on 18 November 1980 to visit Portugal, the Federal Republic of Germany, and France. In Portugal he met Catholic churchmen, business people, journalists, and a delegation from the Social Democratic Party. In the Federal Republic of Germany, according to the Garagua documents, he met delegations from the two opposition parties, the Christian Democratic Union and Christian Social Union, the latter led by Franz Josef Strauss. In France, on 27 November, he met with an adviser of President Valery Giscard d'Estaing. Soon thereafter the MNR opened offices in Portugal and the Federal Republic of Germany, and some support followed.

The second part of South Africa's strategy was to expand the war. On 25 October 1980 Dhlakama had had a meeting at the main MNR training camp in South Africa at the time, Zoabostad, with a South African delegation led by van Niekerk, the MID liaison officer to the CIO-MNR in Rhodesia in 1979. Van Niekerk said they had now concluded training the recruits evacuated from Rhodesia in March 1980. He stressed the need to open new fronts in Mozambique's southern provinces of Gaza and Inhambane. In Gaza, the objective was to create a destabilized buffer zone to curb ANC infiltration into South Africa; while in Inhambane, South Africa could use the cheaper method of landing supplies by sea, as airdrops were proving too expensive and "each parachute costs around R 500." They were also instructed to open an offensive in Maputo province and to conduct urban terrorism in Beira and Maputo. Finally, at a time when Zaire, Zambia, and Zimbabwe were reverting to use of their traditional trade routes through Mozambique and becoming less dependent on South Africa, the MNR were instructed to sabotage these routes.[23]

This is the pattern which now emerged. On 12 April 1981, Dhlakama addressed a meeting in the Gogoi area of Manica province near the Zimbabwe border. He predicted the overthrow of Machel by 1985 and promised there would be no further food shortages because adequate supplies would come from South Africa. And, he added, the oil pipeline from Beira to the Feruka refinery in eastern Zimbabwe would be destroyed.[24] A series of sabotages of the pipeline followed. The most serious was on the night of 10–11 October 1982 when a large MNR group attacked and destroyed a pumping station at Maforga and kidnapped three Portuguese technicians, their wives and a five-year-old child. From the Garagua documents, it appears that the South Africans were counting on the low-level destabilization in Zimbabwe's southwestern Matabeleland to ensure that the Mugabe government would not commit troops to Mozambique.[25] But the Maforga attack had exactly the opposite effect, and for the first time, members of the Zimbabwe National Army (ZNA) were deployed to Mozambique to protect the railway, road and pipeline from the port of Beira to the Zimbabwe border. The ZNA commitment was initially limited to the western end of these routes near the Zimbabwean border. But as the need grew to free Mozambican government forces from static guard duties for operations against the MNR, the

ZNA presence also grew. By early 1985, the ZNA contingent guarding these communications routes had increased to two thousand men operational at any one time along the pipeline from the Zimbabwean border to Beira.

Elsewhere, also acting on South African orders, the MNR escalated their activities and their atrocities against the civilian population. Large groups were observed heading south from Manica province, crossing the Save River into Gaza. Later, other groups were seen crossing the Limpopo River, reaching the South African border, and thereby establishing a link for northbound supplies. The railway to Zimbabwe was blown up in three places on 16 December 1981 and thereafter was regularly sabotaged. Communal villages—one with 709 houses, stores, and schools—were destroyed. Overflights by planes from South Africa were seen and heard regularly.

By 30 December 1981, intelligence sources had reported the presence of a large MNR base in Inhambane "to facilitate resupply of the movement by sea." Captured MNR members said one of their targets was National Highway No. 1, the road linking Maputo to Beira. Soon it became unsafe to travel on much of this road, except in armed convoys.

In the northern Niassa province, a 1 July 1981 intelligence report stated that "large numbers of MNR are entering Mozambique via Dobwe along the border with Malawi. It is as yet uncertain whether these elements are trained in Malawi, or whether that country is just a holding area." In Zambezia province, which provided about 50 percent of Mozambique's export earnings, sabotage also began in 1981. Next the fighting spread to neighboring Nampula province, and it was clear that Malawi, officially or unofficially, at South Africa's behest, was providing a rear base or transit routes for the MNR into the three provinces it adjoins, Niassa, Tete, and Zambezia.[26] In this phase only Cabo Delgado, in the extreme north-east, remained unscathed.

The Mozambican government had not expected South Africa to unleash such an offensive against it. "After independence, when we took off our guns, and exchanged our uniforms for suits and ties, we made a mistake," Machel told a mass rally in Maputo on 23 June 1982. "Now we're putting our guns on once more, and we won't make the same mistake this time."[27] Thirteen months later, opening the SADCC summit in Maputo on 11 July 1983, he said, "We are aware that the fundamental aim of the actions of destabilization against our countries is to render SADCC non-viable. Our land, sea and air frontiers are regularly violated by the Pretoria regime. Destabilization through gangs of bandits is complemented by the operations of special units designed to destroy selected targets that are vital for regional co-operation. Our ports and railways, fuel depots and pipelines, bridges and roads, communications systems and other economic development projects are the targets for this kind of aggression."[28] This was entirely true, as the Garagua documents prove, but Frelimo had become aware of the danger too late; and in some areas of the country, their forces were outnumbered and poorly equipped.

In addition to training, arming and directing their surrogates, the SADF frequently has been involved in direct actions in Mozambique. South African troops invaded the country in January 1981, killing 13 members of the ANC in the capital, Maputo. In May 1983 they rocketed a suburb of Maputo killing six people, only one of whom had ANC connections. The principal damage was to a jam factory. In October 1983 a SADF commando group bombed the ANC office in Maputo, wounding five people. Maputo was again the target of a commando attack in late May 1987 in which three Mozambicans were killed, including a couple executed at home in front of their 18-month-old daughter.

It is, however, the third area of military action, between surrogate support and admitted direct action, which is the most difficult to detail. Former Rhodesian CIO officers admit South African participation in their attack on Beira's oil storage tanks in early 1979, and there is no doubt that the early 1982 Beira attack was also South African. But they have been involved directly in other acts of sabotage inside Mozambique, and the story of Alan Gingles dramatically illustrates this.

In late October 1981, the SADF headquarters in Pretoria announced that a Lieutenant Alan Gingles, 27, had been killed "in action against terrorists on October 15" in the "operational area," a euphemism for the Namibia-Angola frontier area. At about the same time, Mozambique announced that unidentified "Boer soldiers" had been killed in a sabotage attempt on Zimbabwe's transportation route from Beira. Four men had been blown to pieces by their own explosives when attacked by a government patrol. Pretoria dismissed the claim as "lying propaganda."

There the matter rested until a London Sunday newspaper, the *Observer*, unearthed the truth. The crucial pieces of evidence at the scene of the intended sabotage were fragments of a handwritten novel. A "Larne Grammar School" and a girl called "Antrim" were mentioned in the novel. The search took the newspaper to the town of Larne in the Irish county of Antrim where they learned a memorial service had been held in a local church for Gingles. He had attended Sandhurst, served in the British army, and gone to fight for Rhodesia in the Selous Scouts. When Zimbabwe became independent, Gingles, like many other embittered white servicemen, moved to South Africa becoming an officer in the SADF. He was based at Phalaborwa, a camp in the eastern Transvaal where MNR members were being trained. He had not died in the Namibia-Angola "operational area," but 1,700 kilometers away on a sabotage mission in Mozambique.[29]

South Africa was undoubtedly encouraged in the policies it pursued in this period by the election of Ronald Reagan as US president in late 1980. When Reagan took office early the following year, his anticommunist rhetoric, and statements such as "South Africa is an ally of Western interests in Africa," left Pretoria's policy planners in little doubt as to where he stood. So while the United States pursued Reagan's policy, enunciated as "constructive engagement," Pretoria pursued its own policy of a "total national strategy," or "total strategy." But the latter was to backfire against its instigators when the escalating spiral of violence began to threaten Western interests.

When the assistant secretary of state for Africa Chester Crocker visited Mozambique in January 1983, he explained the US perspective.[30] After Mozambique's expulsion of four alleged CIA agents in 1981, the Crocker visit was an important milestone. The US concerns were clear. The escalating level of violence, if left unchecked, could force greater Soviet presence into the region. Mozambique's support for the ANC threatened Washington's major ally in the region, South Africa. And Washington's support for Pretoria was threatening its relations with independent African states.

In June the US under secretary for political affairs Lawrence Eagleburger announced that the Reagan administration now had what he called a coherent strategy for southern Africa.[31] The Frelimo government interpreted this to mean that South Africa was no longer the principal axis of Washington's relations with the region.

Crocker's visit to Maputo had come a month after the first ministerial-level talks between Mozambique and South Africa in December 1982 at the border town of Komatipoort. The two sides met again in May 1983. Such was the level of distrust that nothing substantial emerged from these meetings.

But they met again in December 1983 in the Swazi capital, Mbabane. Mozambican officials say this meeting was "as a result of efforts" of Frank Wisner, then Crocker's deputy in the State Department's Africa Bureau.[32] Despite a subsequent reference to "fiery" exchanges, the Mozambicans felt there was a new atmosphere in which South Africa accepted Mozambique's "sovereignty, its territorial integrity, and its chosen path for development." Why then, when South Africa and its surrogates were moving toward destroying the economic and social fabric of Mozambique, did some of Pretoria's policy makers decide to include negotiation in the ruthless "total strategy" agenda they had been pursuing?

Pressure from the United States, against the background of its regional imperatives spelled out by Crocker, played an important part. So did pressure from European nations. But a critical factor lay in the very nature of the MNR, for it remained without alternative policies or alternative leaders. If Pretoria intended to remove the Frelimo government, then the MNR could not do it. Despite the massive South Africa–MNR offensive of 1981–83, they had come no nearer to removing Machel and his government. South Africa would have to play a far greater and, therefore, public role, and this was a price Pretoria could not afford, politically or economically.

At the Mbabane meeting the two delegations outlined the principles upon which an agreement must be based. When they met again in Pretoria on 16 January 1984, Mozambique laid out a seven-point basis for an agreement which included respect for sovereignty and territorial integrity; respect of borders; nonaggression; neither party to resort to the threat of force against the other; no support or establishment of bases for hostile forces; and no broadcasting facilities for such forces.[33]

Machel's statement after the Mbabane meeting that Mozambique would continue to give political, moral and diplomatic support to the ANC troubled officials in Pretoria. That he was no longer including the word "material" was too fine a distinction for them and their constituency.

On 20 February a South African delegation, led by Foreign Minister Roelof "Pik" Botha and including Defense Minister Malan, flew to Maputo. For the first time Machel entered directly into the talks when he met the South African ministers to receive a message from P. W. Botha. During the meeting, Machel described the atrocities being committed by the MNR. "Are these soldiers?" he demanded of Malan. The South African general, outranked by Machel who was a marshal, snapped to attention and replied, "No, Sir!"

At the Maputo meeting the South Africans continued to press for total elimination of the ANC in Mozambique. The draft agreement they proposed "went so far that it would have meant we could not even have Miriam Makeba in Mozambique to give a concert," a Frelimo official said.

The final significant meeting in the sequence occurred in Cape Town on 2–3 March 1984 when the amended Mozambican draft was accepted with minimal change. Frelimo won its argument to prevent the total removal of ANC personnel from Mozambique and to retain an ANC office in Maputo with a staff limited to 10 people. In addition ANC members with full-time jobs in various sectors in Mozambique would not be affected.

On 16 March on their common border, Machel and P. W. Botha signed the "Agreement on Non-Aggression and Good Neighbourliness," known thereafter as the Nkomati Accord (for full text, see appendix 1). Included in the agreement was the establishment of a Joint Security Commission (JSC) to consider alleged infringements.

The ANC National Executive Committee condemned South Africa's "diplomatic, political and propaganda counter-offensive," adding that South Africa "sought to reduce the independent countries of our region to the level of its Bantustan creations."[34]

Although his organization had not been consulted on the agreement, ANC President Oliver Tambo received two briefings, one from Machel and the other by Security Minister Mariano Matsinhe, in late February. At a press conference in London, Tambo struck a conciliatory note:

> I'm not sure that in their position I'd have gone quite so far, but it must be accepted that the South African regime

had decided to destroy Mozambique, to kill it as a state,
and the leadership was forced to decide between life
and death. So if it meant hugging the hyena, they had
to do it.
The rest of us, we must accept that position, but we
also had to defend our position.

He added that if Mozambique had received adequate political
and material support, it would not have had to do what it hated
doing.[35]

In January 1984, two months before Nkomati and with the
objective of getting its $1.4 billion foreign debt rescheduled,
the government of Mozambique had issued an economic report
compiled by its National Planning Commission. Table 1.1,
showing South African imports and exports through Maputo
for a decade from 1973, starkly illustrates the vulnerability of
Mozambique's captive economy.[36]

From table 1.1, it is possible to see how South Africa systematically reduced its traffic through Maputo after the Portuguese
coup d'état, deliberately undermining Mozambique's economy.
By 1983 South Africa had reduced this traffic to 21.5 percent of
the 1973 level. Similar direct actions of economic sabotage
occurred elsewhere in this period, such as a reduction in high-
tariff cargoes sent through Maputo. These policies reduced
foreign exchange earnings. An independent study for the Mozambican government in 1986 put the direct and indirect losses
to Mozambique's ports and railways at well over $1 billion from
1980 to 1986 inclusive.[37]

A similar trend in the case of Mozambican migrant workers
occurred between 1975 and 1983 when South Africa reduced
their numbers from 118,030 to 45,491. That led to a loss of $568
million in income remitted home by the miners. The figures
spiral upwards, with the total cost from 1980 to 1986, inclu-

Table 1.1

South African imports and exports through the port of Maputo

Year	Traffic/thousand tons	Percentage relative to 1973
1973	6,823.5	100
1974	5,665.1	83
1975	5,638.5	82.6
1976	4,974.4	72.9
1977	4,248.2	62.3
1978	4,064.8	59.6
1979	4,155.2	60.9
1980	3,428.0	50.2
1981	3,023.9	44.3
1982	2,216.8	32.5
1983	1,467.6	21.5
1984	1,122.5	16.5
1985	962.6	14.1

Source: Mozambique Ports and Railways.

sive of withholding cargo from the port of Maputo and direct or surrogate actions, estimated at well over $6 billion. High as it is, this figure is still incomplete. In 1985, for example, defense and security accounted for 43 percent of Mozambique's budget and 58 percent of government receipts as a result of South Africa's undeclared war. And these figures do not include the yet unascertained amount of money diverted from development and social services to military hardware and construction.

In 1980, Mozambique had a small balance of payments deficit. By 1986, the Paris meeting of the consultative group on Mozambique known as the Paris club was told that the current account deficit before transfers was $600 million. The foreign debt, including accumulated arrears, stood at $3.4 billion, with a debt-service ratio of 275 percent.

What economic reports do not cover, or only skim over, is the social cost. Hard-nosed bankers attending a debt-rescheduling meeting are not expected to pay attention to details such as human suffering. But here again statistics, such as those on education shown in table 1.2, reveal an unbelievable magnitude of social disruption. The impact of the current disruption on Mozambican society in the years to come cannot be measured.

One of the most basic requirements for a largely rural population is a good network of rural stores selling basic commodities and other consumer goods. Since 1971 the population-per-store ratio has dramatically decreased, for three main reasons:

Table 1.2
Disruption to education system before and after Nkomati

Province	Schools closed		Pupils displaced		Teachers displaced	
	Before	After	Before	After	Before	After
Cabo Delgado	a	29	a	5,713	a	91
Gaza	98	98	13,374	12,288	219	202
Inhambane	233	247	56,131	55,775	752	807
Manica	49	98	9,653	18,328	145	257
Maputo prov.	36	123	3,532	15,061	82	258
Nampula	43	230	5,454	36,273	95	608
Niassa	a	193	a	19,330	a	354
Sofala	186	228	31,539	39,197	495	597
Tete	18	164	2,239	22,092	39	434
Zambezia	177	453	30,766	89,709	569	1,384
Total	840	1,863	152,688	313,766	2,396	4,992

Source: Minstry of Education.
Note: Under each heading, the figures on the left are those for 14 November 1983, four months before Nkomati. Those on the right are for 31 December 1985, revealing how the situation deteriorated after Nkomati.
[a]In the case of Cabo Delgado and Niassa provinces, no statistics appear in the 1983 report. Bandit activity had not begun in Cabo Delgado at that time; for Niassa, it is unclear whether that province did not make returns or whether no schools were affected at that point.

the flight of the Portuguese settlers in 1974–75, population growth, and bandit activity. In 1985, for example, MNR activity was responsible for the destruction of some nine hundred stores and the closure of an indeterminate number of others.[38] Health clinics, larger health centers, and rural hospitals have been destroyed on a large scale: 102 in 1982, 110 in 1985.

Livestock are another basic need of most people in the rural areas. From 1980 to 1985, the national herd, 50 percent of which belonged to peasant farmers, was reduced from 1,500,000 cattle to 900,000.[39] No stratum of the society has remained untouched by South Africa's "total strategy": schools for children, access to medical care, local stores, livestock, and markets have all been destroyed.

Nkomati was a high-risk gamble for Frelimo arising from their harsh—and painful—assessment of Mozambique's reality. Machel initially hailed it as a "victory," a description many people found easier to understand from a South African perspective than a Mozambican one, by which he meant that it reduced the dangerous isolation of his country. In addition, the aggressor, South Africa, had been forced, on paper at least, to commit itself to nonaggression, a tacit admission that it had been the aggressor.

The two immediate questions arising from Nkomati were whether South Africa would honor the agreement and whether it would bring a cease-fire in the debilitating war.

In the prelude to Nkomati, and in the months thereafter, the Mozambican government pursued a strategy that was diplomatic as well as military. Machel's visit to six European countries in October 1983 was one of the opening moves in the diplomatic offensive. Pik Botha followed a month later on a European tour which received a generally frosty welcome. The message he received was that destabilization was bad for business.

Within a month of Nkomati, a steady shuttle of officials began to ply between Pretoria and Maputo. The Mozambican government's foremost objective was to bring an end to the violence, and it was decided that a Mozambican envoy should meet MNR spokesman Fernandes in Europe. The meeting took place in a Frankfurt hotel on 29 May, and the envoy gave Fernandes a newspaper of the previous day containing his government's amnesty offer.

On 30 June, Machel again met Pik Botha and MID head van der Westhuizen in Maputo. He spoke of Portuguese ties to the MNR which he described as *saudosismo colonialista* (colonialist nostalgia). Eleven days later, van der Westhuizen was again in Mozambique proposing another meeting with Fernandes. This took place in Pretoria three days later, and again it was unproductive. Increasingly, the question arose as to whether Fernandes was speaking on behalf of Mozambicans or on behalf of Portuguese political and business interests opposed to the Frelimo government.

Discussions continued in Pretoria on 27–29 September and again on 1–3 October, with Pik Botha as the go-between. The latter meeting culminated in a joint "declaration on a cessation of armed activity and conflict." The Mozambican government delegation obtained the two most important points they sought: recognition of President Machel and, therefore, his government and agreement in principle on an unconditional cease-fire. The "Pretoria Declaration" established a commission to work toward implementation of the agreement and requested South Africa to "consider playing a role in the implementation."[40]

Two days later, South African Deputy Foreign Minister Louis Nel flew to Maputo where he discussed the modalities and timetable of a cease-fire. But Fernandes had already begun demanding political conditions which had previously been rejected.

The Mozambican government delegation was under no illusions when its members returned to Pretoria on 8 October.

Their objective was to fix the date for a cease-fire and to refuse to be drawn into any further discussion until there was a total cessation of violence. The meeting dragged on for four days, but by the night of 11 October agreement appeared imminent. A total cessation of violence was to occur 45 days after agreement in the JSC.

Then Fernandes asked for a one-week suspension of the meeting. This request came after he took a telephone call which he said came from Lisbon, from Carlos Mota Pinto, the deputy prime minister and minister of defense in the Soares coalition government in Portugal. Fernandes claimed that he had been told not to reach any agreement before going to Lisbon for discussions and that the head of the Mozambique government delegation, the minister of state in the president's Office for Economic Affairs Jacinto Valoso, should accompany him.[41]

Mota Pinto was named in press reports by Mozambican journalists who were accompanying their delegation and by others who were present when Fernandes concluded the telephone call. As far as the authors are aware, he has not denied these reports. However, two other possibilities have been suggested as to who really called Fernandes. One is that it was Manuel Bulhosa, a rich businessman and Fernandes's employer.[42] The other is that it was faked by the MID which opposed the Nkomati Accord and was intent upon blocking a cease-fire. In the light of subsequent evidence, particularly that contained in the Gorongosa documents, this last explanation is the most plausible.

Whether that telephone call sabotaged possible agreement is difficult to determine, but Fernandes's previous behavior had already led the Mozambican delegation to suspect that he, or whoever was giving him instructions, had always intended to demand impossible concessions. Thereafter, the Mozambique government kept the diplomatic option open, but there were no further meetings with Fernandes.

In this period of intensive negotiations and thereafter, the government in Maputo frequently protested to South Africa about violations of the Nkomati Accord. In Cape Town in January 1984, it had raised the point that the Rhodesians had infiltrated many men in the interim period between the Lancaster House agreement and Zimbabwe's independence. The South Africans had replied that they were not Rhodesians whose government was on the point of collapse and would not resort to such measures. But that was exactly what they did. In the weeks before the ceremony at Nkomati, supplies were moved into Mozambique by air and sea to cover MNR requirements for many months. A large number of trained men were pushed across the border from South Africa into southern Maputo province. Attacks began to occur near the capital, and road travel in the area became hazardous. In the north, operations were escalated dramatically from Malawi into Niassa, Nampula, Tete and Zambezia provinces.

In June 1985, Machel, Mugabe and Tanzanian President Julius Nyerere met in the Zimbabwean capital of Harare, where Mozambique's two closest neighbors agreed to increase their military support. Tanzania, under almost as great an economic constraint as Mozambique, agreed to train Mozambican recruits to defend the three northern provinces of Niassa, Nampula, and Cabo Delgado. Zimbabwe, in the midst of a comparative economic boom and with a well-trained and well-equipped army, was able to make a greater commitment. The ZNA, already guarding communications routes to Beira, moved into the three central provinces of Manica, Sofala, and Tete. In mid-July, Zimbabwe deployed three combat battalions numbering about three thousand men, backed by a further two thousand support troops. The Mozambican army undertook defense of the other four provinces: Gaza, Inhambane and Maputo in the south, and Zambezia in the north central area.[43]

On 28 August 1985, the MNR headquarters at Gorongosa in Sofala province was attacked and overrun. Psychologically, it was an important morale boost in the new joint offensive against the MNR, and large quantities of arms, ammunition and supplies were captured. But most important were more than two-hundred kilograms of documents, which revealed the extent of South Africa's duplicity before and after Nkomati.[44]

Extracts from three MNR diaries revealed massive and premeditated violations of the accord. They also revealed the names of some of the principal persons involved in the violations: Pik Botha's deputy Nel; the SADF commander General Constand Viljoen; the head of SADF special forces General André Liebenberg; the head of MID, van der Westhuizen; the MID liaison to the former Rhodesian MNR van Niekerk; and another MID officer, Brigadier van Tonder.

As stated earlier, it had been agreed that in the two months prior to Nkomati, no men or equipment would be infiltrated into Mozambique. Yet on 23 February, three weeks before Nkomati, Dhlakama met van der Westhuizen, who is quoted in the documents as saying, "We, the military, will continue to give them [MNR] support without the consent of our politicians in a massive way so they can win the war." Machel, he added, would only fall by the destruction of his economy and communications.

Van der Westhuizen guaranteed resupply to the MNR, and he defined targets: railways, the Cahora Bassa power grid, foreign-aid workers,[45] and economic targets *such as those involving SADCC.* It was arranged to rearm and resupply the MNR before Nkomati to give them autonomy for a six-month period, and one of the diaries records details of innumerable resupplies by plane and ship in this period. A South African team was sent to Zambezia province to train one hundred MNR instructors and two hundred recruits. The Phalaborwa training camp in South Africa was moved to Louis Trichardt, and a new transmission network was set up between the SADF and the MNR inside Mozambique. So much for the gentlemen's agreement.

In June 1984, when Dhlakama reported to "friend Commander Charlie" that he was short of ammunition, van Niekerk instructed him to avoid clashes and concentrate instead on the destruction of the economy and infrastructure. Dhlakama pleaded in a radio message that "the enemy is bound to recuperate . . . They will go on chasing us all over the place." The South Africans responded by sending in more armaments by air and sea.[46]

In a meeting on 6 September 1984, Viljoen recommended that the MNR not accept the amnesty which his government had proposed to Mozambican officials. The general offered to facilitate contacts with foreign countries especially in Africa, and told the MNR not to be deceived by Pik Botha "because he is treacherous."[47] One diary entry records that microphones were to be installed to bug Pik Botha's meetings with Frelimo and it is clear that the foreign minister's meeting with senior Western ambassadors was also recorded. Mozambique government military communications were also monitored and all of this passed on to the MNR.

On 16 September 1985, two weeks before revealing the contents of the Gorongosa documents, Machel summoned Pik Botha to Maputo and presented him with extracts. According to officials present at the meeting, Botha was "visibly annoyed" to find himself described as "treacherous" and to learn that meetings he thought were private had been bugged by his own military. Botha said he had not been informed that his deputy, Nel, had flown to Gorongosa on 8 June 1985 to meet Dhlakama.

At a news conference in Pretoria on 18 September, limited to South African journalists, the foreign minister tried to minimize the damage. He admitted that contacts had continued with the MNR after Nkomati but described the breaches as "technical." The South African air force had made supply drops, he said, but he characterized these as "mostly humanitarian aid." He later told parliament that, "One can go through all those entries in the diary . . . the information tallies with the flights undertaken by the air force. That is true. The times of our meetings in Pretoria are correct. The times that they indicated I had been present are correct."[48]

On 9 October Viljoen also admitted that the diaries were essentially accurate. Pik Botha had not been informed about his deputy's visit to Gorongosa, Viljoen said, nor had he informed his minister of defence, General Malan, or P. W. Botha. He criticized the handling of the negotiations by the Ministry of Foreign Affairs but claimed the SADF accepted their government's "change of strategy" toward Mozambique.[49] The following day, P. W. Botha publicly gave Viljoen his total support.[50]

There were other serious questions arising from the contents of the Gorongosa documents and the apparent contradictions within the South African establishment. Why had Viljoen described Pik Botha as "treacherous"? Why had his meetings with Mozambican officials and Western ambassadors been bugged? No one commented on the large number of well-documented arms drops to the MNR. Nor did anyone comment on van der Westhuizen's remark that the military would continue to support the MNR irrespective of what the politicians decided to do. The breach of the gentlemen's agreement preceding Nkomati was ignored, as was the fact that the SADF was selecting for the MNR specific targets to destroy in Mozambique.

Whether or not there were contradictions between some politicians and some soldiers over Nkomati is not the point. In the final analysis, government must be held responsible for the actions of its army and in this case, finally, P. W. Botha as the head of government. For many years before becoming prime minister, he had been a very aggressive defense minister, standing on the political right of the National Party (NP). His career, in effect, had been made by the military, and he had brought it to power with him. By 1984, he was increasingly losing the support of the right wing of the party over his reform program. His main constituency at that point was the military.

In all probability, P. W. Botha never wanted Nkomati. But South Africa, like Mozambique, was confronted in 1983 by the US analysis that the two countries were principal ones responsible for the state of insecurity in the region. If there was to be peace in the region, then they must establish it. While Mozambique was certainly willing to consider an agreement leading to peace, this probability looked very slim until the two sides met in Pretoria on 16 January 1984. Thereafter, the real bargaining and details took exactly two months before Nkomati was signed.

P. W. Botha then faced considerable difficulty. He had publicly committed himself in a very high-profile manner at Nkomati. To renege on the agreement would undermine his political credibility internationally and in South Africa. But, the Gorongosa documents reveal, senior members of the SADF were unhappy about Nkomati from the beginning and had no intention of abiding by it. There can be little doubt that they were supported in this course of action by their senior political leaders, including the state president, as most of those named have since been promoted. Van der Westhuizen was moved from MID to the powerful post of secretary to the State Security Council (SSC). Von Tonder is now head of MID. Nel was removed from his post as foreign affairs deputy to that of deputy minister in charge of the state president's information bureau (responsible, among other things, for foreign media coverage). Liebenberg was promoted to army commander. Viljoen's retirement had been announced months earlier and had more to do with Angola than Mozambique.

The timing of the discovery of the Gorongosa documents could not have been worse for South Africa. Machel was about to leave for his first official visit to the United States, and by the time he met Reagan at the White House, the US leader had been briefed about the documents. Reagan expressed "shock" at the South African breaches of the Nkomati Accord, and when the meeting ended, the two leaders were on a first-name basis (Machel called Reagan "Ronnie"). Machel struck the right chord by briefing Reagan on the situation but asking for nothing.

In Britain, a few days later, Prime Minister Margaret Thatcher expressed similar concern, noting that it is a very serious matter when armies do not follow the orders of their governments.[51]

Ten months earlier, and eight months after signing Nkomati, Machel had met Thatcher at the funeral of the assassinated Indian prime minister Indira Gandhi. During their meeting, according to British officials, the Mozambican leader asked for military support. Machel was in a strong position to make this request for two reasons. First, by pressuring Mugabe into accepting the Lancaster House agreement, Machel had saved Britain from a potential catastrophe in Rhodesia. His second major asset was the signing of the Nkomati Accord.

Thatcher regarded Machel's decision to sign the accord, in the face of considerable criticism, as an act of courage. When they met at the British prime minister's residence, 10 Downing Street, in September 1985, the Gorongosa documents had just been published, proving that Mozambique had adhered to the agreement while South Africa had not.

Four months later, in January 1986, the first contingent of British soldiers arrived to begin training junior officers from Mozambique at the Inyanga Battle Training School in Zimbabwe's lush eastern highlands. Sixty Mozambicans were inducted into each of four courses over the next 16 months, filling one of the most pressing needs of the Mozambican army.

On 1 May 1987, the number of trainees was increased to 120 officers every four months. Later in the year, the number of British instructors grew to 13, and they began to train full combat companies. In addition, places were made available at the prestigious Royal Military Academy at Sandhurst (which

Machel had visited in 1985), and some $400,000 worth of medical kits and radio parts were supplied. Within the same time frame, the ultraright in Washington, led by organizations such as the Heritage Foundation, were pressing the Reagan administration to recognize the MNR and give them material assistance. However, the support for Mozambican government forces from Britain's conservative prime minister blunted their arguments.

Malawi's military commitment represented a quite different form of interest. The Malawian government is heavily dependent upon South Africa for trade and financial assistance, and is the only African country to have formal diplomatic ties with Pretoria. Their commitment of soldiers to Mozambique—albeit out of self-interest to guard repair crews on the railway line to the port of Nacala—indicated a growing recognition in some quarters in Malawi that it is an integral part of the region.

Historically, Malawi's octogenarian president, Kamuzu Banda, has never accepted the Frelimo government in Mozambique. When most other African countries agreed in 1965 to recognize colonial boundaries in order to prevent territorial claims and conflicts, Banda, encouraged by Portugal and later South Africa, laid claim to all of Mozambique north of the Zambezi River as part of a "greater Malawi."

He visited Tanzania in this period, taking with him an old atlas which he produced as "evidence" that northern Mozambique should be absorbed by Malawi and Tanzania. He urged President Nyerere to accompany him to a number of African countries and then to Portugal to present his case. Nyerere declined. When the Portuguese dictator, António Salazar, refused to consider the proposal, Banda began supporting a number of anti-Frelimo movements, including the now defunct African National Union of Rombezia which sought to divide the country in two at the Zambezi River. This movement was established by the PIDE in the hope of creating a buffer zone between Tanzania and southern Mozambique.

Infiltration into Mozambique from Malawi began to increase dramatically in the early 1980s, and by 1984 there were large-scale attacks on agricultural complexes near the border.[52] People living in the border area increasingly reported night flights across the frontier on resupply missions to the MNR. It became clear that South Africa sought to cover up its flouting of the Nkomati Accord by infiltrating men and equipment in the north, far from the South African border; but it was a thin disguise.

The deteriorating situation between Malawi and Mozambique reached crisis proportions in September 1986. Machel, Mugabe, and Zambia's President Kenneth Kaunda flew to Malawi to try to persuade Banda to stop supporting the MNR and to resume usage of the Mozambican ports of Beira and Nacala, Malawi's shortest and cheapest routes to the sea. Machel took with him a dossier containing evidence of Malawi's involvement with the MNR.

The bulging dossier included letters and photocopies of passports, as well as other information. Among the photocopies were Malawian passports issued to the MNR chief representative Jimo Phiri in his own name and under an alias.[53]

On his return to Maputo after the meeting on 11 September, Machel angrily threatened to put missiles along the border with Malawi and impose an economic blockade, which would have prevented some 70 trucks a day crossing Tete province carrying Malawi's trade through Zimbabwe to and from South African ports. On 26 September, a Malawian government delegation visited Maputo, and a joint security commission was set up.

While officials of both governments were engaged in these meetings, a massive invasion of Mozambique's north central provinces of Tete and Zambezia was launched from Malawian territory. Large groups of armed men, attacking in up to battalion strength, seized several district capitals and a strategic bridge over the Zambezi River. Their objective appeared to be to reach the Indian Ocean to make resupply easier, to separate the south of the country from the north, and to capture Quelimane, the provincial capital of Zambezia. People fleeing from the district of Mutarara in Tete province said the bandit groups were commanded by "white soldiers."

In August 1986, seven Commonwealth leaders had met in London to endorse a limited package of economic sanctions against South Africa. Similar measures were adopted a few weeks later by the US Congress, but vetoed by President Reagan. The Zimbabwean authorities had received information soon after the minisummit that as sanctions were tightened, South Africa would increase its hostile actions against Mozambique. In a message conveyed through intelligence channels, the South Africans threatened to instruct their surrogates in Mozambique to disrupt road and rail traffic along the Beira corridor, capture towns and hold them, and make the country ungovernable. The subsequent events of September and October 1986 bore out the reliability of this information.[54]

On 12 October, leaders of southern Africa's six Frontline states—Presidents Machel of Mozambique, Kaunda of Zambia, Quett Masire of Botswana, José Eduardo dos Santos of Angola, Ali Hassan Mwinyi of Tanzania, and Prime Minister Mugabe of Zimbabwe—held an emergency meeting in the Mozambican capital and issued a statement called the Maputo Declaration, which condemned "the complicity of the Malawian government with the Pretoria authorities":

> In its activities, and in express violation of the undertakings it has given, the South African regime is using the territory of Malawi to attack the People's Republic of Mozambique. It thus drags Malawi into a conflict that is damaging to the interests of its own people, of the peoples of southern Africa, and to peace in the region.

The situtation worsened at the end of September. Then the Malawian government, at the same time that it proposed negotiations with the People's Republic of Mozambique, organised, facilitated and set up conditions for bandit gangs to occupy frontier zones in the provinces of Tête, Sofala and Zambezia, of Mozambique.

Over the last few days Pretoria has unleashed an incessant campaign of accusation and threats against the People's Republic of Mozambique. South African forces are concentrated along the borders with Mozambique and Zimbabwe and commando units have been infiltrated to carry out acts of terrorism in Mozambique.

The Frontline leaders referred to threats that had begun on 2 October. Pik Botha informed a number of US senators by telephone that if the Senate did not uphold the presidential veto of the Sanctions Bill passed by Congress, then no US grain would be transported on South African railways to the independent states of the region. In effect, he threatened that South Africa would impose further sanctions against its neighbors, as well as against US farmers. This threat was hollow because South Africa can only block supplies to Lesotho which it totally surrounds; and, in fact, one of its neighbors, Zimbabwe, produces a grain surplus. But it was the beginning of a phase of mounting tension in the region, and some commentators wrote that South Africa had shifted tactics and decided to overthrow Machel's government.[55]

On 6 October, a South African military vehicle detonated a land mine near the border with Mozambique, injuring the six occupants. Defense Minister Malan blamed the incident on Mozambique, saying that, "If President Machel chooses land mines, South Africa will react accordingly." He warned that Machel faced a head-on clash with South Africa.

Three days later, Pretoria increased its own economic sanctions by banning the recruitment of Mozambican miners, a decision which would have cost Mozambique $50 million a year had it been fully implemented.

On 11 October, the Mozambican government issued a statement accusing South Africa of preparing a "direct attack against the city of Maputo," with the aim of overthrowing the government: "The raids being prepared involve the use of the air force and of disguised commando groups infiltrated into our country." The land-mine incident was fabricated by "South African militarists . . . forming the pretext for launching direct aggression against our country," the statement said, citing the massive infiltrations into Tete and Zambezia, as well as into the southern provinces of Maputo and Gaza, and fresh arms supplies flown into the central province of Manica.

On 15 October, Malan again threatened military action against the Frontline states, saying they "share the responsibility" for the ANC's "acts of terror" and "would have to suffer the consequences." On 16 October, the Mozambique News Agency (AIM) put out a feature story which said, prophetically:

> President Samora Machel could be one of the chosen targets of the South African military hierarchy. . . . Malan's threats were directed specifically against Samora Machel rather than against Mozambique or its government in general.[56]

Three days later, Machel was dead, killed in a plane crash just inside South African territory. He had been returning from a meeting in northern Zambia in which three Frontline leaders had met Zairean President Mobutu Sese Seko to discuss reopening the Benguela Railway through Angola and had asked him not to allow his country to be used as a conduit for arms to government opponents in Angola.

A factual report by officials from Mozambique, South Africa, and the Soviet Union (as manufacturer of the presidential aircraft) agreed on the technicalities of what had happened and where. But they did not agree on the cause of the crash. South Africa later held its own inquiry which claimed pilot error caused the crash, but did not address the question of why the plane had turned off course, or why a massive disinformation campaign had been mounted, as Pik Botha subsequently admitted.

Many other questions remained unanswered. Had a false radio beacon lured the plane off course? Why did the South Africans put out false meteorological charts showing the weather had been bad when it had not been? Why were there incisions in the necks of the bodies of the two Soviet pilots and why was the suggestion made, and subsequently withdrawn, that they had been drinking?

Why, when the plane was on South African radar all the way from Zambia, was it not warned that it was off course and why was the Mozambican government not informed of the crash until almost 10 hours after it occurred? And why were they first told that the wreckage was in Natal province, south of Maputo, when it was in Transvaal, to the west? Why was a South African military tent rapidly removed from the site, and why were survivors' cries for help ignored, as they later described, while military personnel searched the wreckage for documents?

While the investigations were being conducted, Mozambican officials maintained a public neutrality, but in late 1987, President Chissano began to assert that his predecessor had been murdered. In February 1988, his vice-president for the first time publicly blamed Pretoria.[57] The death of Machel, with 34 officials and staff members,[58] was a shock to Mozambique and to southern Africa. Frelimo leaders, Mozambicans, and their friends wept openly at his funeral. But, once they had buried their president, the Frelimo leadership moved with disciplined determination to replace him, unanimously electing Joaquim Chissano, the popular prime minister during the transition to independence and foreign minister for 11 years.

The tragedy, however, galvanized support for Mozambique, as was the case after the PIDE assassination of Frelimo's first president, Eduardo Mondlane. More Tanzanian troops arrived to augment those involved in training and guarding installations in the north and north central area. Zimbabwe increased its contingent to over 10,000 men guarding the Beira corridor and fighting the MNR in three central provinces.[59] Algeria, Ethiopia, India, Nigeria, and Yugoslavia were among those countries which increased their offers of medical supplies, transportation, uniforms, rations, communications, and other equipment. In April 1987, Malawi committed three hundred soldiers to guarding repair crews on the strategic Nacala Railway, leading to the irony, when the first Malawian nationals were killed a month later, of Malawi making an official protest to South Africa.

In Norway, a leading Lutheran bishop called for military aid for Mozambique, citing as a precedent British military support for Norway during World War II. In such neutral countries as Holland and Sweden, "non-lethal" military aid came under increasing discussion, and a representative of the Canadian government spoke publicly of the possibility of supplying "boots and blankets."

Leaders of 48 Commonwealth countries, meeting in Canada in October 1987, established a technical fund for Mozambique and committed themselves to further assistance for such strategic projects as upgrading of the Limpopo Railway line. Chissano visited France, which approved the sale of helicopters and offered other assistance; and in early 1988 the West German chancellor Helmut Kohl called on the president in Maputo and promised assistance.

Among Western governments, only the United States, as a result of right-wing pressure, waivered. Just hours before leaving for France in late September 1987, Chissano received the credentials of the new US ambassador, Melissa Wells. She is on record as having described the MNR as "bandits," and her confirmation had been held up for almost a year by Jesse Helms, Robert Dole, and others who sought administration support for the MNR against the Mozambican government. She visited seven of Mozambique's 10 provinces in the first weeks after her accreditation and spoke out against the destruction and brutality she witnessed, particularly against children.

The administration's flirtation with the MNR had begun much earlier, during the time of covert dealings with Iran that led to the Iran-contra scandal, but only a handful of senior US officials knew about it. In August 1986, three MNR officials from Europe and the US visited the White House for a meeting with Reagan's then director of communications Patrick Buchanan.[60] Given the timing of their visit and the large amount of still unexplained Iran-contra money laundered in that period, it is strongly suspected that some of the illicit funds went to the MNR.

It was not until 15 July 1987, 11 months later, that the US administration finally admitted to any contact with the MNR. State Department spokesman Charles Redman said that although "low-level" talks had been held, "this meeting does not mean recognition of the group as a political organization. We are not changing our policy in any way."[61]

There were two unrelated reasons for the meeting. On 13 May 1987, the MNR, which by then had murdered or kidnapped over 150 foreign-aid workers in Mozambique including several nuns and priests, took their first US citizen hostage, Kindra Bryan, from a mission station in the center of the country. One condition for the release of a hostage is direct communication with the person's government as a form of recognition. Thus, a hostage deal was part of the reason for the meeting.

The second reason is related to right-wing Capitol Hill opposition to the appointment of Wells as ambassador to Mozambique. When Helms realized he could not block the appointment, he settled for official "contact" with the MNR.

The senator from North Carolina had demanded that Wells answer 247 questions in writing, including, "Did you personally study scientific socialism, Marxist-Leninism or Communism during your youth in Eastern Europe?" Wells was born in Estonia in 1932, when it was still an independent state, and left the country with her parents at the age of three!

After a Senate vote delayed Wells's confirmation in May 1987, the influential conservative British magazine the *Economist* bluntly described the MNR as "a rag-tag anti-communist force [which] has survived with infusions from Portuguese exiles, Brazilian malcontents and South African gun-runners. Its atrocities are well documented." Dole, the magazine said, supported them because "his private anxiety . . . is that he cannot make a convincing run as a conservative presidential candidate next year if he is seen to be supporting a Marxist regime."[62]

A president already in office can afford a different stance. That same month, Secretary of State George Shultz told visiting Mozambican Transport Minister Armando Guebuza that "both he and President Reagan were fully committed to the current policy" of support for the government.[63] A few weeks later, on 24 June, Assistant Secretary of State Crocker took matters further in his testimony to the Senate Foreign Relations Committee.

"No country in southern Africa has worked more consistently than Mozambique with the United States to further the cause of peace and stability in southern Africa," Crocker said. While Mozambique had adhered to Nkomati, "there is credible evidence that South Africa remains a reliable supplier of high-priority items that Renamo is not able to acquire on its own. . . . Credible reports of Renamo atrocities against the civilian population have undercut its popular appeal, as have increasingly apparent divisions among its military and political leaders."[64]

Crocker stressed the Thatcher connection, citing military and economic aid, as well as the visit soon after Machel's death of a British warship to Maputo; and he warned against the dangers for US policy of flying in the face of international opinion. "We will continue with this Western/African consensus," Crocker said.

Early in 1988, it was announced that a US warship would pay a mid-year visit to the port of Maputo, the first such visit since Mozambique's independence.

As the struggle continued on Capitol Hill, so did the struggle on the battlefield in Mozambique. In the north central area, troops from Mozambique, Tanzania, and Zimbabwe rolled back the MNR, recapturing towns and areas that had been lost in the previous year. But these gains led to a new and more vicious phase of South Africa's surrogate war.

On 8 July, the Mozambican newspaper *Noticias* reported that passengers on a coastal ship, *Chiloane II*, had seen an "unidentified" submarine off the Mozambican coast inside territorial waters. Within days, there were reports that several hundred newly trained and well-equipped MNR had been landed by sea in the southern Inhambane province, and military parachutes were found in a lake in the area. On 18 July, a large MNR contingent attacked the town of Homoine, in Inhambane.

The attackers wore new uniforms and were very well equipped, according to a US Mennonite agronomist, Mark von Koevering, who survived the massacre. "Having lived through this I think it's important for Americans to realize that this is not a civil war. These people are not fighting for any ideal. They're fighting to create terror," he said. "This is not a war to win land or support. It's a war of terror. . . . The bandits have absolutely no support from any person or group I have met."[65]

Four days later, the British newspaper the *Guardian* carried a report about Pretoria's support for the MNR, tracing the parachutes to a supply drop at Chitipe, in Inhambane, on 8 May.[66] The 29-metre parachutes of US manufacture can each carry almost 1,500 kilograms in weight and the only air force in the region which uses them is that of South Africa. More than four hundred people were killed at Homoine, including 44 children and some patients in the local hospital. It was the bloodiest massacre perpetrated by the MNR, but not the last. The nearby town of Manjacaze was attacked a few days later, and almost one hundred people lost their lives. Ambushes on commercial convoys increased in Maputo province, near the capital. In one such attack 96 trucks were destroyed; in another, a busload of people were burned to death inside the vehicle.

More information about South Africa's involvement is becoming available from people who have escaped from MNR captivity or have surrendered under the government's amnesty program, as well as from captured documents and prisoners. Now details of recent support have been exposed by some members of a group, recently released from prison in South Africa, who had been collecting information on assistance to the MNR.[67] Another source of inside information was a former senior official of the MNR in Portugal, Paulo Oliveira, who returned to Maputo earlier this year and spoke publicly of South Africa's involvement. He said visits to MNR training camps in Mozambique and South Africa enabled him "to see the degree of control that the South Africans had over the MNR."

Oliveira confirmed that South Africa was still giving material support to the MNR at the time he resigned in 1987. He gave the names of officers whom he dealt with (one of whom he said gave the order to begin cross-border attacks into Zimbabwe), and he said he was told by one of them that the objective was "to create massive confusion and difficulty for the Mozambican government.

One of the most frightening aspects of this surrogate war is the use of child combatants, some as young as 10 years old. Alfredo Carlos Mbulo, another 11-year-old, saw his family hacked to death with machetes, and less than two weeks later he was in training with the killers. He was kidnapped and trained to use a gun. He said he was afraid of guns, but those who refused were beaten. Another boy was made to watch while MNR men first beheaded his grandfather and then paraded the head on a pole. They told the child that if he cried, they would do the same to him.

The United Nations Children's Fund (Unicef) in Maputo has begun collecting these stories, and a Unicef official has described how some kidnapped boys have been conditioned to kill: "First, they kill a pig or a goat as a group. Then they kill as an individual. Finally, they graduate to a human prisoner."[68]

A captured MNR recruit told journalists that there were more than five hundred children serving at one base in southern Gaza province. The MNR prefers using children, he said, because the army "won't shoot children" and because "children do what we want them to do. Adults defect."[69]

US Ambassador Wells says these children are part of a larger pattern of abduction and recruitment. She described to journalists what happens when the MNR occupies an area: abducted civilians are ranged around the network of camps "like a cordon sanitaire"; children are separated from adults; girls are often sexually abused; boys are used to carry wood, water, food, and loot; some serve as scouts and spies, others train with weapons and go on combat missions.[70]

When several MNR bases were overrun in Zambezia province in 1987, dozens of these children were found. They, and many others found since then, have been given special care. One such center in Maputo contains 35 children at any one time, under the care of social workers, doctors, and psychologists. When they are able to leave, to be absorbed into extended family networks or orphanages, others take their place. They tell tragic tales of brutality, murder, mutilation, and use of drugs.

The director of Social Welfare in Maputo said, "You can tell the ones who have killed. When you speak they don't listen.

They're always vacant." The director explained that the child is doing things he doesn't understand: "He is worked like a puppet by an adult." She added that it is important to "note their conditions and behavior when they come in. Some always have to have a stick in hand as a weapon. Tantrums and fist-fights diminish over time, and depression is the long term problem. All of them are very tired and depressed."

The MNR also uses child mutilation as a signature of its terror. When its members struck across the border into Chipinge, Zimbabwe, in November 1987, they killed five children, abducted 20 and sliced off the right ears of seven more. This is not uncommon in what the *Washington Post* called "a chilling new chapter in a war that has maimed a generation."[71]

Some 200,000 children have lost or been separated from one or both parents. Mikas, about 12 years old, is one of thousands of orphans. He has lived at a school at Costa del Sol near Maputo for two years, since the train he was travelling on with his parents was ambushed and they were killed. His forefinger is all that remains of his left hand, and he lost his right leg below the knee. His dream is to have shoes and play soccer.

It is not only children who have suffered. A youth with a bandage over his left eye steps into the street at a traffic light in Maputo. As he passes, the realization that he has no ears, lips or nose is devastating. A young woman sitting on a bench at the airport has no ears. In the rural areas of the southern provinces, this is not an uncommon sight.

An Australian doctor, in the southern Inhambane province, asked if there were any problems she might help with. "Yes," replied an elderly woman. How could they get the bodies out of the well where the *bandidos armados* had thrown them, and get clean water again?

In Maputo's Central Hospital, a young mother with a mutilated face wept as she told of an attack on her village in the northern province of Nampula. Her husband escaped with their three children. She tried to run but was caught. Everything was stolen, including the clothes she wore. She wants to see her children, to go back to her village, but she thinks she cannot live there again.

Another young woman, not out of her teens, walked from house to house in a Maputo suburb begging milk for the baby strapped to her back. She had been in a convoy ambushed 60 kilometers north of the capital a few days earlier, and had come to Maputo to search for her parents.

The human cost of South Africa's undeclared war against Mozambique is estimated at well over 500,000 dead since 1980. According to a Unicef report published in January 1987, more than half of those who died were children under the age of five who, had it not been for the war, would have lived. They have died from easily preventable diseases such as diarrhea and measles, deprived of rudimentary health care as a result of the war, and from the effects of malnutrition.[72] The report predicted that at least another 140,000 children would die in Mozambique and Angola in 1987.

Of the total of 5,900,000 people in need of emergency relief, at least 1,100,000 are displaced within their own country, and the remainder have returned without means or have had their livelihood disrupted by continuing acts of destabilization. In addition to 2,200,000 people threatened with starvation in rural areas of Mozambique are 2,600,000 urban dwellers who rely on the market system for their food.[73] The number who have fled to neighboring countries was over 700,000 by April 1988. A serious consequence of the present situation is the disruption of normal commercial trade patterns between the rural and urban areas. Although drought has exacerbated the problem in some areas, it has not been the main cause.

"We are not simply talking about people who are hungry," says Oxfam (UK) representative Rosemary Feith, "but about people who are homeless and destitute. People who have lost everything." A report from DPCCN, the Sofala province disaster control department, says people in the north of the province are living on wild fruit and roots, and "wearing bits of old sacking."

The number of "displaced" Mozambicans in Malawi doubled between May 1987 and the end of the year, from 200,000 to 400,000, and reached over 500,000 in early 1988. Food distribution must take into account the hunger among the Malawian population in the area as well. Traditionally, a quantity of their food was bartered from across the border, from the surpluses of Tete and Zambezia provinces, but now there is none. Coupled with drought, Malawi is facing its own food shortage.

A Unicef report which revealed that due to war-related causes, Mozambique has the highest infant mortality rate in the world, also showed a startlingly high rate of malnutrition and infant mortality in Malawi, where it is estimated that more than 50 percent of children under five are malnourished.[74]

The number of Mozambicans arriving in southern Malawi was running as high as 1,000 a day in early 1988, according to an independent report commissioned for the US State Department, which also revealed in some detail the level of MNR brutality against civilians. The report, by Robert Gersony, said that many thousands of people are detained against their will be such methods as food deprivation so they are too weak to escape, or through fear after being forced to witness executions. Gersony's findings confirmed a high level of violence including rape and other physical abuse, murder and mutilation, abductions, forced labor in fields and as porters, systematic burning of villages and looting of possessions. "That the accounts are so strikingly similar by refugees who have fled from northern, central and southern Mozambique suggests that the violence is systematic and coordinated and not a series of spontaneous, isolated incidents by undisciplined combatants," Gersony concluded. Commenting on the report, a State Department official, Roy Stacey, described the situation in Mozambique as "one of the most brutal holocausts against ordinary human beings since World War Two."

If the upward trend in its economy had continued from 1981, Mozambique would be comparatively prosperous. Instead, it is the world's poorest nation. Exports in 1985 of just over $80 million were not enough to cover the 1986 cost of oil imports.

Mozambique's mineral wealth is vast and virtually untapped. The country is traversed by many rivers, and drought and cyclones notwithstanding, it has considerable potential for economic growth. However, the destruction of communications routes has made it virtually impossible for Mozambique to get its exports to the coast. At Gurué, in Zambezia, tea worth almost $14 million sits deteriorating, and factory equipment has been destroyed.

Production has halted at the Moatize coal mine in Tete province with a stockpile of high-grade coal worth about $25 million. The railway freight cars that moved the coal and the trucks that hauled cement to build the giant Cahora Bassa Dam now provide shelter to hundreds of families displaced by the war.

Nearly all geological mapping and prospecting has been halted as a result of the security situation, and most mines are closed.

The destruction of one economic target has a ripple effect through the entire economy. Cement is one example. A quarry that supplied the cement factory at Dondo, near Beira, was forced to close because of the security situation. This led to the closure of the cement plant itself, then of an asbestos roofing factory, and finally of an asbestos mine.

Mozambique, which had become a significant post-independence cement exporter, has been forced to import clinker from South Africa, spending precious foreign currency to produce any cement at all. Meanwhile, South African companies have taken over Mozambique's traditional export markets for cement.

In one attack on a successful state farm, $4 million worth of combine harvesters, tractors, trucks, and workers' housing was destroyed. In virtually every agricultural sector, production is at less than one-quarter of its 1981 level.

The state agricultural marketing company, AGRICOM, estimates that the grain (maize and rice) marketed in 1986 amounted to only 40,000 tons, less than one-third of the 1982 figure, and even lower than the initial estimate of 61,000 tons. This is the lowest figure in the 30-year recorded history of agricultural marketing in Mozambique and has put urban dwellers reliant on the market system at risk of hunger.

The Trade Ministry's Food Secruity Department says the main reason for this collapse in marketing is disruption and insecurity in rural areas, especially in the main producing provinces of the north central.

The destruction of major sugar processing factories caused national sugar production to fall to 35,000 tons in 1986 from 115,000 tons in 1980. The minimum requirement for internal sugar consumption in Mozambique is 70,000 tons. In 1986, production of vegetable oil fell to 6,000 tons, while the minimum supply needed is 15,000.

Statistics, however, do not begin to reflect Mozambique's suffering. South Africa's onslaught over the past eight years has affected every sector of the economy and the entire social fabric of the country, as well as jeopardizing the region's transportation routes.

In southern Mozambique, vicious attacks on all main access routes have made them unsafe for civilian traffic, even in escorted convoys, and southern railway lines have been sabotaged. These attacks may be aimed at cutting off the main access roads, making them unsafe for commercial traffic, and trying to prevent reopening of the Limpopo rail line, with the overall aim of trying to force negotiation with the MNR. Or there may be a more ominous plan, strategically reminiscent of

Saigon and Salisbury, of surrounding the seat of government: Maputo.

The escalation of activity in southern Mozambique coincided with renewed attacks along the Zambezi River, the brief retaking of Sena, and the apparent regrouping of MNR forces in the north central area after the successful offensive by Frontline allies in early 1987. These forces began trying to take towns as they did in 1986, but were now unable to hold them against Zimbabwean, Tanzanian and better-trained Mozambican troops.

The MNR managed to hold a few strategic locations, such as Malanje, on the Malawi border, which remains a key transit point. They also began cross-border attacks into neighboring Zimbabwe, on the same pattern as in Mozambique: looting and burning, abducting members of the local population to carry the loot, killing some, mutilating others, and scattering posters of Dhlakama.

At the end of 1987, the Mozambique government passed a law granting amnesty to those who give themselves up during 1988. In October 1987, in a speech reminiscent of the one a year earlier, South African Defense Minister Malan had again threatened Mozambique. Opening a new air force base in the northern Transvaal near the Zimbabwean border, Malan accused Mozambique of supporting the ANC and added, menacingly, that, "When it comes to freedom of action, the point is not whether the Frelimo government falls or Renamo takes over power." For South Africa, he said, whoever provides good neighborliness "which promotes and serves our interests" is acceptable.

Some Western governments and their diplomats in the region have argued that the Mozambique government should negotiate with the MNR. At his first press conference after taking office in late 1986, President Chissano asked what could be negotiated with people who inflict this brutality. "Negotiate with who[m]? What do they want? Will they rule a country of people with no ears, no noses, no breasts?"[75]

While the Mozambican government has rejected negotiations with the MNR, it has not rejected a political solution in favor of a military one. What it has done is to define whom it should talk to at the political level and whom it must deal with at the military level. The distinction was succinctly summed up by one government official who said, "We talk to the organ-grinder, not the monkey."

The "organ-grinder" is South Africa, as the trainer, supplier and director of the MNR. Therefore, it has been necessary for Mozambique to talk to South Africa—before, during, and after Nkomati. That South Africa acted in bad faith and breached the Nkomati agreement is now well documented; but this does not alter the validity of the political solution with South Africa that had to be sought by Mozambique.

2

ZIMBABWE
Apartheid's Dilemma

South Africa's destabilization of Zimbabwe can be divided into seven categories—direct military action including sabotage, clandestine support for banditry, assassination, espionage, economic sabotage, propaganda and disinformation. All of these have been used to varying degrees since Zimbabwe's independence on 18 April 1980. Yet Pretoria's policy planners face their greatest dilemma in just how far to go in destabilizing Zimbabwe.

The seeds of destabilization were sown in a 45-day period from 4 March to 18 April 1980 during the country's transition from colonial Rhodesia to independent Zimbabwe. At 9:00 A.M. on 4 March, the Rhodesian registrar of elections Eric Pope-Symonds announced the results of Zimbabwe's preindependence elections in a live radio broadcast to a hushed nation. The Zimbabwe African National Union-Patriotic Front (Zanu-PF) led by Robert Mugabe had won 57 seats, an outright majority in the one-hundred-seat parliament. Only one of those seats was in Matabeleland bordering on Botswana and South Africa. The Patriotic Front-Zimbabwe African People's Union (PF-Zapu) led by Joshua Nkomo had won 20 seats, 15 of them in Matabeleland. The United African National Council (UANC) led by Bishop Abel Muzorewa, prime minister of the short-lived and discredited "Zimbabwe-Rhodesia," had won only three.[1]

The remaining 20 seats, reserved for whites on a separate roll, had already gone to the Rhodesian Front (RF), whose leader, Ian Smith, had rebelled 15 years earlier against the British crown to prevent black majority rule.

Most Zanu-PF leaders had assembled in Mugabe's temporary home at 3 Quorn Avenue in Salisbury's Mount Pleasant suburb, and as the results were announced, province by province, cheers reverberated through the house. But as the victors celebrated, a convoy of Rhodesian armored vehicles moved menacingly down the street outside. The faces of the white soldiers expressed their bitterness, and their guns were trained on Mugabe's house.

In most white Rhodesian homes there was stunned disbelief. Mugabe, the pariah, the man they had been told was the "arch terrorist," had won. Some began packing their bags, loading their cars and heading for South Africa. Thousands more made plans to follow. Among those who headed south were members of "compromised" Rhodesian units such as the all-white Rhodesian Light Infantry (RLI), the Special Air Service (SAS), and the Selous Scouts, who feared retribution for actions during the war. Others who fled included police officers from the Special Branch (SB), a handful of officers from the Central Intelligence Organization (CIO), members of the Guard Force, district security officers and members of Muzorewa's Security Force Auxiliaries. In all, some five thousand "compromised" military and paramilitary went south. Some took with them invaluable intelligence and military knowledge; others took actual files.

They were gladly received by South Africa, which had pumped more than $2 million into a vain attempt to prevent a Zanu victory, subsidizing Muzorewa's campaign in particular.[2] Many of the Rhodesians went into the Fifth Reconnaissance Regiment, a newly formed specialist unit which was to see action against independent African governments throughout

the subcontinent, particularly in Angola. Others joined the
Military Intelligence Directorate (MID) which was to have a
key role in the destabilization of Mozambique and Zimbabwe.
South Africa built its policy of destablizing Zimbabwe upon a
foundation inherited from Rhodesia.

The shock of the election result was equally acute among
the losing black parties; six of them had failed to win a seat and
in most cases had forfeited their deposits. Muzorewa's humiliation was total. In the stage-managed "Zimbabwe-Rhodesia" elec-

tions of April 1979, in which neither Zanu-PF nor PF-Zapu participated, he had supposedly won a majority. Lord Chitnis, a British peer who observed that election, reported that it "was nothing more than a gigantic confidence trick designed to foist on a cowed and indoctrinated black electorate a settlement and a constitution which were formulated without its consent and which are being implemented without its approval."[3]

The Reverend Ndabaningi Sithole continued to pose as leader of Zanu, but it was clear that he had lost the confidence of the rank and file. He did not win a single seat in the 1980 election.[4]

Among all the contenders in the 1980 election the severest humiliation was reserved for Nkomo. He had been active in nationalist politics for over 20 years and rejoiced in the titles of "Father of Zimbabwe Nationalism" or "Father Zimbabwe." He had had himself declared "President for Life" of Zapu, and defeat at the hands of Mugabe, whom he referred to as "that young man," was unthinkable. Now the unthinkable had occurred.

Mugabe was magnanimous in victory, advocating a policy of reconciliation, offering Nkomo the post of constitutional president and, when he refused, giving him the powerful post of minister of home affairs. The Lancaster House agreement that led to the elections succeeded because each party was certain that it would win; consequently, Zanu-PF's victory left a plethora of embittered parties and individuals in its wake.

Mugabe displayed considerable statesmanship in trying to retain the confidence of all groups. In addition to Nkomo he brought three other members of PF-Zapu into the government. He also appointed David Smith, who had been deputy prime minister in the RF government, as minister of finance, and the head of the white Commercial Farmers Union (CFU), Dennis Norman, as minister of agriculture. However, he rejected a suggestion by Mozambican president Samora Machel that he include Ian Smith! Remarkably, after 30,000 people had died in the liberation war, he retained the services of the Rhodesian army commander Lieutenant General Peter Walls. Walls resigned a few months later when Mugabe refused to promote him to full general. He left for South Africa after disclosing that he had asked the British prime minister Margaret Thatcher to annul the election results when he learned that Zanu-PF had won.

For South Africa the outcome was a bitter blow. It had invested US $300 million in the Rhodesian war against the nationalists and also invested heavily in the election campaign against Zanu-PF. P. W. Botha sought the creation of a Constellation of Southern African States (CONSAS), which South Africa would economically and technologically dominate. Whereas some of the other election contenders might have been malleable, Mugabe certainly would not be, despite his country's heavy economic and geographic dependence on South Africa. In the first place he advocated socialist policies. Second, he was an outspoken critic of apartheid. Third, he was determined to decrease Zimbabwe's dependence on South Africa and reroute his country's trade, traditionally through Mozambique. On 1 April, 17 days before Zimbabwe became independent, Mugabe joined leaders from eight other independent states in the region to establish the Southern African Development Coordination Conference (SADCC). This loose grouping sought greater economic independence from South Africa, a policy diametrically opposed to the subcontinental hegemony Pretoria perceived as its role.

Thus, at the end of the 45 decisive days which embraced the period between the announcement of the election result and Zimbabwe's independence, many of the players who would take part in destabilization had taken their places. But Pretoria faced a dilemma in the case of Zimbabwe, whose geography placed it beyond South Africa's control. Destroying the communications routes through Angola to the west and Mozambique to the east ensured dependence upon South Africa for the landlocked countries of the regional hinterland. But Zimbabwe, located to the immediate north of South Africa, commanded access routes to Malawi, Zaire and Zambia. Of necessity, the destablization of Zimbabwe had to be handled differently.

In a broadcast to the nation on the night of his victory, Mugabe had tried to allay South African fears. The republic, he said, was a "geographical and historical reality. And our reality is that we must coexist with South Africa." Future relations, he said, would be conducted on the "basis of a mutual recognition of the differences which exist between us." Zimbabwe would not interfere in South Africa's internal affairs and, similarly, it would expect South Africa to respect Zimbabwe's sovereignty. Coexistence, however, did not mean keeping silent about apartheid.[5] In May, a month after independence, he banned a visit by the British Lions rugby team who were touring South Africa, and in late June he announced the severing of diplomatic ties inherited from Rhodesia. Ten days later, the South African foreign minister Roelof "Pik" Botha announced the withdrawal of his diplomats from Harare. The diplomatic missions in the two countries were replaced by trade missions.

On 3 August 1981, Joe Gqabi, representative in Zimbabwe of the African National Congress (ANC) of South Africa, who had spent many years imprisoned on Robben Island, was assassinated outside his Harare house. Three weapons were found abandoned at the scene: a silenced pistol and two silenced, Israeli-manufactured, Uzi submachine guns. All had been issued to the Selous Scouts prior to independence. But none was the murder weapon. They had been left, it would appear, to confuse the police investigators. The murder weapon was never found. Later it emerged that Gqabi had been targetted by the South Africans and eliminated by a squad sent into Zimbabwe to do the job.[6]

A small cell of strategically placed whites, at the time serving as members of the CIO, had supplied the vital intelligence for Gqabi's assassination. The cell was led by Geoffrey Price, a former Rhodesian intelligence officer who had stayed on after independence, and he had recruited two of his colleagues, Colin Evans and Philip Hartlebury. After getting compassionate leave claiming his "grandmother was dying," Price escaped to Britain and then South Africa. His flight came only days after Evans and Hartlebury had been arrested and charged with espionage and illegal possession of arms. After High Court judge Mr. Justice McNally dismissed the cases against them, ruling their statements inadmissible as evidence, the two spies were detained under emergency powers legislation.

On 10 February 1983, the minister of state (security), Emmerson Munangagwa, speaking from a brief prepared by a team of lawyers, made a lengthy statement to parliament challenging Mr. Justice McNally's judgement and reading extracts from the statements made by Evans and Hartlebury.[7]

"Immediately after their arrest," the minister said, "South Africa approached us through the mediation of their Trade Mission here in Harare, and admitted that the two spies were their men. Along with this admission came the request that we agree to release them and their families in exchange for 115 Angolan prisoners. We rejected that request. That was in January 1982. Towards the end of January or in early February the South Africans came again with a second proposal, this time offering one Russian spy and the 115 Angolan prisoners in exchange for the two spies at a venue of our choice. Again we rejected that offer." A further approach was made through a third party. "They, the third party, the Western regime, were willing to receive them and later pass them on to Pretoria. Incidentally, the two spies are British." This latter comment appeared to indicate that the third party was Britain.

Both Evans and Hartlebury had admitted to being recruited by Price to spy for South Africa, according to extracts of their statements that the minister read to parliament. Both admitted to supplying information about Gqabi and said their contact, named Erasmus, had said only three people knew the details of the assassination and "it was best if it remained that way." They believed the killers had come from, and returned to, South Africa.

The next incident occurred on 16 August 1981 when a series of massive explosions ripped through the armory at Inkomo Barracks near Harare destroying $36 million worth of armaments. A board of inquiry, including explosives experts from Britain and Yugoslavia, investigated three possible causes— enemy action, negligence and accident. They found the explosions were caused by "deliberate enemy action against Zimbabwe."[8]

Police investigations led to the arrest of Captain Frank Gericke, an explosives expert who had served in the Rhodesian security forces and stayed on in the Zimbabwe National Army (ZNA) as commander of the corps of engineers. He was in charge of the armory at Inkomo, had an office in the compound and complete access to the bunkers containing the armaments.[9] Police investigations and the questioning of Gericke were continuing when the South Africans made a tacit admission that they were involved. Frederick Varkevisser, a detective inspector in the police, obtained Gericke's release "ostensibly to undertake further enquiries." That was the last the Zimbabweans saw of either of them. With the net closing in, the South Africans had opted for what is known in intelligence parlance as "a hot extraction." Gericke and Varkevisser are believed to have flown to South Africa in a light plane. Gericke is now in the South African Defense Force (SADF).[10]

On 18 December, a 10–15 kilogram bomb exploded on the roof of the Zanu-PF headquarters at 88 Manica Road in central Harare. Six Christmas shoppers were killed and more than one hundred injured. But investigating officers were sure that the real target was the Zanu-PF leadership. The central committee had been scheduled to meet on the third floor of the building at the time the bomb exploded. Fortunately, the meeting had been postponed. Subsequent information obtained by the investigators suggested the operation was carried out by former members of the Rhodesian SAS serving in the SADF.

Another major sabotage attempt in this period went unreported. Explosive devices were placed in the fuel tanks of 30 tank transporters, tanks and armored cars at the ZNA headquarters in Harare. The charges had complex, electronically controlled timing mechanisms with a 33-day delay. But the fuses became saturated by diesel fuel and the two or three which detonated caused only minor damage. Had the whole lot gone off as planned, the bulk of the ZNA's armored vehicles would have been destroyed.

Late July 1982 brought two more serious incidents. On 23 July six tourists—two Americans, two Australians and two Britons—were abducted on the road from Bulawayo to Victoria Falls. It was about two years before their bodies were found, and the publicity generated by the incident seriously undermined Zimbabwe's tourist industry.

Two days later, on 25 July, a quarter of Zimbabwe's air force planes were sabotaged on the ground at the Thornhill base near Gweru in the center of the country. This virtually wiped out Zimbabwe's strike and jet interception capabilities. Incendiary devices detonated by a clockwork timing mechanism were used. The investigators were convinced, from information they received and from the level of expertise required, that this was another South African operation.[11]

The most damning evidence of South Africa's direct activities against Zimbabwe came on 18 August 1982. The ZNA, acting on information, ambushed a group of South African soldiers who had crossed the Limpopo River into Zimbabwe three days earlier. Three white soldiers in the group were killed. The remainder, believed to be Africans, escaped across the border. The South African government initially denied any knowledge of the group. But, under pressure from the solders' families to secure the return of the bodies, the chief of the SADF, General Constand Viljoen, held a press conference on 26 August. He identified the three dead men as Staff Sergeant David Berry and Sergeants John Wessels and Robert Beech. Berry had served in the Rhodesian SAS, Wessels and Beech in the RLI. All three were believed to have been serving in the Fifth Reconnaissance Regiment of the SADF special forces, a unit made up largely of former Rhodesian servicemen. Their base was at Phalaborwa in the northern Transvaal where dissidents were trained to fight in Mozambique and Zimbabwe. Viljoen claimed the group crossed into Zimbabwe on an "unauthorized raid" with the aim of freeing political detainees. He was unable to explain why one of the dead men was wearing an Angolan military uniform and another a T-shirt bearing the slogan of Muzorewa's auxiliaries.[12] This incident was acutely embarrassing for Pretoria.

As the election result had demonstrated, Zanu-PF's support lay primarily among the majority Shona who make up about 80 percent of the country's population of seven million and PF-Zapu's support was in the southwest of the country among the minority Ndebele.

Sporadic postindependence incidents between the Zimbabwe African National Liberation Army (Zanla) and the Zimbabwe People's Revolutionary Army (ZPRA), the former guerilla forces of Zanu-PF and PF-Zapu, respectively, spilled over into large-scale conflict in Bulawayo's eastern suburbs on 10 November 1980. A subsequent enquiry by a High Court judge failed to establish exactly what had triggered the fighting. However, another incident, which occurred in the days immediately preceding, but which was not then publicly known, may have been directly related to the Bulawayo fighting.

Before independence, whereas the Zanla forces fought a classical guerrilla war relying heavily on politicizing and mobilizing the rural population, ZPRA had been prepared for more conventional conflict. In September 1979, as the Lancaster House negotiations began, Rhodesian intelligence estimated that 70 to 80 percent of Zanla forces were inside Rhodesia. They also estimated that 70 to 80 percent of ZPRA forces were in Zambia, which was later confirmed by Zapu officials. In the last three months of that year, ZPRA infiltration increased dramatically. Then, when the guerrillas moved from the bush into assembly points for the cease fire as agreed upon in the Lancaster House settlement, and right after independence, Zapu began infiltrating weapons.

Seven trucks which had carried maize north to Zambia, and which should have returned empty, came south with armaments. These were cached near Assembly Point Papa, close to Mushumbi Pools, which contained ZPRA guerrillas.[13] Although no announcement was ever made by the government, these were unearthed and there was a ruling that all armaments held outside the country must be surrendered to the new ZNA. Train loads of Zanla armaments came in from Mozambique and were escorted to the main national armory at Inkomo Barracks near Harare. But ZPRA was not willing to surrender its weapons, and this in part may have triggered the Balawayo fighting.

In the first few days of November, immediately prior to the Bulawayo fighting, a number of trains laden with armaments crossed the Victoria Falls bridge from Zambia into Zimbabwe. These should have gone to the armory at Brady Barracks in Bulawayo. But when the trains stopped at Dett siding, ZPRA guerrillas from the nearby Gwaii River Mine assembly point were waiting. The armaments were unloaded and taken to Gwaii. The shipments included 571 tons of assorted ammunition for the standard AK 47 guerrilla weapon, 234 tons of rockets and grenades, 287 tons of light weapons including pistols, 195 tons of heavy weapons from mortars upwards, 22 tons of 7.62 ammunition, 39 tons of rockets and rocket launchers, 39 tons of various ammunition up to 145 mm anti-aircraft, 234 tons of diesel fuel, two armored vehicles and ammunition, 273 tons of assorted ammunition and land mines, 234 tons of small arms, and six heavy guns from 50 mm up to 105 mm and 155 mm. It was certainly more sophisticated weaponry than Zanla possessed and quite enough to resume the war, this time against the Mugabe government.[14]

There is a clear connection between the arrival of 49 wagon loads of armaments at Gwaii and the outbreak of fighting in Bulawayo a few days later. Mugabe said later that the fighting started when ZPRA began shelling and firing on a Zanla camp in the western Entumbane suburb of Bulawayo. This was borne out by a report in The Times of London on 12 November by Nicholas Ashford, one of the most reliable journalists covering southern Africa at that time. "Judging by the amount of damage done, Zanla had suffered the most," he wrote. "Many of thier huts were riddled with bullet holes and some had been partially destroyed by mortar and rocket fire. By contrast little apparent damage was done to the ZPRA camp."

Fighting broke out in Entumbane again on 8 February and on this occasion, as Mugabe put it, it followed a more "sinister pattern." ZPRA armored columns from Essexvale camp, 40 kilometers to the southeast of Bulawayo, and Gwaii, 230 kilometers to the northwest, began advancing on Bulawayo. And at Connemara Barracks, 160 kilometers to the northeast, ZPRA troops mutinied, breaking into the armory and killing some Zanla members of the integrated ZNA battalion in the camp. Every major access road to Bulawayo was blocked and it seemed clear that ZPRA intended to try to capture the capital of Matabeleland.

Faced with this massive threat, Mugabe acted decisively. With three of his nine integrated army battalions in mutiny, he called in still-existing, former Rhodesian ground and air units to quell the uprising. Seven of the 12 armored cars used by ZPRA to attack Zanla positions were destroyed, and the Gwaii column halted near the outskirts of Bulawayo after threats to bomb it were conveyed by airborne loudspeakers. Entumbane was a turning point. The mauling ZPRA received in their abortive bid to take Bulawayo, and Mugabe's decisiveness, had shown that they could not take control of even part of the country through conventional means.

Mass desertions of ZPRA troops followed from the integrated ZNA battalions and assembly points. Many took their arms with them. And the vast arms cache at Gwaii began to be distributed around the country. Nkomo and Zapu had spent some $20 million buying 52 properties, including farms, around the country in 1980–81, a number of them on strategic access routes around Harare.[15] The Mugabe government was to discover 10 months later that arms from Gwaii had been recached on some of these farms.

There was a strategic shift in ZPRA's tactics after Entumbane. At Hampton Farm, 50 kilometers southwest of Gweru, the caches contained enough arms to equip two infantry battalions and enough medical equipment for two or three district hospitals. At another of the properties, the Castle Arms Motel in Bulawayo, communications equipment was found, capable of jamming or monitoring army and police communications within a range of 100 kilometers. Mugabe announced on 13 February 1982 that enough armaments to equip 20,000 men had been found. These included a total of 2,051, 424 rounds of ammunition. The amount was "astounding and stunning." On 17 February he fired Nkomo and three of his colleagues from the government.

Some defeated ZPRA soldiers and politicians were determined to continue to try to overthrow the Mugabe government. But to do so, once existing supplies of arms and ammunition had been discovered, they needed a source of resupply and a rear base for training and sanctuary. Only South Africa could offer that.

The isolated acts of banditry which had begun after independence increased considerably in Matabeleland after Entumbane. But, initially, these do not appear to have been coordinated, falling largely into the category of "robbery for personal gain." In 1982, however, there was a dramatic increase in reported incidents. Between 1 March and 31 August a total of 1,136 incidents were reported in Matabeleland, Midlands, Masvingo and Mashonaland. Sixty-six people died in these six months, 41 of them civilians and 17 bandits. The others were members of the security forces. In the same period, official police figures show 175 bandits captured, 523 robberies involving bandits, 305 sightings of bandit groups, 46 contacts and 22 ambushes. Over two-thirds of the incidents, 847, occurred in Matabeleland.[16] In late 1982 definite proof was obtained showing that the bandits now had an external source of supply.

On 1 December seven bandits were involved in a series of contacts with Zimbabwean security forces at Dorrington Ranch in the Mwenezi area north of the South African border. Five members of the group, a member of the security forces, and two civilians died. Two others, Benson Dube and Zwelibanza Nzima, were captured two days later.[17]

From this group the security forces recovered five AK 47 assault rifles of Bulgarian manufacture and a Soviet RPG 7 rocket launcher. The original maker's numbers had been removed from the exterior and breechblocks of the weapons with a center punch; and new numbers had been punched onto the AK barrels and engraved on the RPG barrel with an electric Dremel-tool. The objective was obviously to obscure the original numbers of the weapons which could have been traced to South Africa or to a third party buying Eastern European weapons on South Africa's behalf.

But what could not be obscured on live ammunition were the head stamps on the captured 7.62 mm intermediate ammunition for the AKs. The head stamp, "22-80," was stamped on the base of cartridge cases found at the scene. The captured arms, and live and expended rounds, were given to police ballistics experts for analysis, and their findings confirmed conclusively that the bandits now had an external source of supply. The first two digits of the head-stamp, "22," indicated the country of manufacture, Romania; the next two digits the year of manufacture, 1980. The RPG 7 had been manufactured in 1981. Further enquiries revealed that Zapu's last supply of arms had been in September 1979. Thus this weaponry could not have been among the armaments brought back by Zapu, and the Zimbabwe government had not received any armaments from the Warsaw Pact countries.

From captured bandits and other intelligence sources, the Zimbabwean authorities had ascertained that South Africa was arming and training the bandits. But proving an external source of supply and proving that the source was South Africa were different issues, even when logic dictated no other plausible explanation.

As soon as the significance of the weapons and ammunition recovered at Dorrington Ranch was realized, instructions went out that all weaponry recovered at the scene of bandit incidents must be forwarded to the police armory for analysis. During 1983 a total of 1,403 rounds of "22-80" ammunition were recovered in 49 incidents with bandits. A total of 25 AK 47 rifles with their original numbers erased were recovered in these same incidents.[18]

Ironically, the first person to die in 1983 in an incident where it was known that "22-80" was used was an RF senator, Paul Savage. On 4 April, just before dusk, a group of about 20 bandits attacked the 70-year-old senator's Jahunda Farm in the Gwanda area about 230 kilometers south of Bulawayo, close to the South African border. The senator, his 20-year-old daughter, Colleen, and a visitor from Britain, Sandra Bennett, were killed. Mrs. Betty Savage was seriously wounded. Security forces recovered 26 "22-80" cartridges at the scene of the murders. On 11 June a farmer of Afrikaner extraction, Mr. H. Swaart, was ambushed at his farm in the Kezi area. Fourteen "22-80" cartridges were found at the scene. Three days later, a Figtree farmer, Ian Brebner, was killed by a group of eight bandits. Four "22-80" cartridges were found at the scene. On 13 July another RF senator, Max Rosenfels, and his son narrowly escaped death, and one of his employees died, when their vehicle was ambushed in the Figtree area. Six "22-80" cartridges were found at the scene.

Further important incidents involving the use of "22-80" ammunition occurred in Mozambique during this period. The ZNA had gone into Mozambique in late 1982 to protect the pipeline, road and railway linking Zimbabwe to the Indian Ocean port of Beira. In clashes with Mozambique National Resistance (MNR) bandits inside Mozambique, "22-80" ammunition was again found, together with weapons whose original numbers had been obliterated and substituted with false ones. The source of external supplies for the Zimbabwe bandits and for the MNR was obviously the same. As the external supplier of the MNR was already known to be South Africa, another piece of circumstantial evidence was added to the mounting dossier.

Of the two bandits captured at Dorrington Ranch, one, Benson Dube, said he had been trained by the SADF in South Africa. Dube had been in the Rhodesian farm militia and had gone south after Zanu's election victory. He said he had been infiltrated back into Zimbabwe on a reconnaissance and sabotage mission on 20 October 1982.[19] Such statements became increasingly common in this period, and details of Dube's statements, which throughly compromised the South Africans, were given to Pretoria. They admitted he had joined the SADF and undergone basic training. But, they claimed, he had failed to meet the required standards and had been discharged. What had happened to him after that they claimed they did not know, a most unlikely claim from a regime which monitors Africans' movements so closely. But the Zimbabwean authorities did not expect the South Africans to admit that Dube had been on a mission for them. It was simply a case of letting Pretoria know that Zimbabwe knew what they were doing. Early in 1983 the Zimbabweans handed over a dossier of a further 15 cases. The South African rebuttal was again predictable.

By this time, resupply and other forms of support from the external source were causing division within the bandit ranks, and in 1983 they could be divided into three categories. Some were bandits purely for personal gain. They had no ideology and did not pretend to act in the name of any leader or political party. Until some time in 1982, the remainder had been more or less homogeneous in that they said they supported Nkomo and Zapu and were committed to the overthrow of the Mugabe government. Among these were members of the South African-supported group Super-Zapu.

The point of contention which emerged within the ranks of this group was not that there was an external source of supply, but the fact that it was South Africa. Fighting broke out among the bandits, the first recorded incident of which occurred in the Gwanda area on 4 September 1983. Another incident occurred on 29 September in the same area. At first it was unclear why they were fighting among themselves. Interrogations of captured bandits revealed the reason, as well as further evidence of the South African connection.

One of the earliest detailed stories about conflict in the bandit ranks came from Judia Ncube, alias George Thebe Dhliwayo. He had been deported to Zimbabwe by the Botswana authorities on 21 May 1983 after being arrested in Francistown a week earlier. Ncube had been a member of ZPRA since 1974 and had turned to banditry after being demobilized from the ZNA on 23 March 1982. In July he had crossed to Botswana, going to the Dukwe refugee camp where he linked up with other dissidents. On 3 October, at the Marange Motel in Francistown, Ncube and another dissident, Peter Ndebele, alias Tafara, met three whites from South Africa. They were Mat Callaway, a former member of the Rhodesian police's special branch, another named Keith, and a third using an African name, Khumalo, whom it was suspected was a former Rhodesian police inspector, Allan Trousdale. The three said that South Africa would supply weapons. On 14 October a bandit group met the whites at the confluence of the Shashi and Limpopo rivers where the borders of Zimbabwe, Botswana and South Africa meet. A total of 20 AK 47 rifles with 80 magazines, 20 boxes, each containing 720 rounds of AK 7.62 mm intermediate ammunition, 10 land mines and detonators, two RPG 7s and 20 rockets were handed over.

A further meeting occurred in Francistown in December. This was followed by a delivery of armaments at the Shashi-Limpopo confluence on 21 December. This shipment included 56 AK 47 rifles, 16 AK magazines and 20 boxes containing AK 47 ammunition. On 3 January 1983 a further 36,000 rounds of AK ammunition were handed over and, three days later, money to buy two vehicles, a Toyota registration number BA 1438 and a Datsun registration BA 3796. During March 1983, Ncube said, reports began to be received that bandits operating in the Lupane area were dissatisfied with their leaders including himself, Ndebele and Hillary Vincent Ndhlovu. The Lupane group said, "They had their own leaders in the operational area and that they did not like the idea of getting weapons from South Africa. Instead they preferred to be supplied by [the] USSR since it used to supply Zapu during the struggle. The bandits suspected South Africa to be using them to promote its own interests."

Following this meeting, Ncube said, Ndebele sent Jabulani Moyo, alias Mututuki, to Pretoria to meet Callaway. He was "tasked to find out from Callaway if the South Africans were using the group to further their own interests." Callaway's response was to supply nine more armed bandits who had been trained in South Africa. They were deployed in the Gwanda area, where Senator Savage was murdered the following month. During the same month, the group operating from Botswana received a report that three bandits—including one supposed to have been involved in a July 1982 attack on Mugabe's Harare home—had been killed by the ZPRA group as suspected members of Super-Zapu, as the South Africa–aligned group was known. In April 1983, Ncube said, the South Africans handed over the biggest arms shipment to date. This included 60 AK 47s and 240 magazines, 60 light-green kit bags, 60 pairs of jeans, 60 pairs of boots, four bazookas, 12 bazooka shells, 30 boxes of AK ammunition, three boxes of explosives and detonators, and six Russian Tokarev pistols. These were issued to the groups operating in Lupane and Tsholotsho on 2 May.[20]

The testimony of one captured bandit would not, in itself, be sufficent to identify the source of external supply. But the name Mat Callaway occurred in more and more statements from captured bandits, as did details of conflict among the bandits over receiving supplies from South Africa, training in South Africa, and the transfer of armaments at the confluence of the Shashi and Limpopo rivers.

The major breakthrough, positively identifying the external source, began on 6 December 1983. On that date, and over the next two months, the Botswana government expelled 199 Zimbabweans in three groups. Among the 199, many were expelled for being in Botswana illegally, but they also included ZPRA deserters from the ZNA who had been involved in banditry and some of the top leaders of Super-Zapu.

The most important member of Super-Zapu to be expelled was Hillary Vincent Ndhlovu, who had been mentioned seven months earlier in Ncube's statement. He was handed over by Botswana authorities at Plumtree on 9 December. Like many young Africans in Rhodesia, he had been forced to stop his secondary school education at Form 2 and, after a series of menial jobs, had left to join the guerrilla forces in December 1976. He had joined Zapu and gone for a series of training courses in Zambia. He had fought for almost two years in the Tsholotsho area prior to the cease fire, gone to the Gwaii River Mine assembly point and thereafter been demobilized.

Frustrated and embittered, he linked up with other dissidents in March 1982 "so that the revolution could continue." Later he was involved in a series of acts of banditry with other former ZPRA members who had deserted the ZNA or who, like himself, had not been recruited into the new national army. In December 1982 he crossed into Botswana. In late December, in Francistown, he learned from other bandits that they had just met three whites, Callaway, Khumalo (an alias) and Carpenter, at the confluence of the Shashi and Limpopo rivers. They had been supplied with armaments which included 56 AK 47s. This was their second supply. These details tallied exactly with Ncube's earlier statement.

But Ndhlovu was not only to confirm independently what Ncube had already said; he provided a wealth of new information. Ndhlovu, by virtue of the fact that he had been a fighting ZPRA cadre for two years, had immediately been absorbed into the dissident group as a senior officer. During January 1983, Ndhlovu said, he and two other bandits met Callaway and Carpenter at the Marange Motel outside Francistown. A training program in South Africa and resupply were discussed. The next meeting with Carpenter and another white, called Nick, occurred at the Holiday Inn in Gaborone toward the end of April.

Following complaints at this meeting that arms supplies were insufficient, the bandits received a new shipment which included six RPG 7s, six RPKs, 88AK 47 folding butt rifles with approximately 240 rounds per weapon plus four magazines per weapon and approximately 10 TM 57 land mines. A further consignment followed in August. This included 10 RPKs, six

RPG 7s, 30 RPG 7 projectiles, six TM 57 land mines, plastic explosives and more AK 47 ammunition.

Dissent about the external source of supply was mounting among the bandits inside Zimbabwe by this time, Ndhlovu said. They were demanding to know how their commanders had become involved in weapons resupply from South Africa, whether their cause was being manipulated by the South African government and whether payment was being made for the weaponry. The principal person involved in the contacts with South Africa was Tafara Ncube, alias Kanka, another of the group believed to have been involved in the attack on Mugabe's home. Ncube, whose title was "chief of operations," and Ndhlovu were delegated to go into Zimbabwe to explain the situation. In the Inseza forest in October, they met with about one hundred bandits, who showed great hostility, particularly toward Tafara Ncube. At one point he was disarmed and beaten. The bandits allowed Ndhlovu to leave but insisted on holding Ncube. He escaped two days later, reporting that they had become extremely hostile and were threatening to kill him. Ncube said he no longer wanted to work with the bandits and Ndhlovu replaced him as "chief of operations" in the "military high command."

On 13 November they received another consignment of arms from South Africa. This included 100 AK 47 rifles, 10 RPKs, five belt-fed machine guns, six RPG 7s, 24 RPG 7 projectiles and 30 land mines. The weapons were cached inside Botswana not far from Plumtree in the early hours of 14 November. On 1 December, Ndhlovu led a group which attacked a train inside Zimbabwe near Figtree. He returned to Botswana on 8 December, was arrested the same day and handed over to the Zimbabwean authorities on 9 December. Ndhlovu and another bandit handed over at the same time, Kaiser Khumalo, alias Mercenary, who was the "deputy chief of operations," gave the Zimbabwean investigators the location of arms caches buried inside Botswana.[21]

Two buried caches of South Africa–supplied arms were dug up inside Botswana in the Ramokwebana Buthale area and at Selkirk Mine on 13 and 14 December respectively, as a result of Ndhlovu and Khumalo indicating their whereabouts. The caches included 67 AK 47s, 253 AK 47 magazines and 27,371 additional rounds of AK 47 ammunition. The caches also included a variety of mines, rocket launchers and rockets, other types of weapons, 285 kilograms of plastic explosives and 20,446 rounds of ammunition for FN rifles of the type taken by deserters from the ZNA. More significantly, the AK 47 ammunition included "22–80," proving beyond doubt that it could not have come from armaments brought back from Zambia by ZPRA and had to have come from an external source after Zimbabwe's independence. The statements of Ndhlovu and other Super-Zapu leaders handed over by Botswana left no doubt that the external source was South Africa.

On 3 February 1984, Munangagwa, the minister of state (security), announced in Bulawayo that "some of the cream of dissident commanders" had been handed over by Botswana and were in custody.[22] His announcement came during a visit to meet representatives of the Matabeleland branch of the CFU, led by its president, Mike Wood. The farmers had presented details of the deteriorating security situation as a result of bandit activities. Two white farmers had been killed by bandits in 1981; the number had risen to 33 in 1983. Some of the murders were directly traceable to bandits using "22–80" ammunition supplied by South Africa. In addition, they discussed the possibility of the CFU making representations to the South African Commercial Farmers Union and asking them to exert pressure to halt supplies to the bandits.

The Zimbabwe government had by now compiled a dossier of irrefutable evidence of South African involvement in supporting Super-Zapu. It contained details of Callaway's involvement, particularly with Ndhlovu, and his role in supplying arms to Super-Zapu, dates and places where armaments were handed over, the types and quantities of the armaments, vehicles used and where the armaments were taken. In addition, ballistics details about "22-80" proved that there was a post-Zimbabwean independence external source of supply and that the supplier was South Africa. Finally, details were supplied of incidents in which "22-80" had been used, with emphasis on the murders of whites such as Senator Savage.

Two days later, this dossier implicating South Africa in the destabilization of Matabeleland was given to Major General H. Roux, of the South African Chief of Staff Intelligence (CSI). The unspoken question was obvious: was it really the policy of a regime committed to apartheid and white supremacy to arm bandits to slaughter the white population of Zimbabwe?

The South Africans were clearly embarrassed by the amount of detailed evidence accumulated by the Zimbabweans.[23] Callaway, the South Africans admitted, had joined the SADF in 1982 on a one-year contract. They claimed his services had been terminated in July 1983 and that thereafter they had no knowledge of his whereabouts. It was the same story they had used in the case of Dube, captured at Dorrington Ranch, and in the case of several people captured in Mozambique. Denials notwithstanding, the message seems to have been understood. For the next 17 months there was no further evidence of infiltration of bandits or armaments from South Africa. Although there was concern over possible disruption of the mid-1985 national elections, infiltration did not resume until afterwards, in July. When the killing of white farmers in Matabeleland began again in November, after ZNA troops had gone on the offensive in Mozambique, the objective seemed to be to draw ZNA strength from Mozambique back to western Zimbabwe.

While, for obvious psychological reasons when dealing with the South Africans, emphasis had been placed on the number of whites killed, the catalogue of banditry grew on a scale that few realized. The police dossier from 1 February 1982 to 13 January 1986 listed a total of 7,313 incidents. By 22 September 1987 the number of known incidents had risen to 9,852. Many of these were reported sightings. But the list remained far from complete. A considerable number of people were given stiff prison sentences for failing to report the presence of bandits. But, faced with the atrocities being meted out by the bandits against those whom they described as "sell-outs" (meaning collaborators with the government), many still chose to remain silent and risk prison sentences rather than be subjected to the sort of reprisals illustrated by the following list:

11 July 1983, Zabalingwani village, a group of bandits cut off the ears of 16 villagers;

12 October 1983, Nyamandhlovu, Mbembezi Forest Area, two armed bandits accused Moment Ncube of being a "sell-out." They raped his two daughters in his presence and forced his son at gunpoint to chop off his father's head;

24 December 1983, Matopo Hills village in Kezi, two girls aged 13 and 16, returning from Christmas shopping in Bulawayo, were stopped by a group of five bandits. The girls were accused of being army informers and given a sharp knife and ordered to cut off each other's ears and noses. The 16-year-old later told the police, "I was terrified, I only scratched my friend's ears and nose. The dissidents got angry with me and ordered my friend to chop off both my ears. They then cut off my nose too";

4 January 1984, Ruby Ranch, six armed bandits shot Hleki Nyathi and his wife accusing them of being "sell-outs." They put their bodies in their house, set it on fire, and cut off the ears of the couple's two sons;

21 February 1984, Mulelezi school, a group of five bandits accused the teachers of being "sell-outs" for working for the

government. Five teachers were mutilated. Benson Moyo and Timotia Chinamatira had both ears and their noses cut off. David Muhuku had both ears, his nose and upper lip cut off, Obort Masunda, both ears, and Musa Siwela was stabbed in the neck;

10 March 1984, two armed bandits accused Bhedu Dube of being a "sell-out." They chopped off his genitals and ordered his wife to cook and eat them;

2 April 1984, Matikiti village in Dete communal land, six bandits abducted Harold Masini, cut off his eyebrows and burned his genitals before shooting him;

6 April 1984, Mbamba Dam, Gwaranyemba communal land, two brothers abducted and shot their grandmother, Moni Dube, accusing her of informing the security forces about their activities.

Zanu-PF officials became a particular target:

5 September 1983, Lupane, the local Zanu chairman, Amos Mukwananzi, was set on fire, wrapped in plastic, and then hanged by a group of three bandits;

26 November 1983, Dimpanhiwa school, Mackenzie Mpofu, a member of the Zanu Youth Brigade, was killed by bandits who cut one ear off each of two of his friends;

12 June 1984, Zhombe, bandits shot dead the local Zanu vice-chairman, Celestine Jongwe.[24]

The similarity between the atrocities committed by the South Africa–supported bandits in Mozambique and Zimbabwe is unequivocal.

Two other weapons, nonlethal but nevertheless destabilizing, which South Africa uses against Zimbabwe are propaganda and disinformation. Zimbabwean monitors first picked up a new station called Radio Truth on 15 March 1983, not long after the South Africans are known to have become involved with Super-

Zapu. The new clandestine station broadcast initially in Ndebele and Shona at 7:00 A.M. and 7:30 P.M. daily. Reception was
poor and a change of frequency in June brought with it the
introduction of broadcasts in English at 6:30 A.M. and 7:00 P.M.
But reception remained poor. A further frequency change improved the quality of the reception of broadcasts in English but
the reception in Ndebele and Shona remained of a poorer
quality.

The South Africans, of course, claimed the station was based
in Matabeleland, just as they said the Voz da Africa Livre, the
propaganda station supporting the MNR, was based in Mozambique. But Zimbabwean communications experts located
the transmitter near Johannesburg at the Meyerton studios
of the South African Broadcasting Corporation (SABC). The
South Africans continued to deny they were responsible for
the broadcasts. But then, on 25 November 1983, they broadcast
evidence of their own involvement when the tapes were ac-
cidentally switched in the SABC studios. The 7:00 A.M. ver-
nacular broadcast of Radio Truth began with the introductory
music of Voz da Africa Livre. And the Voz da Africa Livre
program began with the introductory music of Radio Truth.
Within a minute the tapes were switched. But by then
Zimbabwe had tape-recorded the evidence that the two stations were in the same place and not in Mozambique or
Zimbabwe.

If the quality of reception left much to be desired, the quality
of content was even more wanting. With almost 80 percent of
the electorate supporting Mugabe and Zanu-PF, personalized
attacks on the prime minister and his party were unlikely to
have much impact on the vast majority of Zimbabweans. Nor
were a people recently liberated from settler colonialism likely
to be impressed by the innumerable broadcasts in defense of
apartheid. The following, broadcast on 30 November 1983, illustrates the type of message Radio Truth was trying to get
across: "For the first time in 35 years, South Africa is taking

steps towards redressing their racial problems. Surely they should be applauded for abandoning traditional attitudes and fears and for taking a giant leap forward towards a more equitable society. By this step the appellation *apartheid* falls away and socialist and Marxist Africa has lost one of its big sticks with which it could beat Pretoria."[25] Such claims from Radio Truth's all-white English language broadcasters hardly tallied with other news people were hearing.

Even for less sophisticated listeners, Radio Truth had a serious credibility gap. Heaping praise upon Pretoria's friends and denigrating its perceived enemies was a clear enough indication where the broadcasts were coming from. Communism generally, and the Soviet Union and Cuba in particular, were bad. Radio Truth broadcasters clearly lacked any sophistication in propaganda. Even the unsophisticated audience in Matabeleland, the only likely listening group of consequence, knew that it was the Soviets in particular who had supported their party, Zapu, during the liberation war. And that the former ZPRA guerrillas who had turned bandit were arguing for the continuation of Soviet support. The line Radio Truth was propagating did not even appeal to Ndebele supporters of Zapu who were opposed to the Mugabe government, a measure of their sophistication. Also in the bad group was the United Nations (UN), a "communist organization," which everyone in Zimbabwe knew by and large had supported their struggle. Also designated "bad," the SADCC, as certainly the knowledgeable listener knew, had sought to reduce Zimbabwe's dependence on South Africa.

In contrast, the "goodies" included "our friends" Britain and the United States. Whitehall's large postindependence aid injections notwithstanding, the highly politicized Zimbabwean audience was well aware of Britain's role in their history in doing virtually nothing to prevent Smith's Unilateral Declaration of Independence (UDI), and of the way in which successive British governments had shown greater affinity toward the white settlers than the nationalist leaders. Israel was in the same group. In a 3 January 1984 broadcast, Radio Truth said, "Of all the countries, Israel has much to offer in the way of expertise and advice on how to successfully create a new nation." Taiwan and South Korea were also mentioned positively. On 13 June 1984, some months before Zimbabwe's first postindependence election, listeners were told: "Remember when our Zanu-PF leaders use the word 'socialism' they mean 'communism.' You will have a chance to vote against this foreign doctrine in 1985. Prepare now. Let us take a stand against communism and win a better life as did the people in South Korea."

In the event, Zanu increased its number of seats in parliament from 57 to 63 and its share of the popular vote from 63 percent to 77 percent. Radio Truth had supported Nkomo, Muzorewa and Sithole during the campaign. The number of seats won by Nkomo was down from 20 to 15. Muzorewa lost the three he had held, thereafter belatedly retiring from politics. Due to the personal unpopularity of the Zanu-PF candidate, however, a relative of Sithole picked up one seat in his home area.

Apart from reflecting South Africa's policies, Radio Truth was to play one other important role in Pretoria's overall destabilization of the region. One of the terms of the Nkomati Accord between Mozambique and South Africa was the termination of clandestine broadcasts. Voz da Africa Livre fell into that category, and on the night of 15 March, the day before the accord was signed, it announced that it was to stop broadcasting for "reorganization." The assumption was that South Africa had simply shut it down in line with Nkomati and that the MNR had been deprived of their propaganda station. On 7 July it became apparent that the MNR message would now be broadcast by Radio Truth which carried a lengthy item detailing the history of the organization and arguing that it was not supported by South Africa. Thereafter, items clearly in support of MNR became more frequent, and the South African line more apparent.

The South African campaign of disinformation against Zimbabwe has been waged in a number of ways, especially through unsolicited publications and circulars, a number of them mailed from Swiss Cottage in London, and attacks on individuals through anonymous letters. Some of them supplemented propaganda broadcast by Radio Truth. The earliest case of disinformation was detected soon after independence when publications were distributed claiming the formation of a new party, Super-Zanu, in which members of the existing Zanu leadership were said to be prominent. There was no truth in this but it caused some confusion.

The disinformation campaign was stepped up in 1983 after the creation of Super-Zapu. Prominent politicians, diplomatic missions and individuals received a series of letters which purported to originate from a "Joe Moyo," said to be a member of the ZPRA high command. One such letter was received by the manager of the Australian airline, Qantas. It raised doubts about the safety of an Australian cricket team due to begin a tour of Zimbabwe. The timing of the letter was significant; Qantas had just announced the cancellation of service from Australia to Johannesburg and that they would be flying direct to Harare.

A more sinister anonymous letter was circulated, to the prime minister among others, following the assassination in Harare in March of the leader of the League of Socialists of Malawi (LESOMA), Attati Mpakati. It accused two white CIO officers of being implicated in the killing and the hope was obviously that the charge would be accepted at face value, causing suspicion within the CIO. But it was not. Investigations revealed that South Africa was the source of the disinformation and that Mpakati was murdered by agents from Malawi.

After the discovery that South Africa was involved in that disinformation, a member of its trade mission in Harare was asked to leave Zimbabwe.

Zimbabwe's geographical and historical ties to South Africa, including the fact that it inherited Pretoria as its largest trading partner at independence, left it particularly vulnerable to economic destabilization. Joining the SADCC 17 days before independence was a public statement that it wanted to do something about this harsh reality. At the same time, from South Africa's standpoint, it was an unacceptable statement which, if left unchecked, threatened to reduce dependence on Pretoria in the future.

As Zimbabwe and other independent African countries sought to divert their trade to the Mozambican routes, all but one of the routes from Zimbabwe were systematically sabotaged. From December 1982, small arms, rockets, explosives and land mines were used by the bandits in southwestern Zimbabwe to disrupt the routes through Botswana. In Mozambique, the MNR damaged the routes to Beira and Maputo. In the eight years after Zimbabwe's independence only one route to the south or east remained unscathed: the direct railway line through Rutenga and Beitbridge from Zimbabwe to South Africa. To the north of Harare the routes carrying South Africa's trade to Zambia and Zaire were also untouched. That was far more than coincidence.

Much the cheapest route to the sea for Zimbabwe's bulk cargo is through Chicualacuala, in the extreme southeast, to Maputo. This route, known as the Limpopo line, was continuously attacked until it was closed down completely in mid-1984. As illustrated in table 2.1, the implications of this for Zimbabwe were that it would have to pay higher tariffs and be forced to use the South African trade routes, although the Limpopo route is much shorter and more efficient.

Table 2.1

Comparative tariff charges showing rate per ton over each route

Commodity	Maputo via Chicualacuala	Maputo via Komatipoort	Durban via Beitbridge	Port Elizabeth via Plumtree
Steel	30.6	64.7	86.44	85.120
Sugar (ex Chiredzi)	29.32	44.01	—	—
Tobacco (ex Harare, box rate)	806.00	1,196.40	1,366.80	1,876.40
Jet Al	99.15	125.94	151.74	173.47

Source: National Railways of Zimabawe.
Note: All figures are in Zimbabwe dollars which at the end of 1985 were approximately Z $100 to US $60.

Thus, through its surrogates and through direct action, Pretoria forced Zimbabwe and other landlocked countries to return to almost total dependence on South Africa's trade routes. But Zimbabwe's response in committing troops to secure the Beira route obviously surprised Pretoria. In the second half of 1985, South Africa introduced a new tactic. This was a two-tier tariff structure, offering lower contract rates than those published. The new contract rates undercut the previous Chicualacuala charges on four of Zimbabwe's main bulk exports—asbestos, tobacco, ferrochrome and steel. The message was obvious. Even if the Limpopo line through Chicualacuala was reopened, it would be more costly to return to the traditional Mozambique routes than to use South Africa. Not only was this a way of further destabilizing Mozambique by denying it foreign currency earnings, but it also exerted pressure on the Mugabe government. Given the competitiveness of world markets, and the fact that the bulk of Zimbabwe's commercial, industrial and mining sector is in private hands, the desire for greater independence from South Africa had to be weighed against the greater cost of using the Mozambique routes. The South African government's decision to offer these contract rates, when its railway system was already losing money, and when the new rates were more favorable than those offered to its own producers, was obviously a political one. Mozambique responded by reducing its own rates. In 1987, Conservative governments in Britain and Canada offered US $23 million and $15 million respectively to facilitate the reopening of the Limpopo line.

The vulnerability of Zimbabwe and other landlocked countries in the region was further demonstrated within a year of independence. First, South African Railways began to extend the turnaround time for railway cars, claiming there was excessive demand for rail transport. Loadings per day, particularly of diesel tankers, were reduced. Then, in April 1981, South Africa withdrew 25 locomotives previously loaned to the government of Rhodesia. It did this on so little notice that the Zimbabwean transport network was under severe strain for some time, forcing the loss of orders and stockpiling of maize, steel and sugar for several weeks. Lost export earnings were estimated at US $4.2 million a week.[26] In September 1986, as the threat of sanctions increased, new restrictions on Zambian and Zimbabwean trade, applied formally and informally respectively, caused delays of several weeks at the South African border crossing at Beitbridge.

One of the ironies of Rhodesia's UDI in November 1965 was that, although it temporarily severed formal ties with Britain, it increasingly reduced the country to the status of a colony or province of South Africa. The UDI years consolidated South Africa's dominion of Rhodesia in areas of finance, trade, investment, military and diplomatic relations. For the Mugabe government, disengagement in the military and diplomatic spheres could be effected relatively quickly but the other three areas posed far greater difficulties.

Insofar as finance is concerned, South Africa's investment in Zimbabwe is larger than in any other country in the region.

Most new investment during the UDI years came from South Africa and during the 1970s the Rhodesian private sector provided up to US $40 million a year in credit loans from South African banks. In 1970 five out of the 10 largest manufacturing companies were wholly or partly South African owned,[27] and at independence about 75 percent of the international debt was owed to South Africa.[28] The South Africanization of the Rhodesian economy was entrenched in sugar, citrus, timber, paper, food processing, fertilizers, copper, chromium, nickel, coal, the press and financial institutions. The new government was able to sever diplomatic and sports ties and to end the relay of SABC broadcasts by the Zimbabwe Broadcasting Corporation (ZBC). South African shares in the main newspaper group were purchased by the government, as were those in the country's largest bank which had been owned previously by the Netherlands Bank of South Africa. However, these and a few other actions barely scratched the surface of South Africa's economic stake in Zimbabwe. Severing the economic umbilical cord will take many years.

Furthermore, at independence in 1980, 19 percent of Zimbabwe's total trade was with South Africa and 41 percent of all Zimbabwean manufactured exports went to South Africa. Sixty percent of these exports were sold under a preferential trading agreement signed between Rhodesia and South Africa in 1964. This agreement gave Zimbabwean exporters preferential tariffs without which they would have been priced out of the South African market with little likelihood of finding new markets elsewhere. Abrogation of that agreement would have caused an estimated loss of Z $50 million a year in foreign currency and a permanent loss of 6,500 jobs in the manufacturing sector.[29] In recognition of his country's reality, Mugabe said on the eve of independence, "We must accept that South Africa is a geographical reality and, as such, we must have some minimum relationship with it." Trade had to be included in that minimal relationship. "We would hope that South Africa would reciprocate,"

Mugabe went on to say, "and not resort unduly to hostile acts against us. We are pledged to peaceful coexistence with it. We are opposed to the politics of South Africa, but we do not regard the people of South Africa as our enemies at all."[30] He said later that while his government fully supported the international community in imposing sanctions against South Africa, Zimbabwe's geographical reality was such that it was "not in a position to implement [them] to the full because of our present dependence on South Africa."[31]

Fuel is another weapon South Africa has used to destabilize Zimbabwe. The rehabilitation of the Beira to Mutare oil pipeline, owned by the British transnational company Lonrho and closed during the UDI years, was a major postindependence priority. The reopening of the line was technically feasible by the end of 1981 but on 29 October the railway bridge over the Pungwe River, which also carries the pipeline, was damaged in a sabotage attack and the road bridge was totally destroyed.[32] The MNR claimed responsibility but it was generally believed to have been carried out by an SADF sabotage squad. Once again, the South Africans had demonstrated the vulnerability of Zimbabwe's hostage economy. In 1982, once fuel was again flowing through the pipeline, it became a frequent target, causing considerable financial losses to Zimbabwe because no insurance company was prepared to offer coverage for the lost fuel. The attack on the fuel storage tanks at Beira by an SADF squad, in March 1982, was clearly designed to check Zimbabwe's decreasing dependence on South Africa.

In December 1982 Zimbabwe suffered an acute fuel shortage which almost brought the country to a standstill and resulted in lines at gas stations that stretched for many kilometers. With Zimbabwe once again entirely dependent upon South Africa for fuel supplies, the authorities there limited the fuel deliveries to Zimbabwe. At one point there was only one day's supply of gasoline and two days of diesel in the country. The revelation that ZNA soldiers had been deployed to guard the pipeline should have come as no surprise. Official records show that from 1982 until 11 September 1987 there were 36 attacks in which the pipeline was ruptured. Fuel losses were recorded in only 18 cases, but these losses (all uninsured and therefore a direct loss to Zimbabwe) totalled over 10 million liters of gasoline, diesel and jet fuel. On six occasions, the fuel loss from a single incident was over one million liters.

Official records also show that between 27 February 1986 and 9 September 1987 Zimbabwe's railway to the port of Beira was sabotaged on average just over once a week. But these incidents were more an irritant than a serious economic threat. Repairs were usually effected within hours, causing minimal dislocation, and the confidence of regional importers and exporters in the Beira route grew steadily from the second half of 1986. ZNA vehicles and convoys along the Beira road were also subject to attack, but the saboteurs, reluctant to become involved in direct confrontations with the well-equipped and efficient Zimbabwean troops, carried out their ambushes from a distance and inflicted minimal damage. The presence of the ZNA in the Beira corridor ensured that one route to the sea, independent of South Africa, remained open.

South Africa's destabilization in the first eight years of independence cost Zimbabwe millions of dollars in additional import and export tariffs, lost orders, property destroyed, and investment and tourism discouraged. Even with the Beira corridor open, Zimbabwe's bulk traffic still had to transit South Africa. By having to use the longer and more expensive South African routes, Zimbabwe was paying at least an additional US $60 million a year in freight costs by the end of 1987, according to Denis Norman, chairman of the private sector Beira Corridor Group.

Beyond that there was the cost of military operations at home, the cost of guarding the Beira route and finally, since

July 1985, the cost of deploying combat units in Mozambique for a joint offensive. The price cannot be fully quantified, but a government official said in September 1987 that some current estimates are as high as US $1.5 million a day. This figure is somewhat misleading, the official said, because it includes the salaries of more than 10,000 soldiers in Mozambique who would have to be paid whether they were there or not. However, the real factor in this cost equation is Zimbabwe's need to maintain an army of this size in defense against South African aggression.

1986, and to a greater degree 1987, brought two worrying, but predictable developments on the war front: a resumption of direct commando attacks on the capital and a sharp escalation in surrogate activity along the eastern border.

Although Zimbabwe had committed itself to giving diplomatic, moral and political support to South African nationalists, material support to guerrillas had been ruled out, as had cross-border operations and transit facilities. However, the porous nature and the length of Zimbabwe's borders, make them difficult to police and provide a ready excuse for any South African action.

Pretoria, in an effort to maintain its pretense that the threat to apartheid is external, struck deep into Zimbabwe on a number of occasions. The most daring and deliberate of these attacks was on 19 May 1986 when a South African commando group blew up the offices of the ANC in the center of Harare and, in a quiet suburb, destroyed the house where ANC representative Gqabi was assassinated in 1981. On this occasion, the South African authorities did not hide their involvement.

"I congratulate the security forces and assure the country that we will do it again when the occasion demands." P. W. Botha said in a written statement after simultaneous attacks on the capitals of Botswana, Zambia and Zimbabwe. The following day, he threatened further military action against the Frontline states.[33] According to Pretoria's policy planners, such strikes against neighboring countries have domestic, as well as international, objectives. Domestically, the raids drew a remarkable degree of praise from a variety of political opponents. Politicians to the right of the Mr. Botha's National Party (NP) gave "whole-hearted" support, describing the attacks as "necessary and highly timely." The leader of the "coloured" chamber (made up of South Africans of racially mixed descent, who are designated "coloured") in the tricameral parliament said he had "no criticism" of the action. Zulu Chief Gatsha Buthelezi observed that neighboring states had been warned that there would be retaliation for attacks on South Africa, and even the white liberal Progressive Federal Party, in muted tones, urged the government only to be "conscious of the grave international implications."

Despite the support of the pliant domestic laager, these audacious attacks on three Commonwealth countries indeed drew sharp criticism internationally. President Reagan's spokesman, Larry Speakes, in an unusually toughly worded statement, described the attacks as "outrageous" and "particularly inexplicable."[34] These "inexplicable" attacks, however, had been carefully timed to abort the mission of the seven-nation Commonwealth Eminent Persons Group (EPG) which was in South Africa at the time.

The group—co-chaired by the former president of Nigeria General Olusegun Obasanjo and the former prime minister of Australia Malcolm Fraser—had been established by the leaders of the 49 Commonwealth nations at their summit in Nassau, Bahamas, in October 1985. Its mandate was to encourage "political dialogue aimed at replacing apartheid by popular government."[35] There was little optimism about the group's chances for success. This pessimism was borne out by British Prime Minister Margaret Thatcher's obstinate refusal to consider sanctions against the South African regime, the mandate thus appearing to have been a concession to preserve a facade of Commonwealth unity.

Initially, however, the group appeared to be making some progress. They visited South Africa twice and had a vast array of meetings, including one with ANC leader Nelson Mandela in prison, where he had been for almost 25 years. Mandela and exiled ANC President Oliver Tambo had a profound impact upon the EPG. The group's most conservative member, Lord Barber, the former British Chancellor of the Exchequer, told a startled P. W. Botha that if he were South Africa's leader, the first two people he would bring into his government would be Mandela and Tambo. Ultimately, the appearance of progress was cosmetic, as is so often the case in South Africa, and the attacks on Botswana, Zambia and Zimbabwe were Pretoria's forthright response.

In early 1987, there were two more South African attacks on ANC targets in Harare. In the first, on 11 May, a young Zimbabwean woman, Tsitsi Chiliza, married to an official in the ANC's Harare office, died when a new television set exploded as she switched it on. The South African agent responsible for carrying the booby-trapped television to the ANC was subsequently lured to Maputo and captured, and more information is expected to be made public at his trial. On 17 May, an ANC house was rocketed in a Harare suburb. Later in the year, on 13 October, as Commonwealth leaders opened their meeting in Vancouver, Canada, to review progress since Nassau, halfway around the world a car bomb exploded outside a bakery in suburban Harare. Most seriously hurt among the 17 people injured was a woman who broadcast South African liberation programs on Zimbabwean radio and her husband.

Of perhaps greater concern, given its implications, was a new development in the proxy war waged by South Africa. Zimbabwean security officials had long feared that Pretoria might use its MNR surrogates to open up an offensive across Zimbabwe's eastern border with Mozambique. The dangers of this were not lost on the ruling Zanu-PF government, whose guerrillas had easily penetrated the same border prior to Zimbabwe's independence.

The first hint that such an offensive might be in the offing came from Washington. On 17 August 1986, a "Friendship and Cooperation Agreement" was signed in the US capital by representatives of the Reverend Sithole, who is living in exile in Maryland, and MNR spokesmen from Europe. The agreement itself exemplified the absence of any substantive political program offered by either signatory; for example, it calls for a multiparty system, which already existed in Zimbabwe where Sithole's cousin was among those holding a seat in parliament who did not belong to the governing party.

Few people inside or outside Zimbabwe took Sithole seriously, his only strength being the external support elicited from his collaboration with apartheid. One of his signatories was a former secondhand-car salesman, Bruce Anderson, who had been arrested in Rhodesia for fraud after previous convictions in Britain for theft, fraud and other offenses. He jumped bail while awaiting trial, soon after Zimbabwe's independence, and fled to South Africa where he became involved in a security firm. On 19 August 1986, Sithole had also signed an agreement with Anderson in Washington, appointing his firm, SACP Services (Pty) Limited, "consultants" on a variety of "projects" in southern Africa including "feasibility" of some ventures. The agreement stated: "On completion of these long term studies I undertake to pay on demand the sum of $100,000,000 Zimbabwe dollars, ... Twenty per cent of the aforementioned sum shall be paid in such currency and in any bank as may be directed by SACP Services. . . . This agreement shall be secured by a bond of US $2.5 million, a copy of which attached hereto." One of Anderson's "duties," Zimbabwean authorities believe, was a planned assassination of Mugabe by three former white Rhodesian soldiers, one of whom had been involved in the attempted mercenary *coup d'état* in the Seychelles.

Sithole had been soliciting support for the overthrow of the Mugabe government since at least 1984. Without success he approached both the US State Department (he saw the Zimbabwean desk officer) and the South African embassy in Washington with a shopping list of military requirements.[36] There were indications by 1986 that he may have received some financial support from ultra-right-wing US institutions. But a report, filed from Johannesburg, in a British newspaper, saying he had raised $20 million was regarded as grossly exaggerated or thinly disguised disinformation planted deliberately in South Africa.[37] It is also suspected that both Sithole and some MNR members may have received diverted funds from illegal US arms sales to Iran.

Although there was no evidence in 1987 that Sithole posed a military, or any other kind of threat, to the elected government in Zimbabwe, the threat from across the border in Mozambique could not be dismissed lightly. In response to a statement by Mugabe (after the death of President Machel) that Zimbabweans would fight to the last man to prevent a rebel takeover in Mozambique, an MNR spokesman issued a statement in Lisbon on 28 October 1986, formally declaring war on Zimbabwe. In the statement the MNR threatened to attack economic and military targets in Zimbabwe from their bases in Mozambique.[38] The MNR declaration came only weeks after Mugabe had increased the pressure for sanctions against South Africa at a Commonwealth meeting in London.

Cross-border incidents at that time were almost nonexistent; "about one a quarter," according to security officials in Zimbabwe. There was an occasional shooting incident, the odd store robbery or cattle rustling, but these gave no grounds for concern. Then, on 15 June 1987, the situation began to escalate dramatically. On that day, a group numbering about one hundred crossed the border from Mozambique and penetrated 30 kilometers into Zimbabwe's northeastern Rushinga District, burning huts and whole villages, looting stores and peasants' property. A crippled child was bayonetted in the buttocks and a woman all over her body, and 70 villagers were abducted. Three weeks later, 29 of those abducted were found massacred inside Mozambique, together with 10 Zimbabwean fishermen who had been abducted nearby.

This initial attack, on the eve of the tenth anniversary of the bloody Soweto uprising in South Africa, signalled the start of a dramatic deterioration of the security situation on Zimbabwe's eastern border. Between 15 June and 27 September, there were 51 recorded cross-border incursions in which 90 Zimbabweans were murdered (almost all of them civilians), 35 wounded seriously enough to be hospitalized, 165 civilians abducted and 27 stores robbed. Only two major economic targets were sabotaged in this period—Katiyo Tea Estate in the Honde Valley and some road-building equipment near Chipinge—but more economic attacks are expected.[39]

The cross-border attacks in that three-month period occurred in all four Zimbabwean provinces that border Mozambique, with more than half of them in Sithole's home province of Manicaland. Thus, his alliance with MNR provided a convenient, if transparent, cover under which South Africa could marshal its Mozambican surrogates against Zimbabwe, thus putting direct pressure on the ZNA to withdraw some forces from Mozambique to the home front.

In the same period, pressure was increased on Zimbabwe's defense forces in the southwest of the country, as the killing of white farmers escalated again to a five-year total of 41 by 1 October 1987. The previous spates of such attacks had, understandably, forced farmers to abandon their farms temporarily, with the result an undermining of confidence and of the economy. These attacks normally increase during the October planting season. Such incidents in Zimbabwe, coinciding with the new infiltration into southern Mozambique from South Africa, are seen as an attempt to force both the Zimbabwean and Mozambican armies to withdraw forces from the north of the country, where the war has been going badly for the MNR.

Thus, 1987 ushered in a new and dangerous phase marking a further escalation of South Africa's strategy to economically and militarily weaken its black-ruled neighbors, directly and through surrogates. Apart from additional and identifiable direct military and economic costs, future prospects indicate that more money will have to be diverted from development to defense as Zimbabwe fights for survival at home and in Mozambique.

Constitutional changes in late 1987, at the end of the seven-year time limit imposed by the Lancaster House agreement, strengthened the internal body politic of Zimbabwe with the removal of the constitutional presidency and of representation by race. Mugabe was sworn in as executive president and the non-racial nature of parliament was maintained with the appointment of several white and brown, as well as black, senators and members to fill the seats previously reserved for whites. A fundamental aspect of this period was the signing of a unity agreement with PF-Zapu, which then received several cabinet positions including a senior ministerial post for Nkomo. An amnesty was declared and implemented for ZPRA ex-combatants still in the bush. One group of 64 armed dissidents who turned themselves in at a remote police camp presented a list of demands that included education and jobs—and the withdrawal of Zimbabwean troops from Mozambique. Although the unity agreement removed any cover for South African operations in southwestern Zimbabwe, the latter point echoed Pretoria's interests and was a sharp reminder of the continuing presence of some of their Super-Zapu operatives should they decide to reactivate them. Even unity is unlikely, in the near future, to remove that problem. Nor will it remove South Africa's massive leverage on the Zimbabwean economy and sustained political and military attempts to keep it economically dependent upon South African trade routes.

Trying to control South Africa, one Western diplomat said, is like trying to house-train a fully grown grizzly bear. The indications in 1988 were that the bear was running amok and that Zimbabwe and the rest of the frontline could expect more of the same.

3

ANGOLA
The Struggle Continues

Among all the independent countries in southern Africa targetted in South Africa's destabilization program, Angola is in
many respects a special case. Many in the West now routinely
ascribe to the Cuban military presence in the country the full-
scale war at the time of independence, continued South African
army attacks, invasions and occupations and, perhaps more
significantly, the intense interest shown by the United States
in Angola's destiny. Some historical background is needed to
show that Western, and particularly US, involvement in Angola dates back to the start of the independence struggle in the
early 1960s.

Angola is potentially one of the richest countries in southern Africa because of its vast array of minerals and substantial
oil reserves. Geographically situated in both central and southern Africa, its Benguela Railway was, before independence, the
main outlet for copper and other minerals from Zambia and
from Zaire's Province of Shaba, the secessionist Katanga of the
latter country's traumatic independence. It was indeed in the
former Belgian Congo (Zaire) that the United States for the first
time deeply involved itself in the political life of a newly
independent African country. After the assassination of Patrice

Lumumba, on the subsequently acknowledged orders of the Central Intelligence Agency (CIA), that country, bordering on Angola, became Washington's main ally in the region.

In the mid 1970s, however, after the fall of fascism in Portugal, when the focus of the decolonization process had shifted to southern Africa, South Africa emerged as a far more powerful ally of the United States. Until 1975, Washington's choice to replace Portuguese leadership in Angola had been the president of the National Front for the Liberation of Angola (FNLA), Holden Roberto, who was brought up and based in Zaire. After the events of 1975, the firm favorite became Jonas Savimbi of the National Union for the Total Independence of Angola (Unita), ever more openly allied with the apartheid regime.

The People's Movement for the Liberation of Angola (MPLA), formed in Luanda in 1956 from the fusion of several anticolonialist organizations, stated from the outset that its goal was to unite all Angolan patriots—regardless of ethnic, regional or racial origin—to win independence. The MPLA put down deep roots in the main urban centers, the detribalized melting pots where patriotic resistance took on its most organized form (the same phenomenon is more than apparent in South Africa today); but when it began armed struggle in 1961, the bulk of its guerrilla forces came from the peasantry.

As a result of these beginnings, the MPLA retained clandestine networks in urban areas throughout the independence war. This was not true of the FNLA, formed among Angolan émigrés in Zaire around the ruling hierarchy of the former Kongo Kingdom. Nor was it true of Unita, also tribally based among Savimbi's Umbundu people, and created on the Zambian border in 1966. Indeed, the various trials of nationalists by the colonial authorities, particularly the renowned 1960 "Trial of the Fifty," were essentially of MPLA members.[1] And when the concentration camps and prisons were opened after the *coup d'état* in Portugal, the well-known persons released were also from the MPLA.[2]

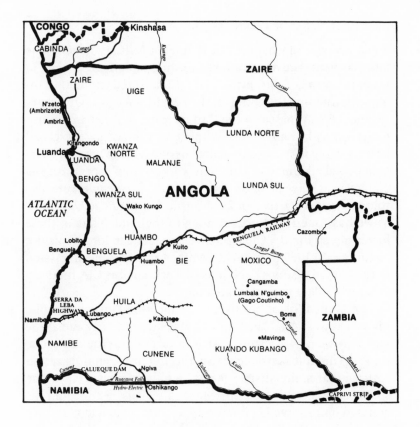

The armed struggle started in the area north of Luanda, in March 1961, after an abortive attempt by the MPLA on 4 February that year to storm Luanda prisons and police stations to release political prisoners. This was followed by ferocious repression and an estimated 20,000 people were slaughtered in the streets of the capital.[3] Many of the survivors fled north to the rural areas.[4]

It was in the Nambuangongo region north of the capital that the first inexperienced MPLA guerrillas started to organize armed struggle in what became their First Military Region. The Luanda events proved a catalyst, leading to uprisings, many of them unorganized, on settler plantations. Intensifying that explosive situation, the Union of the People of Angola (UPA, later renamed FNLA) based in the Zairean capital, Kinshasa, issued directives to kill all whites, all people of mixed parentage, all bearers of identity cards, so-called *assimilados* or educated Angolans, and all Umbundu migrant workers from central Angola employed as slave labor on coffee estates. The people were also told to await the arrival of 25,000 armed and trained UPA men, as well as American forces coming to their aid. None of these forces materialized.[5] The reference to American forces was not fortuitous. In 1959 Roberto had worked at the Guinean mission to the United Nations (UN) in New York, and his CIA links are believed to date back to that time.

The United States consistently supported Portuguese colonialism against Angolan nationalism, both militarily and at the UN. However, as a result of African reaction to the assassination of Lumumba, strategists in the Kennedy administration realized that nationalism was a force to be reckoned with. The solution was to select African individuals who could be counted on to serve US interests.[6] Roberto, who had close ties with Cyrille Adoula, a US protégé who headed the first "government of national unity" in Zaire, was the natural choice in Angola.

Following the FNLA's formation of a "Government of the Angolan Republic in Exile" (GRAE), in April 1962, life for the MPLA in Kinshasa, where they had established an office, became increasingly difficult. Their weapons were seized by the local *gendarmerie* who then fined them for possession of the weapons. Many leaders were arrested, refugee relief services were stopped and, in November 1962, the MPLA offices in Kinshasa were closed down and the movement was expelled from Zaire.

Angola's other borders were with Northern Rhodesia, a British colony later to become Zambia; Namibia, a South African colony; and the Congo (Brazzaville), from which only Cabinda was accessible to the liberation movement. Cabinda, the northern enclave cut off from the rest of Angola by a strip of Zairean territory, became the MPLA's Second Military Region. The Eastern Front, the Third Military Region bordering on Zambia, spread from Moxico province to Kuando Kubango in the southeast, Lunda in the northeast and Bié in the central highlands.

When war against colonialism was launched by the MPLA in the first region, it was UPA/FNLA that appeared as the foreign-backed force used to obstruct it. In the second region, Cabinda, a separatist group called the Front for the Liberation of the Cabinda Enclave (FLEC) played the same role. One of the leaders was Alexandre Taty, former "minister of war" in Roberto's GRAE and then an officer in the Portuguese "special forces" from which most FLEC members were recruited. In the east, the group used to undermine the struggle was Unita, formed in 1966 by Savimbi, also a former "minister" in GRAE.

The Portuguese dictator Marcello Caetano wrote in his memoirs that: "The opening of the eastern front by the enemy was tremendously worrying, and on assuming the responsibilities of defending Angola, Costa Gomes [commander-in-chief of the armed forces in Angola] faced the problem with intelligence and determination." Bettencourt-Rodrigues was given the job of pacifying the region, with quite a lot of autonomy and powers to coordinate all the authorities in the zone, and this he achieved; it included coming to an understanding with the Unita people, an insurgent group headed by Savimbi which was operating there in disagreement with the MPLA.[7]

A chameleon in Angolan politics, Savimbi's switches of allegiance over the years do not reflect corresponding ideological change or development, but appear to have been dictated by an overriding ambition to rule Angola.[8] He likes to boast of his alleged friendship with prestigious revolutionary leaders now dead and unable to set the record straight. These have included Che Guevara and Amilcar Cabral. In a letter to Basil Davidson, written in April 1972, Cabral writes, "Yes, I knew Jonas Savimbi in Lisbon as a faithful servant of the Portuguese colonialists. In 1959 (I no longer remember the exact date) he even made a speech at the Geographical Society in favour of the Portuguese colonialists and their great work. Later he became a 'nationalist,' a 'minister,' 'leader of so-called Unita,' etc., but in my opinion he is still serving the Portuguese colonialists. Jonas Savimbi is well aware of my opinion of him, because I told him in Lisbon as well as in Africa."

Unita's claims about its "anticolonial struggle" in eastern Angola center on acts of sabotage against the Benguela Railway. These were doubtless intended to cause friction between the Zambian authorities and the MPLA. The MPLA had given Zambia assurances that it would not touch the railway, which transported goods to and from the landlocked country then virtually surrounded by minority regimes. Neither Portuguese military bulletins nor foreign observers noted any military activity by Unita which, then as now, was given to dramatic communiqués calculated to exploit the credulity of uninformed outsiders.[9]

The true role of Unita in eastern Angola was revealed after the Portuguese *coup d'état* of 25 April 1974, when officers of the Movement of the Armed Forces (MFA) gained access to the secret files of the former fascist regime in Lisbon. These contained correspondence between Savimbi and high-ranking Portuguese military personnel in Angola. In a letter dated 26 September 1972 to General Luz Cunha, commander in chief in the colony, Savimbi recommended, as a way of ensuring peace in eastern Angola, "weakening the MPLA forces inside Angola to the point of liquidating them," a task which could be fulfilled by the combined forces of the Portuguese "military and para-military forces and Unita forces." He further proposed "liquidating the MPLA camps in the regions on the border between Angola and Zambia," pointing out that Unita's lack of political status made it easy to carry out such actions without being censured by any international body. Indeed, the Organization of African Unity (OAU) recognized Unita only after the *coup d'état* in Portugal.

On 4 November 1972, Lieutenant Colonel Ramires de Oliveira of the Portuguese Eastern Military Zone command wrote to Savimbi, agreeing that Unita's clandestine activist cells in Zambia could be used "to gather information on the MPLA's activities and on the political situation in Zambia and other African states" and "to exert pressure on the Zambian government to make it change its policy towards Portugal." He writes that "as far as UNITA is concerned, the main thing at this stage is to stay in the Upper Lunguê–Bungo region, far from the war, and secretly strengthen its cooperation with our troops. ... At this stage, therefore," he continues, "the mass surrender of the population and guerrillas cannot be contemplated."

Unita's contact with Portuguese military intelligence was maintained through settler timber merchants called Duarte and Oliveira, and also through a Portuguese Benedictine missionary, Padre António de Araújo Oliveira. Costa Gomes and Bettencourt-Rodrigues have since confirmed that there was a "gentleman's agreement" with Unita in eastern Angola. This was, according to Costa Gomes, that "we Portuguese do not fight Unita and Unita does not fight the Portuguese forces." There were, he said, "certain areas especially for Unita," for example, "Lunguê–Bungo ... an area where we cannot go to fight, nor can the authorities collect taxes from the indigenous people."[10]

When the files of the previous regime in Portugal were opened for the inspection of the international press in 1982, one British newspaper, the *Times*, headlined its article "Secret files in Lisbon compromise Savimbi." The report said: "In one dusty file, a telegram from the DGS [new name of PIDE, the security police]... marked Top Secret and dated September 19, 1972, gave an account of a report by Dr. Jonas Savimbi, who at the time was supposed to be fighting the Portuguese. According to the DGS, Dr. Savimbi said his Unita guerrillas had successfully ambushed a 30-man force of the rival MPLA. He now wanted arms, ammunition, syringes, medicines and a safe passage for his men through Portuguese Army lines."[11] Costa Gomes estimated that Unita had no more than six hundred men at the time. In June 1974 a Portuguese newspaper, *Diário de Lisboa*, put the figure at "approximately 300 men under arms."

Copies of these documents and others, including memos and minutes of meetings of the Timber Working Group set up to coordinate Operation Timber, the code name for collaboration between the colonial authorities and Unita, are in the possession of the Angolan government. The Timber Working Group, chaired by Bettencourt-Rodrigues and including members of the military and military intelligence, met with the timber merchants Duarte and Oliveira, acting as intermediaries with Unita, and reported back to and received instructions from the colonial authorities in Luanda, who in turn maintained close contact with Lisbon regarding the operation.[12]

Little is known so far of the precise movement when Savimbi started his collaboration with the Portuguese military in eastern Angola. There are indications, however, that it dates back to well before November 1971, when the first meeting of the Timber Working Group was held.[13]

By 1970, the MPLA had expanded the guerrilla areas to Bié, the Fifth Military Region in the center of the country, and to the Fourth Military Region, Lunda. Costa Gomes admitted as much when interviewed in 1984; and countless foreign observers testified to the advance of the struggle from the liberated areas in Moxico province, where schools, medical care and elected local authorities were being established under MPLA leadership.

In a document issued in January 1970, entitled "Western countries are providing Portugal with arms to fight the Angolan patriots," the MPLA revealed a list of military aircraft supplied to Portugal by the countries of the North Atlantic Treaty Organization (Nato). The list included Thunderjets, Sabers and Lockheeds made available under the American Military Assistance Program, B-26 bombers provided by the CIA, and other equipment provided by Britain, Italy, the Federal Republic of Germany, France and Canada.

Another statement issued two months later announced the presence of South African troops in eastern Angola, consisting of "four commando companies equipped with helicopters, artillery, automatics, bazookas and other types of weapon." The statement said that the "South African military interventionist corps" were "quartered in their own private barracks" in Lumege district of Moxico. "Two of these companies took part in many of the October–November 1969 enemy operations in the Lunda region. The remainder carried out criminal acts against population centres, crops and our people's fishing areas, even making incursions into Zambian territory."[14]

The MPLA repeatedly denounced the use of napalm by the Portuguese forces and also of herbicides and defoliants of the types used by the Americans in Vietnam. Chemical warfare caused the guerrilla struggle severe setbacks. The peasants— who received from the MPLA such rare essentials as soap and salt, together with schooling and medical care—were the main source of foodstuffs to sustain the guerrillas. The destruction of their crops caused a massive movement of peasants to the Zambian border, where the MPLA was faced with having to provide relief for thousands of hungry peasants. This was one of the reasons why despite the April 1974 *coup d'état* in Portugal, the MPLA was in a militarily less favorable position than in the first years of the decade when it had been advancing from strength to strength. Another factor was treachery within its own ranks.

In late 1973 the MPLA revealed that it had foiled a plot to assassinate then MPLA president, Dr. Agostinho Neto and other top leaders. As in the case of the murders of Eduardo Mondlane, president of the Mozambique Liberation Front (Frelimo), in 1969, and Amilcar Cabral, the leader of the African Party for the Independence of Guinea Bissau and Cape Verde (PAIGC), in 1973, members of the liberation movement were instruments in the plot. In the MPLA, Daniel Chipenda, by no means a military commander as he is often described, but a diabetic unfit for military activity, used his post in charge of logistics to devastating effect.[15] Using the tribalist slogans of his so-called Eastern Rebellion, Chipenda further damaged the MPLA by inciting attacks on their camps along one section of the Zambian border. These fratricidal attacks did not lead to ugly scenes of fighting because of the restraint exercised by the MPLA, mindful that the aim was to undermine its relations with the Zambian authorities and the governments of other countries.[16]

Another faction, the so-called Active Revolt, opposed the MPLA leadership after the *coup d'état* in Portugal. This was a small group of no more than 70 people. The overwhelming majority of them were intellectuals in exile who had failed to respond to Neto's appeals to all Angolans to join the liberation struggle, regardless of class or educational background, a policy which had resulted in the relatively large number of university-educated people among MPLA field commanders. That revolt had all the earmarks of a bid for power when independence was already on the horizon. Most members of the group subsequently acknowledged their error and hold responsible posts in Angola today.

These were all weakening factors in the crucial months leading up to the independence process. Yet they also resulted in the closing of ranks around the leadership of the MPLA, particularly behind Neto, whose single-minded determination and refusal to accept the possibility of anything but victory had provided a powerful incentive in overcoming obstacle after obstacle in the course of the struggle.

After the coup in Portugal the Junta of National Salvation headed by General António de Spínola still did not recognize the right of the colonies to independence; and the new democratic freedoms of Portugal were not extended to the colonies, where the war continued. The MPLA issued a statement in Lusaka on 1 May condemning this and demanding that "all Angolan prisoners be released, that Angolans be free to organise themselves politically and that Angolans be given the right to freedom of expression and assembly in our country."

Then began a struggle in Portugal between the right wing of the new regime and those determined that the democratic aims of the MFA should not be betrayed. These internal conflicts were to influence events in Angola decisively, with Western powers, and particularly the United States, moving rapidly to promote their own interests. An MFA representative proposed that a referendum be held in Angola to decide on independence. Commenting on this in June 1974, General Costa Gomes said, "I am convinced that Angola will decide to remain Portuguese. It should strengthen its relations with South Africa and Rhodesia."[17]

That same month Unita signed a cease-fire with the Portuguese military authorities—before Portugal had even accepted the principle of independence for Angola. Padre Oliveira, the missionary who had already carried messages between Unita and the Portuguese military, acted as guide to the cease-fire talks in the bush. The Portuguese delegation to Operation

Dove, as it was called, was led by Lieutenant Colonel Fernando Passos Ramos of military intelligence, "a man who already had Unita's full confidence," according to the padre.[18]

The Portuguese clearly attached no military significance to the cease-fire signed with Unita in June. In July the MPLA denounced the continued bombing of villages by the Portuguese air force and on 8 August 1974, the Junta of National Salvation issued a communiqué that stated: "Once a cease-fire agreement has been reached, the Portuguese Government will set up a provisional government in which all liberation movements will be represented, together with the ethnic groups most representative of the state of Angola, which will obviously include the white ethnic group."[19] The MPLA condemned this as an attempt to divide and rule by resorting to tribalism and racism, stating its own position as: "One nation, one people, and no minorities or sectors of the people with special status."

Although the MPLA sought to iron out the problems with Chipenda's Eastern Rebellion and the Active Revolt group, these factions refused all dialogue and lobbied for external support, internationalizing what the fiercely independent MPLA regarded as internal affairs. The OAU and neighboring independent countries first made themselves intermediaries and then set up a "good offices" commission. Under external pressure and in the spirit of unity, the MPLA agreed to take part in a congress held in Zambia in August 1974. An international press campaign, meanwhile, announced that Chipenda was "tipped for leadership."

On 1 August, a week before the congress, 83 guerrilla commanders signed the proclamation of the constitution of the People's Armed Forces for the Liberation of Angola (Fapla), which constituted unequivocal support for the movement's leadership from the commanders fighting in the field.[20]

The MPLA was obliged to attend the congress with the same number of delegates as the Eastern Rebellion faction, 165, while all 70 members of the Active Revolt were delegates. During the checking of credentials, 14 of Chipenda's delegates were found to be FNLA members. These and other anomalies, including the droves of journalists hovering around what was supposed to be a gathering held in camera, caused the MPLA delegation, headed by Neto, to walk out of the congress. Chipenda then proclaimed himself president of the MPLA. Some months later he joined the FNLA. In September, the MPLA held a conference inside Angola attended by delegates from all the fighting fronts and from the clandestine networks in urban areas.

In addition to the efforts to dilute Angola's independence, or even to exclude the MPLA from the process, there were a number of schemes to carve up the country. In September 1974, a meeting on the island of Sal, in Cape Verde, was reported between the short-lived President Spínola of Portugal and President Mobutu Sese Seko of Zaire, also attended by Roberto. The 28 September issue of *Horoya*, published in Guinea (Conakry), reproduced a letter to President Sékou Touré from a member of the Portuguese MFA who wished to remain anonymous. It said that during the Sal meeting on 14 September, it had been agreed that Portugal should support Roberto in an Angola shorn of oil-rich Cabinda province, which would be controlled by the Kinshasa-based FLEC separatist group. A Zaire-Angola-Cabinda federation was then to be formed with Mobutu as president, and possibly Roberto as vice-president. In exchange, the letter said, Zaire would help Portugal to obtain diplomatic respectability in Africa (the OAU had said it would not recognize the new regime in Lisbon until all the colonies were independent); to ensure that "all Portuguese and multinational companies acting under cover of Portugal should, for a period of at least 20 years, dispose as they please of the vast natural resources of Angola, Cabinda and Zaire"; and to help Portugal "to recuperate Mozambique and Guinea-Bissau, either by provoking *coups d'état* or by undertaking assassinations by infiltrating merce-

naries or corrupting certain cadres in the liberation movements."

However, Spínola was forced to resign shortly thereafter. His
successors in Portugal recognized the principle of independence for the colonies, and the MPLA was then able to sign a
cease-fire in October. In November, the first official MPLA
delegation arrived in Luanda to a tumultuous welcome.[21]

With a view to preventing further hostilities and further
foreign intervention in Angola's affairs, the MPLA went to
Mombasa, in Kenya, where an agreement was reached with
FNLA and Unita delegations to cooperate in all fields and to
start negotiations with the Portuguese government. In January
1975, at a meeting in Alvor, Portugal, an agreement was signed
under which a quadripartite transitional government—made
up of the MPLA, the FNLA, Unita and Portugal—would run the
country until elections in October and independence on
11 November. That same month, when a tenuous platform for
unity was being sought to avoid further bloodshed, the CIA
decided to give $300,000 of military assistance to its own Ango-
lan protégés, the FNLA.[22]

Under the terms of the Alvor Agreement, the various movements were to enter Angola legally and without arms. The
MPLA respected this agreement, and Unita was too small a
force at that time to matter; but the FNLA came in heavily
armed. The United States supported them, both directly and
through Zaire; and Zaire sent troops into Angola. In 1975, the
border between Zaire and Angola was uncontrolled, with
troops pouring in, stolen Angolan coffee and other goods pouring out, and the Portuguese army—which was supposed to be
controlling the situation—removed from that area.

Interviewed in Luanda the previous year, the MFA senior
representative, naval officer José Martins e Silva, referred to an
earlier FNLA plan to invade Angola with Zairean troops, a plan
apparently postponed pending negotiations. He went on to say,
"We are not very worried about the guerrillas belonging to

Unita, because they are not strong . . . Organisations like Unita and FNLA are unwilling to accept peace because they know they don't represent more than a small number of people in a small section of the country. The MPLA is different. It is the only one with sympathisers in all the urban centres of Angola. The greatest number of them were known before the revolution. We know that all the black intellectuals are MPLA."[23]

In the capital, the FNLA was regarded as a foreign force, speaking mainly French and Lingala (the Kinshasa dialect), and, finding it had no political support there, tried to impose itself by military means. The big onslaught started in March. The MPLA instructed its army not to respond to provocations. Over the ensuing months, until July when the MPLA started its counteroffensive, Luanda became a charnel house, with the FNLA shelling the shanty towns, torturing and killing. The mortuaries were overflowing, and MPLA members and leaders were hunted down, going into hiding as in colonial times.

Some insight into what the FNLA and Unita offered to the Angolan people in ideological terms is found in speeches made by their leaders in this period. In a radio broadcast in February 1975, Roberto, after dismissing direct democracy as "utopian," said, "We are a religious people and our faith is unshakeable. We are creating our true democracy based on that great faith, against atheistic materialism which crushes the individual, the group and the collective in its iron jaws." Savimbi was more complex. In the central highland region of his birth, he sought to whip up tribal feelings, speaking in Umbundu of the need to kill whites and people from the north who, he claimed, wanted to take over the country. Speaking in Portuguese to the most conservative sector of the settler population, which flocked to support him, he said that the Angolan people were not ready for independence. Unita was "in favour of a period of preparation of the Angolan people to play the democratic game," he said, according to a report in a Lisbon newspaper, *Diário de Notícias*, on 17 June 1974. "After a period of educating the people," elections should be held for a legislative assembly, out of which would come a government which would "discuss what future relations between Portugal and Angola should be."

The forces brought together under the Alvor Agreement to form a transitional government were therefore totally disparate, making the agreement impracticable from the outset. The United States, as shown by its aid to the FNLA, was determined that it should not work. The Soviet Union, in contrast, did not send any assistance to the MPLA throughout 1974 and the first eight months of 1975.[24] The Portuguese MFA, rent with internal contradictions and conflicting views, was unable to take a clear stand beyond defending what were regarded as Portugal's interests in Angola.

What actually sounded the death knell of the Alvor Agreement was when the FNLA tried to seize power by force. But, as a result of the MPLA counteroffensive, the FNLA and Zairean troops were driven out of the capital in July 1975 and, with the massive support of the population, the MPLA finally brought peace to Luanda. Without troops to back them up, the FNLA leaders left Luanda, followed by the Unita officials. Government in Angola, only four months before the date set for independence, was left in the hands of the MPLA and the Portuguese, the latter due to leave the country in November. Contrary to propaganda claims, the MPLA was not put into power by Cuban or any other forces.

The United States reacted swiftly to the new situation and, also in July, the CIA and President Ford approved a further US $14 million in covert support for anti-MPLA forces. It was now total war. Elite troops of two Zairean commando battalions were pouring in from Zaire and settlers were openly demonstrating in favor of Unita. Having lost the capital, the FNLA and Unita sought to establish their own spheres of influence: the FNLA in the northern provines of Uíge and Zaire, Unita in Huambo, and Bié in the central highlands.

By August the MPLA had established control over 12 of Angola's then 16 provinces. The CIA stepped up its interference. According to John Stockwell, then chief of CIA operations in Angola:

> Paramilitary and organizational specialists flew to Kinshasa, and the [CIA] task force took form. The third C-141 flight was launched. And in long working sessions of CIA paramilitary and logistics officers, the composition of the shipload of arms was carefully formulated: twelve M-113 tracked amphibious vehicles; sixty trucks, twenty trailers; five thousand M-16 rifles; forty thousand rifles of different caliber; millions of rounds of ammunition; rockets, mortars, recoilless rifles, etc. . . . Strategic and tactical radio networks were devised for use by the FNLA inside Angola. Mobutu's army and air force hauled enough arms for two infantry battalions and nine Panhard armoured cars to the FNLA base at Ambriz, seventy miles north of Luanda.[25]

MPLA President Neto appealed to the people to resist and to ensure national unity. The Zairean invasion from the north was followed by a far more serious one from the south when a contingent of South African troops entered Angola in August, allegedly to protect the Calueque hydroelectric dam near the Namibian border. This preceded an invasion by motorized troops which resulted in the occupation of the whole of central and southern Angola. The joint plan called for the invading forces from the north and south to converge on the capital and take it before independence on 11 November.

"During September and October, the CIA, with remarkable support from diverse US government and military offices around the world, mounted the economy-size war with single-minded ruthlessness," Stockwell later wrote. He continued:

> The lumbering USAF [United States air force] C-141 jet transports continued to lift twenty-five-ton loads of obsolete US or untraceable foreign weapons from Charleston, South Carolina, to Kinshasa, where smaller planes took them into Angola. The USN *American Champion* sailed from Charleston on August 30 with a cargo of arms and equipment. Any "snags" were handled by a phone call from the CIA to the White House, Pentagon or State Department, and the problem magically disappeared. CIA officers, eventually eighty-three altogether, were dispatched to the field, where they beefed up the Kinshasa, Luanda, Lusaka and Pretoria stations, and managed the air, ground, maritime, and propaganda branches of the little war. An additional $10.7 million, authorized by the president on August 20, 1975, for the purchase of more arms, ammunition, and advisors for Angola, had brought our total budget to $24.7 million. The deadline was November 11, 1975, when the Portuguese would relinquish proprietorship of the colony to whichever movement controlled the capital at that time."

The entire operation was coordinated between Washington and Pretoria. A South African brigadier, Ben de Wet Rood, led the South African troops who manned the FNLA's artillery in northern Angola. In a 1984 interview, he said, "I was called in to assist with the formulation of an attack on the capital by the FNLA, which was operating in the north of the country with the aid of the CIA, while South Africa and Unita were fighting in the south." He went on to say that, "after discussions with Roberto, I put in a request for some 5,5s [140 mm] guns and in less than 48 hours they were flown in and ready for deployment. This shook Roberto to the core, because the SADF [South African Defense Force] had complied within hours to what the

CIA could not do in weeks." The brigadier described the battle at Kifangondo, some 20 kilometers north of Luanda, which took place on 10 November, the eve of Angola's independence. The FNLA was routed there, according to him, because of its total military incompetence. The brigadier and his 26-man SADF team then decided that discretion was the better part of valor and made their way to the port of Ambrizete, where the South African ship the *President Steyn*, secretly lying offshore, picked them up and carried them back to Walvis Bay in Namibia. The brigadier then flew north to act as chief of staff, and later of command, of the South African forces invading Angola from the South.[26]

Eyewitness reports that the white troops with Unita were South Africans found their way into the Western press, but the South African government continued to deny its involvement in what was supposed to be a secret war. In mid-December, however, the Angolan government announced the capture of four South African soldiers between Cela (now Wako Kungo) and Kibala, 750 kilometers north of the Namibian border. Only then did South African Defense Minister P. W. Botha acknowledge that his army was deep inside Angola.

John Stockwell went into considerable detail about CIA co-operation with the South African Bureau of State Security (BOSS) in this phase. He described South African planes meeting US transport flights in Kinshasa to ferry arms into Angola, and South African planes and trucks turning up "throughout Angola with just the gasoline or ammunition needed for an impending operation."[27] South African Prime Minister John Vorster was later to admit implicitly that his government received a green light from the US administration for its invasion of Angola.[28]

On the eve of independence, there was also an invasion of the oil-rich Cabinda enclave by a Zairean force in support of FLEC. "Seeing his chance in October 1975 to annex the MPLA-held Cabinda, Mobutu approached the CIA," Stockwell wrote.

"We promptly flew in a one-thousand-man arms package for use in the invasion, and CIA officers of the Kinshasa station began to visit the FLEC training camps to coordinate."[29] Fapla, however, continued to hold Cabinda, with the help of a small group of recently arrived Cuban instructors.

The purpose of the Washington-Pretoria operation in support of the FNLA and Unita was not, therefore, to avert an "impending" Soviet and Cuban takeover, as the propaganda made out, but to prevent the MPLA from proclaiming independence. The first Cuban military personnel arrived in Angola in October 1975: 480 instructors to help train the vast numbers of young people flocking to join Fapla. The experienced MPLA guerrillas were too busy on the various combat fronts to handle training as well.[30]

The South African army, with armored vehicles and heavy artillery, took the towns of Lubango and Moçâmedes (now Namibe) on 27 October and started to advance on Lobito and Benguela. South of Benguela was a Fapla training camp where Cuban and Angolan instructors, armed with nothing more powerful than a 75 mm antitank gun, fought the invaders and were defeated. Those were the first Cubans to die on Angolan soil.

Independence took place as planned, to the sound of the boom of artillery north of the capital. The celebrations were a moving event, proud and festive. In the south, the South African advance was halted about two hundred kilometers from Luanda, mainly by blowing up bridges on their route.

During the critical period before independence, the MPLA had appealed to friendly countries for help. Cuba, Guinea-Bissau and Guinea (Conakry) offered to send troops. Having just come out of a guerrilla war, Fapla had neither the numbers of men nor the technology to defend the country against the conventional forces and sophisticated equipment pouring across its borders. But neither could the required numbers of friendly forces arrive before the 11 November independence date, as Portugal was still the administering power in Angola. By this time Zaire was estimated to have 11,200 regular soldiers and officers in Angola. The South Africans numbered about six thousand, a figure which doubled shortly after 11 November when an army brigade moved across the southern border into Angola. Mercenaries of various nationalities had joined the forces in the north, as had an organized group of Portuguese fascists who called themselves the Portuguese Liberation Army (ELP), and the FNLA and Unita.[31].

On 5 November, the Central Committee of the Communist Party of Cuba decided to send the first Cuban combat troops to Angola in response to MPLA requests. Code-named Operation Carlota, it started with 650 Cubans aboard three old, four-engine planes of Cubana Airlines.[32] The Soviet Union supplied arms and equipment to Fapla as did Yugoslavia, and Cuba continued to send men. With this assistance Fapla started to drive out the invading armies. On 14 November, according to Stockwell, the 40 Committee, which supervises the CIA and which had instructed them to "prevent an easy victory by Soviet-backed forces in Angola," now asked the agency to draw up a program that would "win the war."[33] The South Africans were being pushed back, and in the north the invading forces had been reduced to a disorderly rabble, robbing, killing and raping as they retreated. When the FNLA chief of staff, former Portuguese colonial army colonel Santos e Castro, disappeared to South Africa, he was replaced by mercenary Costas Georgiou (the self-styled Colonel Tony Callan) as the CIA made a last-ditch effort to save the FNLA.[34] The story of the mercenaries captured and put on trial is well known. They were put on trial before international observers and four of them, including one American, were sentenced to death and then executed. The rest, including two Americans, were given lengthy prison sentences.

In the urban centers they occupied in the south of the country, the South Africans set up a Unita administration; and it was under a South African umbrella that the FNLA and Unita set up what they called a "democratic republic of Angola" in Huambo, recognized by no government in the world. Fighting later broke out in Huambo between the FNLA and Unita, with Huambo radio broadcasting pleas for peace on 22 December 1975. By 23 December the fighting had spread to Benguela. When Huambo was liberated on 8 February, charnel houses filled with bodies and mass graves were found. Special targets had been Umbundu officials of the MPLA. Wherever the FNLA and Unita had passed, banks, safes and vaults had been broken into and millions of escudos stolen from the country. Nowhere had they set up a viable administration.

Members of the US Congress, angered by revelations of clandestine operations in Angola and by the lying of CIA officials, introduced an amendment to the 1976 Arms Export Control Act, banning all military aid to antigovernment forces in Angola without congressional approval. Known as the Clark amendment, for the chairman of the Senate Foreign Relations Committee, Dick Clark, who proposed it, this became law on 9 February 1976.

Savimbi had already made his headquarters in Kinshasa, from where he had appealed for help. Stockwell recorded that Savimbi approached the CIA station chief in Kinshasa in early February and asked what he should do next. "When Washington finally answered, it encouraged Savimbi to continue fighting. On February 11 the CIA spokesman promised Savimbi another million dollars in arms and money. On February 18, 1976, Secretary of State Kissinger sent the American chargé in Kinshasa a cable, instructing him to tell Unita leaders that the United States would continue to support Unita as long as it demonstrated the capacity for effective resistance to MPLA."[35] This was after the Clark amendment became law.

The South Africans were finally driven out of Angola on 27 March 1976. In their retreat, they blew up every bridge they crossed, plundering vehicles, machinery, pedigree cattle and everything they could transport into Namibia. The Angolan government estimated the quantifiable war damage at US $6.7 billion.[36]

Military means having failed, the United States tried economic warfare against Angola. Stockwell recalls that "CIA and State Department attorneys repeatedly discussed means of blocking Gulf [Oil]'s payments to the MPLA, and pressure was brought to bear . . . [but] Gulf could not be persuaded to deliver the money to Roberto or Savimbi unless they controlled Cabinda. On December 23 [1975] Gulf compromised and put $125 million in an escrow bank account."[37] The Angolan press reported that on 20 December the US technicians had abandoned Cabinda for Zaire after closing down all the oil wells.[38] The money owed to Angola and the three-month halt in oil pumping represented a loss of valuable revenue for both the Angolan government and the US company. Only in March 1976, when the invading forces had been defeated, did the US authorities permit Gulf Oil to resume operations in Angola.

The US government again interfered, blocking delivery of two Boeing 737s which, at the time of the transitional government, the Angolan airline had purchased from the United States. But, to quote Stockwell again, "the CIA, the working group and Henry Kissinger were not about to permit the delivery of new American jet airliners to Luanda. Why provide the means for the MPLA to fly their delegations around the world, drumming up support? In November the State Department withdrew the export licences for the planes."[39]

President Neto spoke about the Boeings in a speech on 26 December. "You know that some planes we bought from the United States have not been delivered to us up to now, although we have paid for them. They are two big planes, Boeings, and the American state feels that it should not deliver the planes, which are ours. Obviously, this is pure and simple theft.

Unless they want to keep the planes and return the money to us. But they have kept the money and also the planes."

The US State Department asked George Wilson, president of Boeing, to deliver the following telex to the Angolan authorities:

> THE UNITED STATES CANNOT STAND BY FOR A SOVIET POWER PLAY IN AFRICA.
>
> IF THE MPLA IS WILLING TO WORK FOR A POLITICAL SOLUTION AND COMPROMISE WITH ITS RIVALS, THE UNITED STATES IS WILLING TO BACK A PEACEFUL SETTLEMENT.
>
> THE MPLA WOULD DO WELL TO HEED OUR ADVICE THAT NO GOVERNMENT CAN PLAN THE RECONSTRUCTION IN POSTWAR ANGOLA WITHOUT UNITED STATES AND WESTERN HELP. NO GOVERNMENT CAN OBTAIN THE TECHNICAL AND FINANCIAL RESOURCES TO STIMULATE ECONOMIC DEVELOPMENT WITHOUT AMERICAN CONSENT. IN FACT, THE UNITED STATES WOULD BE QUITE RESPONSIVE AND HELPFUL TO A COALITION GOVERNMENT THAT WAS NOT DEPENDENT ON THE SOVIET UNION.
>
> THE UNITED STATES GOVERNMENT IS PREPARED TO THINK FURTHER ABOUT THE SUPPLY OF BOEING AIRCRAFT TO ANGOLA AND IS WILLING TO UNDERTAKE FURTHER DISCUSSIONS DEPENDING ON THE COURSE OF EVENTS IN ANGOLA. THIS MESSAGE SHOULD BE GIVEN TO LUANDAN AUTHORITIES. AS THE MPLA IS AWARE, ACCESS TO SOPHISTICATED TECHNOLOGY IS A PRIVILEGE; THE PRESENT BOEING CASE IS JUST ONE, BUT A GOOD EXAMPLE OF THE ADVANTAGES OF HAVING ACCESS TO AMERICAN TECHOLOGY.

However, as with Gulf Oil, the course of the war forced the State Department and CIA to back down over the Boeings. On 29 March, two days after the expulsion of the South African army, the Angolan airline took out a full-page advertisement in the local press announcing the arrival of the Boeings.

The United States, Stockwell records, "launched a major political effort to embroil and entrap as many countries as it could into opposition of the MPLA. Secret agents were sent to third world conferences," including the OAU summit in Addis Ababa in January 1976 and the summit of non-aligned leaders in Sri Lanka in August, with a view to preventing Angola's membership. US officials based in Africa used "whatever leverage they could manage with their host governments to prejudice them against the MPLA."[40] However, Angola became a full OAU member in February and the foreign ministers of the nonaligned movement accepted Angola's admission by acclamation even before the summit meeting. In June that year the United States vetoed Angola's admission to the UN, and it was not until after Republican Gerald Ford was defeated by Democrat Jimmy Carter in November that the United States abstained from voting and Angola became a UN member.

Intimations that the Carter administration would recognize Angola proved illusory. Pursuing a vacilating policy—depending on whether the doves headed by UN Ambassador Andrew Young or the hawks personified by Security Adviser Zbigniew Brzezinski were ascendant—it posed as conditions for recognition of Angola the withdrawal of the Cuban forces from the country and power sharing with Unita.

US analysts were certainly not unaware that the Cubans were in Angola as a result of South African invasion and that their withdrawal would weaken the country militarily in the face of the continuing threat from Pretoria, although the Cuban presence was used as an excuse for continued US involvement in Angola. In April 1976, barely a month after the expulsion of the South Africans, the Angolans and Cubans agreed on a programmed reduction of Cuban forces and in less than a year they were reduced by more than a third. Renewed South African aggression, however, stopped the withdrawal. A further decision by the two governments, in 1979, to reduce the number of Cubans was followed by an escalation of SADF military operations against southern Angola.[41]

On 25 July 1979, the Angolan government presented to the UN a detailed account of South African acts of aggression against the country during the period from 26 March 1976 to 11 June 1979. It described the types of operation, the damage caused and the estimated losses. The report (UN Document S/13473) listed 193 armed mine-laying operations, 21 border provocations, seven bombing raids and one large-scale operation in which both air and ground forces took part. Special mention was made of the 4 May massacre at Kassinga in Huíla province, when two hundred SADF paratroopers, assisted by two C-130 troop transport planes, 14 Alouette SA-300 and Puma helicopters, nine Mirage III aircraft and a number of smaller planes, launched a 6½ hour attack on a Namibian refugee camp, indiscriminately slaughtering the occupants, mainly women and children. Nerve gas was also used in the attack. The second largest operation of this period was the bombing of a Patriotic Front training school at Boma, in Moxico province, on 26 February 1979, a combined operation of the South African and Rhodesian air forces.

Estimated human losses during this three-year period were at least 570 killed and 594 wounded among the Angolan population, 612 Namibians killed and 611 wounded, 198 Zimbabweans killed and six hundred wounded, three South African refugees killed and eight wounded. Material losses were assessed to be almost US $300 million broken down into the categories of agriculture and livestock, construction, transport, machinery and equipment, fisheries, commerce, administration and public services.[42]

Unquantifiable losses have resulted from the forced exodus of people from war areas, interruption of schooling, unemployment caused by the destruction of economic targets, war-related disruptions in social services, serious nutritional and material shortages. The noncompletion of social and economic projects has hurt the economy as a whole. Even less quantifiable perhaps are the psychological traumas caused, particularly to those maimed, orphaned and subjected to relentless bombing.

In 1977, the five Western members of the UN Security Council—then the United States, Britain, Canada, the Federal Republic of Germany and France—set themselves up as a "contact group" to negotiate a Namibian settlement. Through shuttle diplomacy involving the Frontline states, the South West Africa People's Organization (Swapo) and South Africa, a Namibian independence plan was agreed upon by all the parties. It included a cease fire between South Africa and Swapo, the reduction of South African forces in Namibia to 1,500 confined to bases supervised by UN forces and the holding of UN-supervised elections in the territory. Implementation of the plan was demanded in Security Council Resolution 435 of 1978.

The South African government, repeatedly stating publicly that it agreed to the plan "in principle," invented pretext after pretext for not implementing it, while stepping up its undeclared war against Angola. This reached a new peak in 1979, affecting Huíla, Cunene and Kuando Kubango provinces, with ground attacks, the bombing and occupation of villages, and troops landed by helicopter.

South African military escalation continued through early 1980, culminating in June with Operation Smokeshell. Fapla put up fierce resistance and the SADF suffered many casualties, including the pilot of an Alouette helicopter shot down. Losses during the period from June 1979 to December 1980 were estimated as four hundred Angolan civilians killed and 640 wounded, 85 soldiers killed and 95 wounded, and an unknown number of people kidnapped and missing. Precise figures were hard to obtain in semidesert and thinly populated areas. Material damage during the same period was estimated to be US $231 million.[43]

The UN Geneva conference on Namibia, in January 1981, was the first attended by delegations from both Swapo and South Africa. UN sources expressed optimism that the independence process might start by March. But South Africa stalled again, intimating that it was waiting to see what US President-elect Reagan might do. Having "haggled and delayed for nearly three years," one American newspaper said, Pretoria "might well believe that a hardline Reagan administration will relax pressures for the cease-fire and elections" in Namibia.[44] South Africa stepped up its aggression against Angola during the conference.

After the Reagan administration took office, further progress on Namibia was effectively blocked and the "Namibian problem" was transformed into the "Angolan problem." The United States, under Carter, had assumed the leading role in the "contact group" which had arrived at the UN plan for Namibian independence through its shuttle diplomacy. Because the UN was responsible for Namibia under international law (after Pretoria's mandate was ended in 1966 and its occupation of the territory declared illegal in 1969), the "contact group," made up of the then five Western members of the Security Council, had a UN mantle but no UN mandate. By introducing the "linkage" issue—making Namibia's independence dependent upon the withdrawal of Cuban troops in Angola—the United States, under Reagan, not only de facto scrapped the UN plan it had helped to draw up, but caused the demise of the "contact group." France withdrew in protest over "linkage," and the other members ceased to play any active role as the United States made itself sole negotiator. Consequently, the pressure on South Africa to end its illegal occupation of Namibia was replaced by US pressure on Angola to accept "linkage." This diplomatic pressure was added to South Africa's military pressure on the young country, the United States openly allying itself with Pretoria by its support of the South African-backed Unita group.

Referring to reports that the new US administration was actively studying the possibility of providing direct military aid to Unita, Zimbabwe's prime minister, Robert Mugabe, said, "This would be a most hostile act—not only to Angola but certainly to the African states in this region. Africa would obviously condemn it. But I can't imagine that the Reagan regime would be that evil." The *International Herald Tribune* commented on 9 March 1981: "Covert aid to Unita . . . is under active consideration by the Reagan administration. Has the situation in Angola so changed that US intervention, a disaster six years ago, has become an attractive foreign policy option?"

At about this time it was disclosed that a report prepared "for Washington" had recommended that the United States provide Unita with antitank and anti-aircraft missiles, as well as military advisers. US military experts were also reported to have made clandestine visits to Unita bases.[45] The US State Department revealed at the same time that an assistant secretary of state, Lannon Walker, had met Savimbi secretly in Rabat, where the Unita chief has a villa. Speaking at a UN seminar in Paris on the arms embargo against South Africa, Angola's ambassador to France, Luis de Almeida, said, "By sending military experts to the border of Namibia and Angola in order to assess the needs of the traitors and to study the situation on the ground, by official statements and secret meetings in Rabat with Jonas Savimbi, and in Washington between the Central Intelligence Agency and Unita representatives, the Reagan administration has shown its enemy face."

The Namibian *Windhoek Observer*, commenting on these machinations on 4 April 1981, said, "The American envoys who arrived under cover somewhere in the south of Angola but more or less all the time on South West African soil, are erroneously under the impression that they have dealt with Unita; these envoys are to advise Ronald Reagan on the great force Unita constitutes and they were given the full treatment so as to give an enthusiastic report."

In May, US customs officials in Houston, Texas, seized a plane load of arms valued at US $1.2 million destined for South Africa. A customs offical said at the time that "the Unita forces in Angola are the obvious place for the final destination."[46]

An increasing number of high-level meetings between US and South African officials indicated that new moves were probably afoot. Senior South African military intelligence officers, General van der Westhuizen and Admiral Duplessis, visited Washington secretly in March 1981, but left hastily when their identities were revealed. In April the US assistant secretary of state for African affairs, Dr. Chester Crocker, had talks in Pretoria with the South African foreign minister, Roelof "Pik" Botha, and the defense minister, Magnus Malan. Pik Botha visited Washington in May. It was during these latter meetings that the "linkage" policy was formulated.

Documents on the US–South African talks, leaked to the *New York Times*, were given substantial press coverage in June 1981. Among them was a memorandum on Crocker's talks in Pretoria on 15 and 16 April which stated: "SAG [South African Government] sees Savimbi as a buffer for Namibia. SAG believes Savimbi wants southern Angola. Having supported him this far, it would damage SAG honor if Savimbi is harmed. . . . Malan declared SAG view that Angola/Namibia situation is number one problem in southern Africa. Angola is one place where US can roll back Soviet/Cuban presence in Africa. Need to get rid of Cubans, and support Unita. Unita is going from strength to strength while Swapo grows militarily weaker."[47]

The various pretexts used by Pretoria until then for refusing to implement Resolution 435—the composition of the proposed UN force (UNTAG), the alleged partiality of the UN, etc.—had never included the presence of Cuban troops in Angola. But this was henceforth made the obstacle to further progress, the added advantage for Pretoria in the appearance that it was the Angolans who were standing in the way of Namibian independence. Referring to the leaked documents, the *International Herald Tribune* of 2 June described the US–South African strategy as to "use the prospect of getting South African troops out of Namibia . . . as leverage on the Soviet-backed government of Angola [and to] demand from Angola both a withdrawal of Cuban forces from its territory and a sharing of power with Savimbi. . . . The Angolans would be told that Moscow cannot help them economically, that Washington can, that they can get US diplomatic recognition only by acceding to the two conditions and that Washington would consider resuming military aid to Savimbi if necessary."

Under Reagan, Carter's two conditions for recognizing Angola became conditions for Namibia's independence. Thus, the solution of the international problem of Namibia was made subordinate to Washington's Angola policy. Although the US government presented itself as a mediator, an "honest broker" in the negotiations, the joint Washington-Pretoria strategy laid down in 1981 has been followed to the letter.

A massive propaganda campaign was needed to gain acceptance of the strategy. The apartheid regime was to be dealt with through "constructive engagement," a curious concept holding that only the racist minority itself can put an end to minority rule—and that it will do so only if not subjected to external pressure. Tension in the region, the reasoning followed, stemmed from an East-West conflict, a Soviet-Cuban threat. The Reagan administration, totally insensitive to African aspirations, echoed Pretoria's line that those who fought to win or defend their nationhood were mere pawns in an international power play. The victims of apartheid and aggression were thus portrayed as the aggressors.

There can be no parallel between the illegal presence of South African troops in Namibia and the Cuban military presence to which Angola is fully entitled under Article 51 of the UN Charter which recognizes "the inherent right of individual or collective self-defence" of a country under armed attack. No Cuban or Angolan soldier, for that matter, has crossed into or threatened any country in the region, whereas the SADF respects no borders and no country's sovereignty. Angola's repeated complaints to the Security Council have resulted in numerous resolutions condemning South African aggression. Despite its persistent claims of "threats to security" in the region, Pretoria has not once lodged a formal complaint with the world body.

The United States took the Namibian negotiations out of the ambit of the UN (to which the "contact group" had reported back) and chose the arena of secret bilateral talks. Angola, in participating in talks, repeatedly stated that it was prepared to do so if there was any chance of progress on Namibia's independence. It persistenly rejected "linkage" and ruled out talks with Unita.

The secret talks were accompanied by misleading leaks to the press, with US officials stating both in public and in private that Angola was about to accept "linkage" and dismissing as "rhetoric" official statements to the contrary. It was a way of making the Cubans the main issue in the regional conflict and of concentrating more pressure on Angola. In the same disinformative vein, there were said to be divisions among the Angolan leaders between "pro-Western pragmatists" favoring US–South African strategy and "pro-Soviet hardliners" blocking it. Anyone at all conversant with Angola's policy will know that a remarkable consistency was maintained when President José Eduardo dos Santos succeeded President Neto and followed all subsequent party and government reshuffles. Despite all the speculation, much of it involving libellous attacks on individuals and racist insinuations that thinking is determined by degree of pigmentation, the Angolan government has never accepted that Namibia's independence should depend on Angola weakening its defenses in the face of persistent South African aggression.

There was a marked increase in South African aggression against Angola after Reagan came to power, leading to the massive invasion and occupation of part of the south of the country in August 1981. The United States vetoed a Security Council resolution condemning South African aggression. The seeming contradiction of increasing military action against Angola while calling for a Cuban withdrawal indicated that insistence on "linkage" was merely a way of easing pressure on South Africa to proceed with Namibian decolonization, and that the Cuban presence in Angola in fact suited both Washington and Pretoria. Without the Cubans to use as an issue the United States would find it much more difficult to present the conflict in the region in global East-West terms and to align itself so completely with the apartheid regime. Equally, for the South African government, the continued Cuban presence in Angola provided their country with an opportunity to play the role of an active ally of the West against the Soviet Union.[48]

After a substantial increase in South African reconnaissance flights over Angola in the first half of 1981 and other military operations, the Angolan authorities revealed in July that about 40,000 South African troops were massed on the southern border with Namibia.[49] Then, on 23 August, the SADF launched Operation Protea, a massive invasion of southern Angola. Operation Protea involved about 11,000 men, 36 Centurion M-41 tanks and 70 AML-90 armored cars, two hundred at least armored personnel carriers, artillery which included the G-5 155 mm gun and 127 mm Kentron surface-to-surface missiles, and about 90 planes and helicopters. After massive bombing raids on major urban centers in Cunene province and north into

Huíla, three South African armored columns entered the country and moved on the urban centers, where there was fierce fighting with Angolan forces. But South Africa's superiority in the air proved decisive.

That invasion resulted in the occupation for more than three years of about 50,000 square kilometers of Cunene province. It facilitated the infiltration of Unita forces further to the north of Angola while concentrating the attention of the Angolan armed forces on the permanent threat from South Africa's regular army. A full-scale propaganda campaign was now mounted in support of Unita. In November 1981, while the South Africans were bombing and killing Angolans from their bases in occupied Cunene and in Namibia—and at the very moment when South African commandoes sabotaged the Luanda oil refinery[50]—Pretoria's protégé Jonas Savimbi arrived in the United States, where he was received by the secretary of state, Alexander Haig, as though he were the leader of a country.

More and more Western journalists visited Savimbi at his Jamba base on the Namibian border (a place not to be found on Angolan maps) and, sometimes after only a few hours in the bush, wrote enraptured articles in praise of Savimbi, illustrated with maps showing vast swathes of Angola under Unita control. Normally skeptical newsmen, particularly where Africa is concerned, seemed prepared to believe anything Savimbi told them. The selling of the man as a "freedom fighter" has been one of the biggest disinformation campaigns mounted in recent years.[51] Meanwhile, Angolan government and other reports on Unita's massacres and mutilations, particularly in the central highlands reputed to be its tribal support base, were largely ignored, as was Savimbi's smuggling activity organized from his SADF-protected residence in the Caprivi Strip of Namibia.[52]

Increased terrorist activity by Unita, particularly in areas further north where it had not previously operated, added to the strain on Angola's resources and social services, already stretched by massive loss of life and by the damage caused by the regular South African forces in the south.[53] By 1987, losses caused by South African aggression were estimated at more than US $12 billion, an astronomical figure which because based on only calculable data might well prove to be a modest estimate.

The war, disrupting agriculture and transport, led to increased foreign exchange expenditure on food imports. The cost of maintaining the modern and well-equipped army needed to face up to the SADF—mobilizing thousands of able-bodied young men and skilled personnel who, under different circumstances, would be crucial to productive activity— was a great drain on the economy of a young country seeking to rebuild. Angola was fortunate, until the sharp fall in oil prices in 1986, in having a thriving oil industry, which still provides the bulk of foreign exchange earnings and crucial fuel for defense. Contrary to propaganda claims, however, oil revenue is not used to pay the Cuban troops, who receive from the Angolans only their local expenses in Angolan currency, kwanzas.

There are substantial numbers of foreign technicians from both East and West working in Angola's oil and other industries. After South Africa's occupation of Cunene province, Unita started to make them a special target. Previously, foreigners killed by Unita had been missionaries or farmers in remote areas. The kidnappings of foreign technicians accompanied by threats against all foreign workers in Angola, were essentially publicity-seeking operations and Unita's crude way of seeking tacit recognition by blackmailing the governments of those kidnapped into negotiating the release of the hostages. This happened in the cases of Czech technicians kidnapped in March 1983 at a paper plant in Alto Catumbela, Benguela province, and British and other personnel taken hostage in the diamond-mining Province of Lunda Norte in February 1984. Czech and British officials were obliged to go to Jamba to secure the release of their nationals. US support for Unita, despite its hostage taking, and the public condemnations of terrorism are symptomatic of the contradictions in US foreign policy. The United States raised not a murmur over the death of an American on board a Transamerica plane in Lunda Norte, which Unita destroyed.

Yet the military situation was substantially changing. The reorganized Fapla, better equipped and with newly trained commando troops to deal with guerrilla-type subversive action—an entirely different kind of war than that being waged against the regular South African army—started an offensive to drive Unita out of the vantage points gained as a result of South African occupation. This new impetus was behind the outstanding victory in the battle of Cangamba in the Province of Moxico, where an attempt by Unita to take the small town was prevented in August 1983, and an estimated 1,100 Unita men killed, many by crossing their own minefields. Only hours later, the South African air force flew in and razed the town, forcing the Angolan armed forces to withdraw. This was the first time that the South African military openly intervened to save Unita.

Fapla's antibandit operations had profound effects within Unita, the deterioration in their military situation causing deep rifts and dissent. The *International Herald Tribune* of 26 January 1985 reported that, "the Angolan rebel movement Unita appears to be overreaching its military capacity and is showing signs of internal dissent as it intensifies guerrilla and diplomatic activity to secure a significant role in negotiations toward a regional peace settlement."

A number of once prominent Unita officials have disappeared, among them Jorge Sangumba, once foreign affairs secretary, and Samuel Chiwale, former military chief.[54] Other disappearances include António Vakulukuta, once Unita's secretary of the interior. A member of the Kwanyama tribe from southern Angola, he was reportedly arrested by the South Africans at Unita's request amid internal tribal strife, Umbundus from

Savimbi's region killing members of other ethnic groups from the south.[55] Unita members in many parts of the country surrendered in response to the Angolan government's policy of clemency. Large numbers of the long militarily inactive FNLA, including some senior leaders, have also given themselves up.

The South African armed forces launched a vast military operation in southern Angola between December 1983 and January 1984. Cloaked in the usual verbal disguise of a "hot pursuit" operation against Swapo guerrillas, Operation Askari was designed to expand the occupied area. It failed, and even the South African generals were forced to concede that they had not expected such fierce resistance from Fapla,[56] making it the costliest SADF operation in Angola, in terms of their own losses, since the 1975–76 invasion. South Africa's air superiority had proved decisive in previous operations, with bombing and air strikes always preceding the advance of the infantry. This time Fapla were better prepared to withstand this "softening up." More than 10 South African aircraft were reported shot down, the exact number difficult to ascertain because some crashed across the Namibian border. Once fighting on the ground began—when the South African air force could no longer intervene—the Angolan army proved more than a match for the invaders, breaking through several attempted encirclements as the South Africans became increasingly overextended. Even US business and intelligence sources have confirmed that Cuban troops were not only not involved in this fighting but had not fired on the South Africans since 1976. The Cubans are primarily a reserve force, garrisoned well to the north of the area concerned.

The main reasons for the South Africans agreeing to go to Lusaka on 16 February 1984 and to negotiate the withdrawal of their troops from Angola are thought to be the failure of Operation Askari, South Africa's economic crisis to which the war in Angola was adding an estimated cost of US $4 million a day,[57] and the Reagan administration's need for at least one foreign policy victory with presidential elections approaching. Another factor in Pretoria's decision to use the language of peace, was a meeting in Moscow on 11 January between Angolan, Cuban and Soviet delegations, at which it was agreed "to help the People's Republic of Angola to strengthen its defence capability to safeguard its independence and territorial integrity."

Before the talks in Lusaka, the Angolan government stated that the South African withdrawal should be followed by implementation of Security Council Resolution 435 and the start of the Namibian independence process. It was agreed at Lusaka to set up a Joint Monitoring Commission (JMC), composed of Angolan and South African forces, to supervise the South African withdrawal from Angola, which was to be completed within four weeks. US requests to be included in the monitoring activities on Angolan soil were rejected. An Angolan press comment at the time asked, "why are our enemies now so interested in monitoring the end of hostilities against us which they always encouraged and fuelled?'" It was agreed that Angola would ensure that Swapo forces did not enter the areas vacated by the SADF during the period of withdrawal. Lieutenant Colonel Alexandre Rodrigues "Kito," leader of the Angolan delegation, stated at a press conference in Luanda on 21 February, "we concurred, on condition that the restriction of Swapo activities in our country should lead to conditions being created for the implementation of 435 . . . otherwise there would be no sense in Angola restricting Swapo." Angola also made it clear that Swapo was consulted at every step of the negotiations and supported them. It stated that the next stage should be direct negotiations between Swapo and South Africa, the belligerent parties in the region.

South Africa, however, neither withdrew its forces from Angola nor moved forward on the implementation of Security Council Resolution 435. Angola continued to use diplomatic means to seek a peaceful solution in the region and further the

Namibian independence process, showing remarkable flexibility in the face of South Africa's obvious decision not to end its aggression against Angola or its colonial occupation of Namibia. There were further meetings between Angolan and American and South African delegations. In early November a number of articles appeared, in the South African press especially, stating that Angola had accepted "linkage" and put forward a detailed program for the withdrawal of the Cubans. These reports were distorted versions of the continuing negotiations leaked by US and/or South African officials.

President dos Santos detailed Angola's proposals in a letter dated 17 November 1984 to the UN secretary general, Javier Pérez de Cuéllar, putting an end to all such speculations. The letter was published as a full page advertisement in the *Times* of London on 24 November (see appendix 2). The proposals rejected "linkage" and stated as a precondition for any withdrawal of Cuban troops from Angola that South Africa must start the implementation of Resolution 435 and withdraw from Namibia all its troops barring the 1,500 stipulated in the UN plan (under which they were to be confined to bases in Namibia supervised by UN forces).

The letter detailed a subsequent proposed withdrawal of 20,000 Cuban troops over a three-year period, with the remainder staying in northern Angola, where South Africa could not claim they threatened its interests, let alone its borders. South Africa's response was to assail Angola for breaking the confidentiality of talks—despite the fact that the Angolan proposals, albeit distorted, had already been published in the South African and US press[58]—and to put forward counterproposals: all the Cubans must be out of Angola in 12 weeks, the Angolans should provide detailed lists of Cuban personnel in the country, and their withdrawal should be monitored by a commission to include South Africans who would be free to move anywhere inside Angola.

Here, most clearly, the "Namibian problem" had been made the "Angolan problem." Far from contemplating the ending of its illegal occupation of Namibia, Pretoria was proposing a further violation of Angolan sovereignty: monitoring the withdrawal of Cubans legally in the country to help defend it against SADF aggression. The immediate US reaction was to state that there was no basic difference between the Angolan and South African positions and that the only problem was to "bridge the gap between them." There were, accordingly, press reports that the difference was a "clash over time limit for pull out of Cuban troops."[59] Angola's proposals, which had gone a long way toward addressing the purported concerns of its enemies, had come up against the brick wall of US and South African objectives.

All this diplomatic activity was drawing away publicity from the other aspect of the Washington-Pretoria strategy: Unita. In early November 1984, a group of 45 journalists were flown in a Dakota aircraft from Pretoria to the Namibian border for a meeting with Savimbi at Jamba. There he announced, as he had in 1983, that he would take Luanda by Christmas. His aim was "to make the inclusion of Unita in the negotiations a precondition for settling the Namibian issue." He was, however, aware that his South African friends might not succeed in achieving this. "Pieter Botha is my friend," he told the journalists, "but I know that he has to look after the interests of his country first." A British newspaper, reporting the event under the headline "Angolan peace summit soon," quoted diplomatic sources as saying that a meeting between President dos Santos and Savimbi was expected to follow the latter's threat to raid the capital, a blatantly false rumor.[60] Clearly, disinformation had become systematic.

In April 1985, more than a year after agreeing to withdraw its troops from Angola, South Africa finally announced that it was doing so, although it would leave two companies at hydroelectric plants on the Cunene River, near the Namibian border. Western press reports presented South Africa as a "peacemaker," although it was simply doing what it had failed to do many months earlier. At the same time, South Africa announced the installation of a puppet "internal" government in Namibia, making it clear that it had no intention of ending its illegal occupation of Namibia.

A single event served to expose the true facts of the military, diplomatic and propaganda campaign against Angola. On 21 May 1985, a Fapla patrol foiled an attempt by a South African commando unit to sabotage the Cabinda Gulf Oil complex at Malongo, in Cabinda province, the most northern part of Angola separated from the rest of the country by a strip of Zairean territory. The commander of the unit, SADF Captain Wynand du Toit, a member of "special forces" based in Saldanha Bay in Cape province, was captured; two of his men were killed and six others escaped. At a press conference in Luanda on 28 May, du Toit said that his unit had come from Saldanha Bay in an Israeli-built South African destroyer, which lay off the Angolan coast about 150 kilometers while they landed at night in inflatable boats. Admitting that he had taken part in previous operations inside Angola, including the sabotage of the Giraúl Bridge in Namibe province, for which Unita claimed responsibility at the time, he said that in "all or most of the operations that we usually do, we claim or Unita claims the responsibility." Had the Cabinda attack succeeded, "then it shows Unita is active also in the northern part, in the province of Cabinda." Among the substantial amount of material captured by Fapla was a tin of paint with which the commandoes had intended to write "Viva Unita" on the road. This would have been "part of the deception," du Toit said.

That one event shattered the credibility of "constructive engagement," destroyed the peacemaking image the apartheid regime was trying to create for itself, and called into question all the Unita claims over the years. The action of that Fapla patrol averted a crisis in the Angolan economy that could have been deprived of its main source of foreign exchange and of the fuel needed to keep everything going, including the armed forces. One can speculate as to what would have been the reaction of foreign oil companies operating in Angola or the reactions of their governments, if the Fapla patrol had not intervened.

South Africa had initially denied that its forces were in Cabinda, then later amended this by saying that they were engaged in intelligence-gathering activities against Swapo and the African National Congress (ANC) of South Africa, but it no longer convinced even the most right-wing press. So complete was the media turnabout that in a dispatch dated 31 May, Unita—continuing to take credit for Pretoria's military actions in Angola—accused the British press of "racist sentiments" for questioning "Unita's capability to carry out sophisticated sabotage missions."

Meanwhile, the Fapla offensive against Unita was gaining momentum. Conservative elements in the US Congress succeeded in repealing the Clark amendment that banned open US military aid to antigovernment forces in Angola. In the nine years that the amendment had been in force, Unita, despite South African backing, had failed to overthrow the Angolan government and was suffering military and propaganda reversals. The State Department, still bent on making the United States appear an "honest broker" in the region, gave assurances that the repeal did not mean that the United States would assist Unita, but events were soon to prove otherwise.

A beleaguered Unita pushed for rapid US support. On 23 August it announced that a Soviet infantry battalion was operating in Angola, a story to which no serious credence was given. In early September it claimed that Soviet officers were directing the Fapla offensive. South Africa said that the new and sophisticated military equipment used—Mig-23s and helicopter gunships—was piloted by Soviets, referring to intercepted cockpit conversation in Russian. Just as Angolan civil aviation pilots use the internationally prevailing English terms, the military pilots refer to technical matters in the Russian in which they learned the advanced technology. The capture of a "Russian-speaking pilot" was subsequently announced with no mention that he was Angolan. This new military capability of Fapla, until then equipped for an essentially defensive war, rang the alarm bells in Washington and Pretoria. The internal offensive to restore the Angolan government's sovereignty over its territory was presented as a "red" threat to the entire region. Johannesburg radio spoke of "the gravity of Unita's position" as Fapla moved on Unita at Cazombo, in Moxico province, and prepared to push on to Mavinga, in Kuando Kubango, and then Jamba, at the border.

During this period, Christoper Lehman, then special assistant to Reagan on national security affairs, left his White House post to travel with his new employer, Paul Manafort of the public relations firm Black, Manafort, Stone & Kelly, to meet Savimbi at Jamba. Savimbi reportedly took off time from a "fierce battle" to consult with them. A week later they returned to Washington with a "signed $600,000 contract" to sell Savimbi in Washington and organize a trip there for him.[61]

On 16 September, Pretoria announced that its forces had entered Angola, with air cover, "in pursuit of Swapo." On 17 September, SADF chief Viljoen confirmed Angolan reports that a South African doctor had been killed in Moxico province. On 18 September, Unita was driven out of Cazombo in Moxico. South African intelligence sources were quoted as saying that "SAAF [South African air force] aircraft flew Unita troops and equipment to Cazombo between September 2 and September 16."[62]

Angola's Ministry of Defense announced that because of Unita's inability to resist the offensive, the SADF 32nd or "Buffalo" Battalion, equipped with armored cars, transport vehicles, artillery and grenade launchers, was advancing on Mavinga from the south and preparing to enter into combat with the Angolan army, after heavy bombing of Angolan troop positions the previous day. South African press reports confirmed this.[63]

On 20 September, South African Defense Minister Malan admitted in Parliament that South Africa was helping Unita. In doing so, he said, "We serve South Africa and Southern Africa and the West's interests." That same day, Savimbi gave a press conference at Jamba at which he spoke of the possibility of his base being overrun by Fapla and appealed for US intervention.[64] Officials from the South African Foreign Affairs Department were sent to Washington to plead Unita's case.[65]

On 7 October, the UN Security Council voted unanimously to condemn South Africa for its "latest premeditated and unprovoked aggression" against Angola. Explaining why his country had supported the resolution—rather than abstain or veto, as was its custom—the US ambassador to the UN, Vernon Walters, said that the United States, in addition to condemning the raid, "welcomes this resolution as an occasion to reiterate our call for an immediate withdrawal of South African troops from Angola." Only two days later, a US State Department spokesman accused the Soviet Union of fanning violence in Angola. Meanwhile, bills were tabled in the US Congress to authorize aid for Unita.

In New York in November, when he addressed the UN General Assembly, President dos Santos accused the Reagan administration of hypocrisy for trying to present the Unita terrorists as "freedom fighters." He pointed out that, despite forecasts by Ford and Kissinger that, under an MPLA government, bilateral economic relations would be impossible, Angola was Washington's fourth largest trading partner in Africa south of the Sahara and that financial relations with US banks in the first half of 1985 had amounted to more than US $100 million.

Also addressing the General Assembly, President Reagan announced a new "initiative" on so-called regional conflicts, naming Angola as one of a number of countries whose wars were caused by "Soviet expansionism," which he would raise with Soviet leader Mikhail Gorbachev at their forthcoming summit meeting in Geneva.

Two months later, in January 1986, Savimbi made his much-heralded trip to Washington, where the red carpet was rolled out on every possible occasion. He was given all the protocol of a visiting head of state and received by Reagan, among other dignitaries. While anti-apartheid groups campaigned against the visit and the congressional Black Caucus refused to meet him, the State Department dropped any misgivings it had previously expressed over official support for Unita. Up to then it had preferred to use the proposed support for Unita as a threat to make Angola accede to US–South African demands. Now support was a *fait accompli*. Angola called it a "declaration of war."

In February, Crocker told the Senate Foreign Relations Committee that the United States had decided to provide military aid to Unita and that "the process is in motion." Reports indicated $15 million in covert aid—including shoulder-fired surface-air Stinger missiles—which by-passed Congress and did not require special legislation. Angola suspended all talks with the United States.

In the curious reasoning employed by US officials, Angola's efforts to defend its people against South African–backed terrorism and aggression are described as a "military option," and US military interference in Angola as aimed at achieving "peaceful negotiations." What John Stockwell said is worth noting: "Savimbi caused the United States a minor embarrassment in September (1975), when he sent feelers to the MPLA for a negotiated solution. The CIA learned of this move through an article in the world press, and a Kinshasa station officer promptly interrogated Savimbi. We wanted no 'soft' allies in our war against the MPLA."[66]

There were reports that then CIA director William Casey visited South Africa in mid-March 1986 to meet Savimbi and assure him that effective anti-aircraft weapons were on the way.[67] Indeed, behind the rhetorical term "freedom fighter" to refer to Savimbi lies the public knowledge that Unita is an instrument of the apartheid regime. When the 32nd Battalion—a mercenary unit officered by South Africans, based in Namibia's Caprivi Strip and operating solely inside Angola—celebrated its 10th anniversary on 27 March, the South African press reported that "top-ranking officials of Angola's Unita movement were among the guests of honour—and given VIP treatment—at a special birthday celebration in the operational area of the crack South African Defence Force unit, 32 Battalion."[68] The event was attended by Unita Secretary General Nzau Puna, among others.

Despite his powerful friends, Savimbi failed to keep his repeated promises to take Luanda by force. Even the South African press reported that "the fortunes of war in Angola have shifted significantly—and now it is Dr. Jonas Savimbi's rebels who are on the defensive and who are being hard pressed by their enemies."[68] Fapla's growing defense capability was reducing the freedom of action of the SADF itself. In January 1987, South African Major General George Meiring, the officer commanding the "territorial" force in Namibia, complained that the Angolan air force now believed it could challenge South African air superiority in southern Angola and that Angolan air defense systems now extended as far south as Cahama, three hundred killometers from the Namibian border, although it was common knowledge that there had been air defense systems in Cahama for years. The *Cape Times* commented that "Angolan MiG-21s flying regular border patrols for the first time since independence have served notice that the days of 'easy' incursions—with South Africa enjoying almost automatic command of the air—are over for good."[70] A massive 54 percent increase in budget allocations for South Africa's air force announced in June was thought to reflect concern about Angola's air power.[71]

South African aggression in southern Angola did not diminish, but the scale of operations did. This was a further blow to Unita. Grandiose military predictions were therefore replaced by US and South African calls for negotiations and "power sharing," duly echoed by Savimbi's urgent pleas for talks.

Talks with Unita have been consistently ruled out. Speaking to Italian journalists in December 1985, President dos Santos said negotiation would violate a guiding principle of the international community, since it would accept that any state could organise a group of terrorists, give them arms and destabilise another state, and then insist that this state accept the group in its government."

The heads of state of Angola, Mozambique, Zambia and Zaire met in April 1987 to agree on the reactivation of the Benguela Railway, part of the regional program aimed at reducing the dependence of most countries in the region on South African railways and ports. A few days before the summit, Savimbi—obviously informed that it was to take place—announced that he would permit the line to function.

This was intended to make Unita appear crucial to the process and to step up the propaganda in favor of negotiations. US officials in southern Africa were said to be pressing Frontline countries to give de facto recognition to Unita by accepting Savimbi's offer not to attack the railway. The British *Guardian* described it as "the latest effort in a long United States campaign to undermine the authority of the Angolan government through Unita."[72]

The "offer" was also a device to make it appear that Unita was distancing itself from the apartheid regime. Savimbi was widely quoted as saying the South Africans were "not happy" about it. Jeremias Chitunda, vice-president of Unita, rashly told the National Press Club in Washington that South Africa had stopped sending military aid to Unita.[73] Yet, on 6 June, Savimbi was warmly welcomed by South African foreign minister Pik Botha at a dinner at the Carlton Hotel in Johannesburg hosted by Altron, the aviation electronics division of the South African state-run Armscor weapons industry corporation.[74]

Although pressing for negotiations, the United States in no way abandoned the military option. In the midst of the Iran-contra scandal, there were reports of illegal airlifts of arms to South Africa, part of the administration's covert military aid to Unita.[75] Other reports indicated that excess profits from US illegal arms sales to Iran went not only to the Nicaraguan contras but to Unita.

The *New York Times* revealed that the CIA was using an abandoned air base at Kamina, in Zaire's Shaba province, to airlift arms to Unita.[76] Joint US–Zairean military exercises in the area in April 1987 were seen as a threat to the entire southern African region. Referring to the base, the US chargé d'affaires in Harare Ed Fugit said, "we are looking at the region as a superpower needing various options."[77] Another disclosure was a "military contingency plan" developed by Nato's Iberlant Command to cover the African coast between the Tropic of Cancer and a line west of Luanda—at approximately nine degrees south of the equator, a region outside the Nato area. Citing pressing defense reasons, US Rear Admiral Warren C. Hamm, deputy commander in chief of the Iberian Atlantic Area, argued that the Soviet Union had ships and aircraft in Angola.[78] The *Washington Post* wrote of a "major buildup of military facilities" in the Azores and Madeira aimed at providing a "viable forward support base" that could project capability below the Tropic of Cancer and of a recent Nato exercise which included "reacting to simulated scenarios involving a threat from Angola."[79] To posit an Angolan threat to Nato takes cold war rhetoric into the realm of irrationality. Everything points to a US–South African military encirclement of that country, a situation reminiscent in many ways to that in 1975–76.

In June 1987, it was announced that the United States was to provide another $15 million worth of "covert" aid to Unita, including anti-aircraft and antitank missiles.

Persisting in its efforts to ensure Namibia's independence and peace in the region, Angola agreed, about a year and a half after it had suspended talks, to resume discussions with the United States. After several meetings with US delegations, in August 1987 Angola presented to South Africa, through the US, a draft agreement to be signed by Angola, Cuba, South Africa and Swapo and guaranteed by the five permanent members of the Security Council. Based on the 1984 proposals presented to the UN, it emphasized flexibility on the withdrawal of Cuban troops, posing as *sine qua non* preconditions for this the immediate withdrawal of South African troops from Angola, the ending of South African aggression against Angola, the ending of US, South African and other support for Unita and the implementation of Security Council Resolution 435 on Namibia's independence. Pretoria's response was to step up its aggression that same month, launching air and ground attacks in Kuando Kubango and Cunene.

Yet events on the battlefield were the main factor which finally brought Pretoria to the negotiating table to discuss Angola's proposals. On 12 November, more than three months after the start of the invasion, South African Defense Minister Malan said they had intervened to save Savimbi from defeat, because, as he put it, "Savimbi cherishes the same values as those held by South Africa." Over the ensuing days, Pretoria announced a growing number of (white) SADF deaths in Angola. SAAF planes were being shot down. There was mounting public pressure in South Africa for an explanation of what was going on in Angola. Even *The Citizen*, a newspaper close to the regime, wrote that "the sacrifices which our young men have to

make require that their families—and the South African na-
tion—be told what is going on." Mutinies took place among
Namibian troops in the so-called SWATF (South West African
Territorial Force), an integral part of the SADF. The South
African *Weekly Mail* reported on 20 November that "more than
400 members of 101 Battalion of the SWATF have mutinied by
refusing to fight inside Angola on the side of Jonas Savimbi's
Unita movement," adding that members of the unit "were given
Unita uniforms before going into Angola."

The military balance had changed. The right-wing British
newspaper *The Sunday Telegraph*, under the headline "Angolans winning in the air," reported on 18 October that "for the
first time black African pilots have been taking on their South
African counterparts in the air—pitting advanced Mig 23s
against the older and slower Mirages which form the backbone
of the South African air force."

On 25 November, the UN Security Council unanimously
adopted a resolution demanding that South Africa immediately
cease its acts of aggression and unconditionally withdraw its
occupying forces from Angola by 10 December. The fact that
even the US voted for the resolution shows that no one took
seriously South African claims of clashes with "Soviet and
Cuban forces."

Far from withdrawing, South Africa sought to push deeper
into Angola and, using long-range artillery (safer than planes),
bombarded Kuito Kuanavale, in Kuando Kubango, for months.
Fapla have continued to hold the locality, strategic for its
airstrip. At one point, Unita claimed the fall of Kuito, a folly
quickly retracted. Everything indicates that Pretoria intended
to take it and instal there a Unita "government" announced at
the time. This plan, with the possible partition of Angola,
aimed at providing Unita with a territorial basis for its claim to
be a party to be negotiated with.

In January 1988, Cuban forces joined the southward push to
drive the invading SADF forces back to the Namibian border.

Military developments, coupled with the failure of the Reagan administration's policy of "constructive engagement"—the violence in Angola and South Africa itself having worsened—and uncertainty as to the outcome of US elections, explain South Africa's sudden willingness to discuss the implementation of Resolution 435. It therefore went to talks in London in May attended also by Angola, Cuba and the US. At the time of writing, Angola was still awaiting South Africa's counter-proposals.

4

NAMIBIA
Preparations
for Destabilization

Festus Thomas is an ordinary Namibian, one of the many whose story seldom comes through in the sterile atmosphere of United Nations (UN) debates and resolutions, international conferences, speeches and statements about Namibia.

Born in northern Namibia in 1942, he received little formal education. He married, had six children and in 1978 was a driver for the South West Africa People's Organization (Swapo) in the Namibian capital, Windhoek.

He was arrested by the South African Security Police on 10 April 1978 after spending the Easter weekend with his wife and children at Ukwaluuthi in northern Namibia. That weekend, Clemens Kapuuo, a leading South African collaborator, had been assassinated in Windhoek. But Thomas, as the security police could have easily checked, was hundreds of miles away and could not possibly have been involved.

Nevertheless he was detained and what happened to him during the next 74 days—verified by doctors who treated his injuries after his release—reads like a horror story from the Nazi era.

The first 12 days of his detention were relatively "normal," Thomas said later. He was given electric shocks on the genitals and anus, frequently beaten and hung with his hands manacled behind his back.

But, on Friday, 21 April, the torture took a new and horrifying turn. Four security police officers took him handcuffed from their headquarters in a blue Chevrolet. First they stopped to buy beer and meat. Then, after they left town, Thomas was blindfolded and put in the trunk of the car.

Some 30 kilometers out of town they stopped and, when the blindfold was removed, Thomas found himself standing on a dried-up river bed. The police officers lit a fire and began cooking meat. Then Thomas was told to lie down, and he realized he was being measured for a grave.

The officers ordered him to dig his own grave. After he was forced to lie in it, the officers decided it was too shallow. When they were finally satisfied that it was deep enough, Thomas was told again to lie in it and given the choice as to whether his head pointed east or west. Stones were piled on top of him and a hole was left so he could breathe. After 30 minutes, the officers excavated him, ramming stones and shovels into his body. As they did so, they sang "No more Festus," a sadistic version of a song then sung at nationalist rallies, "No more Vorster," referring to then South African Prime Minister Vorster.

After a brief respite, Thomas was ordered to clean the grave and lie in it again. This time he was completely covered and lost consciousness. When he recovered he found that he had been dug out again and was lying on the side of the grave with water being poured on him. Some sort of grenade or firecracker exploded next to his body. Then Thomas was made to stand next to a rock while a Sergeant Botha fired a pistol at it, sending chips into his leg. Finally, as he put out the fire, the officers stoned him.

Late on 22 April he was admitted to ward four at Katutura Hospital in Windhoek's African township. Doctors and nurses said

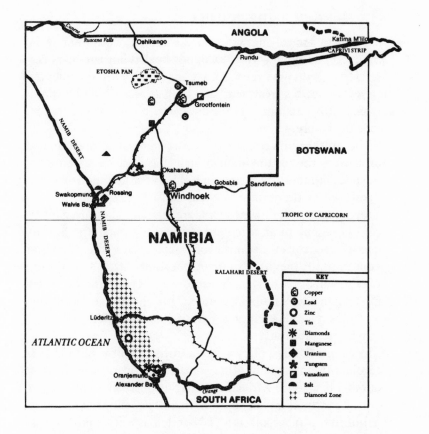

his body was covered with cuts and bruises consistent with his story. When Swapo learned where he was and instituted enquiries, Thomas was immediately transferred back to police custody. His medical records were removed from the hospital, and police officers said he had a fever.

Four days later, the security police took him out again, to a river on the Okahandja Road. There he was severely beaten and his head held under water until he lost consciousness. His shoulder was dislocated and a tooth broken. When he was returned to his cell he was so weak that he could not stand. Finally, on 23 June, with his wounds healed but the scars very visible, Thomas was released. He made a sworn statement to lawyers about his treatment, and they arranged that he should be medically examined. Three days after his release he told his story to the press.[1]

The brutality meted out to Festus Thomas is not unusual. For decades the torture of Namibians has been documented by lawyers, churches and by Swapo.[2] This is the common everyday experience of thousands of Namibians. Beatings, torture and "disappearances" following arrest are regular means used by the Pretoria regime in an attempt to suppress Swapo, the internationally recognized organization representing the Namibian people. But the inevitable outcome of South Africa's continuing illegal occupation of Namibia goes well beyond the enormous suffering of the Namibian people. This chapter seeks to illustrate how Namibia plays a part in South Africa's policy of regional destabilization.

In Namibia this policy takes a different form from that in Angola, Mozambique or other southern African states because Namibia is a South African colonial territory and has been for over 70 years. However, South Africa has abandoned its earlier goal of literal incorporation of Namibia as a fifth province, so the strategy and tactics toward Namibia have become an integral part of the regional—rather than the domestic—front of "total strategy."

Domination and exploitation remain central but Pretoria's tactics have varied—partly as a consequence of deteriorating results in Namibia, partly because of international constraints, and partly because the failure of the Smith-Muzorewa regime in preindependence Zimbabwe showed that initial plans for a neocolonial solution for Namibia would not work. As a result the details, and even some of the main features, of the present South African design for preserving and consolidating control in Namibia are by no means clear, probably not even to deci-

sion makers in Pretoria. Further, Angola and Namibia are interlocking elements in South Africa's regional strategy whose
policies in respect to each country are mutually dependent and
mutually determinant.

South Africa's strategy for Namibia turns on the following
elements:

1. Political developments in Namibia, domestic considerations
   in South Africa and international efforts being made to secure Namibia's independence
2. Economics relating to the gains and costs of continued occupation and the burden of the war
3. War and repression

Since the late 1970s, South Africa has—with strategic fore-
sight or as a consequence of tactical actions or both—created
an ominous structure for the destabilization of an independent
Namibia without major direct intervention by regular South
African troops. While not impregnable, that infrastructure for
destabilization will require substantial diversion of resources
and of policy attention by an independent Namibian government to limit its impact. Even then it will significantly reduce
the room for maneuver open to Namibia at independence, assuming that this predates majority rule in South Africa.

The roots of the present South African position on Namibia
go back to its 1915 military occupation of what was then
known as German South West Africa. After the 1914–18 war in
Europe, South Africa sought to annex this former German colony. At the Versailles peace conference in 1919, the king of the
United Kingdom was granted a mandate over Namibia, to be
exercised through the government of the then Union of South
Africa. This bore the obligation "to promote to the utmost the
material and moral well-being of the inhabitants of the territory."[3]

The South African view of this mandate was clear from the
outset. Within two years, South Africa's prime minister,
General Smuts, told a visiting German delegation that "the

mandate over South West Africa [Namibia] was nothing else but annexation." In 1925 he told his parliament: "I do not think it is necessary for us to annex South West Africa to the Union. The mandate for me is enough and it should be enough for the Union. It gives the Union such complete sovereignty, not only administrative but legislative, that we need not ask for anything more."[4]

Soon after the UN was set up in 1946, South Africa presented its case for the annexation of Namibia, which it had long regarded as a fifth province. Pretoria argued that the territory was a de facto part of South Africa. The UN Fourth Committee rejected the argument and the General Assembly, in a resolution on 14 December 1946, called upon South Africa to place Namibia under international trusteeship. South Africa rejected the demand in 1947 and on ten other occasions over the next eight years. Although it had appealed to the UN in the first instance to annex Namibia, South Africa now questioned the international organization's competence to take over from the defunct League of Nations.

The lengthy legal wrangle over Namibia began in 1949. The following year the International Court of Justice at the Hague, in an advisory opinion, found that South Africa still exercised the mandate over the territory and was obliged to submit reports on its administration of the territory to the UN.[5] South Africa refused, and the legal wrangle that began in 1949 has continued since then. Its disregard for UN resolutions and the opinion of the International Court of Justice was further illustrated in the early 1960s with the establishment of the Odendaal Commission. In 1964 the commission reported its recommendations for the bantustanization of Namibia.

Resolution after resolution followed from the UN. In 1966 it found that South Africa had "disavowed the Mandate" as it had "failed to fulfill its obligations in respect of the mandated territory." Therefore, "henceforth South West Africa comes under the direct responsibility of the United Nations."[6]

Due to the indifferent attitude of Western powers, the Security Council had remained aloof from the debate. But in 1968 they joined the fray, demanding that South Africa stop the trial of 37 Namibians in Pretoria, release them and repatriate them to Namibia. Pretoria predictably ignored the demand and, in a display of contempt for the UN authority over Namibia, proceeded with a second trial and began implementing its "Bantustan," or "homeland," policy.[7] This system sets aside areas, "homelands," for a particular African people, each with its own chief minister but under the control of Pretoria.

On 20 March 1969 the Security Council declared that South Africa's continued occupation of Namibia was illegal and contrary to the principles and decisions of the UN. Five months later, it gave Pretoria until 4 October 1969 to withdraw its administration from Namibia. During that debate the British representative clearly spelled out the lack of will on the part of some member states that made the UN powerless to enforce its decisions over Namibia. The three Western permanent members of the Security Council (Britain, France and the United States) in practice have acted on the basis of his statement that Britain "could not and would not contemplate an economic war with South Africa and sanctions against South Africa under Chapter VII of the Charter," a measure used in reprisal against a country found to threaten international peace and security.[8]

In 1971, the International Court of Justice delivered a second advisory opinion. The court upheld the validity of the revocation of the mandate and, therefore, the illegality of South Africa's continued occupation of Namibia. This made it incumbent on all UN member states to "refrain from any acts" and in particular "any dealings with the Government of South Africa implying recognition of the legality of, or lending support or assistance to, such presence and administration."[9] But all attempts to move South Africa, including a visit in 1972 by the UN secretary general, Dr. Kurt Waldheim, failed.

This visit initiated a technique that South Africa has since used: to seem to negotiate in good faith while simultaneously proceeding with its own program, no matter how inconsistent with what is supposedly being negotiated. South Africa declared that Ovamboland and Eastern Caprivi would be granted "self-government" in the immediate future, thus advancing the "Bantustan" division of the country. Later, Pretoria appeared to be negotiating seriously over UN Security Council Resolution 435 (1978), while at the same time going ahead with its own program to retain and consolidate control over Namibia.

The Africa Group at the UN, in an attempt to introduce more effective pressure, presented a draft resolution to the Security Council in June 1975 proposing an arms embargo against South Africa. It was blocked by vetoes cast by Britain, France and the United States. However, there was growing concern among the three Western members that Pretoria's refusal to consider any solution could lead to greater pressure on them to impose sanctions.

As a result, UN Security Council Resolution 385 was adopted with Western support on 30 January 1976. This demanded that South Africa withdraw its administration from Namibia and that elections be held, under the supervision and control of the UN, leading to independence for Namibia. In the wake of South Africa's invasion of Angola, the US secretary of state, Henry Kissinger, launched his much-publicized diplomatic shuttle in April 1976 in an effort to deflect mounting pressure on the West over developments in South Africa. Britain, France and the United States again used their vetoes in late 1976 to block a mandatory arms embargo resolution in the Security Council. They found themselves in an increasingly untenable position as the veto highlighted their role as South Africa's protectors.

The five Western members of the Security Council at that time (Britain, France and the United States, plus rotating members Canada and the Federal Republic of Germany), began a series of contacts in 1977. The five, who presented themselves as the "contact group," and South Africa, continually tried to give an impression of forward momentum. In September 1977, Pretoria appointed Justice Marthinus Steyn administrator general of Namibia. He initiated a review of Namibian laws, repealed some elements of apartheid legislation and streamlined "security" legislation. But the exercise was cosmetic, and South Africa's determination to continue to wield power in Namibia remained undiminished.

However, in retrospect 1977 did represent a strategic shift. The mock constitution, produced by a gaggle of white and collaborationist parties, was a blueprint toward indirect South African rule of a nominally independent, confederal but white-dominated Namibian state. Pretoria tacitly dropped claims of integrating it as a fifth province, or a set of "Bantustans," and also of maintaining permanent colonial rule. At this point, destabilizing a potentially hostile government was not yet on South Africa's agenda because Namibia's neocolonial status was assumed.

In January 1978, "proximity talks" were held in New York with members of the "contact group" shuttling between delegations from Swapo and South Africa, who refused to talk directly with Swapo. As had consistently been the case during the preceding months of negotiations, Swapo was pressured to accommodate the demands which Pretoria continuously made. The argument was that if Swapo did not make these concessions, then the whole process would break down. The "proximity talks" resumed in early February 1978, but lasted only three days because South Africa's foreign minister, Roelof "Pik" Botha, suddenly left New York, warning that aspects of the proposals "would be totally unacceptable and so dangerous that there is a serious danger of people in the territory being overrun and being governed by a Marxist terrorist organization,"[10] by which he meant Swapo. What became clear from this and other statements by Pretoria was that it would, under no circumstances, accept a Swapo government in Windhoek. It sought to delay a solution and would only agree to a settlement which provided the Pretoria regime with a clear opportunity to install a puppet government with international approval.

After another flurry of "contact group" activity, the South African government announced on 25 April 1978 that it accepted the group's proposals for a settlement in Namibia. Nine days later, in a savage attempt to dissuade Swapo from accepting the proposals, South African forces bombed a Swapo settlement at Kassinga in southern Angola. On 4 May 1978, they massacred more than six hundred Namibians, almost all of them noncombatants. The timing of this left little doubt that South Africa's true motive was to provoke their adversary into refusing the proposals, but Swapo accepted them on 12 July.

Toward the end of that month, the proposals were considered by the Security Council who instructed the secretary general to appoint a special representative to take the matter further. He chose Martti Ahtisaari, a Finnish career diplomat who was then UN commissioner for Namibia. Within a week, accompanied by a 50-member UN team, he was in Namibia.

But events, it would seem, were moving too rapidly for Pretoria's liking. No sooner had the secretary general reported back to the Security Council than South Africa raised objections. Foreign Minister Botha objected to the size of the proposed military component—7,500 men to be called the UN Transitional Assistance Group (UNTAG)—and to the inclusion of a civilian police unit. And he insisted that elections be held before the end of December.[11] This latter point, Botha well knew, was impossible within the timetable of the "contact group" proposals and the secretary general's report. In contrast, on 9 September, Swapo offered to sign a cease-fire with South Africa, an offer which was promptly rejected by Pretoria.

Eleven days later, South Africa announced it would go ahead with its own "internal settlement" elections in December without the UN.[12] The UN responded quickly, adopting Security Council Resolution 435 on 29 September. This formalized the acceptance of the secretary general's report and the action plan for Namibia's independence. (Appendix 3 contains the full text of Resolution 435.)

It is clear that Pretoria has never intended to allow genuine independence for Namibia. But the evidence suggests that the regime was seriously studying the offer from the "contact group." It was, it seems, considering the possibility of Resolution 435 eventually offering a means of securing continued domination of Namibia but with the UN out of the way and Swapo's struggle seriously undermined. To achieve this Pretoria believed that more time was needed to build up an alternative to Swapo and to establish an administration, army and police which were ostensibly Namibian but loyal to South Africa. When independence came, a state apparatus would be left in place, creating major difficulties for any incoming government opposed to the South African regime. Time was also needed to experiment with literally buying out a population during an election process.

This last element took the form of the December 1978 "election" in Namibia and the carbon copy of that election in March 1979 in Rhodesia (Zimbabwe). Swapo boycotted the election as did both Zimbabwean nationalist parties. In both cases, lavish election rallies, with free food and drink, were funded by the South Africans. In both cases there were claims of high voter registration and voting. And in both cases it was claimed that internal parties secured an overwhelming majority. In Namibia the Democratic Turnhalle Alliance (DTA) claimed it had won 41 of the 50 seats. In Rhodesia, Muzorewa supposedly won the majority of seats. Neither result was recognized by any government other than South Africa's which had manipulated it.

Judging from the articles which appeared in the press in South Africa, Namibia and "Zimbabwe-Rhodesia" at that time, Pretoria was working on the theory that the prestige of holding government office would enhance the puppets' chances of victory in any later election. Thus when the Lancaster House settlement was proposed, Pretoria put pressure on Ian Smith and Abel Muzorewa by threatening the withdrawal of supplies from South Africa. The South Africans had convinced themselves that the March 1979 "Zimbabwe-Rhodesia" election results could be repeated in the independence elections. The outcome of Zimbabwe's independence elections, when Muzorewa won only three seats, left Pretoria stunned. The lesson was obvious: a similar fate awaited their puppets in Namibia.

Throughout 1979 and 1980, the South African government raised one objection after another to Resolution 435. It objected to the presence of Swapo bases in Namibia and demanded the monitoring of Swapo bases in neighboring countries. It demanded that its internal surrogates be included in any negotiations and that its external surrogate, the National Union for the Total Independence of Angola (Unita), also be included. UN "partiality" was posed as another barrier to implementation of Resolution 435, and Pretoria demanded the cessation of UN funding to Swapo.

Pressure was again mounting on the "contact group" over South Africa's intransigent position. To deflect this pressure and to give the appearance of forward momentum, a "preimplementation" meeting was held in Geneva, in January 1981, at the instigation of the group. When the meeting began, Swapo immediately agreed to cooperate in implementing Resolution 435 and to sign a cease-fire as the first essential step. South Africa refused and the meeting collapsed.

There is some considerable significance to the timing of this meeting and Pretoria's continuing obduracy. Ronald Reagan had just won the US election and was about to move to the White House. The South Africans, correctly, expected more sympathy from the new administration in Washington. Not long after his inauguration, Reagan confirmed Pretoria's analysis. In a television interview, he described South Africa as a "friendly country" and then, taking up Pretoria's favorite theme, went on to say that South Africa is "a country that strategically is essential to the free world in its production of minerals that we all must have."[13]

Five senior South African Defense Force (SADF) officers were permitted to visit the United States in March—the first known to have done so in some years—despite the mandatory arms embargo and Washington's accepted policy of not allowing such visits. The same month, a DTA delegation and Unita's leader, Jonas Savimbi, visited Washington, and conservative pressure began to mount for the repeal of the Clark amendment which forbade support for antigovernment groups in Angola. Pretoria had read the meaning of Reagan's election well. There would now be another change of direction in the campaign to buy more time for South Africa's occupation of Namibia.

In late May 1981, confidential State Department documents relating to the visit to Washington two weeks earlier by Pik Botha and the South African defense minister, General Magnus Malan, were leaked to the American press. The documents provided an insight into the new approach to the Washington-Pretoria axis. The State Department appeared to accept South Africa's proposition that Angola and Namibia afforded the United States the opportunity of "rolling back Soviet influence in Africa."[14] The approach fitted the cold war scenario that South Africa sought to project in the region and was obviously appealing to Reagan's own ideological idiosyncracies. Changes to Resolution 435 were mooted, and South Africa's determination to prevent Swapo coming to power at any cost was confirmed.

A State Department briefing written for the designated assistant secretary of state for African affairs, Chester Crocker, referred to a "semantical" problem, saying the alterations being sought should be referred to as "attempts to complement rather than to change 435."[15] This briefing referred to these attempts to undermine Resolution 435 as "strengthening" the resolution.

The argument was put forward that if the South Africans were to be persuaded to implement Resolution 435, then their "concerns" with the resolution and with "regional security" would have to be met. There was no question of forcing an intransigent South Africa to agree to implementation. On the contrary, the whole direction was toward making the resolution acceptable to Pretoria, which meant altering it so that it would be a means of retaining effective control of a nominally independent Namibia.[16]

The logic of this approach was that all concessions would have to be made by Swapo. Reopening negotiations would also provide a legitimized delay, which South Africa needed to reshape circumstances within Namibia. Pretoria's objective was to alter fundamental aspects of Resolution 435 and to lay the foundations for continued economic and political dominance or massive destabilization of Namibia.

In June, the US deputy secretary of state, William Clark, visited South Africa, accompanied by Crocker. Their policy was being labelled in Washington as "constructive engagement," a description which inferred that all previous attempts to move South Africa had amounted to "negative engagement." The real motivation was revealed in a memorandum to the secretary of state, Alexander Haig, from Crocker, who proposed that in return for South Africa's help in reaching a settlement in Namibia, the United States should work "to end South Africa's polecat status in the world, and seek to restore its place as a legitimate and important regional factor with whom we can cooperate pragmatically." It was during this visit that the Reagan administration made public the new condition they had attached to the implementation of Resolution 435: withdrawal of Cuban troops from Angola, thereafter referred to as "linkage."[17] The South Africans were delighted by the proposal, which ensured further substantial delay in the Namibian independence process.

The other four members of the "contact group" acquiesced to this, as well as to many points of detail that Washington and Pretoria now littered in the path of Resolution 435. In the Security Council, with the United States abstaining, a resolution proposed on behalf of Swapo and the southern African grouping of Frontline states condemned "linkage."[18] But, by linking South Africa's illegal occupation of Namibia to the withdrawal of Cuban troops (legally in Angola at the request of that government in response to Pretoria's 1975 invasion), the Reagan administration had placed a seemingly insurmountable hurdle as a precondition for Namibian independence.

Pretoria still faced the problem of trying to create a viable alternative to Swapo and its president, Sam Nujoma. When the term of office of South Africa's DTA surrogates expired in September 1982, Pretoria was confronted by an untenable level of corruption and chaos—and an excessively expensive bureaucracy. Finally, at the beginning of 1983, South Africa was forced to return the governorship of Namibia to yet another administrator general. This was followed by a proposed but stillborn State Council and, when this failed to materialize, by the Multi-Party Conference (MPC), a group of eight disparate political parties including the DTA and Afrikaner nationalist groupings. But by the end of 1983, two parties—the Damara Council and the Christian Democratic Party (CDP)—had withdrawn, arguing that the MPC was no more than an anti-Swapo front, anonymously funded by South Africa through a West German source. Another member of the MPC, the South West African

National Union (Swanu), withdrew on similar grounds in 1984.[19] Once again the attempt to create an internal alternative to Swapo failed.

Nevertheless, Pretoria continued to pursue the internal option. The administrator general had said in his New Year's message that South Africa was "pinning its hopes" on the MPC.[20] Soon thereafter, P. W. Botha called the MPC to Cape Town to tell them they were to agree to a concrete alternative to the implementation of Resolution 435.[21]

The interminable, often bewildering and invariably Machiavellian, twists and turns of Namibian politics now brought the Zambian president, Kenneth Kaunda, briefly to center stage. Kaunda, it transpired, had written to P. W. Botha suggesting that if he were serious about finding a solution he should give Namibia its independence as a "Christmas gift." The South African prime minister had replied, indicating a willingness to arrange talks between Swapo and the MPC and offering a guarantee of safety if Swapo would send a delegation to Windhoek. Swapo's leaders declined to meet the MPC but reiterated their willingness to hold direct talks with the South African government.[22]

The illusion that something might at last be happening was maintained for several months. On 30 January 1984, a high-level delegation from SADF military intelligence flew to the Zambian capital, Lusaka, for an unpublicized meeting with Swapo leaders. The delegation included the head of the South African Military Intelligence Directorate (MID), General Pieter van der Westhuizen, Brigadier van Tonder, and Brigadier Hammon. Swapo took the meeting seriously but found that nothing more than negotiation with Pretoria's Windhoek puppets was offered.

The SADF delegation flew home the same day. In parliament, the following day, P. W. Botha gave further momentum to the illusion of progress. He announced that the SADF had begun its withdrawal from Angola as a first step toward a hoped-for cease-fire. He went on to say that the cost of retaining Namibia had become too high, and he urged political leaders to find an acceptable solution to bring the territory to independence. "Our determination [to hold Namibia] has exacted a heavy price—in material, in international condemnation, and in the lives of our young men," Botha added.[23]

The release, early in 1984, of Andimba Toivo Ja Toivo and a number of other Namibian political prisoners, one of the conditions of Resolution 435, served to maintain the illusion. On 11 March, P. W. Botha went a step further. South Africa was willing, he said, to take part in a peace conference involving all Namibian parties, without preconditions. Swapo had already indicated its willingness to meet the administrator general if he was the designated representative of the South African government. Kaunda now invited Swapo to meet in Lusaka with a South African delegation led by the administrator general. The meeting collapsed when it became clear that South Africa was trying to lure Swapo away from Resolution 435 and a seven-month transition to elections, and into protracted constitutional negotiations with the unrepresentative MPC. Swapo would have to disarm, while South Africa's military forces, police and administration would remain in place. It was thus being proposed that Swapo become part of the client administration in Windhoek, thereby legitimizing South Africa's continued illegal occupation. So ended yet another Namibian hope. South Africa remained as determined as ever to prevent Swapo from taking power now that it had the open support of Washington which insisted on linking Namibia's independence to the presence of Cuban troops in Angola.

Swapo had started its armed struggle on 26 August 1966 directly as a result of Pretoria's violent suppression of political activity in Namibia, and the determination of those Western states with the greatest economic stake in the region to protect the Pretoria regime from any form of effective international action through the UN. During the first years of the conflict, responsibility for attempting to contain Swapo guerrillas rested with the South African police. The military began to take over in the early 1970s. In 1974, SADF strength in Namibia was 15,000 men. By 1976 it had risen to 45,000; by 1980 to 80,000; and by 1985 to between 100,000 and 110,000. These figures, especially in later years, included mercenaries, members of Unita, "Bantustan" units, and South West Africa (SWA) territorials, which are in fact part of the South African military command structure. Estimates of 50,000 and 65,000 appear to refer to SADF personnel only. Since taking control of Namibia in 1972, the military has continued joint operations with the police, referring to both forces as the "security forces." This, in part, was the increasingly costly burden of holding Namibia to which P. W. Botha referred.

Behind these cold statistics lurks a sinister objective. Inevitably, sooner or later, South Africa must relinquish its direct, illegal rule of Namibia. It has tried, and failed, to create an alternative to Swapo. It is still trying to do so; but Pretoria must be fully aware that the likelihood of success is, at best, minimal. It can, through "linkage," buy time for a while longer, with the support of the Reagan administration. But, one day, it must recognize the probability of having to deal with a Swapo government in Windhoek. Thus, while delaying that day and trying to find an alternative, it is also building structures within Namibia to limit the options of an independent country. These military and political-economic structures are designed to limit the ability of any Namibian government to rule without South African approval of its policies—and to serve as land mines to destabilize or destroy such a government if it attempts to do so.

Force has been the primary vehicle used by South Africa to retain its domination of Namibia, so it is not surprising that the first neocolonial structures created were military. Within two years of the SADF taking over military responsibilities from the police, they began forming black "ethnic" units. The first of these was a San unit, created in 1974 and today known as 201st Batallion. Other "ethnic" units followed, recruited from among the Ovambo, Kavango, Rehoboth, Caprivian, Damara, Nama, Herero, and Tswana peoples, and "coloured" groups.[24] In essence what South Africa was doing was recruiting Namibians to fight Namibians in defense of Pretoria's illegal occupation of the territory. And, in a country where so few people are in salaried employment, recruitment is not a difficult task, although certainly it sows the seeds of disunity both for the present and the future. The 1980 establishment of the South West Africa Territory Force (SWATF), bringing these units together with a number of SADF units, was an attempt to create a potent force for the future destabilization of an independent Namibia.

It is important to note that the SWATF was created after the passage of Resolution 435. This explicitly states that the SADF would withdraw from Namibia during the transition, with the exception of 1,500 troops who would remain in two specified bases. "Ethnic," or tribal, units would be disbanded. By creating the SWATF the South Africans sought to create the impression that the "ethnic" units no longer existed and that there was now a "legitimate" Namibian force not covered by Resolution 435, which should remain intact and continue to exist as the national army of an independent Namibia.

The SWATF has been set up as if it were a fully fledged SWA army, incorporating a command infrastructure (although ranks used are little different from those in the SADF), a permanent force infantry component, a citizen force, a commando network comprising 26 area force units, a training division, and an administrative and logistics component. Distinctive uniforms give it the outward appearance of a separate force, and military communiqués in Windhoek are now always issued by the SWATF. This, however, obfuscates the fact that it remains an integral part of South Africa's military machine, with Pretoria remaining in overall command and retaining control of its entire operation.[25]

In 1982, the officer commanding the SWATF, Major General Charles Lloyd, spelled out South Africa's view of its position in the event of the implementation of Resolution 435. Essentially, what he said was that the territorials would be partially demobilized for a temporary period during implementation but not fully dismantled. It would retain its command structure, bases, weapons and capacity to fully mobilize within hours. Pretoria clearly hopes to make utter nonsense of the fundamental principle in Resolution 435 that all South African forces in Namibia must be withdrawn, bar the 1,500 who would remain confined to two bases for the transitional period. Since the SWATF is an integral part of the South African forces in Namibia, Pretoria's obvious intention is to have a military force in Namibia which is ostensibly Namibian even if it is commanded, equipped and supplied by Pretoria and owes allegiance to South Africa. In the longer term, the apartheid regime probably hopes the SWATF can be locally staffed, largely locally financed, and backed and run by South Africa less overtly and completely than at present. The goal was, and is, a neocolonial army for a neocolonial state.

Apart from the SWATF the Pretoria regime has developed a motley collection of "special" unconventional units, some of which are used specifically in Namibia while others are used more widely. Although they operate in great secrecy, it is known that the same process of making them ostensibly Namibian is in progress.

Koevoet (crowbar) was the most notorious of these units, responsible for many brutal murders and the extensive use of torture. Officially "disbanded," it has actually been transferred from the South African Police (SAP) to the "South West African Police." Despite the nominal change, it continues the savage practices of the *Koevoet*.

Pretoria's law and order minister, Louis Le Grange, announced in May 1985 that members of the SAP who are members of *Koevoet* or the "security police" would be "seconded or transferred to the South West African Police" and that the SWATF would expand its "counter insurgency" function. Pretoria is using this method to "Namibianize" the names of their surrogates and further their identification as Namibian units.

While the "South West African Police" is formally designated a police unit, it is in fact the cutting edge of the South African military in Namibia. It functions as a military unit and has never had anything other than a military function, operating in much the same way as the Selous Scouts did in preindependence Zimbabwe. In designating it a police unit, Pretoria's reasoning attempts to circumvent a fundamental element of Resolution 435 which makes provision for the withdrawal of all South African forces from Namibia (barring the 1,500 who would be confined to two bases for the transition period) and the total disbanding of all "ethnic" units. But it also provides for the existing police force to maintain law and order during the transitional period. Pretoria can be expected to argue that "South West African Police" units are "police" units and should remain operational during the transition. This type of deception by Pretoria should be firmly dealt with by the UN. The SWA Special Task Force is also technically a police unit, presumably for the same reason. It too is a brutalized, professional military unit into which Pretoria has been transferring members of *Koevoet*.

The so-called "reconnaissance commandoes," the "recces" in South African military jargon, constitute another element of Pretoria's army of occupation in Namibia. There are known to be six such commandoes based at secret locations in South Africa. They are highly trained troops and operate in great secrecy, mainly in destabilization operations in neighboring states.

The 32d Battalion is a very large mercenary force made up of the remnants of Unita and the National Front for the Liberation of Angola (FNLA), as well as black Mozambican former members of Portuguese paramilitary units such as the *Flechas* (Arrows). They are led by a white officer corps of South African permanent force members and mercenaries. It is widely held that they are "32d Battalion" while at rear bases or operating in Namibia and "Unita" while operating in Angola.[26] The 44th Battalion has its origins in the recruitment by South Africa of members of the Rhodesian Light Infantry (RLI) when Zimbabwe became independent in 1980. It is primarily deployed in so-called follow-up operations. The SWA Specialists undertake tracking using San trackers and dogs (including pack hounds). They make extensive use of scrambler motorcycles and horses in their operations. It can be expected that any of these units not yet under the SWATF will be transferred into it within the next couple of years. Clearly Pretoria's objective is to impose military and police structures loyal to South Africa on Namibia as part of the program to retain effective control of the country even after Resolution 435 has been implemented.

Although Namibia's economic history has been characterized by intensive and brutal exploitation of its natural resources and its people, not until the late 1940s did the country become relatively economically significant. From then until the late 1970s Namibia's economic importance—and its contribution to South Africa's coffers—increased dramatically. Throughout that period and thereafter, Namibia remained a grossly exploited, unequal and racist society. The differential between per capita white income and that of African and "coloured" Namibians is in the range of 18 or 20 to one, as against a differential in South Africa itself of 12 or 15 to one and marginally less in Zimbabwe.[27] During the economic halcyon years, foreign enterprises and settlers prospered, and so did Pretoria. Then the bubble burst.

What happened? There are several reasons, by no means all related to the liberation struggle. They include the post-1975 slump in metal prices, reduced diamond output by De Beers to try to stabilize world prices, the collapse of the karakul wool industry, overfishing, and the semipermanent drought since 1977, which has reduced agricultural output and livestock by up to 75 percent.[28] Not all of these factors were unique to Namibia and several were shared by other countries in the region.

Over 1984–86 the economy ceased contracting but did not recover. With improved diamond and karakul prices offset by falling uranium oxide and base metal prices, an end to rapid government expansion and continued net private disinvestment there are no prospects for real recovery.

However special factors affecting the Namibian economy do relate to the liberation struggle and to the response to it by other factors:

1. Major enterprise employers raised real wages for and began to create a stratum of semiskilled wage elite (partly to reduce costs, as white workers were much more expensive, and partly to secure an African group "loyal" to employers).
2. A similar policy toward professional and semiprofessional personnel (especially teachers and nurses) was combined with a strategy of creating a class of well-paid politicians, clerks and home guards, and extending some mobility—both economically and socially—to selected members of this group.
3. Massive recurrent and capital expenditure was incurred—on military camps, cleared border zones and roads—to slow the advance of the guerrilla war.
4. There was an increase in risks and costs associated with the war, for example: the need to move fuel by convoy, to use air passenger and freight transport in the north, to guard ranches and installations, to repair sabotage damage to

transport and power links (as far south as the main Van Eck power station in Windhoek) and to build a new power line to the Cape to supplement the Ruacana Falls Dam supply rendered uncertain by war.

5. This led to an increased exodus of ranchers and other whites, who had been partly bought off by higher wages and subsidies.

6. It also led to a collapse of enterprise investment as the investors calculated the military and political risks of investing new capital (even out of territorial profits) as too high until an independence settlement and peace emerged.

These factors account for the explosive rise in the recurrent budget deficit, met partly by South African transfer increases (largely for a portion of military and police spending) and partly by external commercial borrowing, almost all from South African financial institutions.

By the end of the 1982-83 financial year, South African government spending on Namibia had risen to about R 900-965 million. Local revenue plus the analogue to customs and excise covered R 420-450 million of that figure, South African transfers R 215 million—of which R 115 million was for "territorial" army and police—and external borrowing (mostly from South Africa) over R 300 million. Of the approximately R 750 million in recurrent spending, R 50 million was for debt service and R 240 million for "second tier," "representative authority" or, more bluntly "Bantustan" administration. The latter transfers were to bodies which even the Pretoria-appointed Thirion Commission found to be monumentally incompetent, wasteful and corrupt.[29]

In 1984, P. W. Botha restated South Africa's old refrain that it subsidizes Namibia, but this time from three new angles. He warned the territory's "internal" leaders that South Africa had to look out for its own people first, especially in times of recession and resource scarcity; so Namibians could not expect much help. Second, he made a plea to Western countries, especially the "contact group," to take over the financing of the Namibian deficit from South Africa (that is, take over subsidizing South Africa's occupation). The intention was, quite likely, to cause them to hesitate to take on the costs of a transition to independence and economic rehabilitation. Third, he gave a more complete set of cost figures than had been presented before.

Botha asserted that in 1984–85 the cost to South Africa of holding Namibia was R 1,143 million (almost US $600 million at the average 1985 rate of exchange). This was asserted to include R 663 million for defense; R 250 million for customs and excise transfer; R 318 million in budgetary grants; and R 95 million for the South African Transport Service (SATS) deficit. Some of these items are hardly what they purport to be. Customs and excise represents a purchase of preferential market access and may well be below what Namibia could get on an independent customs/excise system, while the SATS figure appears to combine capital and recurrent costs.

A more complex matrix of costs as of 1984–85 shows a different breakdown and larger total:

1. Defense expenditure in and on Namibia and Angola, which is 33 percent of total South African military, police, security spending—R 1,500 million;
2. Budget grants plus external borrowing guaranteed by the South African treasury and not likely to be accepted as valid by an independent Namibia—R 500 million;
3. The South African Transport Services (SATS) net cash flow loss (assuming that capital inclusion and Walvis Bay exclusion cross cancel)—R 90 million.[30]

That total of close to R 2,100 million was about 9 percent of the South African government's budget for 1984–85. Even more striking, it is only slightly smaller than the likely 1984 gross domestic product (GDP) of Namibia, which is R 2,250 million when adjusted upward from official data to include Walvis Bay and subsistence.

Admittedly, R 2,100 million is not a net figure. Profit and wage remittances plus capital flight to South Africa (offsetting in part loans in the other direction) may come to R 300–400 million, reducing the net cost to R 1,700–1,800 million. South Africa still probably has a slim external balance gain from Namibia. But that surplus is now negligible.

As of 1987 the net cost to South Africa has probably escalated, with inflation and military spending surges of about R 2,200–2,400 million. Borrowing is down—apart from the "asset purchases" from the Electricity Supply Commission (Escom), SATS and the South African state development corporation—but transfers to the territorial budget are up.

Thus from a South African economic perspective, Namibia no longer pays.[31] Recession, drought, military spending and the costs of manipulating Namibian society and the economy to create a broader base for the "total strategy" have achieved that reversal.

In the economic sphere, as in the military, South Africa has created the infrastructure for destabilizing Namibia—whether as a strategic preindependence design or as a result of the tactics of restructuring. This cannot be ignored, nor can one assume it will not be used, given South Africa's regional strategy of domination and history of destabilization, of which at least seven elements can be identified.[32]

First, South Africa has created for Namibia an "external debt" which by the end of 1983 was of the order of R 500 million, with interest and debt service of about R 100–120 million a year and a rate of increase of perhaps R 250–300 million a year. By mid-1986 it may well have been approaching a R 1,000 million principal (100 percent of export earnings) and R 200–

250 million annual overall debt service (20–25 percent).[33] In part this represents nominal transfers of railway, power and selected mining assets from South African entities to the occupation regime, along with parallel debt liabilities to South Africa for their "purchase." This creates a slightly more plausible "external debt," as well as raising its level. To accept that debt would cripple the economy of an independent Namibia. To repudiate it—despite the 1971 International Court of Justice opinion which clearly renders it legally void—might damage Namibia's external financial standing and access to credit.

Second, the debt has made budgetary shambles of both actual revenue and expenditure, and, even more, by the appearance of total, permanent insolvency. The attempt to cast Namibia as a fiscal "basket case," not worth assisting, is quite clear in some of P. W. Botha's statements on the cost of the territory to South Africa. So is the warning that instant cutoffs of South African funding before a new tax and expenditure system was in place could cause a breakdown of governmental ability to function.[34] Since 1984 the budgetary position has been stabilized but is still propped up by transfers and by serious cuts in services such as health and education.

Third, in Namibia's multiple-tiered and racially structured administration, South Africa has created a bureaucratic monstrosity. It is not merely politically unacceptable as an entrenchment of racism; it is corrupt, wasteful and unable to operate competently for any purpose, as even the South Africans have admitted. While these functional weaknesses are now a drawback to South Africa as an occupying power, at independence they will threaten an independent Namibia with paralysis. South Africa can aggravate this paralysis by the sudden withdrawal of key technical, professional and administrative staff.

The "Transitional Government of National Unity (TGNU)" installed in 1985 is neither united, national nor a government; and there is no indication that it is intended to be transitional in any real sense of the word. The South Africans want it and its "constitution" to gain some semblance of legitimacy by being in place and to establish a power base in areas which any new administration would find difficult to change. Despite high-sounding claims, TGNU has remained subject to the administrator general and quite unable to desegregate even one white school.

Fourth, the flirtation of large companies, and of the occupation regime, with creating a stable and skilled black labor force will leave a potential time bomb. The professional, skilled and semiskilled workers are not politically loyal to South Africa. However, their pay scales of R 5,000–12,500 a year pose serious problems. It is economically impossible to set these income levels for all workers. Even if it were, the increasing rural-urban income inequality and siphoning off of resources otherwise available for rural development would be politically dangerous to the extreme. To limit these scales to certain posts would both entrench massive intra-African income inequality and make expansion of basic public services fiscally impossible. To sustain them for present African jobholders only, with new entrants on lower scales, would create great bitterness among returning liberation war veterans. To cut them—by direct scale changes or even by a freeze—would at best lead to loss of morale and resentment that gains "won" from the South African occupiers were promptly eroded at independence.

The "Bantustan" politician, clerk and home guard pose a different set of problems. Their "services," unlike those of the professional and skilled personnel, are not needed. But if they are fired they will provide the core for a political fifth column which could provide a focal point for discontent.

Fifth, by remaining in illegal occupation of Walvis Bay—Namibia's only deep-water port—after independence, South Africa could ensure that it has a choke point. Until Namibia creates alternative ports (for example, by reactivating Swakopmund) or gains access to others (via Angola or Zambia), South

Africa at Walvis Bay controls its basic access to the outside world and can prevent diversification of trade and transport away from South Africa.[35]

Sixth, similar considerations apply to road and rail transport. Rolling stock is highly mobile and, like many of the truck fleets, is South African owned. Major repair facilities are in Upington in South Africa, or Walvis Bay, but not Windhoek. Roads and rail lines without trucks and rolling stock, and without maintenance and repair capacity, do not constitute a transport system.

Seventh, the sea bastion of South Africa's Orange River line at Alexander Bay has within mortar or launch range Namibia's premier economic asset—the Oranjemund diamond complex. Furthermore, the "boundary" of the Walvis Bay "enclave" has within its range the alternative port at Swakopmund. Thus, Namibia's economy is all too vulnerable to South African aggression.

This analysis of the infrastructure for destabilization reveals two things. The infrastructure established by South Africa is alarmingly strong and multifaceted but several, perhaps all, of its seven elements could be rendered less effective by giving priority attention to dismantling or neutralizing them.

First, despite South African claims to the contrary, most of the "external debt" seems to be held by South African financial institutions, and all is fully guaranteed by their government. Thus, repudiation backed by the International Court of Justice opinion and precedents for former colonial debts—plus a firm commitment to honor any debt an independent Namibia would incur—seems likely to defuse the threat of bankruptcy or of lack of access to normal credit. This position is upheld by the 1983 Vienna Convention on "Succession of States in Respect of State Property, Archives and Debt" which bans imposition of colonial debt on a former colony without the newly independent government's consent—even when a colonial administration has been lawful.

Second and third, financial and administrative reform, plus training and upgrading Namibians and securing replacement expatriates, are priorities for independent Namibia. To some extent these can be planned and programmed before independence with the knowledge that an orderly, leisurely transition (of the type which characterized most British colonies at independence) is a luxury Namibia is unlikely to enjoy. Similarly, some professionals will stay if assured of terms and conditions of service, and some have had initial discussions with Swapo on such issues.

Fourth, a scaled-down income policy and an approach to mobilization of professional and skilled Namibians can begin even before independence. Frank dialogue on constraints is not hopeless in respect to the middle class with real skills. The politicians, clerks and home guard are not an economic, but a conversion or security, problem; buying them off would be an economically, as well as politically, bankrupting approach.

Fifth, interim port facilities can be available within months, probably by reactivating Swakopmund by dredging, artificial breakwaters, lighters, among other means, and by road links to Angola and Zambia created over the same period if the priority is accepted and planning begun before independence. The diversion of resources would remain a severe cost but less of a danger and constraint than seeking to operate by using a South African–held Walvis Bay.

Sixth, similarly, vehicles, rolling stock, and maintenance and repair equipment can be in place in a limited period of time—if needs are identified early and priority given.

Finally, action on the economic front cannot prevent cross-border raids, primarily a diplomatic and security issue. However, the careful choice of partners (for example, a continuing De Beers presence at Oranjemund, North European technical partnership at the Rossing mine, Dutch or Scandinavian interim port management at Swakopmund) would raise the costs to South Africa of random sabotage attacks.

Thus, although South Africa has a potentially paralyzing economic destabilization apparatus already in place, there are a number of obvious measures that can be implemented to reduce its potential to do harm. It is also clear that the planning for this defensive action must begin sooner rather than later.

Resolution 435 is not a perfect solution to the problem of South Africa's illegal occupation of Namibia. From the outset Swapo has taken the view that, should the proposals being presented offer the opportunity for a settlement which would broadly reflect what the vast majority of Namibians want, Swapo would cooperate, even though the proposals made considerable concessions to Pretoria. Swapo has been only too aware of the numerous political risks resulting from the concessions made in Pretoria's favor, but has consistently urged early implementation of Resolution 435. Swapo's flexibility arises from a position of strength reflected by its very evident support among Namibians.

Namibia is not approaching independence in a vacuum. The difference between implementing Resolution 435 in 1978 and at some future date is not simply a matter of time. Pretoria seeks to undermine the aims of the resolution by changing the structures within the country and by setting impossible parameters for implementation. Without great vigilance on the part of Swapo and the UN—whose responsibility it would be to ensure fair implementation of Resolution 435—Pretoria could create a situation where the process would be sabotaged, destroying any possibility of future implementation. They could attempt to wipe out the Swapo leadership, or create a situation where the government emerging would find it effectively impossible to govern the country. Basically Pretoria is busy laying the groundwork for a massive destabilization of Namibia in case, at some point, it is forced to bow to the pressure to implement Resolution 435. The only circumstances under which Pretoria might willingly agree to such implementation would be those in which it perceives the opportunity of making gains for itself: by using the process to set up a puppet government; by trying to destroy Swapo; or by so destabilizing Namibia that the government of the newly independent country would be forced to capitulate to Pretoria's demands. Given the financial and military cost of holding Namibia, South Africa may at some point decide it is prudent to pull out, following the 435 process or a simple "truce to withdraw" procedure (analogous to the British evacuation of Aden). South Africa has prepared for this psychologically by gradually distancing itself from the Namibian administration and making plain that it does not view Namibia as an integral part of South Africa.

The UN plan makes provision for the South African administration to organize and run the election with the UN taking on a role of "supervision and control" of the electoral process. Originally, no specific provision was made for the nature of the electoral process. This was superseded by Resolution 539 (1983) which required that Pretoria communicate its choice of an electoral system. In November 1985, Pretoria informed the secretary general that it had adopted proportional representation but gave no further details.

There are numerous ways in which the South African administration in Namibia may attempt to rig the registration of voters or the election itself, and make campaigning difficult for Swapo. Pretoria may attempt to rush the registration of voters at a time when a considerable number of Swapo personnel are out of the country, in the hope of excluding a substantial part of Swapo's organizational capacity from the process and of directly disenfranchizing those still outside Namibia. It could produce misleading information in selected areas, disqualify candidates, intimidate the population, stuff ballot boxes prior to the beginning of the election, or insist that illiterate voters are "assisted" by its own officials. The administration will almost certainly create bureaucratic difficulties for Swapo in importing the vehicles it has in neighboring states which are essential for campaigning in Namibia. Likewise it will prevent or greatly delay campaign materials or paper supplies coming in from abroad. Similar barriers were put in the way in the Zimbabwe independence elections.

Today there are few people, even in conservative international circles who would deny the mass support that Swapo enjoys in Namibia. Certainly South Africa believes Swapo does have support—otherwise it would have held less implausible internal elections or agreed to internationally monitored elections long ago.

Assuming Swapo wins two-thirds or more of the seats in the constituent assembly, Pretoria may still seek to impose procedures in the constituent assembly, making progress difficult. Much would depend on the organizational readiness of Swapo to cope with these eventualities, the adequate training of Swapo cadres to provide its own effective monitoring of the election, the integrity and independence of UNTAG and the arrangements made by the UN Security Council in its enabling resolution. For example, if this Security Council action to enforce changes in South Africa's administration of the election required a positive vote, it would be subject to a veto. This could be avoided by requiring positive approval of the stages in the process, as proposed by South Africa.

At the end of October 1987, the Security Council passed Resolution 601 authorizing the secretary general "to proceed to arrange a cease-fire" between South Africa and Swapo in order to undertake the administrative and other practical steps necessary for the emplacement of the UNTAG. This resolution, which also urged UN members to render all necessary practical assistance, passed by a vote of 14 in favor (including Britain), with none against and one abstention (the United States). It welcomed Swapo's readiness to sign and observe a cease-fire agreement, paving the way for implementation of Resolution 435. Appendix 4 contains the full text of Resolution 601.

The mass resistance within South Africa also serves to weaken the capacity of the regime to maintain its illegal occupation of Namibia. The regime is forced to commit more and more of its troops and police within South Africa; and its violence and brutality are becoming more evident to the international community. As a result, South Africa is steadily gaining a reputation among Western business investors as an area of too great a risk for their investments. In addition, these investments have too great a "hassle factor" (in terms of negative image domestically) to be worthwhile. Coupled with an economy in a state of deep structural crisis, South Africa is no longer able to attract external financing.

For South Africa, as already outlined, Namibia is a fiscal and military personnel drain. The gross cost of holding down Namibia is already 10 percent of South Africa's state budget, about half of its annual external borrowing, and over R 500 per white South African. That is a heavy cost now and likely to become more difficult for Pretoria to maintain.

These economic factors are related to the narrowly military set of issues. South Africa has over half of its front line infantry tied down in Namibia and Angola. Both logistical and military considerations make their speedy redeployment to meet threats to the regime at home virtually impossible. From a military security point of view, a much smaller force on the more easily defensible Orange River line and a substantial home-based tactical force available to meet domestic threats would clearly make more sense. This is increasingly necessary if the current level of physical resistance to apartheid is sustained.

Pretoria's attempt to create a Namibian facade for its military presence there through the establishment of SWATF has run into considerable difficulties. The regime's objective is to establish an army in Namibia, capable of replacing the official South African forces, which can claim to be Namibian. To attain this, the force would have to be largely black, would need to be fairly well trained in order to handle the technical sophistication of South African military equipment and would need to maintain a reasonable level of morale. On all three fronts Pretoria has problems.

The declared intention of the Pretoria regime is to conscript all Namibian males between the ages of 16 and 65. The first attempts—which avoided the northern regions of Namibia, judged by Pretoria to be more committed to Swapo—brought strong opposition from Namibians in the central and southern regions. They objected to being drafted into a military force illegally occupying Namibia and to fighting fellow Namibians. Many potential conscripts chose to leave Namibia and join the People's Liberation Army of Namibia (Plan). More recent attempts to conscript Namibians began with a sudden order that all males in the Sector 10 area (Tsumeb, Otavi, Grootfontein) would have to register within two weeks. In spite of assistance offered by some companies who forced reluctant workers to register, Pretoria again seems not to have followed through with the process. The underlying problem for Pretoria in conscripting Namibians is the overwhelming support Swapo has throughout the country. Conscription holds the grave risks for the regime of having its forces thoroughly infiltrated by Swapo sympathizers. Minutes of a South African military intelligence conference held in May 1984, released to the press in Britain by Swapo, recognized that "Swapo internally is organized on a wide terrain on different levels and possesses the infrastructure to collect information over a wide spectrum."[36] They fear that valuable information could be leaked to Plan or that trained military personnel might desert to Plan.

To counter this problem it can be expected that SWATF will retain a very large South African and mercenary component. This can already be seen in the extensive use of South African officers to command forces which are otherwise largely indigenous. In the transfer of *Koevoet* from the SAP to the "South West Africa Police," South African members of *Koevoet* were also "transferred or seconded" to these supposedly Namibian forces. The South African regime's presentation of a Namibian face in its military occupation is not going to reduce costs to the South African treasury unless, of course, it chooses to reduce the size of its military machine, an option which would seriously weaken the current tenuous hold on Namibia.

South Africa's closest allies are finding it harder and harder to defend the regime, particularly in the case of the United States. In spite of vigorous support for Pretoria by the Reagan administration, in 1986 the US Congress passed less than total but still far-reaching sanctions legislation. The British government, while not under the same degree of domestic pressure, is isolated within the Commonwealth in its refusal to apply sanctions against South Africa.

The period 1986–87 has seen an upsurge of Swapo support and a collapse of TGNU credibility in Namibia. Despite constant harassment, Swapo has repeatedly held mass demonstrations in major towns. In addition, the Mine and Food and Allied Workers Unions affiliated with the National Union of Namibian Workers have organized over 16,000 members and held rallies, negotiations and strikes.[37] All major Namibian organizations signed the Ai Gams Declaration at Windhoek in 1986, reaffirming their commitment to national liberation. The major churches, Swanu, the CDP, the Damara chiefs, and smaller bodies joined with Swapo in this declaration. Meanwhile, the German settler interest group held talks with Swapo in Lusaka and indicated its commitment to early and full implementation of Resolution 435.

The TGNU, in contrast, had nothing to show for its claims. Even its attempt to cobble together a plausible-looking constitution, so as to provide some electoral credibility, was vetoed by P. W. Botha.

Whatever antics Pretoria may be up to with the intention of avoiding a Swapo government in Windhoek, the regime will eventually be forced to capitulate, and then the Namibian people, under Swapo's leadership, will achieve the liberation of their country and genuine national independence. South Africa's occupation of Namibia has reached a dead end on the economic, political and military fronts. How fast it can be pushed down the remaining distance—and forced to accept Namibian independence—depends primarily on the Namibian people and their liberation movement, but this can be influenced significantly by both domestic and external pressures on the Pretoria regime.

Similarly, how successful South Africa can be in perpetuating economic dependence and in destabilizing a genuinely independent Namibia will depend primarily on alertness, planned reduction of vulnerability and commitment to continued struggle by the people of Namibia and their government. But this can be influenced significantly by the price South Africa will have to pay to continue occupation or to effect subsequent destabilization.

5

LESOTHO,
BOTSWANA,
SWAZILAND
Captive States

In a quiet valley of aloes, wattle and poplar trees below Lesotho's parliament lies a curious little graveyard. It has 27 low headstones with the names of the dead and the blunt epitaph: "Massacred by the SADF [South African Defense Force], 9/12/82." Six newly turned graves alongside them are unmarked, but when the headstones are erected they will probably carry a similar statement. . . .

The graveyard is fenced off with barbed wire and separated from Maseru's main cemetery by the Seputana River, a little tributary which runs a few hundred yards into the Caledon River, the border with South Africa. The separation from the main cemetery is deliberate. The dead are all South Africans, members of the African National Congress [ANC]. And the plan is that when "liberation" comes to South Africa they will be leaving, making the trip across the Caledon to some final resting place, another of Africa's "heroes acres."

In the meantime the graveyard serves as a reminder of this tiny mountain kingdom's invidious position, caught between the millstones of white South Africa and black nationalism, and of its diplomatic dilemma.

A couple of miles down the road at the Maseru border post a handful of South African police in paramilitary uniforms make minute examination of vehicles and baggage in search of explosives, guns and ANC desperadoes which they know will not be found, but which provide a convenient excuse to reduce a puny neighbour to a state of seige.[1]

In those four descriptive paragraphs written in Maseru on 14 January 1986, David Beresford encapsulated the dilemma facing Lesotho in particular, as well as Botswana and Swaziland (known collectively as BLS or Boleswa)—the captive states of southern Africa.

LESOTHO

After the ANC was banned in South Africa in 1960, Lesotho became one of many countries where its members and others sought refuge and shelter. Twenty years later the South African refugee population in Lesotho had reached 11,500, mostly refugees from the social system of apartheid—people who left because of the ban on racially mixed marriages, children escaping from "Bantu" education (the inferior curriculum available to Africans), students looking for university places—and one hundred new arrivals were registering each month at the Interior Ministry.

Then, in the early hours of 9 December 1982, the haven for refugees was turned into a charnel house. SADF commandoes, supported by helicopters and armored trucks, sped through border posts on the outskirts of Maseru and shot up several

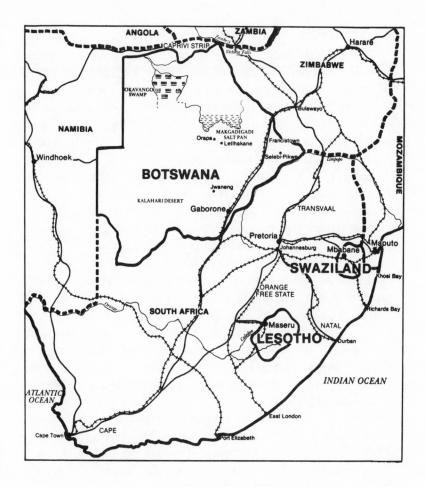

residences, slaughtering 42 people, including Lesotho nationals, some of them women and children. The then minister of information Desmond Sixishe said it was a "traumatic" experience that "destabilized us psychologically."[2] The dead included 30 South African refugees, and 27 of them now occupy those marked graves on the banks of the Seputana River.

The other six graves, as yet unmarked, are those of refugees who died in another attack on Maseru on 19 December 1985. They were killed while attending a Christmas party.[3]

Of the three captive states, Lesotho is the most vulnerable. It is a tiny, impoverished nation of almost 1.5 million people, completely surrounded by South Africa and almost entirely dependent upon the capriciousness of its hostile neighbor. Only 13 percent of the country's 30,355 square kilometers is suitable for cultivation. Its economy is essentially a remittance and subsistence one. Although censuses depict 90 percent of the population as agricultural, only 3 percent of rural households are able to sustain themselves on agricultural production.

About 150,000 people—more than half the adult population—are absentee migrants in mines, in industries and on farms in South Africa. The money they remit accounts for over half of the national income. Lesotho depends on South Africa for 97 percent of its imports and 95 percent of its tourists; and the bulk of the commercial enterprises are subsidiaries of South African firms. The only rail link from the capital, Maseru, to South Africa is owned by South African Railways.

In addition, the country depends on the Southern African Customs Union (SACU) for 70 percent of government revenue. Prior to the military coup of January 1986 in Lesotho, South Africa had consistently attempted to use the fact of this dependence to force Lesotho to recognize the "Bantustans" and to be less critical of apartheid policies.

Over the last decade or so, the country has been transformed into a labor reserve of a single industry—mining. However, development of technology in the mining industry, and consequently upgrading of training and skills, has stabilized the labor demands and restricted them to a core of relatively skilled and semiskilled workers. Thus, since 1980, the number of Lesotho nationals employed in the mining sector has declined to around 115,000.

Given the high level of unemployment inside South Africa, particularly among blacks, and in the "Bantustans," and uncertainties of the political situation throughout the region, new opportunities for Basotho migrants are markedly on the decline.

To understand the recent *coup d'état* and Pretoria's destabilization of Lesotho, it is necessary to put into perspective the country's historical evolution and the contradictory forces arising from this history which gave Pretoria the opportunity to intervene.

In Lesotho, formerly the British protectorate of Basutoland, the dominant political party prior to independence was the Basutoland African Congress (BAC), formed in 1952 with the assistance of the African National Congress (ANC) of South Africa. In 1959, it changed its name to the Basutoland Congress Party (BCP). Its leader, Clement Ntsu Sejabanana Mokhehle, was a student at Fort Hare University, where he was also a founding member of the ANC Youth League.[4]

Both the British colonial administration and Pretoria were dissatisfied with the political orientation of the BCP and sought a moderate political platform to counter it. In these circumstances, acting through the local agencies of the Catholic Church, Pretoria provided the financial and organizational support to found a party of the right. Thus the Basutoland National Party (BNP) of Chief Leabua Jonathan Molapo was formed in 1959 explicitly to counter the radical BCP, with a "moderate" political platform to which the British would bequeath power.

Besides the two main political parties, three smaller ones emerged during the preindependence period. These were the Communist Party of Lesotho (CPL), founded by Basotho and South African communists; the Marema Tlou Freedom Party

(MFP), a breakaway from the BCP over the question of the powers of the king; and the United Democratic Party (UDP) of Charles Mofeli, also a breakaway from the BCP.

The first constitutional conference, held in London in 1964, resulted in the first preindependence constitution, effective May 1965. This constitution gave wide executive powers to the monarchy, including control of the armed forces.

Preindependence elections were held on 29 April 1965 and, with financial support from Pretoria, the BNP won 42 percent of the votes and a razor-thin majority of 31 out of 60 seats. Chief Jonathan did not win his seat in parliament, but became prime minister in July 1965 after winning a by-election.

The Basutoland independence conference, held in London in June 1966, marked the last stage to independence but was shrouded in controversy over constitutional amendments. Tabled by the ruling BNP, these amendments sought to remove executive authority from the king. Despite overwhelming opposition from the delegates, the colonial secretary confirmed the amendments and independence was finally set for October 1966.

Just three months later, in December, an abortive meeting at Thaba Bosiu, at which the king intended to demand executive powers under the 1965 constitution, gave Chief Jonathan the excuse to place him under house arrest. He later went into exile, only to return after he had accepted his role as a constitutional monarch.

Throughout its first five years of independence, Lesotho very much resembled a "Bantustan." The ruling BNP pursued a policy of class links with South African capital. Anton Rupert, a South African industrialist and an Afrikaner nationalist, became Chief Jonathan's economic adviser and helped to set up the Lesotho National Development Corporation (LNDC).

Chief Jonathan's liberal economic policies opened the door to South African capital. This led to domination of the economy by South Africa's commercial capital at the expense of small Basotho traders, largely ignored because of their support for the opposition BCP. Labor force exported to South African mining and other industries expanded, reaching an average figure of 250,000 per year.

The extent of South African domination was probably best demonstrated by their control of the civil service. Key areas of the bureaucratic establishment—chief justice, attorney general, chief electoral officer, permanent secretaries—were packed with Afrikaner bureaucrats recruited from South Africa. It is no wonder that Chief Jonathan emerged as the chief exponent of "dialogue" with Pretoria.[5]

This pro-South Africa policy was to prove unpopular and erode much of the BNP's electoral base. The anti-Boer (the Boers were Dutch settlers of the southern tip of Africa) sentiment, very much a historical tradition of the Basotho, was further fuelled by the fact that there was nothing to show for five years of close collaboration with Pretoria. Despite considerable financial support from Pretoria, the BNP was unable to retain its hairline parliamentary majority.

According to reliable sources, at the time of the government's censorship of election results on 29 January 1970, the figures stood as follows: BCP, 35 seats; BNP, 23 seats; and MFP, 1 seat.[6] It was then that Chief Jonathan declared the election null and void, suspended the constitution and declared a state of emergency. Chief Jonathan's paramilitary coup was the beginning of a political crisis which spanned the next 15 years.

Chief Jonathan ruled for three years through a personal dictatorship, without any semblance of democratic representation. In March 1973, following pressure from international donors, he reintroduced the Westminster parliamentary process through the reconstitution of an 86-member Interim National Assembly, consisting predominantly of his party and a few hand-picked opposition elements.

This split the opposition BCP down the middle. The vice-president, Gerald Ramoreboli, and Phoka Chaolana led a fac-

tion into the interim assembly, while Secretary-General Ko-
enyama Chakela responded by organizing an abortive uprising
in January 1974, in which a number of police stations were
attacked in the northern part of the country. When this failed,
the rest of the BCP leadership and many of its members fled
into exile.

After 1974, Lesotho's relationship to Pretoria began to undergo
dramatic changes. In fact, as early as 1973, Chief Jonathan had
told the newly reconstituted Interim National Assembly that
"while still committed to dialogue rather than force in settling
domestic and foreign policy, Lesotho would not cease to give
moral support and any other possible support to our fellow men
in the liberation movement who are still struggling to free
themselves from the yoke of colonialism and racial oppression."[7]

Chief Jonathan's about-face was influenced by a number of
factors. First, his pro-Pretoria policy and the violence that had
accompanied his paramilitary coup had isolated the ruling BNP
and made it extremely unpopular. By 1973, and particularly
after the abortive uprising, Chief Jonathan was ruling from a
very narrow political base. Because of traditional hostility toward the Boers, the ruling BNP hoped that by appearing to
distance itself from Pretoria it could undermine the political
influence of the opposition and usurp its mantle of radicalism.

Second, proximity to Pretoria continued to be a source of
embarrassment, particularly to the new social forces which had
joined the ruling party since independence. After 1970 the
exiled BCP was able to use the role of Pretoria in the 1970 crisis
as a constant source of diplomatic embarrassment to the
Maseru regime, a fact that no doubt isolated Lesotho from the
majority of independent African states. It would seem, therefore, that the regime was under pressure to shed its collaborationist tag.

Third, from the narrow view of economic self-interest, Lesotho did not seem to have reaped any economic benefits from the collaborationist policy. Pretoria all along showed a lack of interest in Maseru's economic development objectives. In 1969, for example, Pretoria announced sweeping changes in its tax structure without consulting Maseru and, again in 1971, devalued the rand without prior warning to Lesotho. Pretoria's failure to commit itself to the Oxbow water project, an important source of foreign currency, probably led to the final realization that the fruits of collaboration were not forthcoming.

Furthermore, it seemed that it was in the interest of the new class forces within the BNP to disengage from Pretoria, so as to be able to diversify the country's sources of foreign aid. Finally, it appears that the changing balance of power in the subcontinent, particularly the collapse of the Portuguese empire, probably convinced sections of the ruling party that the future of the subcontinent did not lie with South Africa.[8]

By 1976, Chief Jonathan had more or less completed his about-face. Following the outbreak of the Soweto uprising of June 1976, Maseru appealed to Pretoria in a strongly worded statement, to reconsider its domestic policy, which "was bound to lead to tragic consequences for both black and white and unforeseeable consequences for southern Africa . . . ."[9] Chief Jonathan proceeded to conclude relations with the ANC and the following year established diplomatic relations with Mozambique. Thereafter, Maseru announced that it would adhere to the United Nations (UN) protocol and accept and protect refugees from South Africa.

Pretoria was far from happy with these developments and predictably began a campaign to "persuade" Lesotho to return to its orbit. At the same time, the realignment of political forces in the 1970s had provoked yet another split among the exiled. Of the two factions, Mokhehle's was prepared "to ride on the back of the devil to cross the river." This was to form the basis upon which Pretoria established the Lesotho Liberation Army

(LLA).[10] Chakela returned to Lesotho under the Amnesty Act of 1980 and, until he was assassinated in 1982, led the progressive faction of the BCP.

The first LLA attacks took place in May 1979. These were followed by a spate of bombings across the country. However, much of the activity between 1979 and 1980 was amateurish, suggesting that Pretoria initially sought to shake the regime and "persuade" the chief back to the fold.

In August 1980, a meeting was arranged between the prime ministers of Lesotho and South Africa at Peka Bridge on the border of the two countries. After the Peka talks there was a brief thaw in hostilities, and the LLA activities were brought to a temporary halt. However, the bargains hammered out at Peka were not honored in the long run.[11]

Perhaps much more important considerations were the events taking place inside South Africa. The second half of 1980 saw the intensification of the armed struggle and resistance against the apartheid regime. After attacks of Sasolburg, and on police stations at Orlando, Soekmekar, Moroka and at various other places, Pretoria sought to take its war into the neighboring countries. It was under these circumstances that the myth of ANC military bases in Lesotho gained currency. It is against this background that, following the collapse of the "Peka Accord," the years 1981–1982 witnessed the intensification of LLA activities.

However, continued destabilization failed to bring Chief Jonathan back to the fold; in fact, it had the opposite effect. Chief Jonathan responded to Pretoria's threat with the only weapon at his disposal—an appeal for support from the international community. Consequently, Lesotho moved closer to the socialist community, which was prepared to offer political, diplomatic and material support for Lesotho's effort to resist apartheid aggression.

This phase of destabilization culminated in the Maseru raid of December 1982. Concerned that it had so far failed to intimidate Lesotho into abandoning its international obligation of accepting South African refugees, South Africa launched a barbaric attack on Maseru on the night of 9 December 1982, killing 30 South African refugees and 12 Lesotho nationals.

The raid failed to intimidate Lesotho into submission. In the historical context of Basotho-Boer relations, it reinforced the resolve to champion a strong anti-apartheid policy and, to a large degree, strengthened the hand of the anti-Pretoria elements within Chief Jonathan's cabinet. The late minister of information Desmond Sixishe said the attack "rekindled the spirit of solidarity against South Africa in this country . . . [and] it had a tremendous effect on our people in terms of rallying them together and reminding them of the constant threat across the border."[12]

It was probably this that convinced Chief Jonathan to establish diplomatic relations at ambassadorial level with the Soviet Union, Cuba, China, Yugoslavia and the Republic of Korea. Pretoria seemed to have concluded at this point that Chief Jonathan had to go, but it took another four years to dislodge him from power.

The period after the Maseru raid saw further intensification of the aggression against Lesotho, which had two broad objectives: Pretoria sought to overthrow Chief Jonathan and replace him with either a candidate from the extreme right of his own ruling party or one from the right-wing coalition the Basotho Democratic Alliance (BDA), which it was in the process of assembling. Second, after the Nkomati Accord, it sought to pressure Maseru into signing a nonaggression treaty along similar lines.

Particularly important in the postraid period was Pretoria's change of strategy and tactics. Probably, because the LLA was by then in a state of disarray, Pretoria relied less on the military instrument and more on selective economic threats. These included the well-timed manipulation of existing economic agreements, such as SACU, border restrictions and, of course, intervention in internal politics by supporting opposition parties.

In May 1983, Pretoria imposed restrictions on the movement of traffic across the border. Following a ministerial meeting, the embargo was lifted but not before Lesotho had acceded to the deportation of ANC refugees, many of them resident in Lesotho for a number of years. Altogether, 60 South African refugees left the country in what was called "voluntary deportation."

Even this did not seem to satisfy Pretoria, for a similar embargo was imposed in July. This was followed in August by a two-pronged incursion, one at the Lesotho Paramilitary Force base at Ongelu's Neck in the south and another at the Roman Catholic Mission at Pitseng in the north. This state of undeclared war continued right into 1984.

At the same time, Pretoria decided to assemble an opposition grouping against the government. The BDA, formed under the auspices of the South African minister for foreign affairs Roelof "Pik" Botha, brought together the dominant right-wing opposition within the country.[13] Its first president, C. D. Molapo, a former foreign minister and secretary general of the ruling BNP, had earlier been unsuccessful in ousting Chief Jonathan and had been excluded from the party because of his South African connections. Phoka Chaolana, its chairman, was a prominent figure of the internal BCP and had been expelled from the interim assembly because of Pretoria connections.

At the beginning of 1984, therefore, the country was facing increased pressure from a number of quarters—the BDA, military invasion, economic threats and intensification of border restrictions. Midway through the year, Pretoria refused transit for an arms consignment, withdrew from the Joint Feasibility Study of the Highland Water Project and threatened to reduce Lesotho's quota of migrant workers. Because of the structure and demands of the mining industry, this threat was to prove difficult to implement. Lesotho decided to take its case to the UN Security Council, whereupon South Africa relented, and by October it had rejoined the joint feasibility study.

President P. W. Botha continued to demand the reduction of diplomatic representation of socialist countries in Maseru. But more importantly, Pretoria demanded a pact which would give it access to South African refugees entering Lesotho, as well as the right to prohibit the presence in the country of South Africans it considered "terrorists."

According to the late minister of information Desmond Sixishe, the United States was the prime mover behind the South African demands. In 1984, Sixishe told an interviewer that the "Americans were behind the whole thing." The United States, he said, was trying to indicate to Maseru that if Lesotho resisted any longer, "we might not get assistance from them if South Africa decided to bash our heads."[14]

The intensified destabilization of and continued pressures on Lesotho, especially during 1982–85, exposed the factional struggles within the ruling BNP. As indicated earlier, the new class forces that had joined the party in the postindependence period had by the 1970s occupied strategic positions within the party and the cabinet. Invariably, the members of this group increasingly used access to state institutions to advance their economic position.

By 1980, the most prominent and economically powerful of these was Evaristus Sekhonyana, who held three ministries: foreign affairs, economic planning and employment. Sekhonyana's rivals in the cabinet consisted of less-propertied colleagues. Desmond Sixishe, the minister of information, was a relatively new appointee. Vincent Mokhi Makhele, party secretary general and minister of cooperatives and rural development, and later minister of foreign affairs, was also less propertied.

The factional struggles that ensued were primarily over the control of state power in the post-Jonathan era. However, against the backdrop of continued pressures from Pretoria and the less reactionary foreign policy championed over the previous five years, these conflicts were bound to be perceived as ideological and between the left and the right.

The "left" faction, identified with the Makhele-Sixishe camp, posed as custodians of the progressive anti-South African stance. Its opportunism notwithstanding, this position provided room for mobilization against South African aggression. However, this faction's most potent weapon was its control of the government's information apparatus and the paramilitary party youth league.

The Sekhonyana faction, partly because of historical ties with South Africa, tended to favor some form of pact with Pretoria. According to Sekhonyana, then foreign affairs minister, he had understood the inevitability of coming to some form of agreement with South Africa. He was, in his own words, "trying to push for something at a lower level—at the level of Security Chiefs." If this was true, then it is probable that the Sekhonyana faction was not merely pursuing the narrow interests of its class base, but was probably working in the long-term interests of the ruling party.

Lesotho's general election, the first in 15 years, was scheduled for 17 and 18 September 1985. However, on nomination day, the whole exercise proved a nonevent. The opposition parties withdrew from the electoral process, thus allowing Chief Jonathan's BNP to capture all the parliamentary seats without a single vote being cast.

As already indicated, the ruling BNP had not been able to establish its political legitimacy or escape the stigma of usurping power after losing the 1970 elections. By 1983, however, a number of factors had turned the tide in favor of the government, and elections now seemed winnable. First, Lesotho's resistance to Pretoria's aggression had to a large degree discredited the traditional opposition and earned the ruling BNP some measure of popularity, as well as boosting the country's international prestige. Second, opposition to the BNP was at its weakest.

The traditional opposition was at best divided into four warring factions—the Ramoreboli-Chaolana BCP faction that had accepted nominations to the Interim National Assembly; Godfrey Molotsi Kolisang, general secretary of the internal BCP, led the faction that had rejected the Interim National Assembly; the Chakela faction, which had dwindled into a small group since his assassination; and finally the external BCP, which was itself riven with divisions.

In addition to the BCP factions and the smaller opposition parties discussed earlier, two new parties had emerged on the political scene. These were the National Independence Party (NIP), led by Anthony Manyeli, a former BNP cabinet minister, and based in the extreme reactionary sections of the Catholic Church, and the United Fatherland Front (UFF), in which a number of CPL activists were involved. With the exception of the CPL and the UFF, the other opposition parties were to the right of the BNP.

The BDA, founded to unite and coordinate the pro-Pretoria opposition, appeared to have made very little headway. BDA leaders acknowledged South Africa's massive financial backing with uncharacteristic frankness. BDA Chairman Chaolana told the *Rand Daily Mail* that "we will be getting funds from Pretoria. I don't think accepting funds will be irregular . . . . This money would be shared among political parties within the BDA for use in their campaigns. These include the Basotho Congress Party, the United Democratic Party, and the Marama Tlou Freedom Party. . . ."[15] Despite this support, at the beginning of 1985, the BDA had not produced even a manisfesto.

Opinion was unanimous that Chief Jonathan would win the general election with a comfortable majority. However, at the crucial moment the government frustrated the electoral process.

This can probably be explained by the existing balance of power within the government and the ruling party in the period prior to the elections. By 1984, the "left" faction had already captured the ruling party and, for all practical purposes, the key state apparatus; however, its members had little or no political clout and hardly any political base. They, more than any other faction, stood to gain in the event of a nonelection.

The outcome of the September electoral process was at best a recipe for acute instability and conjuncture in the organs of the state. The country emerged from this crisis acutely divided, the ruling party in complete disarray. The Makhele "victory" mirrored in the new cabinet was for all practical purposes hollow. It could only be sustained by the ruthless brutality of the party's youth league.

Thus, at a time when South Africa was tightening its noose around the country, Chief Jonathan faced one of the most serious political situations since his coup of 1970. As early as October 1985, rumors of a coup began to circulate in Maseru. The timing of the commando attack on a Christmas party in December 1985 and the border restrictions that followed immediately were calculated to take maximum advantage of the political crisis in Lesotho.

Consequently, when, on 20 January 1986, the Paramilitary Unit staged the coup in the name of their commander, Major General Justin Metsing Lekhanya, there was hardly any resistance. The coup marked not only the overthrow of Chief Jonathan, but also the end of the Molapo dynasty and the reinstitution of the Letsie dynasty. The coup leaders were the Letsie brothers, Thaabe and Sekhobe, cousins of the king, who are both colonels in the Lesotho defense forces and who are members of, and the real power behind, the ruling Military Council.

The post-Jonathan political dispensation is, in a sense, a reflection of the age-old struggles for power between Molapo and Letsie, the two houses of the ruling Bakoena lineage. The coup has in a way reestablished the 1965 constitution with full executive powers to the king, Moshoeshoe II, whose role in influencing the events of 20 January is still not entirely clear. Chief Jonathan, 73, died in Pretoria of stomach cancer in early 1987.

Soon after the *coup d'état*, there was a move to expel South Africans with ANC affiliations. Initially, the new military regime promised to transfer refugees to third countries for their own safety, and leading ANC figures were flown north to Zambia. The situation, it would seem, has deteriorated remarkably since then. Allegations of interrogation of ANC refugees by South African security police have been made repeatedly. In late 1986, the general secretary of the Christian Council of Lesotho and his wife were deported for reporting these allegations to the press.

In November 1986, two of Chief Jonathan's senior former ministers were abducted and murdered by what appeared to be a military-type hit squad. Sixishe and Makhele, former information and foreign affairs ministers respectively, were known to have been sympathizers of the pro-ANC policy. There are reports of harassment and intimidation of other Lesotho nationals known to be sympathetic to ANC, as well as reports of South African hit squads operating in the country.

Immediately after the coup, Maseru played host to Chief Kaizer Mantanzima, the Transkei Bantustan's first "president," an act which bordered on recognition of South Africa's so-called independent states. This was one of several developments that have helped to ingratiate Maseru to Pretoria.

The expulsion of the ANC and the normalization of relations with Pretoria apparently prepared the ground for approval of the Highland Water Project. The "water treaty" was signed on 24 October 1986 by Pik Botha and Colonel Thaabe Letsie. The project will take 30 years to complete, and Lesotho's earnings will be an estimated R 120 million (US $50 million) a year when complete. Total cost of the water project is R 5 billion.[16] It is understood that the agreement included security cooperation, facilitated through Joint Security Committees. In early 1987, South Africa reported that the two countries had signed an agreement to establish trade missions.[17]

Given the historical animosity of the citizens of Lesotho toward the Boers, however, the incumbents do not have much room to maneuver if they are to retain a popular base or credibility in the region. A member of the Military Council toured Frontline states soon after the coup and told leaders that Lesotho remains committed to regional cooperation and opposed to apartheid. But he added that, first and foremost, Lesotho must consider economic and geographical realities. The implication was that while the government would continue to admit refugees from South Africa, they would be moved rapidly northward, official ANC presence would be curtailed, and the decibel level of opposition to apartheid would be muted.

BOTSWANA

Gaborone, the capital of Botswana, has the charm of a large, rather sleepy, village. Its central feature is a colorful broad shopping mall. There, politicians, civil servants and cattle owners rub shoulders, free from racial tension and segregation although less than 10 kilometers away, across the border, is South Africa.

This tranquility was rudely shattered in the early hours of 14 June 1985, when residents were awakened by bursts of automatic rifle fire, mortars and grenades. Gaborone had become a victim of the South African government's strategy of armed attacks on neighboring capitals.

The raid lasted 45 minutes. Ten houses and an office block in different parts of the city were destroyed. South African soldiers stormed the houses, spraying bullets as they went, and residents who came to their doors were gunned down. In all, 12 people died.

Later that day in Pretoria, General Constand Viljoen, head of the SADF, claimed the targets were "key" activists of the "control centre of the Transvaal sabotage organization of the ANC." Every effort had been made, he said, "to get at the enemy, and not at the Botswana police or members of the public or innocent members of the terrorists' families."[18]

But a very different picture emerged as the identities of 11 of the 12 victims became known. The people caught asleep in their beds were all civilians—a six-year-old boy from Lesotho; his uncle; a recently arrived computer programmer from Somalia; a young government social worker; her husband; the couple's friend visiting from South Africa; a pacifist university student; two teachers; a typist; and a domestic worker. Four of the 12 may have had connections with the ANC, but none were likely candiates for guerrilla training. By no stretch of the imagination could they be construed as "key" ANC activists.[19]

The true motives for the attack seemed to be to try to silence a vocal community of South African exiles, as well as alienating the exile community from the Botswana community, exerting pressure on the government to expel South African exiles, and generally boosting morale in South Africa by dramatizing the attack as a "successful" offensive against "terrorists." Botswana would continue to receive refugees under the Geneva Convention, a senior official said, confirming that, "there are conditions which they [refugees] observe and [they] may not be expelled from a country without any evidence that they have contravened such conditions . . . . The only way we could stop receiving refugees is if they do not come."

The attack on Gaborone was highly embarrassing to the Reagan administration, coming as it did only three weeks after the foiled Cabinda raid in Angola, in which a South African officer was captured and confessed that the mission had been to destroy US-owned oil installations. The US ambassador in Pretoria, Herman Nickel, was recalled "to review the situation." Nickel observed that the raid made "it virtually impossible for

President Reagan not to sign" the divestment bill then before Congress. The State Department called in the South African ambassador-designate, warning him, "If you [South Africans] want to bring down the wrath of God on your head, I couldn't think of a better way of doing it."[20] The British Foreign Office described the attack as "indefensible."

Until that raid, Botswana had been left in relative peace by South Africa. There had been a number of car bombings and other explosions, killing several ANC members, but, for nearly 20 years, the Botswana government had been able to maintain a "dignified pattern of independence" and a "good working relationship with South Africa."[21]

Botswana gained its independence from Britain on 30 September 1966, having been a British "protectorate" since 1884. From the following year until independence, the 600,372 square kilometers of sparsely populated and largely arid territory was known as Bechuanaland. The first prime minister of independent Botswana was Seretse Khama, chief of the Bamangwato. Under pressure from South Africa, the British colonial administration had exiled him for marrying a white woman. But he returned in 1962, entering the Legislative Council as head of the Bechuanaland Democratic Party (BDP), which worked toward a multiparty, democratic, nonracial state and won an overwhelming majority in the preindependence elections. He was later knighted by the British queen.

Despite his conservative traditionalist background, Khama was to play a significant role in southern African politics over the next 14 years until his death in 1980. He was part of the Frontline state grouping, which also included the leaders of Angola, Mozambique, Tanzania and Zambia, and which played a prominent role in the Zimbabwean liberation struggle. As leader of one of the Frontline states, Khama stood in the forefront of opposition to apartheid. While his role was more muted than that of some of his colleagues—and his country's economic and geographic position more difficult—there was no doubting the principles he stood for.

He was a leading advocate of the Southern African Development Coordination Conference (SADCC), and his country hosts the SADCC secretariat. On 3 July 1979, at a Frontline states meeting in the northern Tanzanian town of Arusha, called to discuss plans for establishing SADCC, he made his position very clear. Political freedom had been won, he said, but economic liberation remained to be achieved. He called for the development of the subcontinent as an integrated region "rather than a cluster of impoverished little chauvinistic entities," adding that there was a need to improve regional transport facilities, so that the African nations could "lessen their dependence upon the racist and white minority regime of South Africa. This economic dependence has in many ways made our political independence somewhat meaningless."[22]

Nine months later, on 1 April 1980, he chaired the summit in the Zambian capital, Lusaka, that launched SADCC, and he sounded an ominous warning. "The struggle for economic liberation will be as bitterly contested as has been the struggle for political liberation," he said. But he emphasized that SADCC, while seeking to lessen its dependence on South Africa for trade and transport, was not seeking outright confrontation: "It is not our objective to plot against anybody or any country but, on the contrary, to lay the foundation for the development of a new economic order in southern Africa and forge a united community."[23] Pretoria, however, had other plans and embarked on its program to destabilize the region.

Traditionally, the people of Botswana have held their wealth in cattle and at independence the pastoral sector was the only significant foreign exchange earner. The cattle industry still generates almost 10 percent of export earnings, but is now in second place, far behind diamonds and just ahead of copper-nickel matte, which has fallen due to commodity prices.

Fifteen years ago, Botswana was one of the poorest countries in sub-Saharan Africa. Today, largely because of diamonds, it is one of the richest, with foreign exchange reserves equalling $1.6 million, almost two years import cover. A major economic problem is recycling the huge cash surplus, large enough to put Botswana in the unique position of having to make regular cash contributions to the International Monetary Fund (IMF).

Since diamond deposits were found in Orapa in 1967, Botswana has become one of the world's three largest diamond producers, along with South Africa and the Soviet Union. Diamond sales dominate export earnings and in 1986 accounted for over 78 percent of visible exports, which reached a record $926.5 million. This helped to generate an economic growth rate of 12.4 percent for the fiscal year ended 30 June 1986. Botswana had its first trade surplus in 1985, and in 1986 its overall balance of payments surplus was $332.7 million.[24]

While Botswana has achieved rapid economic growth, it still has a host of economic problems, including, as Khama realized, its dependence on South Africa. Another key problem is that, due to a colonial legacy lacking in adequate planning for future development, priority must be given to the expensive task of creating an infrastructure, to providing education and rural training, and to expansion of productive employment. Third, the drought in the 1980s has ravaged the country, reducing the national cattle herd by over one-third and diverting state funds from development to relief projects. Water shortages and unreliable rainfall continue to cause serious difficulties, with small harvests necessitating large food imports.

South Africa likes to give the impression that withholding food is a weapon that can be used against its neighbors, that "more and more black states will depend to some extent on this country for basic foods" and that "full grain silos will mean that we can talk and negotiate from a position of strength."[25] However, South Africa is actually responsible for the critical short-age of food in some neighboring countries such as Angola and Mozambique, where its surrogates have sabotaged transporta-tion routes, damaging rural infrastructure, and destroying crops and food relief supplies. Furthermore, South Africa's own weak-ness was exposed during the same period of drought, when it was forced to import supplies of the staple food, maize meal, from one of its independent neighbors, Zimbabwe.

Botswana's economic turnabout has been based in large part upon the development of its mineral wealth by the state, in conjunction with largely South African capital. Anglo-American, a South African transnational, and the American Amax Corpora-tion have a controlling interest in the copper-nickel mine at Selebi-Pikwe. De Beers Consolidated Mines, another South Afri-can company linked to Anglo-American, has joined the Botswana government in the development of the diamond fields at Orapa, Letlhakane and Jwaneng; and De Beers' Central Selling Organiza-tion markets Botswana's diamonds abroad. This leaves Botswa-na's vital foreign exchange–earning sector highly dependent upon forces outside the government's control.

In July 1987, De Beers agreed to purchase the entire diamond stockpile of Debswana (De Beers Botswana Mining Company Pty), accumulated during a recession in the world diamond market from 1982–85. Debswana is jointly owned by De Beers and the Botswana government, each with a 50 percent share-holding. The stockpile, with an estimated value of $300–500 million, was transferred to De Beers for an undisclosed sum of money and 20 million shares in De Beers, valued at $380 million, equivalent to just over 5 percent of enlarged capi-tal. Thus, the Botswana government, with an effective 2.6 percent interest in De Beers, is the first black African gov-ernment to have a stake in the mining company that has dominated the production and marketing of diamonds for most of this century. The transaction will boost Botswana's assets and De Beers' image.[26]

Botswana is also heavily dependent upon South African transport, and industrial and processing sectors, with more than 80 percent of its imports passing through or originating in South Africa. Twenty percent of its electricity comes from the republic, as does all its oil. Unable to absorb its own growing labor force and secondary school graduates, Botswana allows over 25,000 of its nationals to work in South Africa. Only four times that many are in formal wage employment at home. The Botswana government receives almost 40 percent of its revenue from the SACU, which has in fact arrested industrial development in Botswana. In a much less precarious position than Lesotho, Botswana is still dependent upon the good will of South Africa and its corporations to keep its cars and trucks running, its lamps lit, its shelves stocked and its people employed.

Physically, Botswana is a country of great contrasts. To the west, the sweeping sands of the Kalahari Desert spill over into Namibia. To the north, close to the Namibian-Angolan border, there is the stark beauty of the Okavango Swamps teeming with wildlife. To the east, the arable lands and ranches with their long-horned cattle adjoin Zimbabwe and South Africa. Because of its geographic location, Botswana has been surrounded by war for most of the past 20 years. Consequently, it has become a refuge for people fleeing from Namibia, Rhodesia (Zimbabwe) and South Africa.

At the end of the war in Rhodesia, there were about 20,000 refugees in Botswana and, on at least one hundred occasions, Rhodesian troops violated the border. Today, there are less than 3,000 Zimbabwean refugees in Botswana, some having fled the conflict in Matabeleland, others economic refugees from the drought that ravages that area.

Tension increased along Botswana's northern border in early 1982 when there were a number of overflights by South African aircraft near Namibia's Caprivi Strip. At about this time, there were also a number of attacks on South African exiles in Gaborone, including the kidnapping of one young man who was taken back to South Africa. A disinformation campaign in the South African press claimed there was a build-up of Soviet personnel in Botswana. Dr. Quett Masire, who succeeded Khama as president, said this disinformation was used to provide Pretoria with a pretext to "eliminate enemies" in Botswana. "I think they're trying to make a Lebanon of us," he observed.[27]

Since that time there has been considerable pressure on President Masire, as there was on Chief Jonathan in Lesotho, to come to some agreement with Pretoria which would ensure that the ANC did not use Botswana as a "launching pad" for operations in South Africa. This pressure has taken at least three forms—diplomatic, economic and military.

After signing the Nkomati Accord with Mozambique in March 1984, the South Africans increased pressure on Botswana to sign a similar pact and, at a SACU commission meeting the same month, they produced "the full draft of a non-aggression treaty—all ready for signing." A number of points were discussed, including South Africa's demand for the right of "hot pursuit," the proposal for the "homelands" to join the SACU, and bilateral economic matters. Botswana officials were "appalled" and refused to sign.[28]

Botswana's government later assured South Africa that "subversive elements" would not be allowed to use its territory, but maintained its refusal to sign a formal security pact, citing the Mozambique National Resistance's (MNR) continued infiltration of Mozambique despite the Nkomati Accord and stating that it would be "difficult to have confidence in what it [South Africa] says it will do." When President Masire met President Reagan at the White House in early 1984, he asked for Washington's support to prevent South Africa from forcing him to sign an agreement.

British and American pressure behind the scenes was credited with relieving South African insistence on a signed agreement. Instead there was an agreed public statement "in which the foreign minister of South Africa said his government no longer required Botswana to sign an agreement because it accepted assurances that it does not allow use of its territory as a launching pad against South Africa. He said that South Africa also undertook not to allow its territory as a launching pad against Botswana."[29]

As opposition to apartheid boiled over in the South African townships in late 1984, Pretoria, wishing to carry on the charade that the enemy was external but no longer having Mozambique to blame, claimed Botswana had become the "channel for sabotage and refuge for saboteurs."[30] Botswana, it argued, was incapable of controlling the activities of the ANC or preventing widespread crossings after the blocking of Mozambican infiltration routes. Early in the New Year, with Pretoria threatening "hot pursuit," the Botswana foreign minister, Dr. Gaositwe Chiepe, met Pik Botha to get some "practical arrangements" under way. But Botswana maintained its refusal to sign any kind of pact with Pretoria.

The most public example of using economic leverage on Botswana was South Africa's vacillation in supporting the $300 million Sua Pan soda ash project. At Makgadikgadi, 150 kilometers north of Francistown, there is a massive dry salt lake containing enough salt, soda ash and potash to supply the subcontinent for the next century. However, to make exploitation of the deposits economical, the South African market is needed. A clause in the SACU agreement, guaranteeing Botswana exclusive marketing rights in territories belonging to the customs union, means that South Africa must stop its importation of soda ash from the United States and cancel its own proposed soda ash project. But Botswana has been unable to get a firm South African commitment, and Pik Botha has made it clear why: Botswana will not get cooperation from South Africa "on certain economic projects" without first coming to an "acceptable understanding" regarding security.[31]

Other economic pressure has included a threat to renegotiate the terms of the customs union, in an effort to bring Botswana into line with P. W. Botha's "comprehensive regional development strategy."[32] And, in an effort to dramatize its economic power and to pressure Botswana into recognizing a "homeland" as "independent," Pretoria, in early 1985, required that railway crews from Zimbabwe and Botswana obtain visas from Bophuthatswana before crossing into South Africa. At stake was about half the north-south railway traffic, including Zambia's metal exports. By April, "quiet diplomacy" was credited with Pretoria's backing down. Business in the "homeland" had been hurt by the slowdown in trade, and Botswana had outmaneuvered Pretoria by building its railway turnaround six miles north of the border and ordering South African crews to collect trains there.

As with the other countries on the frontline, Botswana faces diplomatic and economic pressure from Pretoria, as well as sabotage, disinformation and military force. Without a surrogate force to do its dirty work, the South African military has had to use its own commandoes and undercover agents to destroy and kill in Botswana. A spate of bombings took place in the months prior to the massive June 1985 raid on Gaborone. Two South African refugees living in Gaborone were hurt in February when a bomb exploded at the home of one, and they left Botswana soon after. A few weeks later, a car bomb killed a South African refugee working for a Western aid organization in Botswana. Marius Schoon, a longtime anti-apartheid activist and ANC member who spent 12 years in prison for his views, was forced to leave Botswana when the British organization for which he worked cancelled the post in the wake of threats against his life. He and his family moved to Angola, where they were followed by a parcel bomb which killed his wife and six-year-old daughter.

Botswana has maintained throughout that it has not given ANC activitists sanctuary or permitted the country to be used as an infiltration route, but South Africa creates its own justifications. "We are dealing with a sophisticated terrorist organization . . . [which] is not, perhaps, in the experience of a small Third World country's intelligence organization and police force," Major Craig Williamson of the South African security police stated after the raid in June 1985.[33]

In the early hours of New Year's Day 1987, the 18th victim in two years was killed by raiders at Ramotswa near the border. In mid-April, only hours after a thinly veiled warning by Pik Botha that "dire consequences" would result from Botswana permitting the ANC to use routes through the country to reach South Africa and disrupt the "whites only" election, a South African microbus blew up in Gaborone. The blast destroyed two houses, blew off the roof of another and shattered windows nearby. Five people were injured and three killed—a woman and two children, all Botswana nationals.

The Botswana Defense Force (BDF) was created in 1977 in an effort to combat Rhodesian incursions. Today it numbers about 3,500 but remains powerless to prevent raids into Botswana or to halt the indiscriminate bombings. However, its defense capabilities are being improved, notably by helicopters provided by the United States. And, in what appeared to be a clear signal to Pretoria to refrain from attacks, it was announced in February 1986 that 90 members of the British Special Air Service (SAS) had arrived in Botswana to assist in military training. A subsequent visit by a high-level US military deputation conveyed the same message.

Pretoria's response was relayed at the end of May 1987 when, as part of an escalation of action against all of the Frontline states, it staged a massive airborne military exercise, called Iron Eagle, just south of the Botswana border. The landing of five hundred men in aircraft capable of striking all the way to the equator showed the vulnerability of Botswana and its neighbors.

SWAZILAND

On 31 March 1984, while Botswana and Lesotho continued to resist signing formal security pacts with South Africa, the pressure on them took a new turn. Two weeks earlier the governments of Mozambique and South Africa had signed the Nkomati Accord, and now Pik Botha and his counterpart from Swaziland, Richard Dlamini, met in Pretoria and announced the existence of a two-year-old, hitherto secret, security agreement. Their joint statement said it had been "decided to make public the existence and contents of an Agreement relating to Security Matters."

Under the terms of the agreement, Swaziland and South Africa had agreed to "combat terrorism, insurgency and subversion individually and collectively as well as their right to call upon each for such assistance and steps as may be deemed necessary or expedient to eliminate this evil." They undertook to respect each other's independence, sovereignty and territorial integrity, to refrain from the threat to use force against each other and not to allow foreign military bases or units in their countries except in self-defense, and then "only after due notification to the other."[34]

Unlike the Nkomati agreement, which the Mozambican government insisted must be a public document, the agreement between Swaziland and South Africa has never been made public, despite the joint statement revealing its existence. The agreement itself is a series of three letters.

The first letter is dated 12 February 1982 and was written by P. W. Botha to the Swazi monarch, King Sobhuza II. Botha begins the letter by referring to various discussions and correspondence between the foreign ministers of the two countries which resulted in agreement "that international terrorism, in all its manifestations, poses a real threat to international peace and security and that our respective Governments should take steps to protect our respective states and nationals against this threat."

To this end, Botha proposed an agreement containing four articles, the essence of which, with one omission, was contained in the statement issued by Pik Botha and Dlamini two years later. The deletion is the reference to the UN Charter giving nations the right to call for foreign military assistance in the event of their being attacked.

The Swazi prime minister, Mabandla Fred Dlamini, quoted P. W. Botha's letter verbatim and then signed it, saying that the exchange of letters would constitute an agreement between the two governments. His reply was dated 17 February 1982, the same date that appears on a short note on letterhead over the signature of Sobhuza II, Ingwenyama, King of Swaziland, addressed to "My Dear Prime Minister," authorizing him to sign the Letter of Understanding on Security Matters between the Kingdom of Swaziland and the Republic of South Africa[35] (see appendix 5).

Inevitably, comparisons have been made between the agreements with South Africa signed by Mozambique and by Swaziland. But, in a number of important respects, they are different. In the first place, although a captive state, Swaziland was not confronted with the massive onslaught that the South African authorities were orchestrating against Mozambique, directly or through surrogates. Thus, there is no similarity between the plight of the two states at the time they signed the agreements. In February 1982, Swaziland could have resisted an agreement as Botswana and Lesotho continued to do, but by March 1984 Mozambique almost certainly could not. Further, Mozambique insisted on conducting its negotiations with public knowledge and that the agreement be open to scrutiny. Swaziland chose to do so in secrecy and only agreed to making it public—without publication of the full document—once its actions would be overshadowed by the attendant post-Nkomati publicity.

There are also fundamental differences in the actual agreements. The agreement with Swaziland gives the South Africans the right to operate in Swaziland. The Nkomati Accord does not. In addition, the agreement with Swaziland clearly places the ANC in the category of "international terrorism." In contrast, the Nkomati Accord contains a clear condemnation of the apartheid system when it refers in the preamble to "the principle of equal rights of all peoples."

The intricacies of Swaziland's arrangement with South Africa may never be widely known, but there seems to have been something in it for everyone, all, of course, advantageous to the South African administration. Within four months of the signing of the security agreement, South Africa announced its intention to formally cede to Swaziland two border regions, Kangwane and Ingwavuma, to which King Sobhuza laid historical claim, wishing to bring "all his children together" into a "Greater Swaziland."[36] By late 1981, the quid pro quo was obvious, a crackdown on ANC activities in Swaziland in exchange for land.

Although their peoples are ethnically related to the Swazis, Kangwane on the northern border of Swaziland and Ingwavuma to the southeast are designated "homelands" in South Africa (the latter is part of KwaZulu). The "chief minister" of Kangwane Enos Mabuza, one of the more forward looking of the "homeland" leaders, was offered a post as deputy prime minister of Swaziland, or ambassador to South Africa, in return for his support of the annexation, but the incentive failed to move him.[37] He and other "homeland" leaders initiated a political and legal battle to prevent the transfer, keeping the issue in the courts until long after Sobhuza's death in 1982.

The leaders' argument rested on apartheid legislation, which dictates that before any measure affecting the "homelands" is implemented, they must be consulted. Since they had not been, the court upheld their case. Pretoria responded by establishing a commission of inquiry, the Rumpff Commission, which reported that the free will of the people of the two areas could not be accurately determined and that the leaders of Swaziland and of the "homelands" ought to deliberate the matter themselves. South Africa abandoned the plan in June 1984, three months after signing Nkomati and making public the security pact with Swaziland.

The land deal would have given Swaziland an outlet to the sea at Khosi Bay and would have greatly increased the size of the tiny kingdom. At the same time, it would have favored South Africa's ethnic "homeland" policy, enabling it to dispose of almost one million citizens with the stroke of a pen. The annexation would have also provided a buffer zone for South Africa along the southern border of Mozambique. In addition, the cost of administering the territories would have been transferred to Swaziland, outweighing any economic benefit, perhaps one reason why the then prime minister Prince Mabandla opposed the deal.

Swaziland was already beset by economic problems which grew steadily worse through the mid-1980s: falling export earnings, increased costs for imports, the resulting high rate of inflation, rising unemployment and so on. But Swaziland has recently placed more emphasis on its industrial sector, and, in so doing, has become a beneficiary of the threat by the international community to impose sanctions on South Africa. From mid-1985 to the end of 1986, at least 15 new industries had been set up in the kingdom, and new industrial estates were being planned. Although Swazi ministers have denied that the country will be used as a base for sanctions breaking, this development does offer new investors access to the world market and, specifically, to the European Economic Community (EEC) through the Lome Convention. Swaziland has moved even more firmly into the South African economic orbit since late 1984 when, nine months after revealing the existence of their security pact, the two countries signed an agreement facilitating the exchange of trade representatives with full diplomatic status.

Swaziland's relations with the Boers have always been different from those of Botswana and Lesotho. While the latter two countries fought Boer expansionism in the nineteenth century, the Swazis gave them land in the north and west of their country in exchange for cattle. Until the 1880s, the Swazis and the Boers treated each other as equals. Since that time, though, with the political subjugation of the African kingdoms in the region by British colonialism and with the development of an industrial economy centered on the gold mines, South Africa has dominated the 17,363 square kilometers kingdom.

On 6 September 1968, Swaziland ceased to be a British colony and became an independent state, with King Sobhuza II, who had been monarch since 1899, at its head and with a political system based on the British model. Five years later, Sobhuza abolished the parliamentary system and banned all political parties, introduced a state of emergency, announced the formation of a national army and vested all state power in himself. In 1979, the king created a new state structure, in which power remained with him while the Liqoqo, or inner council, had an advisory role. A council of ministers was created, including a prime minister, but decision making rested firmly with King Sobhuza II until his death in 1982.

The power of the royal family rests upon its traditional role and upon the wealth it controls through the Tibiyo Taka-Ngwane Fund, created before independence to act as a depository of mining royalties. The money has been used to buy land, most of which is under sugar for export, and to establish joint ventures with transnational corporations, many South African. The fund is exempt from taxes, is not accountable to Parliament and revenue accrues to the royal family, not to the nation as a whole.

The population of Swaziland numbers less than one million, the vast majority peasant farmers living at a subsistence level. Not surprisingly, South Africa dominates the economy, buying 20 percent of the exports and providing 90 percent of imports. About 50 percent of government revenue derives from the joint customs union. South Africa also provides employment, and because only 30 percent of secondary school graduates are able to find employment in the local wage economy, the South African job option is vital. About 17,000 Swazi nationals work in South Africa, sending home about R 11 million each year (US $4.5 million). More than a third of Swaziland's electricity comes from South Africa and all its fuel.

Swaziland is landlocked and therefore reliant on its neighbors for port facilities. Until 1985, about one-third of its trade went through South Africa and the remainder through Mozambique. However, in February 1986, a new rail link between Mpaka and Mananga opened, which will tie Swaziland even more firmly into the South African transport system, instead of moving away from it as SADCC colleagues would prefer. Its construction raises questions about Swaziland's—and South Africa's—future plans for utilizing the port of Maputo. The cross-country railway is plugged into South African railways at both ends, carrying traffic from the mining, industrial and agricultural areas of the eastern Transvaal to the port of Richard's Bay in Natal. While revenue from the railway is expected to boost the Swaziland treasury, it will have the parallel effect (like Lesotho's water project) of assisting the local economy while making it more dependent on South Africa.[38]

As in the case of Lesotho, political and financial relations with Pretoria have caused deep divisions within the government of Swaziland, although they have taken a different form. Divisions over the security agreement, the resultant actions against the ANC, the land deal and other economic considerations have developed into a struggle for supremacy in the post-Sobhuza era. In 1982, a strong, conservative economic lobby emerged which hoped to use the death of the king to clamp down on ANC activities in Swaziland and revitalize relations with South Africa to great economic advantage; and no doubt South Africa saw fit to encourage those whom it counted among its allies.

The struggle for power among the financial and political elite in Swaziland was over the direction of the state, in terms of socio-economic and political philosophy, as well as personality. This power struggle can be broken down into four broad phases. The first deals with the subordination of the prime minister to the Liqoqo, which was accomplished in early 1983 when Prince Mabandla fled with his family to Bophuthatswana. His successor, Prince Bhekimpi Dlamini, an ardent supporter of the land deal, was put into office by two powerful members of the Liqoqo, Dr. George Msibi and Prince Mfanasibili.

The second phase saw the subordination of the queen regent to the Liqoqo. This was orchestrated in 1983 when the existing regent, the "old she elephant" Dzeliwe, was removed, and Princess Ntombi was ensconced. The new queen regent signed an agreement limiting her powers, an agreement her predecessor had refused to sign. By the end of 1983, power lay with a small clique within the Liqoqo, a group that supported closer ties with South Africa. Richard Dlamini, another leading proponent of the land deal, was appointed minister of foreign affairs. But it was not long before there was a falling out among the power brokers.

A multi-million-rand customs fraud involving the SACU caused considerable political, as well as financial, damage when it came to light in mid-1984. The finance minister, Dr. Sishayi Nxumalo, revealed that the customs union had been defrauded of about R 13 million (US $5.5 million), depriving the member countries—Botswana, Lesotho, Swaziland and South Africa—of that revenue.

The fraud, involving South African businessmen, consisted of the importation of textiles, electronic equipment and other goods worth about R 50 million (US $21 million). The goods were dutiable and were released by customs at the South African port of Durban only because they were consigned to a bonded SACU warehouse in Swaziland, where duties would be paid when the goods were released. However, papers had been falsified, the bonded warehouse did not exist, and the goods remained in South Africa where they were sold without duty being paid.

Dr. Nxumalo announced a thorough investigation, which he expected would unmask people in "high places" in Swaziland. Within days he was arrested and charged with treason. Several of his associates were also detained or removed from office, including Richard Dlamini.

In early 1985 a number of other officials were forced into "compulsory retirement," while others were arrested and charged with sedition. Among the latter were the commissioner of police and his white deputy, both of whom were regarded as highly professional policemen. They had antagonized Mfanasibili when they were involved in Mabandla's attempt to detain him. Shortly after this arrest, the Liqoqo leadership claimed that there were plans for a *coup d'état* led by relatives of the men in detention, but none materialized.

A commission of inquiry was set up to investigate the customs fraud, headed by the ombudsman, Robert Mabila, who was also secretary to the Liqoqo. His report concluded that 17 South African companies were among the 21 involved and that "the architects of the customs union fraud are largely, if not entirely, South Africans." The remaining four companies were registered in Swaziland. The ombudsman's report recommended legal action against the companies and persons implicated.[39]

During the second half of 1985, the power struggle reached its third phase when the queen regent moved to reassert her authority and that of the monarchy, and ordered the arrest of some of those who had put her in power. A group of disgruntled members of the royal family led a march on parliament, in opposition to the excessive powers of the Liqoqo, which they said had been "hijacked" by Msibi and Mfanasibili. The two were removed from the Liqoqo in October, and their hand-picked police commissioner was dismissed. Within a few weeks, the former finance and foreign ministers, Sishaye Nxumalo and Richard Dlamini, were released, as were the senior police officers arrested earlier for treason.

The political crisis in Swaziland led to the early coronation of the teenage king, Mswati III, in April 1986. This fourth phase has been marked by a reassertion of royal authority, counter-acting measures taken since Sobhuza's death to subordinate the monarchy to the power of the Liqoqo. Immediately after his accession to power, King Mswati dissolved the Liqoqo, while resisting pressure to halt legal proceedings against Mfanasabili who, with his associates, was given a long prison sentence for producing fraudulent evidence against politicians in detention. Prince Bhekimpi was replaced as prime minister by Sotja Dlamini, one of the senior police officers ousted in the 1983 purge and a man who remained loyal to Queen Regent Dzeliwe throughout.

In early 1987, rumors surfaced of a plot to assassinate the new prime minister and others; and 12 leading figures, including members of the royal family, were detained. Mswati III set up a tribunal to hear evidence about the political turmoil that followed his father's death. The young ruler seems well on his way to consolidating his power, and his closest associates seem to be those who favor a foreign policy less hostile to the ANC. There is little indication, however, that the new king will be in a position to initiate any major changes in the economic or political structures of Swaziland, or fundamentally change Swaziland's policies toward Pretoria.

The growth and activities of the ANC provide some understanding of the development of relations between South Africa and Swaziland. Since the early 1980s, Umkhonto we Sizwe, the military wing of the ANC, has stepped up its actions against apartheid. The South African authorities claim that the number of incidents of ANC armed attacks rose from four in 1976 to 12 in 1979, then increased significantly in 1981 to 60. According to their figures, the number decreased in 1982 to 39, but rose again the following year to 56. For some months after the signing at Nkomati, the incidents of ANC attacks decreased but, by the end of 1984, the ANC had made up for lost time and has been escalating their struggle ever since.

South African military forces, which invaded Angola in 1975, began violating the sovereignty of other neighbors in the early 1980s, on the pretense that there was an external threat—despite the evidence of increasing and sustained internal resistance to apartheid. In late 1981 there were a series of raids on ANC residences in Swaziland, the ANC representative was detained, and there was a shoot out near the Mozambican border. The South African defense minister, General Malan, threatened to open a "second front," and South African authorities warned Swaziland privately that it would be turned into an "operational area" if it did not take action against the ANC.[40]

There were some arrests and harassment of ANC members whom the Swazi authorities claimed were "violating the terms of their exile." Tough, new legislation was introduced, to restrict opponents of the government as much as to restrain members of the ANC, but relations in the country long a safe way station for refugees from South Africa remained "politely tolerant" until about the time the security agreement with Pretoria was made public at the end of March 1984.

In early April, a bomb exploded in the South African coastal city of Durban, killing three people. The bombing, and the influx of ANC members from Mozambique, led to strong South African pressure on Swaziland to fulfill its commitment under the agreement. The government of Swaziland responded by ordering police to round up and jail ANC members who crossed the border. A few weeks later, Swazi police claimed that several ANC members had stormed a police station, releasing four of their colleagues. The ANC denied this and insisted that the guerrillas had been handed over to the South African police. Within weeks, more than one hundred ANC members had been flown out to a safer haven farther north.

ANC members interviewed later said four of their number had been turned over to the South Africans and another six were unaccounted for. "Whites in camouflage uniforms were seen at all the big raids," they said, stating, "It seems clear that most of the whites were South Africans and that they actually directed an assault on a house in Manzini which led to a seven-hour gun battle, and killed at least two men."[41]

The situation continued to deteriorate, and late in 1984 students demonstrated at the university campus against the deportation of a student leader to South Africa. Then the deputy chief of the Swaziland security police was murdered, and the government alleged that the killer was an "ANC hit man," a claim the ANC denied. But the murder was used to justify another crackdown on the ANC, resulting in several arrests, as well as a deportation order for the ANC representative. More than three hundred ANC members were deported from Swaziland in 1984, and 23 others were threatened with deportation if they did not surrender to police.

Early in the next year, an ANC member was shot and killed by police and seven others "vanished" from the Mbabane police station, following threats that they would be handed over to the South Africans. The Swazi police claimed there had been another ANC break-in to free the missing men, a claim the ANC again denied. The ANC blamed South African agents, calling the whole affair a Pretoria-inspired provocation aimed at sabotaging ANC talks with Swaziland. Relations deteriorated further in 1985 with the expulsion of students and academics belonging to the ANC.[42] South African forces often crossed the border in "hot pursuit," raiding villages and threatening villagers to report any ANC presence.

In an effort to ensure that Swaziland would not be raided as Botswana and Lesotho had been, deportations of ANC personnel continued throughout 1986. But this policy was a failure, for South African commandoes raided refugees' homes and offices, and abducted ANC members, taking them back to South Africa. In mid-December 1986, five people were kidnapped in two raids, one of them Ismail Ebrahim, a leading ANC member. The commanding officer of the Northern Transvaal Security Branch claimed that the South African police had played no part in this kidnapping, but Pik Botha told a different story. He claimed that he knew of the raid before it took place, but that the Swazi government had not. "We have done them a favour by not involving them," he said. After that incident, the Swazi police again took the initiative, raiding "safe houses," arresting ANC members and deporting them north.

The security situation deteriorated again in mid-1987, apparently as part of a broader South African strategy to assassinate specific opposition leaders inside and outside the country. An ANC member and two Swazi nationals were killed in May in a suburb of Mbabane when their car was stopped by a group of men who opened fire on the occupants. Then, in July, a member of the ANC's National Executive Committee, Cassius Make, another senior party official and a Mozambican woman died in a hail of bullets when their taxi was forced off the road between Matsapha Airport and Mbabane by a South African–registered vehicle containing three white men. The Swazi police commissioner said the armed men came from a "neighbouring country."[43]

South Africa's relations wtih Botswana, Lesotho and Swaziland have been based primarily upon their geographical proximity and almost total economic dependence—and dominated by

South Africa's overwhelming military strength and its willingness to use it against it weakest neighbors. Each of the three states has a different relationship with Pretoria, depending on its political structures and composition of government.

As long as there is apartheid, there will be destabilization, not just for these countries but for all of the independent black-ruled states of southern Africa. They are caught in apartheid's cross fire and, until the shooting stops in the republic, they will be victims of the whims and excesses of the last colonial bastion of white supremacy.

Perhaps the best summation of what the future holds for the three captive states was given by Botswana's foreign minister, Dr. Chiepe, when she said the "sole source of tension is apartheid policy . . . . Until apartheid is dismantled lock, stock and barrel, the confusion which this vile system generates inside South Africa will continue to spill over across the borders and threaten the peace and stability of the region."[44]

The Namibe railway in southern Angola, where 15 meters of track were destroyed and another 20 meters mined by South African troops transported by helicopter. South Africa's sabotage of regional transportation routes is one example of its economic sanctions against the region, keeping its neighbors dependent upon trade routes through South Africa. Photo: Department of Information, Angola

A burnt out truck in Manica province of Mozambique. As many as 100,000 people died of starvation in Mozambique in 1983-84 because food relief trucks were destroyed by bandits trained and supplied by South Africa. Photo: Paul Fouvet, AIM

A block of flats in the Mozambique capital, Maputo, damaged when a powerful car bomb exploded near the center of the city on April 21, 1986. Photo: Alfredo Mueche, AIM

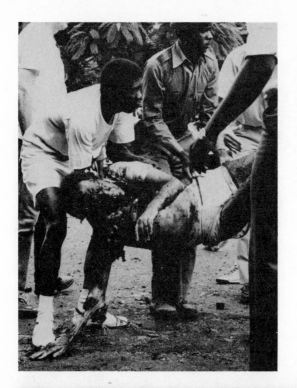

These photos were taken minutes after a car bomb exploded on a main street in Maputo, injuring well known South African writer and lawyer, Albie Sachs. Sachs lost his right arm in the blast on April 7, 1988.
Photo: Jose Cabral

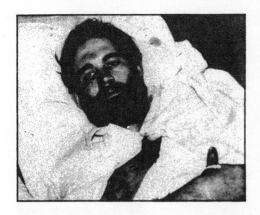

Captain Wynand du Toit, commander of a SADF Special Forces unit, captured in the far north of Angola on May 21, 1985 while attempting to sabotage an oil installation belonging to Cabinda Gulf, partly owned by the US transnational Gulf Oil. Du Toit admitted that the action was to be claimed by Unita.   Photo: COSAWR

A bridge on the Serra da Leba Highway in Huilo province, Angola, sabotaged by South African troops landed by helicopter.
Photo: Department of Information, Angola

Defeated South African troops re-
treating from Angola in March 1976,
several months after their unsuccessful invasion aimed at preventing the MPLA from proclaiming
independence.   Photo: IDAF
insert *Identity card of Rifleman
Smit, one of many young South
African soldiers killed in Angola.*
     Photo: Department of Information,
                              Angola

One of many mass graves of Namibian refugees murdered by the
South African army. This one, at
Kassinga in southern Angola, was
photographed on May 4, 1978.
     Photo: Department of Information,
                              Angola

The town of Ngiva, capital of Cunene province in southern Angola, burns after a South African bombing raid.

Photo: Department of Information, Angola

Angolan government soldier guarding Soviet-made anti-aircraft battery in the southern Angolan town of Cuito Cuanavale, held by government forces in early 1988 in the face of a massive South African attack aimed at taking the town and its strategic air strip.

Photo: Agence France Press

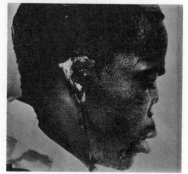

The terror tactics of South African proxy forces are similar in each country where they operate, including murder, maiming and rape, as well as destruction of the economic infrastructure. These photographs show two victims of MNR mutilations in rural Mozambique.

top This woman had her ear cut off in Manica province in 1985.

and This man, Joaquim Mapinda, a teacher in Sofala province, had his ear and his nose cut off. His nose has since been reconstructed surgically.
                    Photo: Anders Nilsson

When the MNR main base at Casa Banana, in central Mozambique, was overrun in August 1985, many rural people being held by the MNR were freed. The only material they had in which to cloth themselves came from the South African parachutes used to drop armaments.   Photo: Tommy Sithole, The Herald

A view of the Casa Banana airfield from inside a helicopter, after the storming of the MNR headquarters. This landing strip was built by the South Africans for ferrying supplies to their surrogates in central Mozambique.   Photo: Tommy Sithole, The Herald

Armored vehicles and anti-aircraft guns dropped by parachute to the MNR by South Africa and captured at the main Gorongosa base at Casa Banana.   Photo: Tommy Sithole, The Herald

TO THE PEOPLE OF ZIMBABWE

SOUTH AFRICAN TROOPS HAVE CARRIED OUT AN ATTACK AGAINST
OFFICES AND HOUSES USED BY ANC GANGSTERS IN YOUR COUNTRY

THESE GANGSTERS INFILTRATE INTO OUR COUNTRY TO MURDER
INNOCENT WOMEN AND CHILDREN OF ALL RACES.

WE REGARD THE PEOPLE OF ZIMBABWE AS OUR FRIENDS AND
NEIGHBOURS. WE HAVE NO FIGHT WITH YOU, AND WE WISH TO
LIVE IN PEACE WITH OUR NEIGHBOURS.

UNFORTUNATELY, YOUR GOVERMENT ALLOWS THESE ANC GANGSTERS
TO TERRORISE INNOCENT PEOPLE IN OUR COUNTRY. FOR YOUR
OWN SAFETY YOU SHOULD NOT ALLOW ANC GANGSTERS TO OC-
CUPY HOUSES AND OFFICES IN YOUR COUNTRY, FROM WHERE
THEY CAN PLAN THESE VICIOUS, COWARDLY ACTS AGAINST IN-
NOCENT PEOPLE IN OUR COUNTRY.

IF THIS HAPPENS IT IS OUR RIGHT TO SEEK OUT AND DESTROY
THESE ANC GANGSTERS WHEREVER THEY MAY BE. SELF DEFENCE
IS NOT ONLY OUR RIGHT, IT IS OUR DUTY.

top left *The house in a suburb of the Zimbabwean capital, Harare, where the ANC representative, Joe Gqabi, was assassinated in 1981. The house was later destroyed in a South African attack in the early hours of May 10, 1986.* Photo: The Herald
and *President Robert Mugabe, then Prime Minister, outside the ANC offices in central Harare which were destroyed in the same attack. The South Africans hired cars from a local touring company for their early morning attack and escaped by helicopter from a rendezvous point outside the city.* Photo: Alexander Joe
above *One of the leaflets scattered in Harare during the South African attack. The simultaneous raids on three Commonwealth capitals—Gaborone, Harare and Lusaka—were condemned worldwide as an act of "international terrorism."*

A South African-supplied AK 47 rifle captured from bandits operating in Zimbabwe's Matabeleland province. The serial numbers have been obliterated in an attempt to make it difficult to trace these weapons to South Africa.

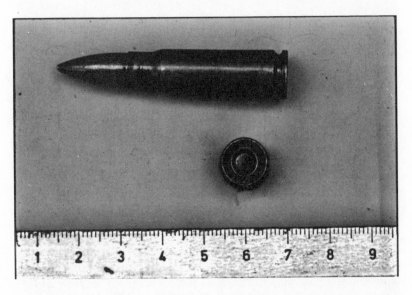

An AK 47 round stamped "22-80," captured from bandits in Matabeleland. South African-supplied ammunition of this type was used in the murder of Rhodesian Front senator, Paul Savage, and other white farmers in Matabeleland.

Burning cars at a popular suburban shopping center in Harare after a car bomb explosion the morning of October 13, 1987, while Commonwealth leaders were meeting in Canada. Three people were seriously injured, all Zimbabweans.   Photo: The Herald

Police and troops of the occupying South African forces break up a SWAPO rally in Windhoek, Namibia. The South Africans have constructed a military and economic infrastructure in Namibia in preparation for future destabilization.   Photo: IDAF

ANC President Oliver Tambo pays his respects at the coffins of some of the 42 people massacred by South African soldiers in Maseru, Lesotho, on December 9, 1982.

MNR representatives inside and outside the White House in Washington, DC in August 1986.

top MNR representatives from the United States and Europe met with then White House Director of Communications, Pat Buchanan, in August 1986 in their effort to gain recognition.

and MNR representatives from Portugal and Federal Republic of Germany outside the White House on the same occasion, with unidentified liaison.

6

SOUTH AFRICA'S MILITARY BUILD-UP
The Region at War

In the ornate assembly halls of the United Nations in New York, the Security Council continues to debate whether South Africa constitutes a "threat to international peace and security." In southern Africa, there is no doubt. Every day people are dying—or are maimed, injured or displaced—as a result of South African military actions. The apartheid regime is at war with its neighbors, as well as with its own population.

Despite a UN arms embargo, the regime has built up an arsenal of sophisticated weaponry that includes nuclear armaments. The defense budget has more than doubled over the past five years. And the decision-making process has been dominated by the military since the accession to power of the former minister of defense in what is often described as a "constitutional *coup d'état*." The South African authorities now use military force to counter resistance to apartheid within the country and have systematically extended its use far across international boundaries. As we have seen earlier, the targets are not primarily guerrillas of the African National Congress (ANC) of South Africa or even South African refugees but include transportation routes and other economic installations, as well as citizens of neighboring countries, both black and white, and other foreign nationals.

The white-power system in South Africa has survived through the use of repressive laws and brutal violence against the majority of the population. The long history of more than three hundred years of colonial domination has recorded many brave challenges which were put down by the use of overwhelming force, in a pattern similar to other colonial situations. But the crude methods of the colonial era were not suitable for a rapidly developing economy in the postwar years; and thus more elaborate and comprehensive techniques of repression were employed especially after the accession to power of the National Party (NP) in 1948. Apartheid was imposed systematically to cover every aspect of human behavior. A series of draconian laws and other measures were introduced beginning in the 1950s in order to create the new apartheid society.

This was also the decade of mass mobilization and extraparliamentary opposition. The regime took extensive powers to cope with the new upsurge of resistance and did not hesitate to use the new laws. The 1952 defiance of unjust laws campaign resulted in the imposition of stronger penalties for any future campaigns of passive resistance. In 1956, a year after the adoption of the Freedom Charter at the historic Congress of the People,[1] 156 national leaders were arrested for high treason. After four years all of the accused were discharged by the courts.

By this time a major confrontation had developed between the mass of the population and the regime. The repressive organs of the state, including the police force, had been expanded to deal with the growing nationwide resistance. It became clear that the regime was determined to answer all protest with the full might of the state security apparatus. It is in this context that Chief Luthuli, president general of the ANC, appealed to the outside world in 1959 to boycott South Africa and isolate the apartheid regime. Luthuli's appeal was directed mainly at South Africa's major trading partners: if they were to implement a program of economic and other sanctions against Pretoria it could help to prevent a major violent confrontation in southern Africa.

But Britain and the other major Western powers had no intention of interfering in the so-called internal affairs of South Africa, let alone adopting specific measures to help to end the system of white domination. However, the crisis that was building up could not be ignored altogether and the British prime minister, Harold Macmillan, warned the all-white parliament in Cape Town early in 1960 to recognize the "wind of change" which was blowing throughout Africa. Within weeks the world was shocked by news of the Sharpeville Massacre.

In March 1960 a crowd of peaceful demonstrators gathered at Sharpeville and Langa to protest against the pass laws which determined where Africans could live, work and travel. The police fired, killing 72 people and wounding 186, most of them shot in the back as they were running away. There followed an upsurge of anger throughout the country, and thousands of Africans burned their passes. The regime responded by suspending the pass laws, declaring a state of emergency and detaining over 20,000 opponents.

The ANC and the newly formed Pan-Africanist Congress (PAC) were declared illegal organizations and driven underground. All effective methods of nonviolent protest were outlawed, and it became clear that the abhorrent system of apartheid would have to be removed through armed resistance.

The regime which had itself created this situation then set about utilizing the crisis to deliberately inculcate a "war psychosis" in the entire white community, as if the country were actually at war. White South Africa was to be trained for war against its own black population: housewives were organized into shooting clubs, and even schoolchildren were given target practice.

"In the same way as the world powers are continually preparing for war, South Africa intends to be ready for internal trouble," the defense minister explained in 1961. A wide variety of military equipment, including armored vehicles, tanks, aircraft, naval vessels and large quantities of ammunition, was acquired from abroad. At the same time, the regime set about developing a substantial internal armaments and ammunition industry in order to reduce its vulnerability to international boycotts.[2]

The initial expansion of the military forces was intended mainly to suppress internal resistance and to intimidate those who might decide to embark upon guerrilla warfare. It is one of the few situations in the world where a regime was preparing for armed resistance well in advance of such a development taking place.

A second factor which led to acceleration of the military build-up was the process of rapid African decolonization. The newly independent African states felt deeply the need to eradicate the apartheid system and spoke openly about it at the UN and in other international forums. Thus, South Africa developed a second objective: to intimidate the new African states by expanding and displaying its own military might.

A third purpose was to utilize its formal military strength to defy the UN over the occupation of the trust territory of Namibia. Indeed, in later years, those who argued for sanctions to be enforced with a naval blockade in order to remove the South Africans from Namibia were countered by Western claims that such action would be impossible in the light of South Africa's substantial naval and military power.

The fourth reason was that a militarily strong South Africa could also be an attractive ally of the West, not only in the subcontinent but in the Southern Hemisphere as well.

It was for all these reasons, with the central purpose being to maintain the apartheid system internally, that the regime embarked on a massive military build-up during the 1960s. This process has continued unabated ever since, so that today, with its acknowledged nuclear weapon capability, the Pretoria regime presents a grave threat to international peace and security.

During the post-Sharpeville period the regime relied heavily on its police force to take on the major responsibility for maintaining internal control. Wide powers were given to a reorganized paramilitary police force which was integrated with the military at various operational levels. At the same time the role of the security police was expanded. Thus a full-fledged police state came into being to cope with the resistance of the 1960s by means of bans and banishments, detentions without trial and solitary confinement, well-developed and widely used techniques of physical and mental torture and killings in detention. The outside world became aware of the brutal and repressive control exercised by the regime over more than 80 percent of the population. Since the police could not fully suppress the growing spiral of internal resistance, the regime began to systematically and deliberately expand the overall capacity of its military forces.

It is by examining the ever-increasing levels of military expenditure that one obtains a clear idea of the true extent of militarization that has taken place since 1960. The figures in table 6.1, showing military budget estimates since 1960, are based on calculations published by the International Institute for Strategic Studies in London and recent figures published in South African Budget estimates. They are in general underesti-

Table 6.1
South Africa's military budget estimates 1960–61 to 1988–89

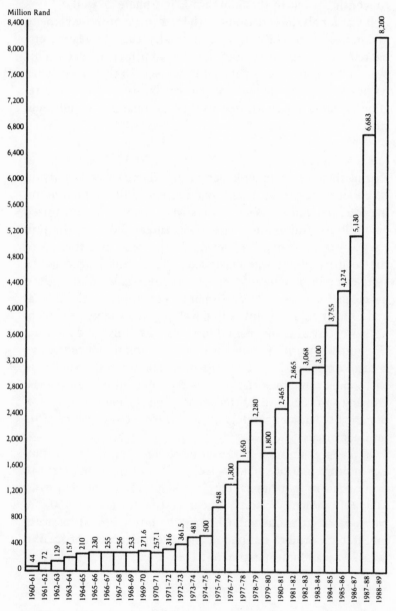

Million Rand

mates and do not cover expenditure by all government departments. Nevertheless, they give a relatively accurate indication of the rate and scale of military expansion since 1960.

Immediately after Sharpeville the annual defense budget of R 44 million in 1960 shot up to R 129 million in two years and reached R 255 million by 1966-67. In less than 10 years this figure almost doubled again to R 500 million by 1974-75, reflecting the growth of armed struggle in the neighboring Portuguese colonies as well as Rhodesia. Thereafter, with Angola and Mozambique independent, and following South Africa's invasion of Angola in 1975, the budget estimate two years later amounted to a staggering R 1,300 million. Over the next two years it increased even more sharply by an average of about R 500 million per year, reaching the record figure of R 2,280 million by 1978-79. This was because 10 years' defense expenditure was contracted into five years in order to cope with the changing geopolitical situation. The military forces also had to cope with the rapidly escalating armed struggle in Rhodesia as well as growing resistance within Namibia and South Africa.

During 1979-80 the figure dipped to R 1,800 million but with the creation of an independent Zimbabwe it rose again to R 2,465 million for 1980-81. Defense spending increased steadily over the next three years, following Zimbabwe's independence and the formation of the Southern African Development Coordination Conference (SADCC), until it reached R 3,100 million in 1983-84. It shot up again by R 655 million in 1984-85 to reach the astounding figure of R 3,755 million, which accounts for about 15 percent of state expenditure. The budget estimate for 1985-86 was R 4,274 million. Thus, in the 25 years after Sharpeville the defense budget increased one-hundredfold from R 44 million to over R 4,000 million. The 1986-87 budget estimate rose again to R 5,130 million and for 1987-88 to R 6,683 million. The 1988-89 estimate of R 8,200 million is 22.6% higher than the previous year, reflecting an increase in internal use of military force as well as South Africa's escalation of the war in Angola.

By any standard this represents a phenomenal rate of expansion and indicates the high level of Pretoria's dependence upon the use of military force—both to impose its authority within Namibia and South Africa and to maintain an aggressive posture throughout the region.

It must be noted, however, that these figures are underestimates since substantial military expenditure is in fact accounted for by other ministries. For example, the Military Intelligence Directorate (MID) is in fact funded by the Department of Finance, and military bases are constructed with funds from the Department of Public Works. In addition, much of the cost of the war in Namibia is drawn from the funds of the "South West Africa Administration." Seen in this context *direct* military spending alone constitutes at least 20 percent, or one-fifth, of all state expenditure.

In order to get an accurate picture of the total cost of the military and security apparatus, one would have to take into account a wide variety of other expenditure, including that of the armaments industry, as well as the police and other security forces. This gives some idea of the central importance of the military and security forces in upholding the apartheid system, as well as the prohibitively high and ever-escalating costs involved in maintaining that system.

The enormous increase in defense expenditure has been accompanied by a substantial expansion of human resources. Most of the military personnel are drawn from the ruling white population and removing them from productive employment adds a further heavy burden to the apartheid economy.

In 1965, according to official figures, the military forces numbered 26,500 (army 19,000; navy 3,500; air force 4,000). By 1985 the total number of regular forces numbered 106,400 (army 76,400; navy 9,000; air force 13,000; medical corps 8,000), with another 317,000 reserves and a further 21,000 listed in the South West Africa Territory Force (SWATF). By conservative estimates, Pretoria is able to mobilize a force of well over half a million—mainly white—personnel for military duties. There is a very high cost to be borne for this level of mobilization which is still lower than what the regime would like to have available at its command.

The economy is generally short of skilled white labor, and for the military to drain it further produces widespread protest from the business community, as well as from those who are conscripted. In addition, active service increasingly involves a risk of death or permanent injury. This and other factors, including conscientious objection, have resulted in hundreds of young white recruits defaulting on the national service and call-up duties, with many deserting the country.

All eligible, young, white males are initially conscripted for a two-year period of national service and thereafter perform regular tours of active duty. Their commitment ends, at the earliest, at the age of 55.

A detailed official explanation about the shortage of human resources was contained in the 1982 Defence White Paper, which says: "It is in the national interest that the White male should no longer be utilized as the only manpower source. Therefore the SA Defence Force will be more and more dependent on other sources of manpower, such as White females and members of other population groups, [and] . . . their utilization is already being based on programmed manpower development plans which extend to 1990."

The white paper disclosed the following composition of the full-time force:

Permanent Force	28%
National Servicemen	46%
Voluntary Service Members	3%

Civilians (including Black Workers)   21%
Auxiliary Service   2%

It went on to state that "by 1987 the Full-time Force will have expanded by approximately 17%. . . . As regards White females, efforts in the short term will be directed mainly at expanding the Permanent Force," and as far as "coloured" and Asian males are concerned "an increase in their numbers is also envisaged."

With regard to Africans, the white paper specified three categories: "namely Permanent Force Members, members of Auxiliary Service and civilians." The permanent force members were trained with those from the "Bantustans," in the 21st Battalion at Lenz near Johannesburg.

The white paper also revealed that, with the exception of a "multinational" African unit still to be established, "Black members who belong to the combat elements of the Auxiliary Service are divided into regional units. These regional units will serve as the nucleus of the independent defence forces of the states concerned." These defense forces will "be able to contribute to the protection of their own territories." It went on to add that the "expansion of Black regional units in SWA [South West Africa] has been given priority" over those in South Africa and that as for the large number of African civilians serving in the defense force "the possibility of placing as many of these persons as possible in uniform is being investigated at present."

Another Defense White Paper in 1984 disclosed that some of the targets mentioned two years earlier could not be met and stated that "the Permanent Force presently constitutes a smaller percentage of the Full-time Force than two years ago." The permanent force had been reduced to 25.52 percent from 28 percent and the main reason given for this was "the lack of accommodation for other population groups as well as for White women in certain centres."

The real reason is undoubtedly the difficulty of recruiting people who do not wish to serve in the armed forces. Another problem is white South Africa's traditional uncertainty about training Africans for warfare when they can so easily utilize those skills to fight the apartheid system itself. Thus, the regime is faced with a situation where it needs to recruit more Africans, whose lives it believes are more expendable than those of whites, at the same time having to balance that with the major security risk involved. How far can it rely upon the victims of the apartheid system to protect it, particularly in times of great internal crisis? Understandably, there are powerful forces within the regime who are deeply opposed to any substantial reliance by the military forces on nonwhite personnel.

The 1984 White Paper stated that while the intake of "coloured" men had increased by 22 percent, there was no "growth with regard to Asian men" and "in the case of Black men there has been an increase of 13 percent." According to the 1985–86 *Military Balance*, out of the total "regulars" in the army of 18,400, some 12,000 are white, 5,400 are black and "coloured," and 1,000 are women.

From the early 1970s the regime has given serious attention to recruiting women for the military forces. Special study teams were sent abroad and considerable attention was paid to the Israeli system. However, all these efforts have not led to any major increase in white women who, since they began enlisting on a voluntary basis, have not been offering themselves for service in great numbers. Those serving at present are estimated to number about 3,500; most are members of the permanent force, deployed essentially in noncombat roles. A further five hundred white women serve through the small, voluntary, national service scheme.

The failure in enlisting an adequate number of white women for the military forces, with the resultant shortage in total white personnel and the inevitable increase in the intake of African, "coloured" and Asian personnel, has caused serious misgivings within the ruling National Party. For example, its Cape Congress in September 1983 had before it a resolution calling for compulsory national service for women. This was turned down by Prime Minister P. W. Botha on the grounds that training facilities for the 24,000 eligible white women who turned 17 each year would cost between R 600 million and R 700 million to establish, and "the country could not afford such expenditure."[3]

With the establishment of special armies for the "Bantustans" the regime hopes, according to the 1982 White Paper, "that such defence forces will be able to contribute to the protection of their own territories." This forms part of the overall strategy to develop a system of "regional" defense as opposed to "border" defense only, mainly as a result of the growing success of underground resistance by the ANC.

Since the early 1960s the South African Police (SAP) force has operated in support of the military, and its paramilitary role on "border duties" in northern Namibia and Rhodesia during the latter half of the decade is well known. This paramilitary role has expanded with the growth of internal resistance, and today is equipped with a wide range of weapons which are primarily designed for military purposes.

The 1983 official yearbook on South Africa says, "The SAP is a national force and is the first line of defence in the event of internal unrest." The nationwide resistance during 1985 exposed the weakness of this first line of defense as thousands of troops were deployed in the African townships. Even then it was virtually impossible to maintain control, and in July 1985 the authorities declared a state of emergency which gave wide powers to the police.

According to a leading South African lawyer, Sydney Kentridge, under the emergency regulations a policeman "may do whatever he pleases to maintain what he considers to be law and order . . . He may shoot, or whip, or tear-gas. However unnecessary or extreme his action, he knows that he is safe as long as he acted in good faith. And he is told anything he does will be presumed to be in good faith."[4] The minister responsible for the police, Louis Le Grange, introduced a bill in Parliament in April 1984 whereby acts or offenses committed outside South Africa by members of the SAP shall be deemed to have been committed inside the country.[5]

Like the military, the police force is acutely short of personnel, and in October 1985 the regime announced that it would expand the 45,000 police force (of whom about half are white) by 11,000 men, or 25 percent, during the next 17 months. As the police force has expanded over the years, there has been a steady reduction in the proportion of white recruits. The police have their own Maleoskop Counter-Insurgency Training Center near Groblersdal which by 1983 could handle five thousand trainees a year in "all aspects of counterinsurgency, combating of urban terrorism and riot control measures."

Soon after the Sharpeville Massacre, a reserve police force was established, consisting of recruits who perform part-time duties in their spare time. Within this force there are special units, such as a diving unit and a radio reserve consisting of radio amateurs.

The military and police forces are integrated in their operational and command structures, and when the first line of defense—the police—cannot cope with internal unrest, the military is called in to assist. On the other hand, specially trained members of the paramilitary police force are deployed in operations beyond South Africa's borders, on sabotage missions and for certain "border duties." Both forces are short of personnel and the police have a much larger proportion of black personnel than the military.

In addition to regular police and military units, there are several special forces (such as the "South West African Police," the former *Koevoet*, in Namibia). For these and other units the regime has recruited several thousand mercenaries from abroad, with the largest number coming from "Zimbabwe-Rhodesia" on the eve of independence. At that time, they also recruited a large number of black "auxiliary" forces from that country, and more than five thousand were kept in camps in the northern Transvaal.[6]

The mercenaries are not restricted to these special units and also serve in the standard army of the South African Defense Force (SADF). Some "special operations," such as the attempted *coup d'état* against the government of President Albert René in the Seychelles in November 1981, include both mercenaries and members of the SADF. That force was led by Colonel "Mad Mike" Hoare, a well-known mercenary commander, but included a senior officer of the SADF, which had also provided the weapons for the group.[7]

South African legislation requires foreign nationals residing in that country to serve in the armed forces. Legislation enacted in April 1984 granted immigrants with permanent residence permits automatic South African citizenship by naturalization, so those aged between 15 and 25 are now liable for two years' full-time national service, plus 12 years on the active reserve.[8] These provisions are not only encouraging a larger group of young white men to resist recruitment but also contribute to the substantial outflow of recent white immigrants, as well as deterring others from settling in South Africa.

It is quite clear that, despite the various measures taken since 1960, the regime is facing a serious crisis of personnel. Moreover, the crisis during 1985 revealed the extent to which the military and police forces are stretched, with the regime unable to assert its authority in many areas.

P. W. Botha's accession to prime minister in September 1978, after serving as defense minister for 12 years, heralded the growing ascendancy of the military in the white political process, in which decision making and planning came to be dominated by security considerations. Soon after taking over from B. J. Vorster, Botha reorganized the power structure and created the National Security Management System, which transformed the State Security Council (SSC) into the most powerful decision-making body in the country. He trimmed the bureaucracy, applying the management methods of the SADF to government. Military men became his key advisers, and Botha's takeover of the administration was referred to as a "constitutional *coup d'état.*"

The SSC was streamlined in 1979 from an ad hoc body—meeting irregularly and subservient to the cabinet—into a powerful planning body whose fortnightly meetings precede cabinet meetings. Technically, the SSC is one of four cabinet committees (the others deal with economic, social and constitutional affairs) but, according to a prominent Afrikaner scholar, the minutes of other cabinet committees are attached to minutes of the full cabinet for circulation; while those of the SSC are not. Decisions of the SSC are not automatically circulated or subject to confirmation by the full cabinet.

The secretary to the SSC who presided over the reorganization was Lieutenant General A. J. van Deventer, a high-ranking military officer and close confidante of P. W. Botha. He was later replaced by General Pieter van der Westhuizen, former head of military intelligence. The SSC, and its secretary, act as a kind of "gatekeeper" through which information is circulated and through which all important government business must pass before submission to cabinet. Technically, the cabinet remains a superior body and may return decisions to the SSC but in practice it rarely does so, due to the powerful representation of cabinet ministers and military leaders on the council.

As a result of widespread speculation about the precise role of the SSC, and to play down claims that the military were taking over the administration of the country, some details of its membership, which was hitherto secret, were officially disclosed in September 1983. The SSC is chaired by P. W. Botha, now state president, and includes the next senior cabinet minister, as well as the ministers of defense, foreign affairs, law and order, and justice, as shown in table 6.2. Other members include the head of military intelligence, the chief of the defense force, the commissioner of police, the head of the national intelligence service, and department heads whom the president chooses to co-opt as "observers," such as the directors of foreign affairs, justice, or information.

The statutory responsibility of the SSC is to advise government on "national policy and strategy in relation to the security of the Republic," and it concerns itself with a wide range of issues not normally associated with defense and security, including foreign and regional policy, labor, sport, cultural and religious matters, among others. The working committee of the SSC draws together government department heads who coordinate departmental activities on security-related matters.

The secretariat of the SSC consists of four branches: administrative; strategy; strategic communication (responsible for "advice and coordination in the war of words"); and national intelligence interpretation. The latter coordinates intelligence provided by the police, the MID and the National Intelligence Service (NIS, formerly the Bureau of State Security [BOSS]).

The SSC also has various interdepartmental committees where representatives of government departments coordinate particular areas of security strategy, as shown in table 6.3. The "grassroots" component of the SSC network is the Joint Management Centers (JMC), officially known by their Afrikaans abbreviation GBS, and the sub-JMCs, mini-JMCs and Local Management Centers. The JMCs correspond roughly with the SADF military command areas; thus there are nine such centers ser-

Table 6.2

South Africa's security establishment relative to political structures

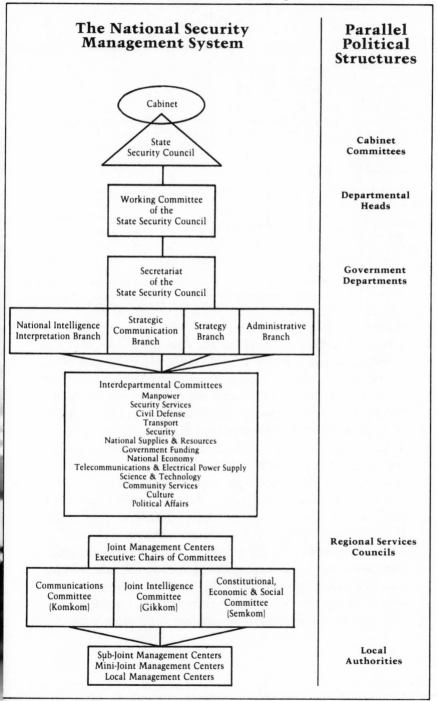

The National Security Management System

Parallel Political Structures

Cabinet

State Security Council — Cabinet Committees

Working Committee of the State Security Council — Departmental Heads

Secretariat of the State Security Council — Government Departments

National Intelligence Interpretation Branch | Strategic Communication Branch | Strategy Branch | Administrative Branch

Interdepartmental Committees
Manpower
Security Services
Civil Defense
Transport
Security
National Supplies & Resources
Government Funding
National Economy
Telecommunications & Electrical Power Supply
Science & Technology
Community Services
Culture
Political Affairs

Joint Management Centers
Executive: Chairs of Committees — Regional Services Councils

Communications Committee (Komkom) | Joint Intelligence Committee (Gikkom) | Constitutional, Economic & Social Committee (Semkom)

Sub-Joint Management Centers
Mini-Joint Management Centers
Local Management Centers — Local Authorities

Source: J. Selfe, *The Sash,* May 1987.

Table 6.3
Membership of the State Security Council

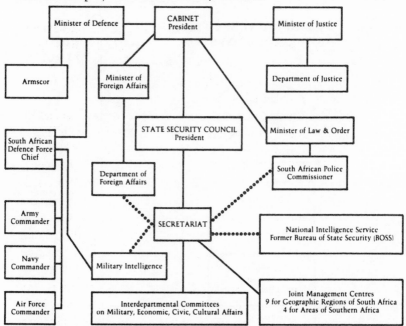

vicing geographic areas within the country and another four covering countries in the region. One study, "The Rise of the South African Security Establishment," says the "most disturbing" result of the shift in power to the security establishment—especially to the defense force—is "the apparent efforts to destabilize the domestic order of foreign states."[9]

Each JMC is made up of about 60 officials and security force officers and is usually chaired by a brigadier from the police or military. The JMCs have specialist committees dealing with intelligence, communications, and constitutional, economic and social issues. These are normally referred to by their Afrikaans abbreviations as the Gikkom, Komkom and Semkom. Below these JMCs are 60 sub-JMCs, roughly coinciding with the metropolitan regions, consisting of civic officials and local military and police chiefs. At the lowest level are 448 mini-JMCs, corresponding to municipal councils and including civil defense officers, fire chiefs, postmasters and other municipal officials. These committees are accountable to no one except the security structures above them. Informal channels have been established in some areas with local community organizations, often without their realizing that they are being drawn into a security and intelligence network.

The preeminent role of the SSC in the overall decision-making system means in effect a dominant role for the military and security forces and diminished responsibility for both the cabinet and white parliament. The establishment of the tricameral parliament in an effort to co-opt Indian and "coloured" people into the ruling white community thus did not represent any major inroad into the white power structure. The constitutional reform has in fact concentrated substantial dictatorial power in the hands of the president resulting in a major erosion of "democracy," even for the white electorate.

In the light of these developments it would be true to say that white South Africa's decision-making system has been transformed in order to cope with growing internal resistance. There are very few aspects of civilian life that are not dominated by military and security considerations, and in the process the military has acquired substantial political power. It is therefore true to speak of a "Botha-Malan" regime since that reflects accurately where effective power lies.

To bring about this transformation, the regime has emphasized during the last decade that the threat to white South Africa is not limited to the border war but represents a "total onslaught" against the republic which it claims is directed by the Soviet Union. This can only be countered with a "total strategy" to resist the "onslaught" at every level. This process has gone through various stages, and in 1982, the chief of the SADF General Constand Viljoen announced a new "area defence system" to meet the growing "area war" assault by the ANC. He claimed that the ANC was planning an "area war" of widely spread attacks aimed at creating "an atmosphere of instability" and at dispersing security personnel.[10]

Unable to contain massive nationwide resistance during 1984–85, the regime proclaimed the first state of emergency, which was lifted in March 1986 and reimposed on 12 June. This has resulted in a martial-law type administration in most of the country, the role of the National Security Management System extended to deal with the day-to-day running of the emergency. The purpose of this "emergency management system" is to counter what the state believes is a revolutionary onslaught: containing political resistance on an ongoing basis; coordinating a "hearts and minds" campaign that includes improvement of some social and material conditions in black areas; and functioning as an early-warning system to locate potential trouble spots and to avert open revolt.[11]

Despite these repressive measures, it has been impossible for the regime to regain total control of the situation, which has led to even more extreme means. Having imposed a news blackout through strict censorship, Pretoria embarked on a massive campaign of repression in which thousands of young children have been special targets. The International Conference on Children, Repression and the Law in Apartheid South Africa, held in Harare in September 1987, heard some devastating statistics about police brutality toward children aged five to eighteen. During the period 1984–86, 300 were killed, 1,000 wounded, 11,000 detained without trial, 18,000 arrested for protest activity, and 173,000 held in prison cells awaiting trial.

General Viljoen predicted that the military would have the task of controlling the situation while the politicians work out a political solution—something that has not happened so far—and he stressed this point again at his retirement in 1985. Inevitably, as the confrontation has grown inside the country, the military has been forced to take on additional responsibility for the day-to-day physical security of the country and its white population; and the loss of political authority and control over the majority African population has resulted in the deployment of massive force throughout the country. Now that the last line of defense, the military forces, are being deployed to maintain civilian order, South Africa has virtually reached its "security ceiling."

The ever-increasing annual defense budgets have contributed to the development of a large internal armaments manufacturing industry as part of an overall plan to make South Africa "self-sufficient" for all its strategic requirements. But even with substantial financial resources at its command the regime has not been able to achieve the intended degree of self-sufficiency in the production of arms and ammunition.

Even before the imposition of an international arms embargo by the UN Security Council in 1963, Western companies had begun to invest heavily in South Africa's new armaments industry. In 1962, Imperial Chemicals Industries (ICI) of Britain joined De Beers in revitalizing the African Explosives and Chemicals Industries Ltd (AECI) and set up three factories to produce tear gas, ammunition for small arms, and antitank and antiaircraft rockets.

Following the two resolutions adopted by the UN Security Council in 1963 and 1964 to prohibit the supply of arms—as well as technology to produce arms—to South Africa, external collaboration in the development of internal arms production intensified. Items which could not be manufactured in South Africa were delivered openly to the Pretoria regime, as either "civilian" or "dual-purpose" products, which were not covered by certain governments' interpretation of their obligations under the arms embargo.

In November 1965, Marconi of Britain constructed a modern radar network along South Africa's northern borders and began a 20-year association with the Pretoria regime, regularly updating the radar systems and providing modern equipment for new installations.

South Africa had little difficulty in securing Western cooperation to undermine the international arms embargo, and in

1965 Defense Minister Fouche was able to boast that he had already obtained 120 licenses to manufacture weapons locally. South Africa, he said was "already practically self-sufficient so far as the production of small weapons, ammunition and explosives were concerned."

Preparations were made in advance to produce military aircraft and by 1967 the Atlas Aircraft Corporation began constructing, under Italian license, the Aermacchi MB 326 under the name "Impala." Most of the vital components of these aircraft were imported from abroad, including initially the Rolls Royce engines; these were later manufactured in South Africa under license granted by Piaggio of Italy, which had in turn received the original license from Rolls Royce in Britain. This was one way to circumvent the partial arms embargo imposed by the British government.

The costly process of developing an internal arms production capability was partially overcome by the massive annual increases in the defense budget. Defense Minister Fouche revealed in 1964 that defense contracts worth R 35 million would be placed with South African industries in that year alone. He added, "The fact that Defence is spending so much is one of the greatest inducements for new industrial development."[12]

The adoption of the international arms embargo and threats of further boycotts served to accelerate industrial development in certain sectors of the economy and in effect amounted to advance preparations for a siege. At the beginning it was generally considered desirable to promote "import replacement," but the threat of more effective international measures changed the goal to one of "self-sufficiency," which was considered vital for national survival. There was, inevitably, substantial state intervention in the economy but, due to the prohibitive costs involved, it was impossible to achieve "self-sufficiency" even in the arms sector which was considered of the greatest strategic significance.

The South African Armaments Corporation (Armscor) was established in 1968 and amalgamated with the government's Armaments Production Board in 1977 to form "an autonomous government organization." Armscor has nine main subsidiaries and claims to have more than one thousand private subcontractors. Annual turnover in 1984 was stated to be R 1,600 million, and its assets then amounted to R 1,400 million. Armscor's chairman, Commandant Piet Marais, said in an interview published in 1984 that the company itself employed 33,000 people but that a total of about 80,000 people are actually involved in armament production throughout the country. He also disclosed that Armscor had facilities "to produce the necessary volume of items such as ammunition."[13]

The cost of simply maintaining existing facilities for the production of arms and ammunition is proving to be quite expensive. Since a constantly diminishing proportion of defense expenditure is being allocated to equipment, that raises the costs even further. The assembly and production of new types of equipment is even more expensive, and when taken together with the large sums needed to pay smugglers, middlemen and others in order to obtain vital parts and components from abroad, one gets an idea of the prohibitive costs involved.

The Pretoria regime has over the years tried to popularize the myth that it is "self-sufficient" in producing arms and ammunition for its military. This is done not only to justify the enormous cost of establishing an internal armaments industry but to discredit the international arms embargo and to give the impression that the SADF is adequately equipped with modern arms. The South African authorities are not alone in perpetuating this impression, which is repeated at times with even greater exaggeration by various Western defense publications. Thus the widespread belief continues that South Africa is in fact "self-sufficient" and meets virtually all of its defense needs from internal production.

The truth is that, despite the development of a substantial domestic weapons production capability, the SADF has been severely hit in certain key sectors, even by the weak and limited international arms embargo.

The South African armed forces acquire military security equipment in a variety of ways. Arms which are "made" in South Africa are those manufactured under formal licensing and other similar arrangements, or those based on "borrowed" foreign technology. Those described as "indigenously developed" items are essentially adaptations of existing overseas products. Most of these involve a large percentage of foreign-made components which are imported either as normal commercial products or smuggled into the country by various devious means.

Second, a large quantity of so-called dual-purpose equipment, including sophisticated military radar systems, are acquired on the open market. Where necessary, the overseas government concerned even provides export licenses for restricted items on the grounds that these do not amount to a breach of the arms embargo. Export licenses are also issued for purchases made directly by the South African military and police forces.

Third, items which cannot be acquired by the above methods are obtained by means of well-established clandestine smuggling operations which are overlooked by the respective overseas governments and their security and intelligence services. The few cases which have come before the courts, with some resulting prosecutions, have been exposed largely by the vigilance of the anti-apartheid organizations and the media, or because of prompt action by customs officials.

Fourth, some arms and components which are generally prohibited for export to South Africa by the major Western countries are acquired through Israel, Taiwan, Chile or other allies.

Many of the problems faced by the internal armaments industry arise out of the fact that the industrialized sector as a whole is highly dependent on foreign technology and components. A recent Study Group Report issued by the Department of Industries and Commerce confirmed that "South Africa is largely dependent on imported technology" and went on to state that "the acquisition of expertise is facilitated by South Africa's close ties with many multi-national enterprises controlled from the developed countries." The dependence on foreign technology and components becomes a much more serious problem for the internal arms production industry because of the high degree of sophistication involved, together with the relatively low production runs which result in massive overhead costs.

Although there is considerable secrecy surrounding South Africa's overseas arms purchases, it is not impossible to make some realistic estimates. According to a finding of the World Campaign against Military and Nuclear Collaboration with South Africa, "more than half of the total amount spent by ARMSCOR in acquiring military hardware is in fact spent abroad." Evidence presented to the UN Security Council's Arms Embargo Committee in 1984 stated that "out of an annual expenditure of R 1.62 billion, over R 900 million is spent overseas and only about R 700 million at home."[14]

Of course claims of "self-sufficiency" can be made more easily if one refers to the total payments made by the SADF for its purchases to enterprises based in South Africa *without* taking into account the cost of plant, parts and components acquired from abroad. The figures can be further distorted by including items which are made entirely abroad but purchased via either a local subsidiary of a multinational company or an agent in South Africa. Thus, the degree of "self-sufficiency" is directly dependent on the way in which the figures are actually calculated.

Moreover, this method of assessing whether all of the needs of the SADF are in fact met by "internal" purchases does not point to the acute shortages in various critical sectors which are not being met. A close examination of official documents gives some idea of the problem even if, for obvious reasons, they are gross understatements and merely reflect the tip of the iceberg.

For example, paragraph 37 of the 1984 Defence White Paper opens with the following sentence: "*The provision of spares for highly sophisticated equipment in the SA Air Force has been a serious problem.*" The gravity of the situation comes through in a later sentence: "As regards the provision of spare parts, priorities have been identified in respect of 10 types of aircraft which require specific attention." Since the air force has relatively few types of aircraft, shortages of 10 types of aircraft spare parts affect the entire air force.

Paragraph 39 opens with another disclosure: "With the phasing out of the Shackleton maritime aircraft towards the end of 1984 the SA Air Force will have no long-range maritime reconnaissance capability." The South African authorities have been making strenuous efforts in recent years to acquire new reconnaissance aircraft but have so far failed to obtain any replacement due to the arms embargo. The white paper describes the situation thus: "The replacement of the long-range maritime aircraft continues to receive attention."

The situation with respect to the navy is no better. Although South Africa claims to "manufacture" a few small, missile-strike crafts, the 1984 white paper concedes that "these vessels only meet part of the current and future needs of the SA Navy." In the next paragraph it is pointed out that the three Daphne submarines "have already seen thirteen years of service" and that the "replacement vessel, SAS Tafelberg, has also become obsolescent and is being modernized and modified." It is expected that this will enable "the needs of the SA Navy" to be met "until a new replenishment vessel replaces SAS Tafelberg." Thus items which would otherwise have to be scrapped are having their service life temporarily extended by costly modifications.

In its conclusion, the 1984 white paper claims that the success of the SADF during military operations "can be ascribed to the sound armaments development of the RSA [Republic of South Africa] and the manufacturing capability developed over the past decade." The next sentence explains: "Achievements in the field of local armaments manufacture include the R4 rifle, the G5 gun, the Ratel infantry combat vehicle, mine-resistant vehicles, missiles and strike craft." Allowing for the fact that these "manufactured" items involve a heavy external dependence, a large variety of arms and related equipment still has to be acquired directly from abroad—or done without.

Thus the white paper itself concludes: "A major problem is that some of the most reliable main armaments are obsolescent." Earlier, it stated: "Objectives in respect of preparedness programmes and the manufacture of arms could not be fully achieved owing to a restricted SADF budget during the past five years and also as a result of the economic recession."

These extracts from just one Defence White Paper point to the serious problems faced by the military forces in terms of simply maintaining the existing level of operational capability in certain crucial sectors, let alone expanding it to meet the growing crisis faced by the regime. It also exposes the grave problems associated with having to keep relying on major items which are in fact "obsolescent." These difficulties point to the following conclusions:

1. Those items which are "made" in South Africa are highly dependent on external sources of technology, plant, parts and components.
2. Items "made" in South Africa are not able to meet the overall needs of the SADF, and the regime itself admits that "some of the most reliable main armaments are obsolescent."
3. Even the limited and weak arms embargo is depriving South Africa of some vital military equipment and forcing it to

allocate massive resources to try to "manufacture" certain items internally while acquiring others from abroad through expensive smuggling operations.

4. Despite substantial efforts to recoup some of the costs of weapons production through exports, South Africa has so far failed to win any important markets. Earnings have not been adequate to make a significant contribution to the exorbitant costs involved in internal weapons production.

5. Faced with an acute and growing economic and political crisis, South Africa is unlikely to be able to proceed with its present weapons production plans which will have to be seriously curtailed.

6. The SADF will increasingly have to make do with a *smaller* percentage of its budget available for the purchase of arms and will consequently have to rely on fewer and more out-dated weapons in several vital areas, resulting in a serious weakening of its overall military capability.

The UN Security Council first imposed an arms embargo against South Africa in August 1963 when it adopted Resolution 181 calling on all states "to cease forthwith the sale and shipment of arms, ammunition of all types and military vehicles to South Africa." In December 1963, through Resolution 182, a second decision was taken which also covered "equipment and materials for the manufacture or maintenance of arms and ammunition in South Africa." In 1964 a third resolution was adopted, reaffirming the earlier decisions and calling upon all states to implement the embargo.

Britain and the United States applied a limited partial embargo while France, and later Italy, openly flouted the decisions. The French newspaper *Le Monde* stated in May 1968 that "France had become the principal supplier of arms to South Africa." By that year South Africa had become France's third biggest arms customer, after Israel and Belgium. It is in this period that South Africa ordered from France modern submarines, radar and missile systems, as well as helicopters and Mirage fighter planes.

Those early decisions of the Security Council were undermined in various ways by several Western governments which did not have the political will to impose a strict arms embargo, with the result that the South African regime was able to obtain a substantial amount of its military requirements from abroad. Inevitably, there were repeated efforts by African and nonaligned states to impose a mandatory arms embargo but these were all defeated by the joint veto power of Britain, France and the United States.

In October 1977, when yet another triple veto was cast, it produced so much protest that the Western powers felt obliged to submit a much weaker text. This was adopted on 4 November as Resolution 418 (1977).

Despite its weakness, this represented a major success and was the first ever mandatory decision taken by the UN against one of its members. Moreover, the resolution had the potential to make a significant impact since the text of operative paragraphs 2, 3 and 4 is very clear:

2. Decides that all States shall cease forthwith any provision to South Africa of arms and related materiél of all types, including the sale or transfer of weapons and ammunition, military vehicles and equipment, paramilitary police equipment, and spare parts for the aforementioned, and shall cease as well the provision of all types of equipment and supplies, and grants of licensing arrangements, for the manufacture or maintenance of the aforementioned;
3. Calls upon all States to review, having regard to the objectives of the present resolution, all existing contractual arrangements with and licences granted to South Africa relating to the manufacture and maintenance of arms, ammunition of all types and military equipment and vehicles, with a view to terminating them;

4. Further decides that all States shall refrain from any cooperation with South Africa in the manufacture and development of nuclear weapons [for full text see appendix 5].

In an address to the UN Special Committee against Apartheid in December 1977, a representative of the British Anti-Apartheid Movement stated: "If the present mandatory decision is applied strictly, then I am convinced that the South African defence forces can be denied any further arms and defence equipment as well as spare parts and components which will make much of their existing weaponry inefficient and non-operational: that is, provided that nobody sabotages the embargo."[15] However, since the adoption of the mandatory resolution results have resembled those following the earlier decisions of the Security Council: the objectives of the embargo have been seriously undermined by the way in which it has been interpreted and implemented by South Africa's major trading partners and certain other countries.

In order to try to avoid some of the earlier evasions, the Security Council decided to establish a committee to monitor and supervise the mandatory arms embargo. Despite its relatively weak mandate, the committee initially issued some important reports, including one in September 1980 "on ways and means of making the mandatory arms embargo more effective."[16] After reviewing the various problems encountered in the implementation of the embargo, the committee submitted 16 important proposals to make it more effective.

One of the proposals was that "the embargo should include imports of arms and related material of all types *from South Africa.*" Acting on this proposal, the Security Council adopted Resolution 558 (1984) which requested member states to "refrain from importing arms, ammunition of all types and military vehicles produced in South Africa."

The Security Council has therefore only partially adopted one of the 16 proposals; Resolution 558 does not cover the importation of military "related material" and, even more important, it is a nonmandatory decision. The Western countries refused to yield on these two points despite intense efforts by the nonaligned members of the Security Council.

Since then the Security Council has adopted further nonmandatory resolutions in an attempt to reinforce Resolution 418 (1977), but, at present, there is no immediate prospect of further mandatory measures being adopted by the Security Council. Meanwhile, its 421 Committee has been left with virtually no effective role since 1980, largely due to blocking by Britain and the United States.

One of the main deterrents to making the arms embargo more effective is the fact that each UN member state determines how to interpret its own obligations in terms of the mandatory resolution. There is no reference to the Security Council in drawing up the necessary legal measures, and no systematic reports are submitted about their actual operation. Thus we have a situation where every country uses different rules to enforce the same embargo; and even the same country has different regulations from time to time, depending on changes in government or in government policy.

The existence of major loopholes in national legislation usually comes to light only when specific cases are publicly exposed. Then, in most cases, the government in question explains that the particular transaction is not in breach of the embargo because it is a "civilian" or "dual-purpose" item, or that the item is not intended to be used for an essentially military purpose.

Even where there is clear prima facie evidence of a breach of national legislation, enforcement still depends on the level of enthusiasm of the authorities to ensure that adequate investigations are conducted, the offenders apprehended and proper criminal proceedings instituted. The general experience of anti-apartheid organizations is that most Western governments attach very little importance to enforcing even their limited national embargoes and are reluctant to prosecute alleged offenders.

In the few cases where criminal prosecutions have in fact taken place, yet another major weakness in national legislation has been exposed. The penalties provided for offenses against the arms embargo are so weak that they do not serve as an effective deterrent. Besides, most offenders calculate from experience that the risk of actually being caught and convicted is so low that they can confidently engage in highly profitable deals on behalf of the South African regime. Even where particular cases are exposed and some lead to prosecutions, the governments concerned do not feel obliged to provide all the available information to the UN.

The World Campaign has repeatedly emphasized the importance of making a comprehensive study of all of the relevant national legislation enacted by individual states with a view to blocking existing loopholes and making the embargo more effective. But the Security Council's 421 Committee so far has not been able to act on this suggestion. As a result, the World Campaign has had to conduct some of its own research about particular aspects of national legislation in order to follow up specific cases. But such information is only of limited value.[17]

In July 1985 the British Anti-Apartheid Movement published the most detailed report so far, *How Britain Arms Apartheid.* This comprehensive study of British policy and legislation provides detailed information about specific breaches and identifies all existing loopholes and other weaknesses. It also offers concrete proposals for making the mandatory embargo more effective.[18] Similar studies for several other countries, including the United States and Federal Republic of Germany, were prepared for the UN seminar on the arms embargo against South Africa, held in London in May 1986. These studies confirmed the gross inadequacy of most national legislative measures, which enables the South African authorities to circumvent and undermine the mandatory arms embargo.

In September 1983, six years after the embargo was imposed, no government had yet informed the Security Council "about particular licences and patents which may have been revoked or discontinued by companies or other enterprises within its jurisdiction."[19] The Italian government claimed, in June 1979, that with respect to the licenses granted for the Aermacchi MB 326 and the Rolls Royce engines "the licences were ceded in 1964 *una tantum*, that is, without a provision for their termination. As the supply of technical assistance and spare parts for both the MB 326 and the Rolls Royce Viper engines has been discontinued since 1972, the unilateral withdrawal of the licences at this stage would not affect in the least the production, and in fact would just result in a net benefit for South Africa."[20]

Thus, the Italian government was claiming that a decision adopted under Chapter VII of the UN Charter to counteract a threat to international peace and security could not be implemented because there was no provision for "termination" of the respective licenses in the original agreement with South Africa. This raises important questions about the binding authority of mandatory decisions adopted by the UN Security Council within the Italian legal system. However, in the above answer, the Italian government appears to be only concerned about the possibility of South Africa continuing to produce the licensed aircraft and engines even if the licenses are terminated, claiming that this would "just result in a net benefit for South Africa." Presumably their concern was that South Africa would stop payment of fees and royalties to the holders of the licenses in Italy.

In November 1986, the World Campaign confirmed that two companies based in the Federal Republic of Germany had illegally supplied South Africa with submarine construction plans and called upon the Bonn government to prosecute the offenders. The West German parliament appointed a special investigating committee to establish the facts. The evidence submitted disclosed that P. W. Botha, during his visit to Bonn in June 1984, had requested Chancellor Kohl to grant permission for the deal. Ten days later, the companies signed a contract with South Africa.

Later the Kohl government stated that official permission had not been granted and that the matter was under investigation. Representations were made throughout 1987 by the UN, the Organization of African Unity (OAU) and several governments, as well as the World Campaign, but the Bonn government insisted that since the illegal deal had not caused any "severe damage to the external relations of the FRG," there were no legal grounds for instituting a prosecution. Despite further representations during June and July 1987, there was still no indication by the end of September that the authorities would take any action.

By December 1987, the newly established Ciskei Aircraft Industries was expected to manufacture the Austrian-designed HB23 Scanliner and HB23 Hobbyliner light aircraft at its plant near the Ciskei's new Bisho International Airport, opened in July 1987. The aircraft were to be manufactured under license granted by HB Aircraft Industries of Haid, Austria, in clear breach of the UN's mandatory arms embargo against South Africa. When representations to this effect were made, the Austrian government at first hedged, saying it was "still engaged in thorough investigations," and later admitted that Austria's regulations had a "loophole" which it claimed had not been noticed. The government said that the minister was considering which legal measures to take but it might take several months and probably a year to decide. The Hobbyliner is ideal for surveillance and military observation duties; and the Scanliner can perform direct military duties.

The arms embargo is extremely weak in the field of licenses, patents and other arrangements that provide technology to

South Africa for its internal arms production. The situation is made worse by the fact that virtually all of the major Western multinationals have subsidiaries or associate companies in South Africa and are therefore able to pass on technical information easily without any monitoring.

In those areas where it is impossible, or too expensive, to manufacture or assemble particular items within South Africa, the embargo is undermined by the way in which "arms and related material" are defined by individual governments.[21] For example, it was revealed that a British firm, International Computers Ltd (ICL), had supplied computers to the South African authorities for use by the police and for a South African plant involved in weapons manufacture. The British government responded to these representations by stating that since the computers themselves did not form part of a weapons system, they were not covered by the embargo.

A second problem related to the fact that although in April 1979 the US administration had announced that it prohibited *all* supplies to the South African military establishment—a policy that was relaxed under the Reagan administration—several other states continued to provide what they considered to be "nonmilitary" items direct to the South African military.

A third problem related to "dual-purpose" or "civilian" items—such as aircraft supplied to various companies or civilian purchasers in South Africa—which later were found to be used by the South African military establishment. A wide variety of aircraft from the United States had been obtained in this way.

There were also difficulties relating to communications and radar equipment. For example, the Advokaat communications system based near Simonstown was described by the South African defense authorities as a joint maritime operations center from which the operational command of the maritime forces was carried out. However, the Federal Republic of Germany, from whom it was purchased, maintained that the Advokaat was an entirely civilian project and did not have much military significance.

These and other cases show the need for a precise definition of what constitutes "arms and related material." It has been suggested that an international checklist of items should be issued in order to avoid difficulties in determining what items are prohibited by the arms embargo. Some of the major areas in which the embargo needs to be tightened have been described in detail in several expert studies. A comprehensive study about computer exports to South Africa published in 1982 revealed that the policy applied by Washington was not as comprehensive as was generally understood.[22]

In May 1981, a document published in London showed that the Plessey AR-3D radar system supplied under license by Britain amounted to a breach of the mandatory arms embargo. The foreign secretary, Lord Carrington, stated that "the equipment is to be used in the South African civil and military air control system" and explained that "integration of the operation of national air traffic control systems is standard practice in most countries." Furthermore, when conclusive proof was provided of a South African military officer being trained by Plessey to operate the system, Lord Carrington explained, "I do not regard the presence of the SADF personnel [in the UK] as having constituted a breach of the government's policy of non-collaboration with the South African government on military matters since they were here as part of a private arrangement directly between the company and their customers."[23]

The AR-3D radar was finally integrated into the overall South African air control and command system by 1982. This system facilitates attack missions by South African Air Force jet fighters, with targets predetermined and programmed into a computer. The AR-3D radar also enables computerized interception of aircraft movements in the region, both automatically and manually; and it is not inconceivable that this type of equipment could be used to disrupt an aircraft's navigational systems. This capability suggests the possible cause of the mysterious air crash which took the life of Mozambican President Samora Machel. At the very least, there is no doubt that South African radar operators saw the presidential plane stray from its flight path as this equipment enables them to monitor flights throughout the region. Why no radio interception or warning was issued remains a mystery.

A major Marconi contract with South Africa for the supply of a tropospheric long-range communications system came to light in 1975 as a result of the refusal by one of its engineers, Mr. Jock Hall, to work on the project. He was suspended and ultimately left the company, but the system was still exported directly to the South African Defense Department.[24] There was another revelation involving Marconi in 1983, which again involved radar equipment licensed for export to South Africa. The British government explained to the House of Commons that the license was granted on the grounds that "it is for use in air traffic control in South Africa and involves no infringement of the UN arms embargo." A Marconi spokesman said, "We are updating the existing S247 surveillance radar system which we installed in the 1960s." The *Jane's Weapons System Yearbook* describes the S247 as a "high-power static radar system used for defence purposes."[25]

A major problem with most of these sales is that Britain and several other Western countries refuse to disclose, even to their own parliaments, details of licenses granted for the export of listed items to South Africa. Because of this secrecy, the facts become known only if there is some unexpected disclosure, and so there is no way of knowing how many such sales are negotiated. A wide range of external military and security collaboration with South Africa also is not covered by the existing embargo.[26]

The 1982 Defence White Paper in South Africa stated that due to the over-production of arms in the world and the difficulty of penetrating "this highly competitive market," Armscor relied "mainly on the fact that the products available from the RSA are operationally evaluated and tested and the highest quality standards are maintained throughout." Its subsequent campaign of advertising in overseas defense publications was launched under the slogan "Born of necessity. Tested under fire."

In September 1982, Armscor invited foreign news correspondents to a champagne breakfast to announce the launch of the G6 artillery vehicle, with the G5 155 mm gun mounted on a mobile six-wheel chassis. Armscor marketing officials claimed it to be a "world beater" since the self-propelled G6 had speed and mobility not normally associated with heavy artillery, which is usually pulled on trailers or mounted on tanks.[27]

Armscor announced that its arms exports for the previous year amounted to R 10 million but that it intended to raise this figure to between R 100 million and R 150 million per year. A senior official identified the sales target areas as those countries with similar conditions to South Africa in South America, the Middle East, the Far East and Africa.[28] Earlier reports that South Africa had made an agreement to supply Morocco with Eland armored cars were confirmed in the *Military Balance 1981–82*, published by the International Institute for Strategic Studies in London, which stated that delivery of the armored cars had been due in 1980.

Despite all the secrecy surrounding South Africa's arms exports, it is not too difficult to identify some of its major customers. Israel has, over the years, developed a close military relationship with Pretoria; several of its weapons have been sold to South Africa and some have been made there. There are several joint weapons production schemes, and Israel is obviously an important customer, as well as a transit point for exports to other countries. Several fellow-pariah nations, including Taiwan, Chile and Paraguay, have decorated Armscor officials and

South African military officers, evidence that these countries constitute some of its main customers.

During Britain's war over the Falkland Islands there were widespread reports of arms and ammunition from South Africa being airlifted to Argentina. Relying on Armscor sources, one newspaper claimed that the South African frequency-hopping radio devices "amazed British soldiers who captured them from the Argentines."[29]

During 1987 there were extensive reports about South African weapons being obtained for the US-supported contras fighting against the Nicaraguan government. During the revelations of the Iran-Contra scandal further reports suggested that Iran had also obtained arms of South African origin.

In October 1982, Armscor managed to display some of its products at the Defendory Expo '82 held in Piraeus, Greece. When after the second day of the exhibition the Greek government was informed of its inclusion, the exhibits were removed and the Armscor delegation was expelled from the country. How Armscor managed to gain entry to the exhibition is still not clear. But its chairman, who was also expelled, was reported to be expecting "good business" despite the premature closing of the exhibit. He added that "it was especially satisfying that our first international show took place in a NATO [North Atlantic Treaty Organization] country."[30] Among those items on exhibit were the newly announced frequency-hopping radio devices, the G5 155 mm howitzer and the Kukri artillery rocket, as well as videos and slide shows of the G6 and the Valkiri air-to-air missile.[31]

During 1983 and 1984, several Western defense publications carried major feature articles, applauding South African-made military equipment and helping Pretoria to promote its arms exports. They, naturally, also carried expensive Armscor advertisements as part of the overall export drive.[32]

The South African Samil line of military vehicles and trailers are in fact a mix of several overseas models, owing their origin mainly to the Magirus-Deutz and Unimogs of the Federal Republic of Germany. The four-ton Unimog chassis is also the basis for the Valkiri 127 mm rocket launcher.

The Valkiri artillery rocket system, claimed to be indigenously developed, is similar to the Taiwanese Working Bee–6 system. The "indigenously" developed Skorpioen antiship missile was originally the name under which the South African Navy deployed the Israeli Gabriel 11 missiles, which are similar to the Taiwanese Hsiung-Feng naval weapons. The similarities between several weapons systems claimed to be "indigenously" developed by South Africa, Israel and Taiwan indicate the existence of high-level cooperation between them on several projects.

The Kukri air-to-air missile which the South African government claims to be "indigenously" developed is said to have a unique helmet-mounted sight for target designation but is otherwise similar to the Matra Magic missile and uses similar technology. The Kukri is also described as the V3B air-to-air missile.

That both South African and Taiwanese missile boats are versions of the Israeli Reshef fast-attack craft further points to cooperation between these governments.

The production of the well-publicized G5 155 mm howitzer was first announced by P. W. Botha in April 1979 when he claimed that it was South African designed and made from local steel with South African know-how. This was considered a "remarkable" achievement for Armscor which had "taken only 24 months from the design to the production stage." Subsequently it became known that the gun was in fact acquired from the Vermont-based Space Research Corporation. The elaborate smuggling operations involved South Africa purchasing shares in the company, as well as having the system tested in Antigua before arranging for the smuggling of the equipment, including thousands of shells, to South Africa. Because of the ease and speed with which much of the equipment was exported by the United States and other intermediaries, there were several investigations about possible official complicity in these sales. According to one report issued in Washington by the House of Representatives Subcommittee on Africa, there must have been high-level involvement in bending the rules on the part of the State Department, the US Army and the CIA to enable South Africa to acquire the system.[33]

In an interview in 1984, the chairman of Armscor, Commandant Piet Marais, disclosed details about the Space Research sale and explained that it arose in the aftermath of the South African invasion of Angola in 1975 when they were "being outgunned by quite a few Russian weapons." It is not known to what extent the G5 has been used in operations by the South African military forces, and some experts claim that it is not a system of great value to the SADF. The G6 was only a prototype and estimated to cost over US $1.3 million, for the mobile vehicle alone *without* the gun.

The South African Eland armored vehicles (based on the French Panhard AML 60/90) and the Ratel combat vehicle (similar to the French Berliet VXB-170 but believed to be based on West German automotive parts) also form part of the export drive.

In March 1984, the South African media reported Armscor's participation in the Fida '84 international military show in Santiago at the invitation of the Chilean Air Force. Following its ejection from the Greek exhibition in 1982 and its failure to participate in any other international exhibitions since then, the Armscor officials were jubilant and said that in "contrast" with their Greek experience "our reception has been excellent."[34] This is not surprising since South African–Chilean relations are at a high military level; the former South African ambassador to Chile, Lieutenant General J. R. Dutton, was replaced in 1984 with the retired chief of the air force, Lieutenant General A. M. Muller.

It is important to recognize that with the end of the Rhodesian war South Africa lost its most lucrative arms market. At almost the same time the SADF had to reduce its percentage of arms purchases due to increasing operational costs. Thus, not only were there increasing overhead costs to be met by reduced sales but new plants which needed more funds. For example, in 1982 a R 176-million expansion of Pretoria Metal Pressings, one of Armscor's three munitions companies, was completed; and these and other capital costs could not possibly be recovered from an expansion of arms exports. The efforts to penetrate the international market since 1982 have not produced any significant results and consequently investment in new production facilities have virtually come to a halt. Short production runs inevitably result in very high costs, and when the items produced have in turn to be offered at low prices, in order to compete on the international market, Armscor is forced to bear massive losses.

The South African arms industry is facing an extremely serious crisis and to continue to produce at the existing level, let alone expand any of its facilities, an increasing proportion of very scarce resources will have to be allocated to it.

In the confrontation that is building up in the region, the Pretoria regime is becoming very anxious about the improved ability of several neighboring states to protect themselves militarily. For over two years, senior South African officers have been warning that Angola, Mozambique and other states in the region have improved their defenses, and are now equipped with modern MiG jet fighters and early warning radar systems.[35]

Toward the end of 1985 these concerns became so acute that South African defense publications printed lengthy reports on the relative force strengths of neighboring states and military officers began to give special briefings on the subject. In November 1985, one Western defense publication reported warnings by South African military experts "that a sophisticated radar network has been installed by the front-line African states capable of monitoring aircraft movements within South Africa." They were also reported as believing that "missile fighter aircraft in hostile African states may now outnumber the South African Air Force by as much as two to one."[36]

The SADF is clearly in some difficulty. While it may be able to inflict considerable damage to the economies of individual African states through destabilization and acts of aggression, it has long borders with these states and cannot possibly gain any comfort from the prospect of turning them into hostile countries.

According to its own admission, South Africa can no longer count on total air superiority. Shortage of tanks is overcome by concentrating on equipping itself with antitank missiles. Lack of new fighter aircraft means that it relies instead on fitting the existing old ones with new types of missiles. Shortage of naval vessels, submarines and helicopters has for years been addressed by claims that they will soon be manufactured locally. So far, South Africa claims to have produced two types of helicopters which are in fact adaptations of existing ones. Similarly, the new Cheetah fighter aircraft is the old Mirage, modernized with assistance from Israel. In November 1986, the World Campaign also established that Israel had provided South Africa with two converted Boeing in-flight refuelling aircraft, which enable the Mirages to have an extended range as far as Tanzania.

The South African authorities have anticipated that they will be unable to maintain the white power structure by themselves and have made strenuous efforts to secure formal treaties with the major Western powers so as to guarantee direct external military support at times of crisis. In order to forge a closer alliance with the West, Pretoria has always emphasized the "strategic" importance of the Cape Sea Route and even offered the use of the Simonstown Naval Base to Nato.

South Africa entered into a formal defense agreement with Britain in 1955 in the form of the Simonstown Naval Agreement, which was based on an exchange of letters between the two countries. Twenty years later, Britain was forced to abrogate it as a result of domestic and international anti-apartheid pressure. The agreement has been used not only to facilitate extensive naval cooperation but also to supply a wide range of military equipment to South Africa on the grounds that there was a legal obligation to do so under the Simonstown agreement. Under this guise, the Heath government even wanted to supply helicopters during the early 1970s and this almost led to the breakup of the Commonwealth at the Singapore summit in 1971.

South Africa wanted something more than the Simonstown agreement and, during the late 1960s, set about preparing for a hemispheric pact to include not only countries across the South Atlantic but also Australia and New Zealand to cover the Indian Ocean. South African ministers visited various South American countries and developed close military links with Argentina. The South African press began to speculate about the establishment of a South Atlantic Treaty Organization (SATO).[37]

The 1969 Defence White Paper states: "The considerable harbour and repair facilities at Simonstown and elsewhere in our country, as well as the modern communication and control facilities, all provided at great expense, are indispensable to Allied naval forces in the Southern Atlantic and Indian Ocean areas." It then disclosed that a worldwide communication network was to be constructed to enable South Africa's maritime command to keep in touch with any ship or aircraft operating between Australia and South America. This project, together with the new tidal basin and submarine base at Simonstown, involved enormous expenditure, all aimed at making South Africa a more attractive ally.

The Advokaat military communications system was inaugurated in March 1973. It was built at a cost of over R 15 million by West German companies, with components obtained from a number of Western countries.[38] At that time it was reported that it had substations in Walvis Bay in Namibia and was directly linked by "permanent channels" with the Royal Navy in Whitehall and the US Navy base at San Juan in Puerto Rico.[39]

The British Anti-Apartheid Movement submitted several documents to the UN Security Council in 1975 which revealed details about the construction of the Advokaat system with the use of official Nato Codification System for Spares and Equipment. In the face of conclusive evidence that South Africa had been provided with the Nato system, it was claimed that this did not amount to military collaboration with the Pretoria regime.

Australia apparently stopped using the Advokaat system by early 1975 and South African press reports complained openly about this. Pretoria thereafter claimed that its system extended only to the Bay of Bengal in the Indian Ocean.

Whenever Nato officials and members have been asked about links with Pretoria, the standard answer has always been that South Africa is outside the Nato area and therefore there is no question of military relationship. However, by 1973, Nato had authorized the Supreme Allied Commander Atlantic (SACLANT) to undertake special studies for operations outside the Nato area, especially covering "the sea lanes for petroleum or other vital supplies."[40] The British parliament was told in November 1974 that "studies have been made, but there is no commitment on the part of NATO members to engage collectively or individually in activities outside the NATO area."[41]

It is interesting that the Advokaat system, which became operational in 1973, covers the northern point of the South Atlantic where the Nato area ends—the Tropic of Cancer. Because of the extensive operational area of the system, South Africa claims that it acts as the virtual nerve center for Western defense in that part of the Southern Hemisphere.[42]

In November 1975 the chairman of the Nato Military Committee, Admiral Sir Peter Hill-Norton, suggested that three or four Nato members could combine with a group outside the alliance to monitor what was going on in the Indian Ocean and in this way a Nato "area of interest" could be established, in addition to Europe.[43] One month earlier, in October 1975, the West German representative on the Nato Military Committee, Lieutenant General Gunther Rall, was forced to resign by the Bonn Government when the ANC disclosed that he had visited various atomic and military installations in South Africa during 1974, under an assumed name.

One issue on which repeated assurances have been sought from Nato is the question of whether meetings occurred with South African officials. When its secretary general refused to give clear assurances, the British Anti-Apartheid Movement took up the matter. As a result, Nato Secretary General Luns wrote to the Anti-Apartheid Movement on 9 June 1976: "There are no contacts between members of the International Staff of the Alliance with the Republic of South Africa." However, the World Campaign established that Dr. Luns himself met secretly with the foreign minister, Roelof "Pik" Botha, in Brussels on 14 November 1980. Dr. Luns then informed the World Campaign that this did not amount to a breach of his undertaking since it was a private meeting at his own residence.[44] There was increased anxiety about Nato links with South Africa when it became known that this was in fact the third such meeting between Secretary General Luns and Foreign Minister Botha, all in clear breach of an official written undertaking. The British government explained that the South African foreign minister had met "Dr Luns, not in his official capacity as Secretary-General of Nato, but as a respected and experienced European Statesman."[45]

Several press reports in 1983 once again led to serious concern about the Nato links with South Africa. The commanding officer of the Simonstown Naval Base, Dieter Gerhard, and his wife, Ruth Gerhard, were charged with spying for the Soviet Union. This followed the arrest of Dieter Gerhard by US authorities who handed him over to South Africa. After a secret trial, they were both convicted of high treason in December 1983. Various press reports disclosed that Gerhard had access to highly sensitive Nato information, as well as detailed technical knowledge about the Seacat missile system, the Sea Sparrow surface-to-air missile, and the Selenia fire and weapon control system.[46]

On the basis of reports about the Gerhard case, as well as other substantial evidence, one may conclude that there exists substantial military and security collaboration between South Africa and certain major Nato powers, as well as with Nato itself. However, despite these and other links, it has not been possible so far for Pretoria to obtain replacement naval surveillance aircraft for their aging Shackletons. This is due largely to the current strength of international anti-apartheid opinion and the vigilance of committed organizations and individuals.

The overall relationship that exists between the major Western powers and apartheid South Africa raises an important question as to the nature and degree of future external intervention that can be expected on the side of the Pretoria regime—particularly when the survival of the white power system is seriously threatened. There is no doubt that in the growing internal confrontation the number of white casualties will begin to increase, and then both Pretoria and its allies will try to subvert Western public opinion by appealing for support against "terrorist violence." Pretoria will try to mobilize anticommunist sentiment in other countries by suggesting that any victory for African freedom will represent a serious threat to vital Western interests. Whether, and to what extent, this succeeds will depend on many factors, including the way in which the Western media present the situation.

For the Pretoria regime it is almost past the point of no return; it cannot put the clock back. In September 1981, Defense Minister Malan told the white parliament that "the next five years are of vital importance in the history of the Republic of South Africa and our actions in many spheres will be decisive." He explained that he was "not speaking only of the sphere of security, but also of the constitutional, diplomatic and economic spheres," concluding, "I believe that time is an extremely important factor, and I also believe that there is not much time left."[47]

It is abundantly clear that despite the various measures taken by the regime since then to consolidate its power through so-called constitutional reforms, "Rubicon" promises and other maneuvers, none of them have succeeded to date. Virtually all such initiatives have had a boomerang effect and have served instead to mobilize increased resistance on the part of the majority of the population. Armed struggle and nation-wide resistance are now permanent features, processes not easily reversed.

Western bankers and business people have realized that South Africa is no longer safe for their loans and investments and, like many South African white business leaders and others, they are looking to an alternative future and seeking meetings with the ANC.

If the economic and political crisis persists, the regime may decide, instead of making major concessions, to simply put the shutters down and operate as a garrison state with a siege economy. It may respond to various critical developments by resorting to massive military retaliation and the fact that it has nuclear weapon capability makes it extremely dangerous. However, while it is important to correctly assess its military capability, it is also vital not to exaggerate it.

On the basis of past experience it is possible to say that the ability of the Pretoria regime to survive for so long is related in part to the massive political, economic and military support that it has received from its external allies. The future is also dependent on the nature and degree of support that it is able to enlist from its major Western allies.

7

SOUTH AFRICA'S NUCLEAR CAPABILITY
The Apartheid Bomb

There is no longer any doubt about South Africa's nuclear weapon capability. What is not known is the number of devices it has in stock and the precise nature of the weapons.

Most of the two hundred aircraft operated by the South African Air Force can easily deliver nuclear weapons. In addition, it has both ground-to-ground and air-to-ground missiles, and there are even reports that it is working on the deployment of cruise missiles. Thus, it has the means of delivery.

There is a long history of Western nuclear collaboration with South Africa. Under the "Atoms for Peace" program, the United States and South Africa signed a 50-year agreement for nuclear cooperation in 1957. In 1961, South Africa purchased the Safari 1 research reactor from the United States and has received extensive assistance in the nuclear field from that country. But Britain, the Federal Republic of Germany and France are also heavily involved, as is more recently Israel, which has given a new dimension to the growing international concern and anxiety about South Africa's weapon capability.

In 1976 the then president of the South African Atomic Energy Board, Dr. A. J. A. Roux, said, "We can ascribe our degree of advancement today in large measure to the training and the assistance so willingly provided by the USA during the early years of our nuclear programme, when several of the Western world's nuclear nations cooperated in initiating our scientists and engineers into nuclear science . . . even our nuclear philosophy, although unmistakably our own, owes much to the thinking of American nuclear scientists."

All the available evidence confirms that South Africa's nuclear program has been initiated, supported and developed to its present level as a direct result of the ready assistance provided by its Western nuclear partners. It is these nations that bear the full responsibility for the development and manufacture of the apartheid bomb.

Although South Africa may by now have several bombs in its cellar, it is still highly dependent on external sources of know-how, plant, technology and finance in order to proceed with its ambitious nuclear plan. Most of this assistance continues to be provided by the major Western powers in various forms. When challenged by anti-apartheid protests, each one individually insists that its own collaboration with South Africa is "exclusively for peaceful purposes"—a claim persistently made for over 25 years.

It is of the greatest importance to ascertain the nature and scale of all external nuclear collaboration. If all of the evidence could be assembled together, it would help to throw light on the specific current needs of the apartheid regime, indicate more clearly the nature and scale of its nuclear plan, and focus attention upon those companies and countries most directly involved.

However, because of the general secrecy surrounding nuclear relations—and especially those connected with South

Africa—it is impossible to establish *all* the facts. Even a cursory examination of the available information reveals that the Reagan policy of "constructive engagement" has made a substantial contribution to enhancing South Africa's military and nuclear capability. If this process continues, then the major Western powers will enable Pretoria to emerge as a significant, and highly dangerous, nuclear-weapon power.

South Africa is known to have substantial uranium resources. According to the latest official figures, its known "reasonably assured resources" amount to over 313,000 tons while those in occupied Namibia are 135,000 tons, making a total of around 450,000 tons under its control. This is a conservative figure and other more general estimates are much higher, calculating an amount that is double the above figure for South Africa. These calculations relate to uranium recoverable from existing production centers at costs of less than US $130 per kilogram.

In addition, there are substantial quantities of uranium resources which have not been tapped so far. If all the potential uranium-bearing deposits are taken into account, then the estimated *additional* resources amount to a further 1,351,000 tons in South Africa, and just under 200,000 in Namibia—all still considered to be recoverable at costs of less than US $130 per kilogram. Of course, if the calculations are made at higher costs of recovery, then that substantially increases the quantity of uranium resources.

South Africa has been producing uranium for over 30 years. Its current level of production is around six thousand tons per year, having almost doubled since 1977 when it produced 3,360 tons. Most of its production is for long-term contracts with a small quantity being sold on the spot market, making it less vulnerable to short-term price variations.

South Africa is considered to be the Western world's third biggest producer of uranium, after the United States and Canada. However, when one adds Namibia's production of almost four thousand tons to that of South Africa, it makes a total of 10,000 tons under the control of the Pretoria regime, which is close to the 10,300 tons and the 10,500 tons produced by the United States and Canada, respectively.

These figures take on an added significance in the context of the overall Western uranium production capability for 1984, estimated at around 45,000 tons. Of the major consumers the United States alone accounts for over 12,000 tons for its reactor requirements, followed by France (6,700 tons), Japan (5,000 tons), West Germany (2,800 tons), Britain (1,550 tons), Canada (1,500 tons) and Sweden (1,300 tons).

Multinational enterprises based in the United States, Canada, Japan and Western Europe are directly involved in South African and Namibian uranium production and sale. Some of them have a long record of collaboration with the apartheid regime, the most notorious being the British-based Rio Tinto Zinc which manages the Rossing mine in Namibia and has South African, British, Canadian, West German and French shareholders. The fact that South Africa's occupation of Namibia has been declared "illegal" by both the United Nations Security Council and the International Court of Justice has not deterred foreign interests from exploiting Namibian uranium. Indeed, encouraged by the "business-as-usual" policy of their own governments toward Namibia, they have effectively become partners with the apartheid regime in imposing its illegal rule over the Namibian people.

South Africa's role as a major producer of uranium has not only helped to legitimize its illegal occupation of Namibia but has also provided Pretoria with substantial—and much needed—foreign exchange earnings. Moreover, taken together with its huge reserves of uranium, they amount to a formidable advantage in securing extensive Western support for its own nuclear program.

The main governmental research body concerned with nuclear matters is the National Nuclear Research Center, which is based in Pelindaba, not far from Pretoria. Its main facility is the US-supplied Safari 1 research reactor, which began functioning in 1965. Under the general nuclear cooperation agreement with the United States, South Africa has received substantial know-how, training and technical assistance since 1957. This included adequate quantities of enriched uranium for operating the Safari 1 reactor until 1975—when deliveries were suspended in an effort to get South Africa to sign the Nuclear Non-Proliferation Treaty (NPT).

Also at Pelindaba is Safari 2, claimed to have been designed and manufactured by South Africa, which began to function in 1967. Its enriched uranium and other needs were also provided by the United States. These two research reactors enabled South Africa to acquire vital experience for the subsequent development of its nuclear programs.

The Safari 1 reactor, as a result of an agreement between the United States, South Africa and the International Atomic Energy Agency (IAEA), was placed under international safeguards in 1967. The reactor is at present operating on fuel which is manufactured by South Africa itself.

At Pelindaba, a hot-cell complex is being built in order to carry out postirradiation examination of fuel and of materials irradiated in the Safari reactors and the two French power reactors at Koeberg.

Since 1960 South Africa had been working secretly on a uranium enrichment research program, and in 1970 Prime Minister Vorster disclosed that they had developed their own "unique" process for enriching uranium. A year later the Uranium Enrichment Corporation was established to make South Africa an independent manufacturer of nuclear fuel.

No one really believed the South African claim of a "unique" process and very soon evidence was forthcoming of close nuclear collaboration with enterprises in the Federal Republic of Germany. The African National Congress (ANC) of South Africa published several documents and concluded that the enrichment plant was developed with the cooperation of the "State-owned Society for Nuclear Research, Karlsruhe, the State-controlled company STEAG in Essen and with the agreement and active participation of the Federal Government in Bonn."

There were vehement denials from Bonn, and by 1976 there were reports about STEAG's withdrawal of cooperation with South Africa. South African officials admit that their enrichment process is related to the West German "jet nozzle" method but also point out that it owes more to the US vortex-tube concept. With such origins it is certainly not possible to claim that the enrichment process is "unique" to South Africa.

A pilot enrichment plant was established at Valindaba, very close to Pelindaba, and Prime Minister Vorster disclosed its existence in April 1975. The Valindaba plant was expected to begin commercial production by the end of 1987, with a design capacity of three hundred tons of separative work a year, enough to provide 75 tons of 3.25 percent enriched uranium, thus ending the Electricity Supply Commission's (Escom) dependence on foreign enrichment facilities. If it performs according to design, the Valindaba plant will supply enough enriched uranium for three reactors of the Koeberg type. At the current cost on world markets of more than $100 a separative work unit, the plant is expected to save R 20 million a year in foreign exchange, although it may not be economically competitive for export at present because of a world surplus of enrichment capacity.

It is also important to note that South Africa has shown interest in the use of lasers for uranium enrichment and that, among others, Israel is conducting research into this method.

The details about South Africa's uranium enrichment process are secret, and its enrichment plants are not under any bilateral or international safeguards.

South Africa has built a nuclear power plant some 30 kilometers north of Cape Town at Koeberg. France has supplied the two pressurized-water reactors, each able to generate 920 megawatts of electricity. Koeberg 1 was due to become operational at the end of 1982, with Koeberg 2 to follow a year later.

However, on 18 December 1982, a series of four bomb explosions caused extensive damage to the R 1.8 billion nuclear power station. The ANC claimed responsibility for the blasts, in retaliation for the South African military attack on Maseru nine days earlier in which 42 people—South African refugees and Lesotho nationals—were killed.

The Koeberg plant suffered substantial damage with the result that the commissioning of its first reactor was delayed until March 1984. It became fully operational a few months later.

Earlier there was a serious shortage of fuel for the Koeberg reactors due to the suspension of deliveries by the Carter administration in an attempt to induce South Africa to sign the NPT and place all its nuclear facilities under international safeguards operated by the IAEA. South Africa refused to comply with the requirements stipulated by the US Nuclear Non-Proliferation Act of 1978.

In November 1981, the Pretoria regime announced that it had obtained the fuel required for the Koeberg plant. It transpired that deals arranged by South Africa's Escom—via two US-based companies—resulted in enriched fuel belonging to the Swiss nuclear unit Kaiseraugst being delivered to the French company Framatome for fabrication into fuel rods. The 130 tons of uranium fuel originally had been enriched for the Swiss plant at the Tricastin facility in France, where it had been stored until it was delivered to Framatome.

Since Framatome is partly state owned, the French government must have known about the deal but refused to try to block it. When US legislators raised the possibility of taking action against companies which undermined its non-proliferation act, the Reagan administration refused to act, claiming that it had no jurisdiction over commercial activities which take place outside the United States and in any case did not want to take actions which would "produce a deteriorating relationship" with South Africa.

The Koeberg nuclear power plants are the subject of a safeguards agreement entered into between France, South Africa and the IAEA. The plutonium produced by these reactors can in theory be secretly diverted to uninspected facilities for reprocessing so that it can be used for manufacturing a plutonium bomb. However, most experts point to the use of enriched uranium as most likely in constructing the apartheid bomb.

South Africa has obtained considerable benefits from its membership in the IAEA, which it joined in June 1957. Much of its nuclear program, and particularly its exploitation of South African and Namibian uranium resources, has been advanced as a result of the direct and indirect advantages of membership.

As the most advanced member on the African continent, South Africa was accorded an important role within the IAEA and served as a member of the Board of Governors until June 1977. Its growing nuclear weapon capability led to increased pressures from other African and nonaligned members, and, at the IAEA General Conference in New Delhi in 1979, its credentials were rejected.

Representations had been made earlier (by the World Campaign against Military and Nuclear Collaboration with South Africa) to several member states calling for the exclusion of South Africa from the IAEA in view of the potential danger in the substantial benefits obtained from its membership. Although South Africa was prevented from participating in the 1979 conference and has not been allowed to attend any of the subsequent annual conferences, it still retains full membership in the IAEA and continues to enjoy all of the benefits that accrue from it.

The UN General Assembly has adopted numerous resolutions calling for an end to all forms of nuclear collaboration with the apartheid regime, but until recently these did not result in any special initiatives being taken by the IAEA. However, due to increased anti-apartheid pressure and growing concern about South Africa's nuclear weapon capability, some limited measures were taken during the 1980s. The first action by the Board of Governors was taken in September 1981 when it decided to exclude South Africa from participation in the Committee on Assurances of Supply (CAS).

All efforts to exclude South Africa from the IAEA itself have so far not succeeded because of the determined opposition of the Western governments which insist that it remain a full member on the grounds that international bodies should be "universal" and open to all states. It is also claimed that by retaining South Africa's membership the international community is better able to restrain the apartheid regime, which should also be encouraged to sign the NPT and place its unsafeguarded facilities under international inspection.

In May 1982, the World Campaign ascertained that the director of the South African Atomic Energy Board was a member of the Nuclear Energy Action Group on Uranium Exploration Techniques, organized jointly by the IAEA and the Organization for Economic Co-operation and Development (OECD). This was in clear breach of UN resolutions calling for an end to all forms of nuclear collaboration with the apartheid regime. Despite protests, South Africa was not excluded from any symposium on Uranium Exploration Methods organized by the group in Paris from 1–4 June 1982.

Further investigations by the World Campaign revealed that South Africa's membership of the IAEA was of even greater importance to the apartheid regime than was at first expected. The IAEA confirmed that South Africa was a member of several special working groups on uranium. In six groups established jointly by the IAEA and the OECD, South Africa was a member of all six and served as chairman of two. It therefore played a central role within all these groups and was not censured or excluded despite common knowledge of South Africa's illegal occupation of Namibia and the plunder of its uranium resources. Representations made to the relevant authorities in the OECD produced the response that since South Africa became a member of the joint working groups as a result of its membership in the IAEA, all representations should be addressed to the latter organization.

The World Campaign appealed to the IAEA Board of Governors at its June 1982 meeting to remove South Africa from the joint IAEA/OECD Working Groups on Uranium Resources and Exploitation Techniques but no action was taken by the board, which later explained that it needed a decision of the full IAEA General Conference.

On 17 September 1982, a letter was addressed to the General Conference, repeating the request to exclude South Africa from the working groups. The UN Special Committee against Apartheid sent a supporting cable to the IAEA stating that it was "most concerned that [the] South African regime is enabled through these groups to obtain nuclear technology and maintain close relations with nuclear experts from other countries." It called for "immediate action to exclude South Africa from IAEA working groups and joint working groups in which IAEA participates."

Despite these representations no action was taken by the IAEA General Conference in September 1982. It became clear that much more was needed to get the matter even raised within the organization. The World Campaign thereafter worked in close cooperation with African and nonaligned countries, so that by the next General Conference, in 1983, it became impossible to avoid the subject.

Nigeria submitted a resolution on behalf of the Group of 77 States which recalled some of the earlier resolutions of the UN Security Council, demanding that "South Africa [submit] all its nuclear installations and facilities to inspection by the Agency," and calling upon states to "end all nuclear co-operation with the South African regime." It further requested the Board of Governors and the director general to consider implementation of the relevant Security Council resolutions "in what relates to the Agency and especially the request to the Agency to refrain from extending to South Africa any facilities which may assist it in its nuclear plans and in particular the participation of South Africa in the technical Groups of the Agency."

The resolution was adopted on 14 October 1983 with 50 in favor, six against and 19 abstentions. This created a serious problem for the IAEA and its members since the resolution called for action which would be firmly opposed by South Africa and its close friends. The matter was handled in an unusual manner: it was suggested that since most of the working groups were about to complete their task it was not necessary to exclude South Africa from any of them but simply to wait for the groups to stop functioning. The major Western countries claimed that any action to remove South Africa from the groups would be tantamount to restricting its membership rights and privileges, which they would not permit.

A few months after the 1983 General Conference, the South African regime sent a letter to the IAEA, stating that South Africa's nuclear customers "will have to guarantee that the technology, material and equipment will not be used for nuclear explosives, but only for peaceful purposes." It also went on to state that South Africa was prepared to "resume" discussions "on safeguards in respect of its semi-commercial enrichment plant but not its pilot enrichment plant." This response, though limited and without much real substance, confirms that the South Africa regime cannot normally be persuaded to comply with international requirements unless some action is taken against it.

The stalemate that had developed regarding the working groups was reflected in the resolution adopted at the 1984

General Conference which repeated some of the earlier points. However, it made the important new call that all states "stop all purchases of Namibian uranium." The vote this time was 57 in favor, 10 against and 23 abstentions.

By 1985 South Africa still had not been removed from any of the working groups and, as the IAEA itself explained to its General Conference that year, "South Africa, as a member of the Agency, has the right under the Statute to participate in activities open to all Member States, including attendance at meetings."

Meanwhile, as efforts were being made to secure South Africa's exclusion from the various technical and other groups, another development came to light. In the 1982 edition of the uranium "Red Book," published by the OECD and prepared by the joint OECD Nuclear Energy Agency (NEA) and IAEA Working Group on Uranium Resources, there was a special entry for the "Republic of Bophuthatswana," with the South African "Bantustan" described as "a newly independent state in Southern Africa."

This entry apparently went unnoticed for almost two years until the World Campaign protested to the IAEA in October 1983. A request to insert a correction in unsold copies was refused but an assurance was given that the next edition would not contain the "erroneous" entry.

The next edition, published in December 1983, contained a map of southern Africa which had *three* "Bantustans" listed with Lesotho and Swaziland, all five described as "independent states." Once again the matter appears to have gone unnoticed by anyone within the IAEA or the OECD until it was raised by Nigeria at an IAEA board meeting on 8 June 1984. An assurance was given that a correction would be made.

It is not too difficult to ascertain how these illegal entries came to be made. The joint working group responsible for preparing the "Red Book" includes South Africa as a member represented by Dr. P. O. Toens, head of its Atomic Energy

Board (later known as the Nuclear Development Corporation of South Africa [Pty] Limited).

Western governments which insist on retaining South Africa as a full member of the IAEA do not appear to notice how the Pretoria regime stretches the "universality" principle to gain international recognition for its "Bantustans." Even after this is done there is no public protest, let alone censure, about such a gross abuse of membership—not even after attention has been drawn to the specific improper entries.

At the 1985 General Conference, the resolution submitted by Nigeria on behalf of the African Group took matters a few steps further. It repeated some of the earlier demands and made the clauses referring to Namibian uranium more comprehensive. However, two crucial new clauses were added, requesting the IAEA "to exclude South African participation from all expert meetings, panels, conferences, seminars, etc. where such participation could assist South Africa to persist with its exploitation of Namibian uranium," "to stop publishing the entry provided for Namibia by South Africa in the Red Book" and "also to ensure that no reports or information relating to Namibian uranium extraction, production and exports are published without the full consultation of the United Nations Council for Namibia."

This time the resolution was adopted without any votes against, though several Western members abstained. Some of those which had abstained in earlier years now voted in favor but explained that they still had reservations about excluding South Africa from any activities of the IAEA since that would amount to interfering with its membership rights. This shift in voting pattern was due to the fact that it was becoming politically impossible for even the staunchest defenders of South Africa's membership to appear to vote against a resolution setting nuclear policy with the Pretoria regime.

With regard to the "Red Book," it is in future to be prepared not by the working group which includes South Africa but instead by the secretariat of the OECD/NEA and the IAEA. Once again, special arrangements are made to end the role of the working group and make both organizations responsible for the publication rather than exclude South Africa from the group.

The way the South African controversy has been dealt with within the IAEA shows the powerful pressures which prevail: South Africa has not been excluded from any of the several uranium working groups and technical conferences. This situation persists despite the narrowness of the resolutions, none of which, so far has called for the suspension or exclusion of South Africa from membership of the IAEA. All of the working groups of which South Africa was a member have had their activities terminated rather than excluding South Africa.

At the time of the controversy, the IAEA maintained that the working groups were in any case ending and that there was therefore no need to exclude South Africa from any of them. However, the OECD/NEA explained to readers of one of its publications in March 1985: "At this point in time, the sixth Newsletter 'R and D in Uranium Exploration Techniques' should have been issued." It mentioned that the previous one had appeared in January 1984 and continued: "However, during the intervening period, developments of a political nature led to the disruption of the NEA/IAEA joint work in the uranium area."

There is no doubt that membership of the IAEA provides a great benefit for the South African regime and specifically for the development of its nuclear program. Through membership it is invited to take part in all technical meetings and other activities organized by the IAEA and is able to participate in the same way as other member states. Through such links South Africa is able to acquire vital technical and other know-how and to make contacts which are invaluable for its nuclear plans. It is able to recruit experts, not only for employment in South Africa but also to participate in conferences held there.

In a very real sense membership in the IAEA enhances South Africa's all-around nuclear capability—including its capacity to develop and manufacture nuclear weapons.

Contrary to the argument that by retaining South African membership it is possible to restrain its nuclear ambitions, there is no evidence that membership over all the years has had this effect. Besides, the arrangements made for IAEA inspection of the Koeberg nuclear plants arose out of formal agreements made with France, the supplying country. These arrangements can be retained.

Another related argument is that if South Africa is excluded from the IAEA it will not sign the NPT. Despite strong pressures from some of its closest friends, including the United States and Britain, South Africa has persistently refused to accede to the NPT. Repeated calls by the international community, including several resolutions of the IAEA which have demanded that South Africa submit "all its nuclear installations and facilities to inspection by the Agency," have had no effect.

In any case, there is considerable doubt as to what extent would South Africa abide by any international undertaking since it has a unique record of violating most of its international obligations. All moves to try and persuade South Africa to sign the NPT apparently involve continued cooperation with it in the nuclear field. In some cases where such collaboration is increased it is even suggested that it can serve as an inducement for Pretoria to sign the treaty.

At the request of the IAEA General Conference in 1986, the Board of Governors recommended the suspension of South Africa's membership in the 1987 conference. Initially, it appeared that such a resolution would pass with the required two-thirds majority. However, on the first day of the conference, the US delegation informed the media that, on the following day, South Africa would make an offer to sign the NPT. The next morning, P. W. Botha announced that South Africa would consider entering into negotiations to sign the NPT, depending on the outcome of the IAEA conference. Later the same day, the media were told that "the Soviet Union and the United States have found a common ground for the South African problem, and they will not be expelled." There seemed to be little doubt that the Botha statement had been deliberately secured in order to discourage the conference from excluding South Africa; and a decision was postponed until the next General Conference in 1988.

This is not the first time that the Pretoria regime has engaged in maneuvers intended to buy time and give the impression that it is serious about its "peaceful" intentions. The long record of negotiations with IAEA reveals its true intentions. As recently as last year the agency had to break off talks when Pretoria demanded that it should have the right to withdraw from agreements "if supreme interests" were "jeopardized." Such conditions would vitiate any agreement entered into with South Africa.

In terms of its obligations to the work of the IAEA it is important to note that South Africa has, since 1979, refused to make any voluntary contributions to the IAEA's Technical Assistance and Cooperation Fund. Even more significant is the fact that by 1984 its outstanding contributions to the regular budget of the agency amounted to over US $930,000. It made a payment of about half this sum during 1985, aware that its default in meeting contributions would result in increased anti-apartheid pressures during the 1985 IAEA General Conference. Though its default was not raised by any delegate it is an added reason for suspending or excluding South Africa from membership in the IAEA.

This account of South Africa–IAEA relations gives some indication of the powerful role played by South Africa in the nuclear field, largely due to its importance as a producer of uranium—and the controller of Namibian uranium—as well as the general political attachment of the major Western powers to the Pretoria regime. It also illustrates the enormous pressures and vested interests that come into play in favor of South Africa once any anti-apartheid initiatives are taken to reduce or end external nuclear collaboration with the Pretoria regime.

Although the Carter administration attempted to impose certain limitations on sales of nuclear technology to the South African regime, the Reagan administration has reverted to more comprehensive nuclear collaboration with Pretoria.

Early in 1982, the US secretary of commerce, Malcolm Baldridge, stated that the administration would permit the export of some nuclear-related items to South Africa and disclosed that five licenses for specific items had been approved in the past two years, among them: vibration test equipment which can be used to test warheads and ballistic reentry vehicles; the Cyber 170-750 computer which can be used to simulate a nuclear explosion; multichannel analyzers for processing data from cables at a nuclear test site; 95 grams of helium 3, which can be used to manufacture tritium for thermonuclear weapons; and a hydrogen recombiner for the Koeberg nuclear power plant.

In addition, the Commerce Department also intended to permit the sale of a hot isostatic press that can be used for making vital components for nuclear weapons, but this (together with the helium 3) has been held up due to congressional pressure.

In September 1983, the US administration approved a request from seven companies to provide an estimated $50 million worth of technical and maintenance services for the Koeberg plant.

In November 1983, reports were published about US attempts to prevent the smuggling of VAX computers from South Africa to the Soviet Union. Certain items were impounded in the Federal Republic of Germany, and the rest eventually confiscated in Sweden. This advanced computer system was said to be useful for conducting nuclear weapon tests, as well as for tracking cruise missiles. Apparently US agents were able to act in time to prevent the equipment from reaching the Soviet Union but what has not been established is how many such systems have in fact been supplied to South Africa and for what purpose.

The Reagan policy of "constructive engagement" with the apartheid regime has already resulted in substantially increased US nuclear and military collaboration with South Africa. With support emanating from other Western powers, the Pretoria regime is determined to press ahead with its ambitious nuclear program.

On 6 August 1977 it was revealed that the Soviet Union and the United States had confirmed, through satellite pictures, that South Africa had made advanced preparations for an underground nuclear test in the Kalahari Desert. President Carter and several Western European government leaders appealed to Prime Minister Vorster not to proceed with the detonation. No explosion was recorded at that time.

However, two years later, on 22 September 1979, the US Vela reconnaissance satellite detected, in the South Atlantic, a double flash of light, resembling the signals from an atmospheric nuclear explosion. This information was kept secret by the United States until the following month when it was revealed by the ABC television network. The State Department then asserted that it had "no corroborating evidence" to verify the explosion and "no independent evidence" to link it to South Africa.

Because of considerable domestic and international pressure, the White House appointed a special panel of experts, who, after their first meeting, according to the *Washington Post* of 1 January 1980, ruled out almost every other explanation for the event except an atomic explosion. Subsequently, the same panel met again and produced several revised findings, eventually deciding that the evidence was "inconclusive."

Meanwhile, the media reported that, according to the Central Intelligence Agency (CIA), a force of South African naval ships had been conducting a secret exercise at sea on the night of 22 September 1979, at about the same latitude and longitude as the recorded explosion. In addition, a US radio observatory at Arecibo, Puerto Rico, detected a disturbance in the ionosphere, a ripple whose path and velocity could only have been caused by a nuclear explosion.

Moreover, at the Los Alamos Laboratory in New Mexico, scientists were certain that the Vela satellite had accurately recorded a small atomic explosion, about seven kilometers into the atmosphere, over the ocean, on the night of 22 September 1979.

All the available evidence pointed overwhelmingly to the fact that a nuclear explosion had been carried out and most experts allocated the responsibility to South Africa, with some suggesting that it could have been done with Israeli involvement.

If the United States or any other Western power had placed the blame on South Africa, they would have had to reduce or cease their nuclear collaboration with Pretoria and would have been under serious domestic and international pressure to take further action against the apartheid regime. The consequences for South Africa would have been extremely serious; hence the later "indeterminate" findings of the White House panel were very convenient for both Washington and Pretoria.

Nevertheless, the major Western powers, like the rest of the world, in fact believe that South Africa does have nuclear weapons. There is also general consensus about this among international scientists, and some have even suggested that the 22 September explosion could have been a neutron bomb.

There was further anxiety when, in December 1980, a US reconnaissance satellite was reported as having sighted another flash over the South Atlantic, with underwater detectors recording unexplained heat and sound originating from the same point. By February 1981, US intelligence experts once again discounted reports of a possible nuclear explosion and explained that the underwater recordings were probably caused by the descent of a large meteorite. There was an unconfirmed report in late 1987 of a small nuclear test in northern Natal, just south of the Mozambique border. This is in the area of an existing coastal rocket-testing range and suggests the testing of small nuclear warheads.

Even if South Africa had not actually tested any nuclear devices, it is the confirmed judgement of the United States and the other Western powers that Pretoria has nuclear weapon capability. There are thus more than adequate grounds for ceasing all forms of nuclear collaboration with the apartheid regime.

Yet the major Western powers persist in their nuclear collaboration. In particular the Reagan administration has increased its support for the South African nuclear program, a dangerous and puzzling policy given the instability and desperation of the apartheid regime.

This of course enables South Africa to intimidate and blackmail African states in the region to submit to the will of the apartheid regime. In the context of overall Western security it seems unjustifiable that South Africa should provide a nuclear "umbrella" in the Southern Hemisphere. Moreover, the threat of an apartheid bomb can be used to persuade the world, at a future date, not to impose effective sanctions or support the African liberation struggle, for fear that it may provoke a deadly form of retaliation by an increasingly desperate regime.

It is vital that the world understand and appreciate to what extent the South African bomb is intended to ensure the survival of the apartheid system and the grave implications of this for the international community.

8
RISING COST
OF APARTHEID
The Economic Crisis

Contrary to the claims and pretensions of South African business the economy is not and never has been entirely capitalist
in nature nor in the manner it mobilizes and deploys the forces
of production. True enough there is a market economy in
which private property relations predominate. But it is also an
economy dominated by wide-ranging institutionalized barriers
to the right of the black population to sell their labor freely in
the highest market, or to gain access to the world of capital
accumulation, or even the right to own land and other property
freely. These barriers emerged not by accident nor by the spontaneous evolution of the economy; they are the outcome of a
consciously designed socioeconomic system. The objective of
this system has been, and remains, the production of a unique
rate of surplus extraction. Its essential function is to sustain
the costly superstructures of white minority privilege, the high
rate of return on investments, and the commanding power of
capital in the South African economy.[1] It is the cheap labor
system which stands at the heart of the apartheid economy.

The system itself is substantially the product of British colonial policy in the years before the Act of Union in 1910. All subsequent apartheid laws and policies have their roots in this colonial past which continues to give the South African economy its essentially colonialist character. Since 1910, this colonial form has been systemically extended and enforced to the point where today the African worker and the black population are little more than dehumanized objects of labor—unequal and without rights in their relations with capital, and allowed to earn an income barely sufficient to continue to produce and to subsist.

As long as the black population remained subdued or were cowed into accepting their miserable existence, the apartheid economy flourished, at a rate which transformed it into the most advanced on the African continent. It has evolved a substantial industrial base and capacity, technologically advanced and with a supporting infrastructure of banking, finance and a service sector.

The country's economic growth has been accompanied by an extraordinary degree of capital concentration and centralized ownership. Seven large corporations control 80 percent of the shares quoted on the Johannesburg stock exchange. They not only work closely together but have structural links with the parastatal institutions which manage the generation of electricity, the production of iron and steel and oil from coal, the manufacture of arms and military equipment and much else. Indeed South Africa is a "cartel economy," akin to the system created in Germany in the Nazi period. It rests on three pillars—the state, three insurance groups and the Anglo-American Corporation. Their tentacles spread far and wide, with the latter occupying a commanding place in the private sector.[2]

South Africa has been the recipient of vast inflows of foreign capital in the postwar years, amounting to about 20 percent of domestic capital formation, as well as transfers of foreign technology and know-how, all on the basis of a rate of return on capital of around 22 percent a year. This is *three times the average rate in the advanced industrial countries.* The state has played a major role in fashioning the parameters of the country's economic modernization process in close partnership with the cartel of corporations, creating what is in essence an organic unity in pursuit of a high rate of return on capital, on cheap labor, the infusion of foreign investment capital and technology and of imperial dominance of the economies of the southern African region.

However, this burgeoning industrial power, and with it the high-cost privileges of the white minority, have always rested on a narrow colonial-type economic base: the mineral, mining and agriculture sectors and those branches of manufacturing and distributive industries which remain heavily dependent upon an unconstrained supply of cheap black labor. The profitability, and indeed the viability, of the more advanced modernizing sectors of South Africa's economy have been critically dependent upon the intensity and scale of the surplus extraction rate. This in turn depended on the intensity of black labor exploitation so that—as in the gold-mining industry—the volume of profits extracted remained about twice the aggregate wage bill of the mining companies and four times the wage costs of their black work force. In agriculture, the systems of bonded labor relations, hitherto protected by law and now by convention, ensured a similar high rate of surplus extraction.[3]

This describes the dual nature of the South African economy, in which an active internal colonialism produces the resources required for a fast-developing industrial economy. The latter has all the trappings of banking, financial and overblown service sectors, with exceptional living standards for the white minority and a degree of openness which has firmly integrated the economy into the world capitalist market.

Sustaining this dualism in the past decade or more has not been easy, in the face of rising black political consciousness, opposition and struggle, increasing workers' militancy, the collapse of Portuguese colonialism, the pressure for Namibia's independence and the international movement of boycotts and sanctions. All these factors put a new, much higher price tag on sustaining the political status quo and the structures of the apartheid economy.

The regime and capital generally responded to the emerging difficulties and costs in diverse ways. The state's involvement and intervention in the national economy was sharply accelerated. The instruments of coercion and repression were refined and considerably enlarged. The bureaucracy required to manage and administer the ever-increasing body of legislative controls and restrictions on the black population was similarly increased. A specific militarist social formation aimed at securing military self-sufficiency and controlling the southern African region was set in motion, with the armed forces occupying an increasingly political role in directing the state's policies. Out of these essentials, the massive growth of the apartheid state machine emerged from the difficulties of keeping the economic duality in place.

Those difficulties have now reached the point of crisis—the gravest yet in the history of the state. The 1985 state of emergency signified that the dual economy was under severe threat. This threat came from three sources. First of all, the transformation of the black population's alienation into open revolt, including labor strikes, cast doubt on the capacity of the regime to govern. Second, there was a ground swell in favor of international sanctions, and the ban on bank loans was beginning to hurt. Third, and most damaging, was the fact that the costs of managing the apartheid system and sustaining the dual economy were beginning to exceed the surpluses generated by the system. In a word, the raison d'être of the apartheid economy was now in question.

For capital, both domestic and international, South Africa suddenly became a high-risk and high-cost investment. The profit rate slumped. The inflation rate, at 15–16 percent, eroded the real value of assets. And the collapse of the currency suggested a breakdown of confidence on a substantial scale, with large amounts of capital leaving the country. The refusal of foreign banks to extend credit or grant new loans to South Africa was traumatic; it meant that this source of funding to meet the rising costs of apartheid and the wars in southern Africa had been interrupted. With the economy in a deep slump, it became clear that overpowering economic and political forces had combined to produce a comprehensive structural crisis for the apartheid economy, generating schisms of varying significance within capital, the regime and some sections of the white population.

Unmistakably, the totality of the crisis now generates the pressures for what is called political reform within the structures of capital (inside South Africa and among Western corporations). "Reform" has become the magic word for ending the crisis. By definition, "reform" consists of an adjustment of the variables within a given institutional structure, or simply "reform" through changes within the system. In the case of South Africa this would amount to no more than rearranging the furniture of apartheid and opening certain windows to make the system *appear* more equitable, without altering it in any fundamental way. This, quite clearly, is not what the majority of the people and their liberation movement can or will accept. A prairie fire has been ignited and there now exists in South Africa's body politic more inflammable material than the Pretoria regime can extinguish. In this sense, there exists no serious long-term hope for the apartheid economy.

Resting as it has on the narrow base of a traditionally high-profit primary goods sector, the South African economy has expanded through a substantial growth in the country's industrial base. Today this accounts for over 32 percent of the gross domestic product (GDP). Between 1963 and 1981 the industrial sector expanded at an average annual rate of around 7 percent. But the slump in the economy since 1981 has caused a reduction in manufacturing output and thus a sharp increase in unemployment. The primary goods sector—agriculture and mining in the main—has been more or less stable, contributing 20 percent of the GDP since 1963, growing in terms of output by 2.3 percent in the period of 1963-72 and by 0.8 percent between 1973 and 1980. Since then sharp declines have occurred, largely as a result of the drought which caused the 1983 farm output to fall by 20 percent.

The three years prior to 1986 have seen little change in real output in either of these sectors of the economy. But slight growth in the GDP (in real terms) has been due to sharp increases in government spending, associated directly with the rising costs of the Namibian occupation, the armed interventions in southern Africa and the intensified repression within the country. Between 1980 and 1984 state expenditure more than doubled, reaching almost 18 percent of the nominal GDP. The state budget, incurring deficits rising to R 4.3 billion in 1984, has been financed in large part from domestic and foreign borrowings. This deficit is now running at over 4 percent of the GDP, compared to around 2 percent in 1980. While military expenditure is officially put at R 3.7 billion, or 20 percent of the total state expenditure for the 1984-85 financial year, actual expenditure may be considerably larger since much military spending is hidden in what is described as "other current" and capital spendings. Taken with the expenditure on the police force, these total about 40 percent of the state budget, or about R 10 billion. Estimates for the current financial year suggest that these expenditures could rise to R 15 billion. The South African defense/police budget has increased by what some observers calculate as eight hundred percent since the early 1970s.

The substantial decline in real private capital investment in the years since 1980 is reflected in the absorption by the state

Table 8.1

South African economy in crisis

	1982	1983	1984	1985	1986
Value of Gold Exports (US$ billions)	8	8.7	8	6.5	7.5
GNP (US$ billions)	72	72	70	68	51
Value of the Rand (annual average, in US¢)	90	80	60	51	45
Inflation Rate (percent)	14.8	13.2	15.1	16	19
Government Deficit (R billions)	2.4	4.0	4.3	3.9	6.5
Treasury Bill Rate (percent)	15.6	13.4	19.3	23.0	16.5
Foreign Currency Holdings (US$ millions)	485	823	242	310	370
US Bank Claims on South Africa (US$ billions)	2.2	2.8	2.9	2.0	?

Source: South African Reserve Bank and International Monetary Fund.

of a growing share of domestic savings—of which a large part is business profits. Gross fixed investment (in real terms) fell in 1982 by 1.1 percent over the previous year, by a further 8.6 percent in 1983, and by almost 15 percent in 1984. Since then there has been no upward movement in such investments. Gross fixed investment in 1986 was lower than that in 1979 and some one-third below the peak in 1981. Last year witnessed a record increase in the number of insolvencies and business liquidations, reaching almost seven thousand compared to 2,400 in 1980.

Table 8.2
GDP volume change by sector 1963–1984

	1983 R millions at current prices	1963–72	1973–80	1980–83	1983–84
		percent change in volume			
Primary Goods Sector	16,129	2.3	0.8	−14.5	−3
Industrial Sector	26,012	8.9	5.0	− 0.3	−2
Service Sector	39,206	5.6	3.9	6.7	1
GDP at Factor Cost	81,347	5.4	3.6	0.4	−2

Source: South African Reserve Bank, *Quarterly Bulletin.*

The disequilibrium in the economy was compounded by the seemingly confused monetary policy pursued by the authorities. On the one hand the money supply was sharply increased to around 20 percent a year, which is undoubtedly an easy way to fund the state deficit. On the other hand, money market rates of interest were pushed to unprecedented heights of as much as 25 percent in a bid to reduce the high rate of inflation and to force public and private corporations to arrange short- and medium-term loans from foreign banks. Within three years such borrowing totalled at least US $14 billion. International estimates put the figure even higher. The South African authorities also floated long-term bonds in Europe which have raised an average of R 2.9 billion a year since 1977.

South Africa's aggregate debt at the end of 1983 (short-, medium- and long-term) was estimated by the International Monetary Fund (IMF) at $26.8 billion. More recent estimates put this debt at $32 billion, of which about $14 billion is in short-term loans. The ratio of this debt to the GDP is now over 33 percent and to annual exports 115 percent.

One key factor, which contributed to the growing pressures on the economy and to prolonging the slump, has been the shift in the wage-profit relationship following the militant upsurge of the black trade union movement and the passage of legislation which, for the first time, permitted black workers to organize legally. The membership of black trade unions has tripled since 1979 to about nine hundred thousand. The country's industrial relations system, once employer-dominated and arbitrary, has suddenly become the center of agitation and militancy, with wage demands increasingly linked to quasi-political demands. The outcome was that while money wage earnings rose by 15-20 percent a year until 1983, this was immediately offset by consumer price increases of 15-18 percent a year. Between 1980 and 1983, unit labor costs (adjusted for productivity gains) rose annually by 18 percent, while wholesale prices direct from factory rose by 10-12 percent a year. The impact on the level of profits must have been considerable, especially if account is taken of the fact that throughout the 1970s wholesale price increases in South Africa were always ahead of changes in unit labor costs. Manufacturing production slumped in 1985 and 1986 by some 5 percent. The mainstay of the economy remained gold and other metal and mineral mining—the classic base of the apartheid economy.

Another key factor which transformed the recession into a structural crisis was the change in the traditional cushion of

Table 8.3

Gross fixed investment 1983

	1983 R million at current prices	1983 Percent of Total	1981-83 Percent Change in Volume
Private Enterprises	12,780	54.9	+ 8.3
Public Corporations	4,569	19.6	−23.9
Government	5,926	25.5	+ 2.9
Total	23,275	100	− 1.6

Source: South African Reserve Bank, *Quarterly Bulletin.*

flexible black wage earnings, which had hitherto absorbed the shifts and changes in the terms of trade (the relation between prices paid for imports and prices received for exports). This cushion may no longer exist, in view of the wage pressures coming from the black trade unions. Since 1980 the unit value of South Africa exports (export prices) has fallen by 22 percent, whereas import prices have come down by only 11 percent. Since 1979, when the price of gold rose to a peak of US $840 an ounce, the terms of trade have fallen by over 20 percent. The outcome has been a persistent decrease in the exchange rate, not only to maintain the volume of exports but to try to increase it. The exchange rate was brought down in the hope of overcoming the damaging impact of the deteriorating terms of trade on the profitability of exports, especially the export of gold and other minerals. At the same time, imports were sharply reduced. In 1983 imports fell by over 11 percent, in part due to the recession in demand and in part to the efforts of the authorities to enhance the level of import subsitution by producing more goods locally. The depreciation of the rand and the temporary imposition of an import surcharge in 1982 (reimposed in late 1985) on some 60 percent of imports sharply reduced the demand for foreign produce. The balance of payments was kept stable but at heavy cost in terms of domestic inflation (in part the result of the currency devaluation) and growing international indebtedness.

The stability of the balance of payments has thus been largely contrived. In 1981 and 1982, the sharp fall in the price of gold and other mineral prices sent the South Africa current account balance into sharp deficit. This led to a major borrowing from the IMF amounting to $1.2 billion, and others on the international capital market. However, this did not stop the steady outflow of private capital because confidence in the South African political situation and in the value of the rand was eroding as early as 1982, reaching crisis proportions in the first half of 1983. At this point, the capital balance (inflows minus outflows) went into a R

1.3 billion deficit. The situation worsened in 1984. According to IMF statistics, the "errors and omissions" item in the capital balance—an estimate of capital flight out of the country—amounted to $2.09 billion (about R 5.5 billion). In 1985 capital flight is estimated to have been some $1.2 billion. The sudden end to fresh international bank lending to South Africa in 1985 caused a panic leading to what amounted to an almost free fall in the external value of the rand, the closure of the stock exchange and the reimposition of severe exchange controls. The two-tier value of the rand was restored—with one rate for trade/current transactions and the other a depreciated rate for capital transactions—in an effort to prevent further outflows of foreign and domestic private capital.

The third factor contributing to the transformation of the recession into a structural crisis concerns the growing absorption of the country's resources by the state machinery. These resources had to come from somewhere, but they could not come from further exploitation of the black population, which had been pushed to its limits. Nor could the resources come from some miracle increase in black labor productivity since such an outcome depends upon the wholesale dismantling of the structures of apartheid. Finally, recent developments suggest that resources available from international borrowing have now dried up and are unlikely to be resumed for some years to come. Public pressure against bank loans to apartheid has become a major political force in the United States and several countries of Western Europe. Hence, the needed resources can now come only from corporate profits—and from the white minority through a calculated cutback in their privileged living standards. (P. W. Botha actually called for cuts in the salaries of white civil servants, but was firmly rebuffed!)

It is in this context that, for the first time, the major multinational corporations have been forced into an agonizing reassessment of the value of their interests in South Africa and into making a choice as to whether they will continue the risk of remaining committed to the apartheid system. There are at present about three hundred American companies operating in South Africa with an estimated capital stake of $3 billion. In 1985, some 40 companies halted all or a part of their South African operations, or some five times as many as in 1984. In 1986 this rose to 50 and in the first half of 1987 to another 33.

Several American companies are gradually reducing their South African exposure by selling out to South African corporations. British multinational corporate exposure in South Africa is of course extensive. Of the estimated direct foreign investment, amounting to about $25 billion, some 60 percent comes from Britain and other member countries of the European Economic Community (EEC). The latter's trade interests are substantial, and their profit income from South African operations has in the past been a major component of their aggregate income. But even here there are indications that a choice of sorts is under way. A number of British companies have liquidated their holdings in South Africa by selling to South African interests; and most significant has been the sale of the South African interests of Barclays and Standard Chartered Bank, both of which dominated the South African banking scene for well over a century. Whereas, in the past two decades, about a third of the growth in the domestic product was attributed to the operations of foreign capital, this has markedly declined in the past three years to around 10–15 percent.

How choices will ultimately be made now depends upon whether the costs of managing and administering the cheap labor structures of the apartheid economy can be contained, and it is here that some serious doubts exist. The mining of gold and other minerals, as well as farming, has traditionally provided the riches which sustained not only the 20 percent rate of return on capital but also the vast state machinery needed to administer the maze of race laws.

Even in good times the system was expensive. The country maintains the expense of 15 different education departments, one for each of the so-called homelands and several others. The administration of the pass laws, which determined where blacks could live, work and travel, costs over US $150 million a year (almost R 400 million).[4] The budget of the so-called Department of Co-operation and Development, in the ministry that controls black affairs, came to $1.15 billion (or almost R 3 billion) in 1984, which amounts to 10 percent of the total state

Table 8.4

The big investors in apartheid

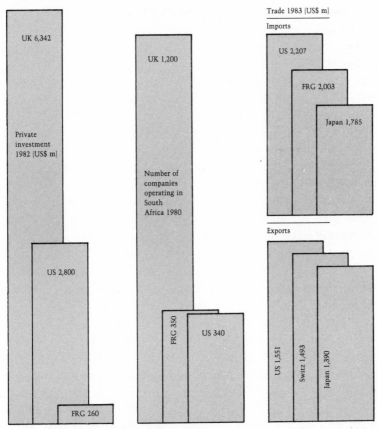

Trade 1983 (US$ m)

Imports

UK 6,342

UK 1,200

US 2,207

FRG 2,003

Japan 1,785

Private
investment
1982 (US$ m)

Number of
companies
operating in
South
Africa 1980

Exports

US 2,800

FRG 350   US 340

FRG 260

US 1,551   Switz 1,493   Japan 1,390

Source: The Guardian, 15 September 1985.
Note: Foreign investment in South Africa in 1982 totalled US $20 billion, of which 54 percent was from Britain and other EEC countries. In the first half of 1983 disinvestment totalled $650 million.

budget. These funds were used largely for the forced removal of thousands of blacks from urban townships to the barren and jobless "homelands." The cost of running these "homelands" reached an estimated $1.1 billion in 1985, nearly 9 percent of the state budget. Another $500 million will be paid out to industrialists for relocating factories in the "homelands." These funds do little more than finance puppet officials and the bureaucracies concerned with controlling the black population. The provision of facilities such as segregated toilets in factories, separate canteens, separate coaches and other segregated railway transport simply adds to the cost.

To this must be added the $1 billion annual military costs of occupying Namibia (although there is some return from mineral exploitation) and waging wars of destabilization against the Frontline states. In addition, vast sums are spent on propaganda to prop up South Africa's increasingly embattled society and win friends abroad.

Into this equation of the rising cost of apartheid must be added the increasingly nonproductive, parasitic profile of white employment. Well over 60 percent of white adults are now directly or indirectly involved in managing the institutions of apartheid—in the police and armed forces, in the various departments of state, in executive and managerial positions of the economic infrastructure, and in other forms of nonproductive employment. As opposition to the regime mounts, this sector of white employment can only become more extensive and, since the distribution of income heavily favors whites, more expensive. Capital will ultimately have to bear these costs without any certainty of social and political stability or a resumption of high rates of return on investment. However, when an Afrikaner millionaire—such as Anton Rupert, owner of the Rembrandt tobacco empire and much else—declares, as he did following P. W. Botha's "Rubicon" speech, that "time has run out for South Africa," he is clearly indicating that capital may no longer be willing to meet the costs of the apartheid system. This fact and its potential implications give a particularly severe twist to the structural character of apartheid's economic crisis.

How far will capital, both domestic and foreign, go toward abandoning the Botha administration? This is certainly the central problem confronting the regime. The regime is aware that its apartheid policies have supported the profit rate and provided a system of security for the cheap wage structures which produced the exceptional economic surpluses that made South Africa such a profitable area for international investment and accumulation. Capital is equally aware that keeping the lid on a revolt by the majority of the population through mounting repression and armed violence not only puts in question that security but undermines the capital accumulation process. For domestic business and international corporations, South Africa certainly remains too important a prize to surrender. Unless driven by overwhelming pressures, they will not easily accept as a solution anything approaching a far-reaching redistribution of wealth, income and power—or which could have a damaging effect on profitability. Despite all the past rhetoric of business about codes of conduct and the need for advances in the relative position of black workers, they do not countenance any basic change in the relative endowments of wealth and economic power between black and white or in the political superstructures required to retrench those endowments. Here a difficult but seemingly necessary set of compromises from capital may be available for barter. These doubtlessly aim at producing elements of reform of the kind defined above—rearranging the furniture of apartheid, making it superficially less abhorrent and less inequitable, and creating a small black middle class which can either control or absorb the tensions inevitable in an otherwise continuing cheap labor economy. As Harry Oppenheimer of the Anglo-American empire declared in a recent interview with *Fortune* magazine, if the ANC "will be willing to think again about the use of violence and about the *rate of change"* (emphasis added), then clearly a deal in favor of stability becomes possible.

The pressure in favor of a specific reform process—which, like the Red Queen in Alice's adventures in *Through the Looking Glass*, would produce all the signs of movement in an otherwise unchanging and entrenched situation[5]—is critically dictated by the requirements of the mining industry in South Africa.

Gold remains of supreme importance to the South African economy. This is the position today as it has been for the past one hundred years. In 1986 the value of gold production amounted to R 17.4 billion and that of all mining activity (gold, silver, diamonds, platinum and base minerals) R 28.9 billion. That latter figure constituted over 25 percent of the GDP and over 75 percent of aggregate exports. Gold alone now accounts for one-half of South Africa's exports. The mining industry absorbs some 700,000 workers, or 14 percent of total nonagricultural employment. Over 90 percent of these workers are black, and over 60 percent are employed on the Witwatersrand–Orange Free State mining complex. Thus, gold production is, and has been, the principal engine of overall economic growth and the dominating force in shaping the dual structures of the apartheid economy, with its unique system of labor mobilization and control. All industrial growth has depended on the continued viability of the gold-mining industry, a fact which has led South African economists to view the economy as taking the shape of an inverted pyramid, with gold and other mining activity supporting the expanding industrial sector and the privileges of the white minority.[6]

The domestic and international significance of gold arises from its very history—as the money-commodity which, by virtue of its scarcity and other properties, instantly commands purchasing power and has for a long period served as the central medium of international monetary settlements. The South African gold fields of the Witwatersrand, Evander, West Wits, Klerksdorp and the Orange Free State—extending in a five hundred kilometer arc—represent the largest known concentration of gold reserves in the world. This is today controlled by a mining cartel of 38 interlocking companies and managed by seven mining houses of which the Anglo-American–De Beers group is by far the most powerful and influential.

With South Africa's gold production running at 650 tons annually in recent years, comprising about 51 percent of world output, the mining industry is very large by any standard. The seven interlocking mining (and finance) houses control 100 percent of the gold output, as well as the output of uranium and several other important minerals. They manage assets of over R 50 billion and employ in gold mining alone some 400,000 workers. From gold mining alone this cartel enjoyed net profits of R 8.3 billion or some three times the wages paid to the 400,000 black workers employed in the industry. No other industry in the world can boast of such a unique profit-wage relationship. This, clearly, is only possible in apartheid South Africa. Few industries in the world can boast of such overwhelming power— in the national economy, in the degree of capital concentration, in the command of labor and in fashioning the institutions of the political, economic and social order. In this fundamental sense, all South African politics since gold was discovered in 1886 have been dominated by gold and by the requirements of the gold-mining industry. The wider question of black labor mobilization is directly associated with this, and so are the economic and political superstructures which it necessitates. The central theme of South Africa's recent history has been the interaction between the gold producers, the flow of capital investments from abroad, and the regime and infrastructure required to mobilize black labor. This is as much true today as it has been over the past one hundred years.

A major problem for South Africa and its mining industry is that the price of gold is largely determined by the outside world. The relationship between domestic cost of production and the externally determined price governs the viability of the industry—and hence the inflow of foreign exchange and foreign capital—and the overall stability of the economy. As long as production costs are constantly minimized in relation to the fixed gold price, the inverted pyramid and the economic base stay in place. Since 1886 this cost-minimizing exercise has led to the mine owners acquiring the right to control the recruitment of labor and to fix the wage rate in a manner that prevented any competition in the market for black labor in general. In time this was institutionalized, with a supporting structure of race laws, in a system of contract labor. The system involved formal controls over the freedom of movement of black workers, concentrating surplus labor in the "reserves," since replaced by "homelands," and imposing on the economy a wage-setting mechanism that deliberately seeks to minimize

Table 8.5
Sources of labor on gold mines, 1951–1982

| | | Foreign Migrants | | | | | Total | | |
Year	South Africans	Les.	Bots.	Swaz.	Moz.	Others*	Foreign Migrants	Grand Total	% For. Migr.
1951	113,092	31,448	12,246	6,322	91,978	31,602	173,596	286,688	61
1961	146,605	49,050	20,216	6,784	100,678	65,012	241,740	388,345	62
1971	86,868	64,056	20,498	5,640	95,430	98,055	283,679	370,547	77
1973	81,375	76,403	20,352	4,826	83,390	112,480	297,451	378,826	79
1975	101,553	75,397	17,440	7,356	91,369	28,731	220,293	321,846	69
1978	204,318	91,278	17,647	8,269	35,234	32,048	184,476	388,794	48
1982	257,954	99,034	18,148	9,422	47,150	16,262	190,016	448,170	42

Source: M. Lipton, *Capitalism and Apartheid* (1985).
*These are mainly Malawians.

mining costs and maximize the surplus generated from gold production.

This system now faces serious difficulties. A sharp downturn in the gold price since 1979 has forced the South African authorities to pay the mining companies for gold produced in a depreciating rand currency. This gives the mines sufficient income but leaves the state to face the problem of declining foreign exchange revenue from sales of gold abroad. A second factor has been the growing wage demands by black mine workers. In 1982, the Chamber of Mines, the mining industry's wage-setting and labor-recruiting cartel, finally extended recognition to the black unions. In 1984, the chamber was confronted with its first legal strike by black miners (the last strike, an illegal one, took place in 1946 and was violently suppressed with the support of the armed forces). The 1984 strike was quickly settled, though not without violence, deaths and police intervention, and a 20 percent wage increase was won. In 1985 another strike was rapidly halted with threats of mass firings and lockouts, though average wage rates were increased by a margin just below that demanded by the black union. In 1987 a challenging strike of over 350,000 black miners, lasting three weeks, was brought to an end after a number of killings and the threat of mass firings. Wage increases led to a rise of about 30 percent in the cost of producing a kilogram of gold between 1983 and mid-1985. In 1983, the average cost was R 7,680 per kilogram; in the first half of 1986 it was R 13,799, despite the increased exploitation of higher grade mining ores.

An important outcome of this pressure on gold-mining profits has been the reduced flow of mining taxation into the state coffers. In 1984 the state received gold-related tax revenue of about R 2.2 billion, amounting to 11.7 percent of total revenue. In 1985 this revenue declined to about R 1.8 billion, or 8.4 percent of total state revenue.

Another factor affecting the mining industry has been the sharp cutback in international investment, as reflected in the

Table 8.6
Gold mining—wage costs and working profits 1983

Number of White Employees	47,083
Number of Black Employees	440,678
White Salaries and Wages (R million)	904.9
Black Salaries and Wages (R million)	1,514.1
Average Annual Cost per White Worker (R)	19,220
Average Annual Cost per Black Worker (R)	3,435
Working Profits of Gold-mining Comapnies (R million)	4,732
Profit: Black Wage Ratio	3.1

Source: South African Chamber of Mines, *Annual Report 1985.*

steady liquidation of foreign holdings of mining stocks and shares until the recent official clampdown on such capital flight. This was done through the imposition of the two-tier exchange rate for the rand and the limitation of payment of dividends on shares held abroad. Finally, the growing international ban on the importation of Kruger rand coins is having a serious effect. Until recently, well over a quarter of the country's gold output was converted into coins for sale abroad as part of a $2 million advertising and sales campaign, crucial for holding up the price of gold in general.

In this situation the mining houses cannot easily consider the ending of the migrant labor system. For them the costs of creating a stabilized labor force, involving the provision of housing and services, would be too onerous to contemplate in the context of the uncertainties mentioned above. The traditional rhetoric about the need for a skilled black labor force rings hollow so long as the companies and the white trade unions maintain a "colour bar" which provides white workers with an implicit monopoly to occupy all the skilled jobs in the industry.

In the past decade several of the major mining houses have sought to extend their investments abroad in wide-ranging primary and secondary activities. Anglo-American has become a major investor in Latin American mines and, through its ownership of shares in the New York commodity house Philbro, has acquired a small but important stake in Salomon Brothers, the powerful New York investment bank. Consolidated Goldfields, through its London arm, has been acquiring shares in mines and other ventures in the United States, Australia and elsewhere. Barlow Rand and Central Mining are similarly expanding abroad. But this expansion has now come up against rising international opposition to business links with South African companies. For example, Salomon Brothers, despite its links with Anglo-American, has ended its banking and capital-raising connections with South Africa. While these pressures are still in their infancy, it is clear that the mining companies are now caught in a double squeeze coming from within and from without. This undoubtedly augurs an escalating crisis for the colonialist base of the apartheid economy.

Shifts and changes in the level of employment are generally associated with swings in the capitalist business cycle and with technological and other structural changes arising from increases in capital-labor ratio in the production process. In South Africa this association manifests itself with a vengeance. The black worker bears virtually the entire burden of each cyclical adjustment, and this burden multiplies as capital searches for lower production costs and labor-saving production systems. Thus the crisis since 1981, first cyclical and then structural, has produced a sharp deterioration in the economic and social conditions of the black working population.

South African economists, even of progressive persuasion, have been discussing the process of "capital restructuring" in the economy following the onset of the recession and the wider crisis of profitability. They see some movement toward both further capital concentration and greater reliance on capital-intensive production processes, and, most remarkably, in the hitherto labor-intensive sectors of white-owned agriculture and mining. These are the sectors which, historically, have been organized along essentially colonialist lines. There is no doubt that there have been some increases in the capital-labor ratio in mining and agricultural production; but there must be some doubt as to whether this transformation toward a capital-intensive primary sector has proceeded to the point where the colonialist character of the South African economic base has been drastically eroded. In mining and farming, as in certain areas of manufacturing, there has never existed the easy option for capital to engage in a systematic trade-off between black labor input and increasing capital investments. Rather, the dependence on cheap black labor has remained crucial since without such a dependence the surpluses required to support the high-cost industrialization process, the privileged standard of living of the white population and much else would be virtually impossible to generate.

It may well be that capital is in a dilemma. Any move toward higher capital investment is an act of confidence—that markets will expand and that profits sizeable enough to repay the capital within a reasonable time scale can be generated. That confidence has been seriously challenged since the onset of the recession and may indeed have collapsed. By contrast, all labor-intensive processes are by nature flexible. Shifts in market demand can be easily absorbed by hiring or firing elements of the labor force. In the latter case, the costs to capital of changes in confidence or of market demand are minimal.

This seems a necessary context for defining what happened to the South African labor market in the period since 1980. The liberalization of trade union regulations in 1979 opened a new period of adjustment in the wage-profit relationship. This was followed by severe recession and a structural crisis (whose causes were of course wider than this factor alone). Hence the crisis may be seen as functional in nature in the critical sense that it was needed in order to produce the counteracting tendencies of high inflation and a sharp increase in black unemployment—that is, counteracting tendencies toward reasserting the cheap wage structure of the apartheid economy. However, where the capital restructuring argument has validity is in the fact that the recession and the crisis have led to a quantum leap in capital concentration and centralization. Huge conglomerates of capital now dominate all key sectors of the economy, with balancing interests and stakes in both the colonialist and the modernizing sectors. This reinforces the traditional inverted pyramid structure of the economy—with giant monopolies now decisively managing the economic duality. Their power has risen sharply and without their support the Botha regime cannot survive.

The regime does not collate statistics on black unemployment nor on unemployment in the unskilled sectors of the economy. Unemployment among the white working population has remained insignificant at no more than 2 percent despite falling output and declining markets. On the other hand, unemployment among the black population has risen to unprecedented heights. Out of a total black population of 27 million, some 9.5 million are what is described as "economically active." According to an IMF report in 1984, "unofficial but highly regarded estimates put the number of black unemployed at between 2½ and 3 million." The *Rand Daily Mail* of 29 October 1984 also used the figure of 3 million. This amounts to an unemployment rate of 30 percent. The South African Research Service (SARS) has estimated that unemployment in the "Bantustans"—in particular the Ciskei, Bophuthatswana, KwaZulu and Gazankulu—has climbed to more than 50 percent.[7] According to an economist with the Johannesburg Consolidated Investment Company, the actual figure for black unemployment in 1987 was 4.5 million (instead of the official 3 million) and could reach 7.8 million by the year

2000 given the likely continuation of the experience over the past years of economic growth averaging only 1 percent a year.[8]

When confronted with these facts, the regime, and business people generally, argue that the trend is for black wage earnings to rise, suggesting something in the nature of a catching-up process. Between 1976 and 1983 monthly earnings in the mining industry rose by 350 percent to an average level of R 304 a month; in manufacturing the monthly earnings rose by as much again to R 385 a month. The gap has been narrowing between black and white earnings although white earnings are still four times higher on average. In the past eight years the cost of living has tripled, however, leaving real wage incomes only marginally higher.

Wage rates may continue to go up as they have since the legalization of black trade unions in 1979, but the rising unemployment also suggests an absolute decline in per capita incomes for the black population and hence in substantial increases in poverty and inequality. According to a paper presented to the Carnegie enquiry in 1985, 93 percent of poverty manifests itself in the "Bantustans" and among African families working on white-owned farms. In the Transkei—the most developed of the "Bantustans"—some 60 percent of families live below subsistence level.[9] A total of 1.4 million people in the "Bantustans" have no income and nearly nine million people (or one-third of the black population) live below the poverty line. The conditions of life in the urban townships are only marginally better. In Soweto, with a population of well over one million, between 20 and 40 percent live below the poverty datum line. Some 85 percent of black workers in gold mining earn wage incomes below the "minimum living level" of R 419 a month as calculated by the Bureau of Market Research of the University of South Africa.

Despite the supposed improvements in black wage rates, the erosion of living standards takes diverse and insidious, though seldom acknowledged, forms. For example, in the "Bantustans," thousands of African farmers have been systematically dispossessed of their land, with the best land being taken over by state and private businesses for commercial agriculture. Significant segments of the population have been—and are being—converted into landless peasants with little or no prospect of employment. Compensation is rarely given for the loss of these lands, and when given is often pocketed by chiefs who work closely with the regime. Next, wages for black workers are negotiated on the basis of changes in the cost of living index. The index is an inflation measure and has little to do with social needs, the burdens placed on the employed by increasing unemployment within families and communities (the "dependency ratio") or from the loss of subsistence earnings resulting from the forced removals program. In these terms it has been estimated that employed workers require annual wage increases of 34–40 percent annually just to maintain existing living standards.

There is no doubt that today the "Bantustans" are key instruments in the hands of the regime and of capital for enforcing the relative poverty of the black population. The concessions made to the urban working class tend to be immediately counterbalanced by a reduction in social conditions of the people living in "Bantustans." Indeed, as a recent study establishes, the "Bantustans" are now the "bulwarks of white domination. . . . [I]ronically, the security and longevity of apartheid lies not so much in the South African police but in the black government appointees" in these "Bantustans." They serve to "fragment black solidarity" and are "concentrations of irrepressible black frustrations."[10]

The black trade union movement has made notable strides since 1979. Today nearly two million workers of all races, or 20 percent of the working population, are unionized (compared to 50 percent in Britain). Despite the fact that there exist on the statute books some 17 laws that can still be used to restrict the freedom of the trade union organizations and harass trade union officials (the most notorious is the Trespass Act), the black unions have become a potent force in securing changes in the wage-profit relationship and in providing a substantial workers' base to the general liberation struggle. In the three years 1982–84 there have been 1,199 strikes and work stoppages. According to a recent report of the National Manpower Commission, 1985 saw 389 strikes involving 240,000 black workers. In 1987 a number of significant strikes took place, among others, in the railways and gold mines, which involved over 500,000 workers. The state of emergency has been employed to detain a large number of trade union officials and to cripple their trade unions. Lockouts and mass dismissals of striking workers have become a feature of business policy as became evident in the mineworkers' strikes of 1985 and 1987.

The further development of the trade union movement remains heavily circumscribed by legal restrictions and constraints on the occupational mobility of workers, the freedom of association and the geographical mobility of workers under the influx regulations. These restrictions have been enjoined by the disparities in education and training, producing virtually insuperable barriers to the movement of black workers into skilled jobs. As table 8.7 shows, there was no dramatic change in the racial and occupational composition of employment between 1970 and 1980. Apart from the legal impediments, there persists a range of informal and social conventions which also entrench the concentration of black labor in the most menial and unskilled jobs. It has been suggested that with the general elevation of the white worker into the managerial classes and into the burgeoning bureaucracies of the apartheid system, the resulting shortage of skilled workers opens new opportunities for black workers to rise up the ladder of skilled jobs. However, what in fact appears to be happening in the manufacturing industry is the diminishing need for skilled workers in the labor process, thus producing built-in barriers to black advancement.

Table 8.7

Composition of the labor force in 1970 and 1980

	Percent of total	
	1970	1980
Skilled Workers		
White	68.3	59.7
Black	21.1	28.5
Administrative and Management		
White	94.1	91.7
Black	1.7	2.9
Semi-skilled		
White	72.9	61.0
Black	15.9	24.2
Unskilled		
White	8.5	10.5
Black	79.7	77.2

Source: South African Central Statistical Services, *Bulletin of Statistics.*

The structural crisis of the 1980s has spawned considerable debate on whether South Africa's apartheid laws and structures have now emerged as major constraints on the evolution of a liberal "capitalism" and to further economic growth. The industrialists and businessmen who met Oliver Tambo, president of the African National Congress (ANC) of South Africa, in Lusaka in September 1985 undoubtedly held to this view. According to press reports at the time, they argued that economic growth and the creation of wealth were now critically necessary for improving the condition of blacks and that this improvement is only possible through the proclaimed "rationalizing" process of the market economy. They see that process as both a necessary and sufficient condition for making the institutions and structures of apartheid increasingly irrelevant. In their view, capitalist industrialization will be a sure factor in dissolving the significance of race in South Africa's economic and political life.

The arguments they used are deceptively simple. Capitalism and free market relations place a premium on economic productivity and the efficient operation of all useable resources. Thus workers are hired solely on the basis of industrial aptitude, management personnel are selected on the basis of managerial efficiency, contracts are awarded to the lowest qualified bidder, industrial opportunities exploited on the basis of entrepreneurial ability, and so on. In this impersonal world, factors such as class origin, family connection, and race become irrelevant. South African economists such as Horowitz, Hutt and O'Dowd hold to this position.[11] It also underlies the current pleading of South African capital to the outside world not to impose sanctions and to assist instead by providing capital, technology and trade which would allow South Africa to cross over from apartheid to nonracist but full-blooded capitalism. Gavin Relly, chairman of the Anglo-American Corporation, presented the philosophy this way:

> Which economic system would best create wealth? Which political system would best secure the stability required *inter alia* to encourage investment both local and foreign? The answer of the ANC to these questions (universal suffrage with a measure of nationalisation of the commanding heights of the economy) would have a devastating effect on the country and subcontinent . . . . Growth will depend on a great number of factors, investment confidence, the availability of capital and the untrammelling of the people to participate fully in a free enterprise society.[12]

This comes from the man who represents the Oppenheimer empire through the Anglo-American–De Beers group—which has absorbed very substantial chunks of the South African economy into its own feudal-type fief. M. C. O'Dowd, also of Anglo-American, has argued that capitalism and apartheid are incompatible and predicted that by the 1980s economic growth would so erode apartheid that a Western-style welfare state would be inevitable outcome. He wrote this in 1965 and we are in the 1980s already.

Some of these positions were considered by Herbert Blumer in a seminal essay published in 1965. He examined a number of countries including his own, the United States, and found that the claim that industrialization dissolves the racial factor was not borne out by the facts. In the southern United States, in South Africa, and in many colonial and former colonial countries, the prevailing pattern of racial alignment and its accompanying codes become firmly fastened to the industrial structure. He concluded that

> the picture presented by industrialization in racially ordered societies is that industrial imperatives accommodate themselves to the racial mould and continue to operate effectively within it. We must look to outside factors (political struggle and international pressure) rather than to the maturation of these imperatives for an explanation of the disintegration of racial mould.[13]

What Blumer does not discuss are the factors which entrench this racial mold; namely how race becomes more than a surrogate of class, given the fact that race is more easily defined and easier to manipulate through the instruments available for propagating the ruling ideology, including education and social policy. This gives the racism of apartheid its distinctive character, and this is why South Africa's industrialization has been built around and within the "racial mould."

Despite this definitive analysis, the debate goes on and in fact has been heightened by the extraordinary nature of the crisis now engulfing the country. A recent book by Merle

Lipton takes up the case of Gavin Relly in what is described as the "dynamics of South African capitalism." Lipton argues that the trend of capitalist opposition to apartheid is accelerating, that the power of the capitalist class has not grown along with their opposition to apartheid, that capitalist dependence on cheap unskilled labor has been declining with the alleged increasing capital-intensive nature of production, and that these, with other factors, have led to the surprising situation where apartheid is sustained not by capital as such, but by politics. This is the political power of what she calls the "oligarchy." In a word, there is no simple correlation between economic and political power in South Africa.[14]

What is absent from this account is a clear recognition that a decisive change has occurred to the relative costs and benefits of apartheid for capital in general, arising not so much from the "dynamics of South African capitalism" but from the challenge to the hegemonic mold in which apartheid has been historically structured. This challenge arises from the transformation of the black majority's alienated mood into active revolt and struggle for liberation; the Namibian people's struggle for independence; and the collapse of the southern African colonial system. The costs of resisting these profound changes have become an exceptional burden on capital itself. This explains the desperate efforts by capital to restore stability through "reforms" and to prevent the further economic and political isolation of South Africa.

The hopelessness of the apartheid economy is now no longer in question. But its breakup and collapse could well take time and will surely be accompanied by even greater violence and killing. The speeches of P. W. Botha suggest that the capacity of the South African system to undergo fundamental, or even meaningful, changes remains severely limited. Even the exercise of intrasystemic change—rearranging the furniture of apartheid—is proving extremely difficult and complex. The influx controls and the group areas regulations are difficult to abandon, as are the separate and unequal education system and the "Bantustan" structures. What remains of "reform" are a series of cosmetic and irrelevant shifts here and there, such as bringing a few blacks into the largely advisory President's Council and acknowledging a national citizenship for the urban black population. Gavin Relly speaks vaguely about the need to alleviate deprivation and poverty, but fails to define the structural changes required for this: the redistribution of wealth, income and political power for the economic liberation of the black populations.[15]

The people's liberation struggle is sure to escalate. Further, the international pressure for sanctions is certain to be important as an associated force, causing a more acute phase in the crisis of power and the ability of the country's ruling forces to govern. The Western powers have been pushed by public opinion into adopting partial sanctions, which by themselves will have only a limited effect. The termination of new commercial bank loans and the inability of South Africa to borrow from the IMF, however, are serious attacks on the country's financial stability, as is the spreading ban on the import of Kruger rands.

In these ways, the liberation struggle within the country has been widened by the internationalization of the crisis of the apartheid economy, and the West is clearly engaged in a complex and difficult damage-control exercise. Western capital's large-scale stake in apartheid and its trade links are certainly important factors in determining crisis-management policies, and in this respect it is very much on the defensive. If it becomes evident that South Africa is ungovernable, Western capital will be forced into a policy course which, as in Zimbabwe and elsewhere, accepts the new reality while striving to sustain its influence, and strategic and economic interests. At the same time, Western capital is transfixed by other equally crucial and wide-ranging strategic calculations. These concern sustaining the surrogate imperial role of apartheid South Africa in the southern African region, with the aim of transforming the region into an anti-communist bastion—even at the risk of costly military forays by South African armed forces into the Frontline states. But here again the West faces severe problems. The policy of "constructive engagement" with the apartheid regime has thoroughly alienated the entire region's black population, who now view Western capitalism as their enemy. In this respect, the dilemmas facing South African capital as a result of the explosive contradictions within South Africa are compounded by the contradictions and dilemmas implicit in Western policy. At some moment, not far off, these contradictions will have to be resolved and in a significantly new way—the West may have to move toward negotiations with Oliver Tambo and the ANC in much the same way that Britain was forced to negotiate with Robert Mugabe and his colleagues for a settlement in Zimbabwe. This possibility, if not eventuality, is now clearly on the political agenda for South Africa and occupies those minds inside South Africa who manage and benefit from the apartheid economy.

9

POLITICAL
ECONOMIES
IN CONFLICT
SADCC, South Africa
and Sanctions

In the Republic of South Africa, and between it and the independent states of southern Africa and occupied Namibia, the most dramatic forms of conflict are military. However, in South Africa itself, and between it and the southern African region, the major underlying contradictions are economic. These economic contradictions are fundamental and often violently antagonistic. They arose out of the European conquest of southern Africa; and they center today on attempts by the South African regime to sustain and expand white economic supremacy at home and in the region, while the peoples of the independent states of southern Africa, with Namibians and black South Africans, struggle to overcome it.

Clearly not all South African goals or tactics are, at least in any narrow sense, economic. Indeed some have significant economic costs to South Africa. The raids on Botswana and the political blockade of customs negotiations would appear to be counter to Pretoria's economic interests. Similarly, not all military-political tactics are pursued for solely security or power reasons; sabotage, especially in respect to transport, is an integral tool of South Africa's regional economic policy.[1] Nor are all the tools used to preserve political-economic hegemony necessarily violent. The customs union, export credits and discount rates on rail traffic are in any normal sense nonviolent; but they are all instruments used to maintain an exploitative regional economic supremacy and this by its nature inevitably leads to violence.

The separation of South African political-economic goals, strategies and tactics from those more narrowly related to security and power is, therefore, somewhat artificial, even at an analytical level. As the above discussions of each country have demonstrated, South African regional policy is based on a "total strategy" aimed at what is perceived by the South African regime as a "total threat" to its basic interests—and ultimately to its survival. However, it is useful to look more specifically at political-economic aims and instruments, both to understand a central element in the regional struggle and to underline the fact that the conflict in southern Africa is not merely a tale of random, episodic violence. The present economic relationship between South Africa and the independent southern African states is sustained and sustainable only by the threat and reality of quite overt economic and military violence. South Africa's economic relations with its neighbors, so long as it retains the apartheid system, cannot be basically complementary nor mutually beneficial. At best, the "partnership" South Africa seeks is that which Lord Malvern described as existing in the Federation of Rhodesia and Nyasaland: a white rider on a black horse.

South Africa's basic objectives in the region are economic, political and security hegemony. The three interlock and are mutually reinforcing, even if they conflict in any one case.

Economic hegemony is important because it pays. South Africa's economic growth in the 1970s was relatively modest, under 4 percent annually. In the 1980s it has been even lower. The most dynamic element was exports to independent southern African states, which accounted for as much as a quarter of total growth.[2] Further, the South African economy is constrained by its domestic market and by foreign exchange. The relatively small home market is more restricted for many products than its size would suggest because of apartheid's impact on black incomes and, therefore, purchasing power. Consequently, export expansion is critical to sustained growth and profitability, particularly in manufacturing. Furthermore, while South Africa has a relatively internally integrated economy (remarkably so for a country of its economic size and level of development), it is crucially dependent on imports of fuel, certain capital goods and a number of intermediate inputs. The demand for these imports tends to grow more rapidly than overall output.[3] Therefore, rapid export growth is necessary to avoid crippling import capacity constraints. Despite its diversified raw materials and traditional gold export base, South Africa can sustain the needed rate of export growth only if it can build a dynamic export sector in manufactured goods. The most logical markets for many products—due to lack of domestic alternatives as well as physical and institutional proximity—are in the independent states of southern Africa.

Regional economic predominance is perceived by the current South African regime (as it was by its Afrikaner republican and British colonial predecessors) as far too important to leave to market forces, let alone to free market forces. This economic predominance is the result of systematic, selective state and enterprise policies in transport, fiscal matters, enterprise structuring, investment, and provision of personnel and knowledge.[4] Present

South African state and enterprise regional policy is in large measure directed toward consolidating, protecting and expanding that pattern of economic predominance and dependence.[5]

Security hegemony interacts with economic hegemony, which reinforces South African security because it renders attempts to effective liberation in any sphere difficult. This is especially true in respect to transport, where denial of access to South African routes could at present throttle the economies and state apparatus of Lesotho, Botswana, Swaziland, Zimbabwe, Malawi and, probably, Zambia. However, it is also the case in respect to revenue for customs union members and to import sources and export markets (including that for labor). All these dependencies could be reduced, but their multiple existence allows South Africa to impose high initial costs in sectors of its choice. It is a deliberate and serious act when Pretoria brandishes the threat of economic sanctions against its neighbors in an attempt to defuse the growing international trend toward sanctions against itself. Those economies would be much weakened by forced, instant disengagement by and from South Africa.

Equally, however, violence by South African "security" forces and their proxies is critical to the maintenance of economic hegemony. Dominance in the key transport sector is neither geographically nor economically natural. Ultimately, it can be ensured only by action to keep other southern African routes wholly or partially nonfunctional.[6]

Both the Southern African Development Coordination Conference (SADCC) and South Africa perceive transport as vital. For SADCC countries—Angola, Botswana, Lesotho, Malawi, Mozambique, Swaziland, Tanzania, Zambia, and Zimbabwe—transport is the key to liberation; to South Africa, it is a tool for continued domination.[7] South Africa has used sustained violence, as well as direct economic means, to ensure that the transport links to Lobito Bay, Maputo, Beira and Nacala have been intermittently available, limited in capacity, or closed entirely. The war on the Beira-Zimbabwe transport links, for example, is a war about economics as much as politics.

Political dominance is also linked to economic hegemony in a two-way relationship—at least in the sense of ensuring that independent states do not seriously pursue economic liberation, successfully mobilize international pressures on Pretoria, or provide effective external support to the South African liberation struggle.

Since economic disengagement is costly in the short term, it can only be carried out by a government with a clear political program. South Africa's strategy—using whatever means possible from economic incentives through sabotage deterrents—is to ensure that such programs are not pursued on a sustained basis. Thus, influential groups in neighboring countries must be convinced that disengagement from South Africa is not in their interests, so that such programs will lack a firm national base and may even cease to be canvassed seriously.

Economic power can also be used as a weapon for influencing other political programs. Economic pressures, as well as terror raids, can be applied against those who support the South African liberation struggle or mobilize external pressures on South Africa. Lesotho's *coup d'état* in January 1986 is a case in point. Conversely, acceptance of South African consent, or mild disapproval, as a binding constraint on political programs would guarantee that these did not threaten South Africa's regional economic interests. The seminal consultancy study in South Africa by Deon Geldenhuys, outlining the uses and tactics of economic destabilization, related primarily to limiting political projects of independent states and not to the defense of economic interests as such.[8]

This relationship between politics and economics presumably underlies South Africa's vehement, and often violent, antipathy to SADCC and passive attitude toward the Preferential Trade Area (PTA).[9] SADCC is overtly political and has an explicit political project of economic disengagement for which it mobilizes external and domestic resources. The PTA is much more technically economic, more market and less state interventionist; perhaps as a result, it is to date far less oriented in any political project of economic liberation than SADCC, even though in 1986 it denounced South Africa and very sketchily advanced the idea of regional trade as a route to disengagement.

South Africa's regional objectives interlock; therefore, it needs a strategic approach to achieving them, not an episodic tackling of one case at a time without regard to the broader picture. South Africa has perceived this requirement. Even if the "total strategy" and "constellation" formulations (South African military, economic and political hegemony over all southern Africa) include a good deal of rhetorical overkill for domestic purposes (and in their fullest presentations seek the impossible), they do constitute operational strategies which may be, to a substantial degree, attainable.[10] They form a framework for particular actions and for gauging their relative success or failure, their strengths and limitations. This fact can be missed because there are at least five strategic elements, and these are not totally consistent in the abstract: economic incentives, economic threats and penalties, a dual outward-looking approach involving a forward or "strike kommando" policy coupled with one of "constellation" or political-economic domination, and an inward-looking laager approach.

The first strategic element is the provision of economic incentives to cooperation. South Africa, and especially, but not only, its business community, has a preference for this approach when it does not perceive its interests to be under severe and immediate threat. One reason for this preference is that the use of force disrupts exports and related profits, while incentives do not. Another reason is that the use of incentives or "carrots"— and of "mutually advantageous" agreements—when successful, gives a degree of consent and stability unlikely to be achieved by either naked economic force or physical violence.

The range of possible incentives is very broad. The Southern African Customs Union (SACU)—whereby railway income, import duty and other related charges are collected jointly and distributed by South Africa to other members (Botswana, Lesotho and Swaziland)—is a major example.[11] So are the various arrangements providing locomotives, wagons (over three thousand in the case of Zambia and six thousand in total) and technical assistance to southern African state railways; and preferential rail rates offered to exporters and importers using South African Transport Services (SATS) railways and ports.[12] Export credit is another "carrot," one which is increasingly effective in the current foreign exchange crisis in most of southern Africa. Even if prices are marked up 20–30 percent to cover the credit cost, 18 months to pay is a major incentive to an importer or central bank with almost no foreign exchange to hand and little or no access to normal commercial credit. Specific, and often transitory, incentives are also numerous, such as the South African market quotas given for television sets and fertilizer made in Swaziland (since effectively withdrawn).

It should not be assumed, however, that the incentive element of the overall strategy is benign. In the first place, benefits to one southern African state may be highly damaging to the economic interests of others—and may increase the difficulty of operating a regional project of political-economic liberation. The customs union, for example, protects South African exports to Botswana, Lesotho and Swaziland from competition from other SADCC states (except for Zimbabwe and Malawi). South African credit facilities greatly hamper Zimbabwean exports to Zambia even when they are substantially lower in cost. The contract rates on external traffic are carefully tailored in an attempt to undercut those of the Mozambican rail and port system.[13]

Further, the appearance of generosity is often either totally false or at the least conceals a radically unequal division of gains. Because SACU payments are effectively made two years in arrears, inflation and import growth fully cancel out the apparent 41 percent revenue bonus. In most years, Botswana, Lesotho and Swaziland would derive more revenue from an independent tariff and excise system than they do from SACU.[14]

However, the barriers to greater domestic production, increased regional trade through SADCC or PTA, and imports from low-cost sources outside Africa, are very real. Even in the short-term, concentrated dependence on South African sources of goods and services entail higher import bills and transportation costs; and in the medium- and long-term, there are significant obstacles to structural change and development. Provision of rolling stock and technical assistance to railways also serves South African interests.[15] This service creates an incentive to, and a body of lobbyists for, using South African routes; and it improves the efficiency of the southern African railways using SATS. As SATS has a surplus of obsolete equipment, the rental fees almost certainly exceed any alternative earnings on the loaned equipment.

These "positive" incentives have always been combined with "negative" aspects, such as penalties and deterrents—the second strategic element. The threat or reality of withdrawal of the incentives is in itself a powerful stick, as shown when SATS withdrew locomotives loaned to Zimbabwe in 1980–81. As with incentives, deterrents vary. Cutting back on the hiring of migrant labor or reducing the terms of transfer of earnings are weapons that have been used against Mozambique and, less systematically, against Lesotho. Selective interruption of the flow of key goods—especially petroleum products, fertilizers and grain—to SADCC states purportedly for "technical" reasons has in fact been linked to political and security demands. All the independent states of southern Africa, except Angola and Tanzania (which do not import or export via South Africa), have been beaten with this stick more than once since the formation of SADCC in 1980.[16] "Technical problems" in relation to moving exports, such as Zimbabwe steel and Botswana beef, are the complement to similar import delays,[17] such as those in late 1986 following the passage of sanctions legislation by the US Congress and the Zimbabwe- and Zambia-led campaign for effective Commonwealth sanctions.

The most dramatic deterrents are specific acts of economic sabotage and the promotion of general insurgency. These have formed the core of the strategy with respect to Angola and have become the dominant element with respect to Mozambique. In Zimbabwe and Lesotho these tactics have been used selectively, and elsewhere in the region they have been used on a more occasional basis. This "outward-looking strategic orientation" runs parallel to incentives and deterrents, and its most dramatic variant is the "strike kommando" policy. This is the third strategic element, typified by the South African raids on Maseru, Maputo, Harare, Lusaka, Livingstone, Mbabane and Gaborone at the single strike level and by repeated invasions of Angola at the level of sustaining advances beyond South Africa's frontiers.

This strategic element makes use of economic sabotage against targets such as bridges, dams, railroads, pipelines, mines and oil installations; and it makes use of general economic destabilization through direct actions by the South African Defense Force (SADF) combined with surrogate activity. Thus the cost of this policy to the target states and their people is very high, in both military and economic terms.

The aims of the "strike kommando" policy are not entirely economic gains sought by South Africa. Indeed, in narrow economic terms it is costly to South Africa; extra military expenditure probably exceeds $2 billion a year; the disuse of the Maputo port escalates freight costs to South African firms; power shortages result from loss of Cahora Bassa power supply, and so on. Only if South Africa's aim in Angola is to install a regime that would resume trade and provide a dependable petroleum supply, do these forward policy tactics there appear to offer specific economic benefits to South Africa. The outward-looking strategy is designed to protect the political economy of apartheid by keeping opponents far from the frontiers and by reducing to rubble the economies and polities of unfriendly neighbors, especially those whose geography provides alternative outlets to the sea and who depend little on South African investment. In that sense, this policy is economic, protecting systemic profitability even at the penalty of particular costs and losses.

The other aspect of the outward-looking approach—the fourth strategic element—is political-economic. This is complete South African regional hegemony, as articulated in P. W. Botha's 1979 Carlton Center presentation of the "constellation plan."[18] This strategy seeks a "co-prosperity sphere," with common economic policies, coordinated security, and at least tacit acceptance of South African political leadership in a region stretching from Zaire through Mozambique and from the Cape to the Ruvuma and Congo rivers. In less ambitious variants, the political element is reduced to demands on neighboring states to prevent mobilization of opposition to Pretoria, and the security aspect to forcing these states to refuse bases, or presence, of South African liberation movements and external armed forces. The economic elements—trade, transport, technical and financial assistance—are then dominant and the number of regional participants flexible, with Botswana, Lesotho, Swaziland, a "multiparty" Namibia, Zambia, Mozambique, Malawi and Zimbabwe as the desired core.

This approach is attractive to the private sector, from the point of view of production, export and profit expansion, but it is not by any means benign and does not confer equal gains. By strengthening economic links with South Africa, it increases the leverage against a political economy of liberation. An example is the 1980–81 threats by Pretoria to end its trade agreement with Zimbabwe. Further, while primarily based on incentives and benefits, this approach can and does make use of threats or penalties to secure specific policy changes by southern African states.

Finally, the fifth strategic element is an inward-looking or "into laager" approach. This element seeks to concentrate South African strength within its borders, behind strong defenses and with minimum dependence on external sources of supply.

South Africa has few critical imports from the region, with the short-term exception of labor for the gold mines. The reduction in use of the port of Maputo, Cahora Bassa power and migrant labor, and the freezing out of certain Swaziland, Botswana and Zimbabwe goods could be viewed as inward looking. On the export side, a comparable strategy of retargetting outside the region does not appear to exist. Indeed, the thrust of the South African Foreign Trade Office (SAFTO) is in quite the opposite direction.[19] However, a strategy highly inward looking in respect to security, political stance and South African imports could also seek to preserve export markets, especially those for transport services, as a means of creating dependency and retaining vital foreign exchange income.

The tactical instruments used to implement South African strategy are numerous and varied, as the presentation of strategic elements suggests. Tactics vary in channels of operation and therefore in degree of coordination and control. For example, the customs union arrangements are government to government, regularly reviewable and instantly terminable. In contrast, existing South African investment in other African countries is historically determined, not speedily (if at all) removable, and owned by private enterprises whose interests may or may not be consistent with Pretoria's overall strategic concerns. An example of the latter point is Anglo-American's stake in Angolan diamond mines which are a target of South

African surrogates. However, because the continued operation of many South African investments is critical to the host economies (such as the diamond mines in Botswana), their continued operation could be put in peril by Pretoria. Thus, existing investment is to some extent a lever the South African regime can use.

New investment is an intermediate case. The South African authorities can directly, via pressure on companies, or indirectly, by creating economic chaos in the potential host country, ensure that such investment does not take place. But it has no power to ensure the reverse unless the investor is a South African state corporation. Private firms will not rush in unless they see a realistic prospect of stable profits, including a continuation of the South African economic tactics which led it to favor the investment. Thus, when Pretoria favored—or appeared to favor—investment in Mozambique after Nkomati, there was a flurry of visits but very little actual investment because the general economic situation was unpromising and because businesses were skeptical of how long the detente might last.

South Africa has used several tactics simultaneously or in sequence in relation to particular countries or sectors, and it has developed multipurpose tactics suitable for furthering several strategic elements. The first point is well illustrated by the transport sector and the second by Renfreight, the South African clearing and forwarding agency dominant in the region.

As stated earlier, the bottom line in blocking the implementation of SADCC's transport policy has always been sabotage. The costs, both financial and to independence, of using the SATS system have been perceived to be so high that most states in the region are firmly committed to SADCC routes to the sea and will not divert their traffic unless forced to do so. The exceptions are Lesotho, which has no overland options, and Swaziland, which benefits from South African transit traffic. From the 1975 blockage of the Benguela railway to Lobito Bay,

Angola, which has never been effectively reopened, through the current defense of the Beira route by Mozambique and Zimbabwe against South Africa's proxy forces, much of the South African violence has centered on transport disruption and blockage.

However, a variety of other tactics have been used, such as the provision and then withdrawal of railway rolling stock. A 1985 development was the use of "fighting rates," or cut-price contracts, designed to offset the advantages of the Mozambican rail and port routes. This tactic can be potent, especially in relation to Zimbabwe.[20] The emergence of "fighting rates" has been facilitated by SATS' increasingly commercial orientation and by the increasing overvaluation of Mozambican meticais and undervaluation of the rand. From late 1985 to late February 1986, as the Mozambican government moved to offer counter rates, the rand rose from US $.35 to US $.46, undercutting the SATS campaign.[21]

Trade promotion also reinforces transport dependence, as imports from South Africa and exports to South Africa must go via SATS routes. Further, SATS insists on relatively balanced traffic, in its own commercial interest. This means, for example, that Zambian imports from or via South Africa lead to effective pressure to balance traffic by rerouting copper exports away from the Tanzanian port of Dar es Salaam to East London.

The last major tactic used in the transport sector is a less evident one: clearing and forwarding. South Africa's two major clearing and forwarding groups, Rennies (a SAF Marine subsidiary, and thus SATS) and Manica Freight Services (an Anglo-American group) have been merged as Renfreight. The new company is controlled by Old Mutual (an insurance company), which has acquired SAF Marine, with a significant minority holding by Anglo-American and additional cross-links via Barclays National. This company dominates not only South African clearing and forwarding but also that of the landlocked SADCC members and of Mozambique. Its links with SAF Marine and its dominance of shipping agencies mean that it directly and indirectly dominates the South African Shipping Conferences which cover Beira and Maputo, as well as South African ports.[22]

Renfreight is a multipurpose instrument. At the simplest level it earns profits and foreign exchange because clearing and forwarding is lucrative. It is also in a position to route freight via SATS (with whom SAF Marine has strong mutual-interest links even if now separately owned) because, in practice, shipping agents have wide latitude in recommending and choosing routes for their clients. Renfreight has every reason to use that position since its associates in SATS—Anglo-American, SAF Marine, Old Mutual and Barclays National—stand to profit from business routed via South Africa, through rail and port charges, insurance, ancillary services, related goods purchases, ship cargoes and so on. In gross terms, these gains are larger than the clearing and forwarding fees themselves. Further, Renfreight prefers to take its profits in rands not in inconvertible regional currencies.[23]

Finally, the internal commercial logic of a regional clearing and forwarding company means that detailed data on cargo by content, bulk and weight, value, source and route must be on a computer in Johannesburg. Effectively, this means it is available, by one means or another, to South African authorities for analysis (of sources and prices to counter with trade credits or data to SAFTO, and of stocks and flows of key commodities) and, when desired, as a means for implementing selective delays and/or sabotage.

As the chapters on individual countries have shown, South Africa does not act in an identical way against all independent southern African states. Dominant strategic elements and tactics differ markedly and are used in different combinations.

In the case of Zambia, the dominant strategic element has been the "co-prosperity sphere," with a systematic campaign since 1965 to build up export trade and transport linkages. This has been notably successful despite Zambia's very real effort to identify alternative sources of imports and to develop intra-SADCC transportation routes.[24] An additional factor is that South Africa has perceived the Zambian president, Kenneth Kaunda, not as sympathetic, but as committed to dialogue. Therefore he is seen as a potentially valuable interlocutor with the leaders of liberation movements and other Frontline states, but also as one who would react very negatively to sustained economic and military aggression.

This is not to overlook a persistent subtheme of more violent actions, such as the campaigns in southwestern Zambia adjacent to Namibia, the training of the Mushala gang, the delays in goods deliveries, in addition to the raids on African National Congress (ANC) offices in Lusaka and on non-ANC camps, offices and houses in Lusaka and Livingstone. These appear to have been designed to warn Zambia of the dangers of more active support for liberation movements, of breaking off dialogue or of failing to develop economic links.

From a South African perspective, the approach has worked rather well. First, Zambia's severe economic and technical problems—flowing primarily from the sanctions imposed on Rhodesia (Zimbabwe) and the collapse of the copper market—have made the government unable and unwilling to incur additional costs. Extended trade credit and massive rolling stock loans are critical to Zambia. Second, South Africa has built up a perception of itself as a relatively fair economic dealer and a competent economic partner in the eyes of elements of the Zambian elite and even of the urban labor force.[25] These perceptions have been critical to its trade and transport campaigns, but have been undermined by the raids and by the restrictions on transit traffic. Zambia is now shifting its trade toward Dar es Salaam and Beira.

A somewhat harder line has been taken by South Africa with respect to Zimbabwe—one constrained by the fact that Zimbabwe is an important export market and investment site. Another constraint is the reality that a prosperous Zimbabwe using Mozambique transport routes and taking SADCC export markets away from South Africa would be a major disaster for both the economic and security aspects of the political economy of apartheid. South Africa has apparently had difficulty in identifying ways to reconcile this dilemma, but the strategy seems to be to exacerbate internal conflict in Zimbabwe, to prevent the use of Mozambican transporation routes and to keep its economy, much more resilient than Zambia's, off balance.

One aspect of South Africa's policy toward both Zambia and Zimbabwe, which is physically external to those states, is the blocking of intra-SADCC transportation routes. In the case of Zambia, this means primarily the Lobito Bay line; and in the case of Zimbabwe, the Beira and Maputo links. Here, too, Zimbabwe's response has posed a dilemma for Pretoria. The Zimbabwe army not only defends the communication routes to Beira and Tete, but acts with the Mozambican armed forces against South Africa's proxies, the Mozambique National Resistance (MNR). Tanzanian soldiers joined the Zimbabweans in this role in 1986, as did Malawian forces which aided the defense of repair crews on the Nacala line.

South Africa's stance in respect to the three small BLS states also varies. With Botswana, it has used the largely "co-prosperity sphere" of economic dependence (markets in, investment in, and mine workers from Botswana matter to South Africa but also keep Botswana dependent). This has been backed by threats in order to deter the government from pursuing any political-economic liberation beyond the verbal level. However, Pretoria has begun to perceive this approach as increasingly unsuccessful. Botswana has rejected advantageous customs union revisions linked to recognizing "Bantustans," turned down water export deals even when this imperilled other desired investments, begun to canvass alternative import sourcing and transportation routing. Botswana has been a driving force in the formation and promotion of SADCC, which is headquartered in Gaborone. Each step has been cautious and limited, but the direction is the same and the impact cumulative. The attacks on Gaborone and the crescendo of threats preceding and following them, represent fairly desperate efforts to force Botswana to reverse its course. As there is no evidence that it has succeeded in that, South Africa is presumably considering what new coercive tactics might be more effective and meanwhile threatening more raids.

Since Swaziland perceives itself as so vulnerable to South African sabotage and economic destabilization, Pretoria's overt strategy has been overwhelmingly one of offering—though often not delivering—incentives. There, South African aggression has been almost wholly against liberation movements and sympathizers, in addition to the sabotage of Swaziland's alternative routes to the sea in Mozambique.

In respect to Lesotho, the South African blockade amounted to the imposition of sanctions, and there have been few incentives other than limiting the market access to Lesotho labor. The bottom line of the proposed water project is that South Africa needs the water and thus will eventually have to support the project. Coercion until 1986 mainly involved raids, both direct and by proxy. These were partly for domestic political consumption, partly out of genuine belief in some quarters that ANC military operations were mounted from Maseru, and partly to remind Lesotho of its vulnerability. The blockade, the most serious form of economic destabilization, was used in spite of the fact the economy is almost entirely South African owned and supplied.

The question arises as to whether South Africa's strategy and tactics for regional hegemony take the form of a seamless web of diabolically Machiavellian (or "Kissingeresque") cunning; a wandering minstrel show lurching from one flurry of crisis management to another; or an inchoate mass of internal contradictions and insoluble conflicts among South African objectives. The answer is probably none of the above alone, but a combination of all of them.

South Africa does have regional interests, which have been defined in fairly stable terms for almost two hundred years, since the early nineteenth century. Regional strategy since 1970 has been intensely ideological and remarkably consistent in objectives—the preservation of apartheid at home and the acquisition of Lebensraum, especially economic and security, throughout the region. However, the balance among strategic elements and tactics has shifted sharply over time with temporary, selective reversals of course overlying a secular trend toward rising levels of violence. The political economy of regional hegemony has been operated pragmatically, responding to perceptions of attainable targets based on changes in domestic and regional, national and international contexts, and adjusted in light of the results.

While a coherent regional policy has emerged from the consistency of objectives, the interests of white South African individuals, subclasses and institutions are not identical, nor are their perceptions of the most effective ways of pursuing them always congruent. Indeed, as demonstrated by the documents captured by Zimbabwean and Mozambican troops who took the MNR central base at Gorongosa in August 1985, there can be quite antagonistic factions within the same institutions. It is worth reviewing some of the divergencies and shifts in balance to gain insight into their underlying causes.

At an individual level, for example, the Gorongosa documents suggest that the hardline militarist advocates of the "strike kommando" approach viewed some politicians as sharing their perceptions while seeing other politicians and some military leaders as having different and antagonistic perceptions. The debate within the armed forces among advocates of the forward strategy, a mixed approach, or an inward-looking approach has been visible for over five years. While apparently emotionally attracted by a "strike kommando" forward policy stance, President Botha has a real concern for direct economic interests and a perception that Portugal's overextension on the colonial periphery led to its collapse at the center. He and his colleagues on the State Security Council (SSC) have developed from their divergent individual opinions a mixed approach, involving the five strategic elements.

Institutions have interests and perceptions which are not necessarily identical to those of the state. SATS, particularly under former General Manager Loubser, is a clear example.[26] The officials of SATS view "transport diplomacy" as a hegemonic tool and the organization itself as a major, quasi-independent actor, which has led to a fairly consistent "co-prosperity sphere" approach. Loaning wagons and rolling stock, setting rates and discounts to get business, and strengthening the role of SAF Marine (then a SATS subsidiary) in regional clearing and forwarding have been among its tactics.

SATS needs traffic, especially for its Eastern Cape ports, and has limited chances of finding this domestically.[27] Thus reasonably functional internal rail services in the independent states funnelling into the SATS network provide the necessary volume of operations. However, perceptions of SATS officials are not wholly based on narrow self-interest, nor are they benign. They see continued regional transport dependence as critical to South Africa's economic and regional dominance and SATS itself as an agent able to work toward those ends with independent African states and institutions that could not or would not readily negotiate or work with the South African government.[28]

They also see provision of rail links and rolling stock in terms of leverage. A decade-long program of constructing the two link lines which make Swaziland a rail corridor from the Transvaal to the Natal ports increases flexibility for SATS in respect to South Africa's own external trade. It is a means of ending South African dependence on the port of Maputo and increasing SATS' ability to compete with Mozambique's transport system for Zimbabwean and Zambian cargo.

Since transport dependence is key to South Africa's regional strategy, undoubtedly any attempts to break from this dependence will be forestalled by the apartheid regime. If Dar es Salaam, Nacala, Beira and Maputo are eventually able to handle the external trade of the core landlocked states of Botswana, Zimbabwe, Zambia and Malawi, then South Africa is likely to step up economic and military harassment of these states.

Subclass interests also differ. The standard conflict is business versus the military, which is an oversimplification. There are three distinguishable capitalist subclasses in South Africa, which broadly correlate with the main white political groupings.

The first can be termed "high capitalism" and encompasses the South African transnational corporations (especially the Anglo-American–De Beers–ex-Barclays National and Rembrandt groups); the large domestic corporate groups (Gencor, Old Mutual); some local subsidiaries or affiliates of transnational groups, with headquarters abroad (Standard Bank, Shell, BP); and certain parastatals (notably SATS, Electricity Supply Commission [Escom] and SAFTO). For this subclass, the bottom line is the preservation of capitalism in South Africa (with apartheid dispensable if necessary to that end) and expansion within the region. Violence and destabilization are perceived as costly and damaging to profitability, though not unacceptable as tactics to attain a "co-prosperity sphere," or "constellation," in the region or to avert socialist revolution at home. Economically, this subclass totally dominates South Africa. Politically—for historic reasons and because its perceived interests are distinctively different from those of most white South Africans—it is surprisingly weak and able to influence state policy only at the margins.[29] It is the "colonial" capitalist class, primarily English-speaking, "liberal" and most often aligned with the Progressive Federalist Party (PFP).

"Middle capitalism" comprises a greater number of firms, ranging from moderately large corporations to efficient family enterprises, and is predominantly Afrikaner in character and culture. This subclass is less able to perceive its capitalist viability as separable from the apartheid state or from South African regional hegemony. Exports are important to many firms in this group (who are SAFTO's main clients), and for some (such as the Kirsch Group founded in Swaziland) regional links go deeper. While broadly in favor of a "co-prosperity sphere," this subclass is less certain of its ability to cope with independent African states or to compete with domestic or other foreign interests in them. Politically, this subclass is National Party (NP), with all of the contradictions which characterize that party.

What the above interests have in common is the promotion of export markets to generate profits, with government support for their expansion. Economic destabilization and sabotage designed to force economic policy changes, though not similar measures related to purely political objectives, can be useful if the pressures are effective, the "sanctioned" state reverses its policy, the destabilization is wound down and the independent state's economy snaps back. Permanent destabilization directed at creating and perpetuating economic chaos as an end in itself (as in Angola and Mozambique) has little attraction for these profit-centered enterprises.

"Petty capitalism" can be typified by the small-town commercial establishments and the small capitalist or large-scale peasant white farmer. Its direct interest in regional economic links is low and its perception of any broader class interest almost equally so. This is numerically the largest, though economically the weakest, of the capitalist subclasses, and its does not perceive itself as able to survive in any context except apartheid. For these "petty capitalists," P. W. Botha's domestic "reforms" are much too radical and far reaching; and the basic aim of their desired regional policy is to combat the *swaart gevaar* (black peril) by force and outside South Africa's borders. They are generally Conservative Party (CP) backers.

That South African strategy is flawed and its tactics not consistently successful—or on occasion counterproductive—is no reason to write it off as insignificant or easy to overcome. Neither is the fact that domestic resistance and regional animosity cannot be cured by "co-prosperity spheres" or "strike kommando" policies, but only through an end to apartheid.

South Africa is much more powerful than the independent states of southern Africa, both economically and militarily; it is willing to use that power to inflict damage on its neighbors and to reward acquiescence. Its identification of its own interests may be flawed and its post-1975, and especially post-1980, strategy largely a series of ad hoc responses to unexpected (but not always unpredictable) external events. But its identification of methods that most inflict costs on SADCC (in terms of human suffering as well as dollars) has been only too accurate. Its ruthlessness in inflicting these costs—especially with respect to transport which both South Africa and SADCC perceive as the backbone of regional political-economic hegemony—is apparently virtually unlimited.

SADCC is the symbol and tangible embodiment of the political economy of southern African liberation. It is a political-economic project of the independent states of the region—Angola, Botswana, Lesotho, Malawi, Mozambique, Swaziland, Tanzania, Zambia and Zimbabwe—perceived by apartheid South Africa as a dangerous enemy of its regional hegemony. If SADCC is able to carry out its programs, especially in transport, it represents a potentially mortal threat to South Africa's political-economic predominance in the region. To assess this program for economic liberation, a more detailed analysis is necessary of SADCC's historical, institutional and operational character.

In 1979 there was hope that Rhodesia (Zimbabwe) would soon be independent under black majority rule. The cost of the war was becoming too high for Rhodesia, and right-wing attempts in both Britain and the United States to recognize the internal "Zimbabwe-Rhodesia" settlement had been forestalled. But the leaders of the Frontline states (Angola, Botswana, Mozambique, Tanzania, Zambia) knew that Zimbabwe's political independence would not mean economic independence. President Seretse Khama of Botswana, who became the first chairman of SADCC, summarized their assessment that "economic dependence has in many ways made our political independence somewhat meaningless." In July 1979, the finance ministers of the Frontline states met in Arusha, Tanzania, to discuss a new type of economic cooperation, which would include independent Zimbabwe, recognizing its geographical and economic centrality in the region.

SADCC was launched in Lusaka on 1 April 1980, a few days before Zimbabwe's independence celebrations. The new group had been expanded in the interim to include Lesotho, Swaziland and Malawi, in order to encompass all the independent states in the region. The African leaders were fully aware of the difficulties of the new venture. Their economies had suffered from the crisis of the international economic system. Terms of trade for their major exports, such as copper, cotton and coffee, had deteriorated by 50 percent in just four years, 1975–1979. Foreign debt had risen to over 30 percent of export earnings for most.[30] They had no illusions that regional coordination could change that global context. Zambia and Mozambique had been victims of economic sabotage when their bridges, rail lines, and irrigation works were bombed by Rhodesia during the Zimbabwe independence talks at Lancaster House. The Frontline leaders realized that a desperate South Africa would use the same tactic.

It was also clear by 1980 that "autonomous" national development projects were not working in the Third World, particularly for low income economies. The Frontline economies were fragmented, dependent on primary commodities and very much tied to their former colonial masters. Botswana, Mozambique and Zambia were dependent on South Africa for regular food supplies, trade and transport. International sanctions against Rhodesia (Zimbabwe) had left the Zimbabwean economy more fully integrated into South Africa's, which provided alternative sources, markets and trade routes. However, the members brought to SADCC experience of multilateral cooperation among their economies. The most innovative example was the Tanzania-Mozambique Permanent Commission of Cooperation, which directly influenced some SADCC provisions, such as production complementarity and countertrade.

In the closing speech of the SADCC summit in Gaborone in July 1984, the late President Samora Machel of Mozambique summarized the nature of the new regional cooperation when he said, "We have built an organization from our own realities and experience and not from patterns imported from abroad."[31] SADCC is a multigovernment organization, not a supranational one, and decisions are made by consensus. Implementation is decentralized as each project is the responsibility of one or more states. Projects are proposed by directly involved states, and agreed to, ordered according to priority, or rejected as regional program elements by all the member states.[32] Consequently, the central bureaucracy is small although technical personnel in the sectoral coordinating units and associated programs number almost one hundred.

The choice of this centralized series of consensual conferences reflects the bitter experiences of Tanzania in the East African Community (EAC), of Zambia and Malawi (before independence) in the Central African Federation (CAF), of Portuguese colonial rule in Africa, and of SACU. The EAC became an entity in itself, almost a fourth state in East Africa. The CAF drained revenue from Zambia and Malawi to expand production in Rhodesia. SACU benefits South Africa, as once "Portugal in Africa" did Portugal.

SADCC is explicitly political, not in the sense of any overall domestic ideological congruity—that could be counterproductive even to try—but in declaring that economic links are not made in a vacuum. Economic conditions and relations in southern Africa had never been left to "market forces." In addition to the bias of the economic unions mentioned above, the colonial states intervened regularly to force labor production from Africans and to limit access of their goods to markets. Lucrative subsidies from the colonial governments went to white farmers and mining companies, while Africans were taxed to the point of malnutrition. Examples abound from each state,[33] but a few from Rhodesia (Zimbabwe) can serve as reminders. The Kyle Dam was built there to aid the sugar industry. The South African Huletts Corporation persuaded the government to finance construction of the dam ($4 million), with the corporation contributing only $600,000.[34] In another example, data from independent Zimbabwe show that white commercial farmers had not been particularly "efficient," with many continuing to farm solely because of the largesse of the state, through price subsidies, extension services, provision of irrigation, and other inputs.[35] As far as their contribution to state revenue, even in 1980 three in four paid no income tax.[36]

SADCC analysts are, therefore, wary of using "apolitical," expert-controlled, cost-benefit analysis, which has been high cost and low benefit to Africans for centuries. Efficiency is a contributing factor but not a sufficient condition for economic growth and in any case can be defined only in relation to specified objectives. Diversity in production, sources and markets, and distribution of goods and services are greater priorities in economies trying to emerge from colonial domination. SADCC's ultimate goal, therefore, is restructuring the southern African economies. The colonial legacy of infrastructure, production and distribution is not acceptable, economically or politically. However, equally important, SADCC has no powers to impose any changes; restructuring will occur only to the extent determined by each government. SADCC's more modest role is to create a new regional economic context for national change—with new infrastructures, agricultural research, shared training facilities, production coordination and intraregional trade expansion. SADCC is equally committed to constructing equitable patterns of regional interaction in order to pursue common interests.

This SADCC analysis clearly complements its first stated goal: to reduce economic dependence on South Africa. This is a practical goal, for even with a free South Africa, dependence would be undesirable. However, this goal is also a political expression of repugnance for a regime and an economy which survives solely by repression of the domestic majority and of its regional neighbors. Again, SADCC is realistic about the difficulty of achieving this goal. First, dependence can be reduced, not eliminated. Second, since SADCC members include Botswana, Lesotho and Swaziland, whose economies are captives of South Africa, and Malawi, whose government has made heavy use of South African project finance and maintains substantial trade links, the economic ability and political will to reduce dependence varies considerably. Despite this, at the Harare annual conference in January 1986, held just days after the South African blockade provoked a coup in Lesotho, the new minister of planning and economic affairs Michael Sefali said Lesotho would "resist any attempts aimed at reducing her to a status of subservience . . . and fully participate in all SADCC programmes."[37]

The objectives of SADCC to increase economic development through regional coordination and to reduce dependence, especially on apartheid South Africa, were not simply left at vague declarations. The steps toward these long-term goals have been small, but many; they have been determined, but practical. SADCC now has over four hundred projects, costing almost

$6 billion, of which half are either completed, implemented or actively under negotiation.[38] Transport is considered the first priority—to refurbish old lines, build new ones, and improve training and operational coordination. For the five landlocked states, Mozambican ports can serve overseas markets, and the Southern African Transport and Communications Commission (SATCC), coordinated by Mozambique, has been praised by the donors. Of 207 projects (over $4 billion), 37 percent are fully financed and another 6 percent are under negotiation. Since 1982, over 20 projects ($50 million) have been completed, including a microwave link among all the states.[39]

Second in the priority list is promotion of food production to reduce economic vulnerability; only Zimbabwe, and possibly Malawi, are likely to continue to be food exporters in the near future. Over 58 agricultural projects have secured some funding (exceeding $214 million), and many are under negotiation.[40] One typical food project is the sorghum, millet, groundnut and legume research, all peasant-produced, drought-resistant food crops. The field tests are occurring at multiple points in the nine countries, with emphasis on small peasant usability.[41]

The agriculture sector also coordinated requests for relief during the drought of 1981-84, so that the different countries would not be competing with each other; $23 million was secured, and $113 million for rehabilitation was partially secured.[42] This cooperation continues to be important since drought persisted in 1986-87 in Botswana and parts of Angola, Lesotho, Malawi, Mozambique and Zimbabwe. By 1986, the early warning system to detect impending food shortages nationally and throughout the region was largely in place. In this first regional system of its kind, each member coordinates one to three sectors.[43] For example, Botswana is in charge of agricultural research and animal disease control, while Lesotho is responsible for soil and water conservation.

The third priority is industry, coordinated by Tanzania. The objective is to set up production complementarity, with industry promoted in all the economies, but planned to avoid competition. For example, each state will produce textiles, but textile chemicals will be produced only by Botswana and Tanzania.[44] With regard to cement production, since all but Botswana, Lesotho and Swaziland produce this material SADCC potentially is able to export cement. No new plants will be started, and studies will ascertain demand for additional cement products. Movement toward coordinated implementation of natural fertilizer production plans appears to be progressing. In contrast, plans to coordinate tractor production seem to have failed.[45] Licenses to transnational corporations have been given for the same product: Leyland has spent 3.6 million kwacha in Zambia to make the same type and range of vehicle as the Mutare plant makes in Zimbabwe.[46] Production complementarity can be seen as an attempt to preclude Zimbabwe's potential domination, since it already accounts for 37.5 percent of SADCC industrial output and 54 percent of SADCC heavy industry.[47]

Mining, directed by Zambia, is a vital sector to many of the economies, but coordination began late and has not yet progressed very far. The mining sector is the most fully integrated with South Africa and more particularly with one corporate group. As one SADCC official joked, "SADCC does not have to worry about regional co-ordination of mining; Anglo-American Corporation already does it!"[48] Or as economist Duncan Clarke points out, "Investment linkages thread a financial and economic pattern of regional interdependence which is deeply rooted"—and which has survived major upheavals in the region.[49] To date, SADCC has not addressed minerals marketing or mining legislation, but has concentrated on the easier decisions of inventory of mineral resources, small-scale minerals studies, training and identification of diversification, downstream processing and production.

In a real sense, SADCC will always be on the brink of failure, for its goals are very long term, but its projects and its new

1986–1990 perspective plan look only to the next five years. Development and dependence reduction constitute an ongoing process, and there will be no "final victory." Partly due to the drought, the international economic crisis and poor national planning—but also substantially related to South African aggression—seven SADCC economies had declines or stagnation in output per capita since 1980; real gross domestic product (GDP) of SADCC as a whole has fallen. Several SADCC members have reduced imports since 1979.[50]

Yet the first years of SADCC also show real successes. SADCC seems to have passed the first test of economic coordination in that cooperation, not rivalry, has increased. Member states attend meetings enthusiastically to argue through problems; counterparts in specific ministries know each other personally and learn to resolve differences more easily. These less tangible benefits now have some concrete results. The Malawi road spur to the Dar es Salaam road in Tanzania was completed in six months, and a fishery project is assessing possibilities for coordinated exploitation of Malawi's Lake Nyasa marine resources although only a few years back, Malawi and Tanzania had very limited relations and argued acrimoniously over their precise boundary.[51] In October 1984, Zimbabwe ameliorated the Malawian fuel crisis, caused by MNR attacks on the rail line, by shipping 3.5 million liters of gasoline to Malawi.[52] In addition, capital has entered the region which might not have come otherwise; and certainly, aid to Angola and Mozambique has been at a higher level than it would have been if received bilaterally.[53]

As regional coordination moves into the second half of its first decade of existence, more difficult questions will arise. The coordination of SADCC has not threatened the political status quo of any of the states. In fact, the decentralized nature is designed exactly to avoid that issue. However, if the ultimate goal is to restructure economies, elements of the ruling classes and of basic national economic interests will be challenged at some point.

The crisis of the international capitalist system will not go away; since the 1970s the "upward swings" have been shallow and for short periods. To deal with the crisis situation, SADCC economies will have to make hard choices about production, not simply promote full capacity of existing industries. It may not make sense to rescue parts of the Tanzanian industry or to modernize parts of the antiquated Zimbabwean industry. As SADCC is organized now, those decisions will be made solely at the national level. For the region to ameliorate the vagaries of the international crises, however, such national decisions should more regularly and fully include coordinated consideration of the regional context. If not, SADCC will remain quite vulnerable to outside forces.

SADCC also has not established an investment code for the region. Until a uniform code is signed, international capital can play one economy against the others; but to sign one code would mean far greater economic congruence than SADCC officials can envisage today or perhaps in the future.

Foreign exchange shortages in all member states except Botswana have deterred trade; SADCC has responded with encouragement of bilateral countertrade. If Mozambique's trade is in deficit to Tanzania, it is up to Mozambique to find goods to export that Tanzania needs. The deficit is eliminated by additional trade. SADCC says that the foreign exchange crises will only be resolved by beginning with greater production and then promoting trade to absorb that production—the opposite of normal common market theory.

Questions that SADCC has not yet addressed also affect its long-term effectiveness. The wage differential among workers on various projects from different countries has not been discussed. The nature of management has not been discussed by Swaziland, which coordinates manpower training, or by

SATCC.[54] It appears that SADCC is accepting, without question, hierarchical management, with the technically skilled in quite superior salary categories and with little worker participation in decision making, or at least the member states pursue various formulations and modifications of that model. The preoccupation seems to be to find and train personnel, not to raise questions about social relations of production. This approach avoids controversy in the short-term, but may undermine SADCC, as the process of development even at present differs greatly between member states.

Dependence on South Africa is being reduced only at the price of greatly increased dependence on Western capital. Until recently, the Soviet Union ignored SADCC, stating that the problems arose from colonialism, and preferred bilateral links. However, all the developed socialist countries, except Hungary, attended the 1986 and 1987 consultative conferences, and discussions are under way concerning a working relationship between the Council of Mutual Economic Assistance (CMEA) and SADCC. The People's Republic of China is helping to repair the Tazara railway and a line in Botswana. The vast majority of funds, however, are coming from Western donors. For example, the sectoral offices, such as SATCC and the food security office in Zimbabwe, have only small portions of their budgets provided by the members. The Scandinavian countries are the primary source of SATCC finance, and the United States, Australia, Canada and the Federal Republic of Germany are supporting the food security division. SATCC officials admit that there are no short-term plans for full financing by members. One suggested that technicians could be transferred to SATCC as a contribution, but that has not yet occurred, even in Zimbabwe which has qualified personnel who might be spared from national service.[55]

In addition, the local currency component of most projects remains modest. For example, 87.1 percent of the food security budget is in foreign currency; as is 100 percent of the agricultural research budget.[56] In industry, 75.5 percent of the budget will be financed by foreign exchange.[57] In several cases, however, domestic input and national contributions have clearly been understated or left out because the published information was designed to attract the external funds needed to complement them. Flows of capital to SADCC to implement these projects are a short-term success, but plans for regional self-financing are necessary to sustain SADCC.

To date, donor interference has been limited, and SADCC has protested sharply and effectively when it has occurred. The United States financed the sorghum-millet research project at the regional level, but put in an exclusionary clause saying that Angola, Mozambique and Tanzania could not benefit. This precipitated several discussions, as well as condemnation by President Nyerere who singled out the United States for reprimand at the 6 July 1984 SADCC summit meeting at Gaborone.[58] The United States altered its formulation to one specifying what it would (as opposed to what it would not) finance, accepted that all findings would be available to all SADCC members and financed the regional and six country components. But it took another year before other donors, such as Canada, agreed to support the three initially left out.

The Western donors will continue to offer funds to try to insert their own agendas into SADCC. The United States Agency for International Development (USAID) prides itself on helping "small farmers," by which it means private farmers who may become "master farmers," and producer cooperatives are not on its agenda. The Scandinavian countries have criticized SADCC members for their agricultural policies, without mentioning the role of international commodity prices in contributing to the African food crisis.[59]

The SADCC leaders are quite aware of outsiders' agendas. The question, which will only be determined by the process, is whether SADCC will reject, modify or accept the "suggestions." To date it has acted on its stated view that all suggestions, comments, criticisms and dialogue are welcome but that, because SADCC and its members are responsible to their peoples, decisions must be southern African.

However, the policy may be different for energy, coordinated by Angola, than for forestry, coordinated by Malawi. The decentralized nature of SADCC makes funding procedures complex for donors, but on occasion gives them much room to maneuver. One critic of SADCC's dependence on Western capital stated that Western strategy is no longer to divide and rule, but to "regroup and dominate; SADCC is only co-ordination of donors, for donors."[60] An alternative view is that SADCC has coordinated the donors and set a regionally determined agenda which has reduced the leverage of donors over individual SADCC states. Certainly, in its first eight years, SADCC has set its own priorities and has halted the more blatant attempts at interference. Further, its annual conferences are the only regular multilateral consultative group meetings called, organized, documented and run by the recipients. However, plans for a greater share of national capital in the projects and for national experts as consultants on projects, as well as policy studies, must progress substantially before SADCC will escape such criticisms.

Moves to secure foreign enterprise technical and financial participation have increased since 1983 within and outside the region. The Beira corridor is backed by an interlocking set of largely private-sector–financed Zimbabwean and Mozambican companies. The 1985 industrial sector and 1987 annual consultative conference specifically provided for foreign enterprise participation, as did the 1987 SADCC mission to the United States; and the 1987 *Overview* paper focussed on productive sector investment and the role of enterprises.[61]

To concentrate solely on overall foreign funding proportions, which SADCC itself said, in its 1985 Organization of African Unity (OAU) summit paper, were unsustainably and undesirably high, is to miss two critical points. First, they are higher than envisaged in 1979–80 because the external economic position of SADCC's members has been much worse than could reasonably have been foreseen—largely as a result of world recession, drought and South African aggression. To make a rapid start and to sustain concrete action, SADCC had to resort to increased use of external resources. While this does lead to a medium-term problem, no other choice would have led to a significant operational program.

Second, SADCC's dependence-reduction objective is not theoretical and undifferentiated but contextual and specific. Dependence on South Africa is the immediate threat. Substituting dependence on grants and soft loans from a range of donors—to restore and upgrade the five SADCC port corridor transport systems—for dependence on SATS is seen by SADCC as a step forward. SADCC's claim is not that it has achieved its aims but rather that it has taken the first step.[62]

South Africa initially ignored SADCC, apparently in the hope it would disappear, but has since decided that SADCC is an enemy. At Nkomati in March 1984, Prime Minister Botha called it the "counterconstellation." In contrast, Pretoria sees the PTA as posing little threat; and it can be easily penetrated by South African transnationals, which can maintain at least 49 percent ownership of their subsidiaries and still benefit from the lower tariffs. The rules-of-origin code allows major exceptions to local-origin-content rules for products. This means that Swaziland, for example, could help South African goods enter the PTA via SACU.[63] Finally, the history of preferential trade areas shows that the stronger sectors dominate. What may look like a surge in Zimbabwean trade could well be South African, with Zimbabwean products largely produced by South African subsidiaries in Zimbabwe. Zimbabwean public and private capital might have 51 percent or more of the shares, but corporations such as Anglo-American have no problem controlling production and financial decisions with limited ownership interest if they dominate management and external marketing, and determine access to technology via licensing and patents.[64] The PTA only requires that a "majority" of the management be nationals.

The result of years of economic sabotage by South Africa underlines the necessity for SADCC. As the Botswanan vice-president Peter Mmusi stated: "It had been said that good fences make good neighbours. We know the hard realities of living with bad neighbours—and we will keep our fences in good repair."[65] Certainly, SADCC needs peace, or coordinated defense, for the new transport links to work and for production to increase.

The choice by South Africa to attack SADCC projects shows, in fact, its vulnerability to coordinated economic links in the region. Having most regional external trade in goods and services flow through apartheid South Africa does not make good economic sense. Zambia, Zimbabwe, Malawi and Bostwana could save over $300 million a year on transport costs alone if the Mozambican lines were open to regular traffic. Furthermore, for many imports, South African sources are more expensive, even with tariff preferences, than regional or global sources.

The first comprehensive estimates of the cost to its neighbors of South African aggression were prepared by SADCC for the 1985 OAU summit.[66] These cover the period 1980–84 and total just over $10 billion. For comparison, this exceeds total foreign grant and loan aid to the region, 40 percent of exports from SADCC countries and 10 percent of their GDP for the five-year period. In fact, the SADCC estimates appear to be low; and even $12–13 billion would be a conservative figure. By 1985, on this basis, the annual loss was running at $4 billion a year, about $70 per capita for a group of countries whose average annual output is perhaps $500 per capita. For Mozambique the costs now exceed 50 percent of GDP, and for nonoil GDP in Angola the share is close to half.

In 1986, a more elaborate analysis of the cost addition and GDP loss side was carried out for a report to the United Nations Children's Fund (Unicef).[67] This concluded that loss-based estimates for 1980-86 inclusive were of the order of $25-28 billion, equivalent to an entire year's regional output. Working from output under actual conditions, as opposed to probable output trends in the context of peace (based on 1979-81 trends), GDP losses were estimated at $25-30 billion. For Angola the estimate was $15-18 billion; for Mozambique $5.5-6.5 billion; and for the other seven SADCC member states $5-6 billion. The Angolan and Mozambican economies have been totally crippled by war; the others have borne heavy additional defense and transport costs, as well as limited sabotage losses.

The Unicef report *Children on the Front Line* presents a stark picture of the human costs of South Africa's "destructive engagement" with the independent states of southern Africa. Several million Angolans and Mozambicans have been driven from their homes by terrorist action. Most are displaced internally but over one million have fled to neighboring countries. In Mozambique, the disruption of production and transport, and of export earnings to buy food, has placed 5.9 million human beings at risk of starvation.[68] In Angola the number at risk is almost two million.

Deaths caused directly by South Africa or its surrogates are probably of the order of 200,000 people. Another 200,000 people have died from starvation, half of these in the 1983-84 famine in southern Mozambique when terrorists disrupted or destroyed both the means of production and the ability to deliver relief food. However, the greatest number of lives have been lost through the dislocation and destruction of health services. The Unicef report estimates that in the 1980-86 period 534,000 Angolan and Mozambican infants and children under five died who would have lived had there been peace, and predicted 130,000 similar deaths in 1987. In total, counting other health-related deaths, over one million human beings have died in southern Africa as a result of South Africa's actions. This is, in the words of the Unicef representative in Mozambique, "a holocaust."[69]

SADCC is not a mode of production or a transition-to-socialism project. There is no consensus among its members for such a project and to promote it would abort its program of economic liberation, for which consensus does exist. Equally, however, while SADCC operates on the basis of consensus, it is not a least common denominator organization. Its relentless condemnation of South African aggression and destabilization— and its growing involvement in the question of sanctions against South Africa[70]—clearly are less radical than those some of its members take nationally, but also go well beyond the purely national positions of others. These coordinated statements and actions do have more impact than those that are purely national—and disparate. In the process of coordination (and, some would say, consciousness raising), SADCC members now see more clearly the overall nature of South African political economic hegemony, as well as the different national abilities to bear costs and assume risks to overcome that dominance.

Sanctions against South Africa as a means of inducing or coercing changes in its internal system, its withdrawal from Namibia or—less frequently—an end to its regional aggression have been advocated more or less seriously for over 20 years. Action, however, has been limited to concentrating on military equipment, sports and entertainment, and in certain professional fields. A parallel oil sanctions effort by the Organization of Petroleum Exporting Countries (OPEC), while imposing real costs on South Africa, was systematically evaded and dissolved in the buyer's market of the early 1980s. Only for a brief period at the end of the 1970s did extensive economic sanctions on a global or near-global basis appear even remotely likely.[71]

The position changed sharply in 1985–86, when there were greater and more general demands than ever before for economic sanctions against South Africa. This was due to the increasing use of violence to protect the apartheid system at home, the continued duplicity of "reform" promises and a growing realization by the international community that apartheid was inherently evil and not reformable. Also the failure of attempts to negotiate a South African withdrawal from Namibia and the rising tide of regional aggression, notably the strikes against Gaborone, Harare, Lusaka and the Gulf Oil installations in Cabinda, increased international demands for economic sanctions.

Actual steps were taken on trade and trade promotion, investment and loans, technical cooperation, petroleum, air links and some consular facilities. These reached a new level of intensity in late 1986 with the imposition of substantial sanctions measures by Canada, Australia, New Zealand, the United States and the Scandinavian countries, and the lesser measures adopted by the European Economic Community (EEC). Sanctions pressure increased in late 1987, with Sweden and Norway imposing full trade embargoes, and 48 Commonwealth countries agreeing to "widen and tighten" economic sanctions against South Africa. While not in themselves crippling, these measures did impose costs and create momentum for further pressures. Ironically, the most effective sanctions came from investors and lenders. The rising crisis of apartheid at home and the costs of regional aggression have rendered South Africa's economy less dynamic and more constrained by foreign exchange. Increasingly, corporations have seen it as prudent to phase down or sell all or part of their South African interests, while world currency and financial markets have passed a resounding vote of no confidence with the rand falling 50 percent against the dollar and over 60 percent against stronger currencies.

As a result, South Africa has been forced to reschedule external loan repayments and has negligible prospects of securing net new-loan or investment capital from abroad until its domestic situation and international image alter radically.[72] In this period, the foreign exchange earnings from trade and transport with SADCC countries have been crucial to South Africa, and the magnitudes now estimated suggest the net earnings are roughly equivalent to amounts needed to pay the interest on outstanding debt.

Broader, more effective economic sanctions against South Africa than those currently in place would impose heavy costs on its neighbors and would certainly include the tightening of South African retaliatory sanctions in the region, as well as intensification of "strike kommando" strategies. This would cause great difficulty for several SADCC states and could bring some economies to the verge of collapse.[73] However, studies carried out at the end of the 1970s suggested that the costs to the region could be sharply reduced, especially once Zimbabwe attained independence.

South Africa has threatened that economic sanctions against it will be matched by retaliatory actions against its neighbors— most specifically by expelling hundreds of thousands of migrant and seasonal workers from Lesotho, Mozambique, Botswana, Malawi and Swaziland, and by cutting off petroleum products.[74] What action the regime will actually take is less clear. Upgrading "strike kommando" raids would be virtually certain. Petroleum supplies would be halted because they are based on imported crude oil. Exports based on South African inputs might well continue since sanctions evasion requires maximizing, not minimizing, export earnings. Transit traffic restrictions might be selective for the same reason. Even labor import cutbacks would probably be selective; neither the crippling of the gold-mining sector (the one export sector which is, in practice, sanctions proof), nor the creation of an explosive enclave of desperate people in Lesotho, would seem a rational course of action. In 1986–87, mining industry pressure led to partial retraction of the decision to repatriate all Mozambican miners by early 1988.

Pretoria's reaction would depend in part on whether it believed that damage to a particular neighbor would cause that neighbor to collaborate in sanctions evasion and/or to press the world community to relax sanctions. Just as South African threats have joined the global chorus saying that sanctions would be bad because they would injure the independent southern African states, so carrying out the threats might undermine global support for sanctions once imposed.

SADCC's response to the potential reality of economic sanctions against South Africa has evolved rapidly. At the 1985 Arusha Summit, seven member states, including Lesotho, made clear their support for sanctions.[75] Two remained silent, but did not dissent. Claims that the seven have said otherwise in private are fraudulent. SADCC members have also made clear their belief that the basic cause of violence in the southern African region, as in South Africa itself, is apartheid and that South Africa's attempts to sustain apartheid are imposing crippling costs on governments and people in the region.[76]

SADCC has commissioned studies and consultations on the impact of sanctions against South Africa, and probable South African response, with a view to identifying concrete measures to speed up the process of reducing economic dependence on South Africa and vulnerability to South African action. SADCC has chosen to view sanctions as within the parameters of intensified struggle and as an opportunity to advance the political economy of liberation. Its most evident responses—accelerating work on the Dar es Salaam, Beira and Nacala transport corridor projects over 1985–87 and planning the reopening of the Limpopo line in 1988—are practical measures to reduce short-term costs of South African sanctions against the region and long-term dependence on South Africa, as well as to prepare for international sanctions against South Africa.

The costs to the region of economic sanctions against South Africa can be broken down into six main components: transport and communications, imports, exports (including labor), finance, security and Lesotho. Lesotho requires attention as a special case because it is not just landlocked but "South Africa-locked."

Any costing must be schematic and tentative for three reasons. First, detailed information has not been collected and analyzed. Second, the extent and nature of the sanctions will affect the costs; and, third, as will the nature, extent, timing and effectiveness of southern African responses. The following analysis presupposes that sanctions would cover at least petroleum, military and technology imports. It also presumes that SADCC states will not serve as sanctions-breaking conduits, nor will they instantly sever all economic links with South Africa, and that South Africa will, for its own reasons, continue some links. The analysis also takes account of the fact that South Africa will almost certainly increase "strike kommando" raids on key economic targets, especially transport and energy, and continue high levels of support for proxy forces (National Union for the Total Independence of Angola [Unita], MNR, Lesotho Liberation Army [LLA], Super-Zapu), but assumes it will stop short of full-scale invasions except in the case of Angola.

Transport relates to the six SADCC members crucially dependent on South African routes. Only Tanzania and Angola would be unaffected. Of the others, only Mozambique, Swaziland, Zambia and, with the reopening of the Nacala line, Malawi could survive economically using presently functional transport routes which do not transit South Africa. In respect to petroleum transport, however, only Lesotho could not be supplied—assuming that both the Beira and Dar es Salaam pipelines were functional, as well as the refineries at Dar es Salaam, Ndola, Maputo and Luanda. Similarly for air transport and communications, the SATCC project has already reduced the use of South African facilities and links to the point that total severance would be inconvenient rather than crippling.

In respect to imports, South Africa is a major source for several countries, but in every case alternative sources exist and quite often at a lower cost. Some examples of regional sources for basic imports are: Zimbabwe and Malawi for grain; Zimbabwe and, to a lesser degree, Malawi and Tanzania for manufactured goods; Mozambique for coal and cement; Angola for petroleum, and so on. The problems are twofold. First, no source is effective unless existing transport routes function. Second, in Botswana, Lesotho and Swaziland, where 85–95 percent of imports come from or via South Africa, there is virtually no commercial capacity to make use of global sources, a gap compounded by the South African company Renfreight's dominance of clearing and forwarding.

South Africa is not the primary market for the goods export of any SADCC member except Lesotho. Most exports to South Africa could be redirected, albeit at a cost. Again the transport routes for exports, other than to South Africa, are crucial. For labor, the situation is different. Lesotho is totally dependent on the earnings from migrant workers in South Africa, and the dependence of Mozambique, Botswana, Swaziland and Malawi is also significant.

Financial flows from South Africa to SADCC states are primarily of two types: via SACU and export credits. SACU flows are critical to Botswana, Lesotho and Swaziland, but the actual underlying import-excise revenues depend on there being imports to tax, not on their sources or the fiscal structures used. For the heavily indebted countries with limited access to trade credit, a rupture in South African supply could cripple imports.

Lesotho faces very particular problems. All ground transport is via South Africa. Virtually all imports are from or via South Africa. About three-quarters of employment and foreign exchange earnings flow from migrant labor exports to South Africa and SACU payments. Total sanctions against Lesotho by

South Africa could, without corrective action, quite literally mean economic strangulation and widespread starvation.[77]

The nature of the costs, in effect, outlines the countermeasures required. The transport requirement is easy to identify. Except for Lesotho, it consists of rehabilitating and protecting the Nacala, Beira and Maputo (Limpopo line) trade corridors. Rehabilitating and protecting the Lobito trade corridor is highly desirable but not essential. In effect this would reverse the effects of South Africa's sustained campaign against SADCC transportation routes by implementing the priority project in the SATCC program on a selective and accelerated basis. The problems beyond that are logistical and manageable. These involve rerouting Botswana traffic, developing onward transit facilities for petroleum products from Mutare and Ndola, coordinating traffic flow and route capacity allocations, adding to rolling stock, locomotive and truck fleets. While SATS would likely recall loaned equipment, presumably its return could be denied or phased to allow arrival of replacement units.

Trade problems, apart from labor, turn on transport and commercial institutions. Alternative sources exist. The basic problem is getting the goods to and from the landlocked states. In the special case of electricity, the basic requirement is three high tension lines: Cahora Bassa to Maputo; Maputo (or the Cahora Bassa–Maputo line) to the Swaziland grid; and connecting the Zimbabwe and Botswana grids with a high capacity link.

To use external trade sources and markets, Botswana, Swaziland and Lesotho each needs an independent import/export house with global information sources and contacts. The practical way of creating them rapidly would be joint ventures of the respective development corporations, either with northern trading houses, including major international trade co-ops such as the Scandinavian Wholesale Cooperative Federation, or with existing Zimbabwean external trade houses. Similarly, with respect to clearing and forwarding, joint ventures with non-Renfreight firms with external contacts are needed along the lines of Mozambique's joint venture with Agence Maritime Internationale (AMI of Belgium). These steps are desirable and would pay even in narrow cost terms, sanctions or no sanctions.

Reducing the loss of jobs in South Africa requires forward planning of alternative employment, especially in rural areas. Numerous public works programs for afforestation, irrigation, anti-erosion, water supply, schools and clinics, roads, local warehouse and community center projects can be undertaken largely by unskilled and semiskilled labor. The problems are in identifying programs and their design, determining the requirements for skilled personnel, tools and materials, then mobilizing these and the finance to procure them.

In respect to finance, the "loss" of SACU can be fully offset by fairly moderate upgrading of existing national customs and excise services to undertake collection. National import and excise tariffs must also be instituted, if import flows are maintained. Alternative trade finance would need to be mobilized—possibly from noncommercial sources—to substitute for South African.

The transition to new transport and trade patterns would not be instantaneous or problem free. Thus, reserve stocks would be needed for key goods such as fuel, food, fertilizer and tools, inputs into manufacturing, spare parts (especially for the transport sector). These stocks should be built up to 90–120 day levels in the landlocked southern African states. Given the present uncertainties in delivery dates, and South African engineering of shortages to exert pressure, such reserves are desirable whether there are sanctions or not.

Lesotho's survival will require international support, including an airlift capable of carrying 150,000–500,000 tons a year, depending on whether only petroleum products or all imports have to be moved. This could be mounted from Maputo to the new Maseru international airport. The Tanzania/Zambia airlift after sanctions were imposed on Rhodesia was technically more difficult. The problem is one of cost. Similarly, to provide income for 50,000–200,000 workers expelled from South Africa and to sustain the foreign exchange for imports (and therefore tax revenue) would require major external financial support.

Security aspects of sanctions relate to the fact that, to survive, SADCC states need operative transport, communication and energy installations. South African strikes against existing, rehabilitated or new facilities in the context of sanctions could be even more devastating than its existing pattern of armed aggression. Security issues extend well beyond the scope of this chapter. However, the recent past makes two points clear. First, sabotage can render many projects key to the political economy of liberation impossible to implement or nonoperational. Second, national and coordinated southern African security operations, such as those undertaken by Mozambique, Zimbabwe, Tanzania and Malawi can limit the damage done by South African aggression.

Without improved security, all cost reduction measures and projects, especially in transport and energy, will be vulnerable to South African military strikes; but broader regional defense coordination could substantially reduce the damage of such strikes, as well as increase the costs to South Africa in fuel, personnel and equipment. Further, it is likely that the interposition of a multinational or northern blocking force (Commonwealth or Scandinavian) with real damage-infliction capacity would deter South Africa from carrying out a high-profile strike program.

A rough estimate of 1987–1990 costs to SADCC states to prepare for South African retaliations against sanctions is $6 billion. Of this, about $1.8 billion would be for transport and energy rehabilitation and development (approximately one-half funded); $1.5 to $2 billion for enhanced security; $1.5 billion for employment (labor intensive public works) and creation of self-employment (agriculture, artisan production) for workers expelled by South Africa; and the balance, trade loss or diversion costs, plus a Lesotho airlift. However, by 1990, gains (on transport and energy cost savings, production by repatriated workers, increased regional trade) could be in the $1.25–1.75 billion range and would tend to grow thereafter while costs decreased.[78]

It would be dangerously romantic to assume that, even if these steps are successful, sanctions against South Africa would not impose severe costs on Lesotho, Botswana, Zimbabwe, Swaziland and Zambia. But these steps could reduce them to bearable levels. Furthermore, almost all of the sanctions cost-reduction measures are part of the political economy of southern African regional liberation and once completed would provide substantial gains.

Finally, with the present annual cost of South African aggression and economic destabilization already running at perhaps $6 billion a year, and rising, it serves no practical purpose to talk of the costs to southern Africa of imposing sanctions on South Africa. The costs of coexisting with apartheid are immeasurably higher, and the region is already suffering from selective sanctions imposed by its powerful neighbor. The imposition of comprehensive international sanctions would mark another stage in the struggle for regional economic liberation and, to the extent they succeeded, would further the welfare of the states and peoples in southern Africa.

10

DESTRUCTIVE ENGAGEMENT

The United States and South Africa in the Reagan Era

There is an enormous wisdom in this land, and one prays it will be granted the necessary time to manifest itself.... The machine gun will guarantee reasonable time, I think. When you return to America assure your people that Afrikaners will use their machine guns if forced to do so.... [We can] buy time, probably through the remainder of this century. But with every moment gained, more wisdom is gained too. And the day will come when the bright lads from Stellenbosch and Potchefstroom will lead the way in conciliation.

Our Zulu and Xhosa—they're the most patient, wonderful people on this earth.... I think they can wait, intelligently, till the sick white man sorts things out.

—James Michener, *The Covenant*

In *The Covenant*, Mrs. Laura Saltwood, James Michener's fictional Anglo-South African liberal who expresses these hopes, is "banned" by the South African government after a 1979 speech advocating that Africans should learn English, not Afrikaans, so that they can read "the greatest body of learning and literature in the world." Saltwood's offense is an improbable one for a "banned" person. And so are the opinions she expounds to her distant American cousin Philip Saltwood, a visiting geologist. Her words would fit more appropriately a South Africa Foundation executive, or Chester Crocker, who, by 1979, still an academic, was already sketching out the policies he would later oversee as President Ronald Reagan's assistant secretary of state for Africa.

Michener's mammoth book, published in 1980, incorporated wholesale the prevailing historical myths characterizing South Africa's racial groups. His saga gives the leading role to the Afrikaners, portrayed as intolerant and racist but far more vivid as individuals than his black characters or even the Anglo-South Africans. South African history is depicted as an epic of warring tribes, the conflicts rooted in the prejudice of the more backward Afrikaners. But there is still hope: "The Afrikaner politicians I've met are at least as prudent as the American politicians I know," concludes Philip, "I'm going to put my faith in them."[1]

Under President Reagan, the United States did place its faith in South Africa's political leaders, relying both on their guns and their wisdom. Reassuring Pretoria that the two powers shared a common interest in a Soviet- and Cuban-free stability in the subcontinent, Washington argued that long-term security also required movement toward power sharing at home and an international settlement in Namibia. With an activist diplomacy of "constructive engagement," the United States tried to persuade South Africa and pressure its African opponents to arrive at a settlement.

Other Western countries were more skeptical about the possibility of solutions, but they were willing to let Washington take the initiative. No major power took active steps to disengage itself from Pretoria. By the end of 1984, it was clear that Western policies had again helped to buy time for the South African state. South Africa's neighbors, meanwhile the victims of intensified attack, had lost time for desperately needed development. Pretoria's steps toward detente in 1984 proved tentative at best. Namibia was no closer to freedom. In South Africa the reform process had produced a new constitution excluding Africans, which the overwhelming majority of blacks saw as entrenching a slightly modernized apartheid.

As Reagan's second term began it was increasingly difficult to maintain even the pretense that US engagement was "constructive." Sustained rebellion in South Africa's black townships, beginning in late 1984 and continuing through 1985 into 1986, ignited an unprecedented response abroad, not least in the United States. Daily demonstrations by the Free South Africa Movement at the South African embassy in Washington expressed outrage at US complicity, as well as South African repression. The drumbeat of publicity sapped the confidence of foreign bankers and businessmen, who feared both continued instability and critics at home.

As several Western countries banned new investments in South Africa, President Reagan was forced by members of his own party to accept limited sanctions to head off stronger action by Congress. The action was only temporarily successful because in 1986 Congress overrode a presidential veto to impose limited sanctions against South Africa.

Simultaneously, however, both Congress and the administration were giving in to the far-right campaign to aid South Africa's Angolan surrogate the National Union for the Total Independence of Angola (Unita), thus bolstering Pretoria's regional aggression. Aid to other Frontline states was beset with crippling congressional restrictions.

This seeming contradiction, penalizing both the apartheid regime and its regional victims, was deeply rooted in patterns governing US policy long before the advent of Ronald Reagan and reflected the diversity of forces in US society affecting Africa policy.

THE POLICY CONTEXT

The faith the Reagan administration placed in Pretoria was not an original invention. Analyzing policies by contrasting those of one US administration with those of another pays insufficient attention to the tendencies, policy lines and coalitions that persist from the term of one president to the next. There is a continuity in policy, which sets parameters and limits significant new directions. Serious sanctions against South Africa, on the one hand, and open proclamation of support for the apartheid regime, on the other, are ruled out of the policy debate in advance. Within any one period, policy is not totally unified—the State Department, the Central Intelligence Agency (CIA), the White House and other executive branches, Congress, transnational corporations and private pressure groups, each has different emphases and separate effects on policy.[2]

The difference lies in the balance of emphasis within each administration. This in turn depends both on its internal political base and on the changing objective reality in southern Africa. Since 1960, the dominant tendency in US policy, under both Democratic and Republican administrations, has been conservative *Realpolitik* or pragmatism, which subordinates most foreign policy issues to preserving US world leadership vis-à-vis the Soviet Union and the more general threat of social revolution. The most common corollary is that the United States should stick with familiar allies, even if they are colonial powers, white-settler regimes, or right-wing dictatorships. Adjustments to rising nationalism or concern with racism or human rights are, from this perspective, sentimental distractions from the real business of defending US interests.

With respect to southern Africa, the most explicit formulation of this perspective was in the Nixon-Kissinger National Security Study Memorandum of 1969, which postulated that the white regimes were destined to stay in power and control the pace of change.[3] In practice, this assumption dominated policy both before and after 1969, until it was rudely challenged by the fall of Portuguese colonialism. Even then, it remained the operating assumption when dealing with South Africa.

The dominance of this assumption, in Democratic as well as Republican administrations, is reflected above all in consistent US opposition to substantive sanctions against Pretoria. Even the arms embargoes adopted by Presidents Kennedy in 1963 and Carter in 1977 were primarily symbolic and hedged with qualifications. They also left Pretoria's economic lifeline to the West—and thus the basis of its military power—intact.

What did distinguish Democratic administrations was their relative openness to the variant theme of "establishment liberalism." This perspective can be summarized in the theses that adjustment to "moderate" nationalism is the best bulwark against radicalism and Soviet-bloc expansion; that the United States must be flexible and undogmatic in analyzing Third World developments; and that there must be some effort to identify with Third World aspirations. Democratic sensitivity to African opinion and greater willingness to take symbolic steps that would offend Pretoria were heightened by the need to pay attention to black opinion and human rights sentiment at home.

Yet the more liberal variant of Africa policy held only a marginal position within the foreign policy mainstream. It had most influence in the opening years of the Kennedy and Carter administrations, which coincided with the periods of uncertainty following the massacres at Sharpeville in 1961 and Soweto in 1976. But in each case idealism lost its bloom, reform becoming less urgent as the white regimes in the early 1960s, and South Africa again after Soweto in the late 1970s, reestablished "stability." The Carter administration did persist with negotiations on Zimbabwe and Namibia, but these rested on the premise of cooperation with South Africa. Reform in South Africa, officials argued, could be encouraged by the progressive involvement of Western capital, under such reformist codes as those for factory workers advocated by the Reverend Leon Sullivan, a black American clergyman.

For Democrats as well as Republicans, moreover, the common axiom of anticommunism and de facto ties with South Africa paved the way for regional intervention, which had the effect of buying time for Pretoria. In the 1950s, the Republican Eisenhower administration made the strategic decision to eliminate Patrice Lumumba in the Congo (Zaire) for fear that his nonaligned stance might give advantages to the Soviet Union. But Eisenhower's Democratic successors also gave priority to securing a pro-Western Congo over advancing the demise of white minority rule to the south. As an Africa Bureau memo during the Johnson administration puts it, "The need to prevent a major Communist success ranks above almost every other consideration."[4] The maxim was well illustrated by US cooperation, albeit embarrassed, with white mercenaries in repressing the 1964 Congo rebellions.

A decade later, the second act of direct US intervention in the region was played out in Angola, again on the initiative of a Republican administration. The United States joined South Africa in trying to block the People's Movement for the Liberation of Angola (MPLA) from power. This was defeated when Cuban troops came to the aid of the MPLA and the US Congress barred further CIA involvement. A crucial factor in this different outcome, was the greater strength of anti-interventionist and pro-African sentiment in the United States, stemming both from the Veitnam War experience and from the growing influence of blacks among Democrats in Congress. But the legislative check to US intervention was an exceptional event. The cold war mainstream, among Democrats as well as Republicans, saw Angola primarily as a case of Soviet-Cuban gains against the United States rather than in the context of African liberation and South African invasion.

In the aftermath of Angola and Soweto, anti-apartheid sentiment in the United States continued to grow, with solidarity groups supporting Zimbabwe, the divestment movement blossoming in universities, churches and local governments, and the formation of the national black lobby, TransAfrica. In Congress, both the Black Caucus and the House of Representatives Subcommittee on Africa became more prominent loci of expertise on and sympathy with African concerns. But such views had little direct influence on foreign policy. As the Carter administration finished out its term, old cold war priorities were already being revived, supplanting greater sensitivity to African opinion.

US policy makers with a more liberal bent could congratulate themselves on Zimbabwe's successful transition to independence. Against strong pressure from the right to endorse the internal settlement of Ian Smith and Abel Muzorewa, a wavering US administration and British realists had listened to African insistence that the guerrilla leadership could not be excluded from power. Pro-African lobby groups and congressional liberals helped prevent the premature lifting of sanctions. In the end a classic British decolonization scenario had been played out, ending the guerrilla war and the prolonged international legal crisis. With vigorous diplomacy, the West had provided the framework for a broad-based settlement, pressuring black guerrilla movements to compromise and reassuring whites that their essential interests could be preserved. Mugabe's victory smashed the expectation that "moderate" Africans chosen by whites could win a free election against guerrilla liberators, despite South African subsidies and the sympathy of an interim administration. Yet the new government was ready to cooperate with the West.

There was even some indication that leading circles in the United States might apply a liberal reading of the Zimbabwean outcome to South Africa. If violence comparable to that in Rhodesia (Zimbabwe) should engulf the South African heartland, the results would be unpredictable, greater international involvement inescapable. The United States, with its assumed global responsibility and history of racial conflict, was particularly concerned. "The formulation of new approaches to the problem is urgent," said an influential US government report in early 1981, adding that violence could intensify and spread. "Time is running out," it warned.[5]

The report *Time Running Out* was the most visible result of "establishment-liberal" efforts to find an appropriate US response. The Study Commission on US Policy toward Southern Africa, sponsored by the Rockefeller Foundation and chaired by Ford Foundation head, Franklin Thomas, had begun its work in early 1979 with a budget of over $2 million. As the Rhodesian drama moved to its climax, the commissioners undertook an elaborate process of study and consultation on the crisis in South Africa.

In spite of the urgency of its title, this report issued two years later went only slightly beyond the policies of the early Kennedy or early Carter years. Moreover, it came when Washington opinion was moving in the opposite direction, against expanding symbolic disengagement from the white-ruled regime. Its conclusions were destined to serve less as a guide to government policy than as a marker of the leftward limits of respectable opinion.

Strikingly, the commissioners made no recommendations regarding Namibia or South Africa's role in attacking Angola and backing Unita guerrillas there. Avoiding these controversial topics, they proposed the general regional goal of aiding economic development in black states. In South Africa, the commisioners concluded that white minority rule was doomed and affirmed the need for "genuine power sharing," preferably achieved with a minimum of violence. Allying the United States with such constructive change could minimize growth of communist influence and the prospect of all-out civil war, they argued.

The commissioners rejected sanctions such as trade embargoes or divestment, while acknowledging that these eventually might be needed. Instead they recommended far more limited actions. The US government should broaden export restrictions on arms and nuclear technology, continue strong public condemnation of apartheid, expand contact with blacks and aid for black organizations within South Africa, and prepare for possible cutoffs of minerals from the area. US firms should refrain voluntarily from new investment and abide by the Sullivan principles.

Even measures such as voluntary restrictions on new investment were seen as daring, in the context of mainstream opinion among US leaders. Opinion polls indicated that public opinion might have been willing to go further; however, a survey among members of the elite Council on Foreign Relations showed no significant support "for any action that might bring effective sanctions in any forms against South Africa."[6]

As the commissioners recognized, the military threat facing South Africa was far from that which had defeated Ian Smith in Rhodesia (Zimbabwe). New student demonstrations and strikes in 1980 marked the most intense resistance activity since 1977. The African National Congress (ANC) of South Africa carried out its most dramatic sabotage attack to date, inflicting some $8 million damage at the SASOL coal-to-oil plant. In Namibia, South Africa had failed to eliminate the guerrilla capacity of the South West Africa People's Organization (Swapo), in spite of repeated claims to have destroyed their base camps in Angola. But there was no immediate challenge to South African control. Time had not yet run out.

Without the expectation of an imminent collapse of South African authority, the liberal call to adjust to a future of majority rule was easily drowned out by the clarion calls of anticommunism. The caution of the post-Vietnam War era had limited staying power in the US political arena; and Africa policy was inevitably affected by the resurgence of cold war perspectives.

This trend was already in evidence under the Carter administration, where National Security Adviser Zbigniew Brzezinski rivalled his predecessor, Henry Kissinger, in willingness to give priority to superpower competition over other issues. A striking indicator of the rising influence of this perspective in African matters came in May 1978, when Brzezinski hinted that the United States should restore aid to Unita and Carter denounced Cuba as responsible for the uprising in Zaire's Shaba province. Simultaneously, a South African raid killing hundreds of Namibian refugees at Kassinga went without effective US rebuke. The message was clear—in the US policy context, the Cuban "threat" to Africa far outweighed the threat from South Africa. US negotiators gained South African agreement to the principle of independence for Namibia, but Washington was unwilling to exert similar pressure to implement the plan.

More generally, events far removed from southern Africa—in the Horn, Afghanistan, Iran and Central America—were all by 1980 pressed into service to portray the need for the United States to stand up against the threat of Soviet-backed world revolution. Reagan's election both reflected and reinforced this trend.

In the Carter administration, the cold warriors had to pay some attention to more cautious or pro-African constituencies in the administration, in the Democratic party and among the public. In Reagan's Washington, however, such voices were excluded from the internal policy debate. The "regionalists," the human rights advocates, the moderates advising recognition of the limits of US power, lost the fragile beachhead they had held during the Carter administration. Instead, the right wing contended with the extreme right wing for influence in the halls of executive power, while radical, liberal and even centrist forces could only build counterweights and check the tilt from the outside. The Reaganauts were riding a rising wave to the right, their only question how far and how recklessly to ride it.

THE REAGANAUT LINEUP

Most accounts of Reagan-era Africa policy have focussed on the ideas of Assistant Secretary of State Crocker. As important and skilled at bureaucratic survival as Crocker has been, this emphasis is misleading. In previous administrations, the Africa Bureau generally held a perspective more accommodating to African interests than other power centers within the government. Although its political spectrum was shifted considerably to the right, the Reagan administration was no exception to this general rule—its ideological center of gravity has been to Crocker's right.

Reagan himself provided the best characterization of his own regime when he joked in mid-1981, "Sometimes my right hand doesn't know what my far right hand is doing."[7] The Africa Bureau's *Realpolitik* evolved within the context of more extreme views. The right hand accommodated itself to the far right, seeking to achieve what was realistic in the goals they shared.

The internal balance between right and far right was affected by a variety of factors—the stances taken by different individuals within the administration, the weight of public and congressional pressure on the left or on the right, and the objective constraints of events overseas. Although the media's rough categorization of Reagan's men as "ideologues" and "pragmatists" was generally a useful guide, individuals could and did shift their positions. In comparison to Central American policy, where the far-right campaign to overthrow the Nicaraguan government clearly dominated any tendency toward detente or negotiation, the Africa Bureau gained greater protection for its professedly conciliatory strategy. Compromise was more possible in the case of Mozambique, for example, than in Angola which was already a potent symbol for the far right.

Even at the height of diplomatic conciliation, in 1983–84, the purportedly "evenhanded" constructive engagement still tilted decisively toward Pretoria. But the shifting balance between pragmatist and ideologue did affect the nuances and timing of policy. And the results deviated sufficiently from the ideologues' hopes that they repeatedly attacked the State Department's willingness to "conciliate communists" in southern Africa.

The heart of the extremist approach was a virtually exclusive emphasis on the need to combat revolution and Soviet expansion, combined with lack of embarrassment at alignment with South Africa. The settlement in Zimbabwe was seen as a victory for "Marxist terrorists," in spite of Mugabe's postindependence moderation and cool relationship with the Soviet Union. The United States, it was asserted, should back efforts to roll back guerrilla victories and install pro-Western governments in Mozambique and especially in Angola, a special target because of Cuban troops there and the memory in the policy community of US defeat.

President Reagan's instinctive sympathies lay with this globalist ideology he had preached for years. "All he knows about southern Africa," one of his own officials privately commented, "is that he is on the side of the whites."[8] He might have added, without fear of contradiction, "and against the Cubans." The hardline perspective, benefitting from its correspondence to the president's world view, had significant support within the Republican party. Lobbyists for South Africa, such as Donald de Kieffer and John Sears, were well connected in the Reagan camp.[9] Senator Jesse Helms was only the most prominent of its advocates among Senate Republicans.

Within the administration, "neoconservative" Jeane Kirkpatrick at the US mission to the United Nations (UN) preached opposition to the Soviet Union and Third World revolution as fervently as any pure-bred rightist. In a 1979 *Commentary* article that impressed President Reagan and led to her appointment, she argued that rightist "authoritarian" regimes, whatever their faults, were natural allies of the United States and potentially reformable. Leftist "totalitarian" regimes and movements, however, were irredeemable.[10]

Another advocate of giving priority to anticommunist causes was William J. Casey, director of the CIA.[11] Casey, one of the founders of the CIA, had been a tax lawyer, head of Nixon's Securities and Exchange Commission, and a founder of the National Strategy Information Center, a right-wing think tank in New York. Casey took over as Reagan's campaign manager for the last six months preceding the 1980 election and retained close ties to the president. In his confirmation testimony he spoke of the necessity of "unleashing the ability of the organization to initiate and carry out its objectives," and during his tenure the pace of covert operations quickened, despite the caution of some experienced CIA professionals. According to Leslie Gelb, writing in the *New York Times* of 11 June 1984, covert operations had increased fivefold since 1980, to an ongoing total of 50. About half were in Central America, "with a large percentage in Africa as well." Casey repeatedly argued for giving increased support to Unita in Angola.

At the State Department, the abrasive and forceful Alexander Haig initially filled the top post. The general, who had served as deputy to Kissinger, White House chief of staff during Nixon's final days, and North Atlantic Treaty Organization (Nato) Supreme Commander, held views well positioned between right and far right. Several of his appointments, including Crocker, disappointed right-wing ideologues.

In many respects, however, Haig faithfully hewed to the extremist line, earning the praise of neoconservative pundit Norman Podhoretz.[12] Haig spoke of "going to the source" in Cuba to stop revolutionary ferment in Central America. In

1979, while serving as president of United Technologies Corporation, he had testified to the House Subcommittee on Mining, echoing a favorite South African theme. The enormous mineral wealth of southern Africa, he said, was threatened by a "resource war" fostered by "Soviet proxy activity in the Third World."[13] The "loss" of southern Africa "could bring the severest consequences to the economic and security framework of the Third World." His racist insensitivity was well illustrated by his habit, in Nixon's National Security Council (NSC) staff meetings, of playfully beating the table like a jungle drum whenever African topics were discussed.

Reagan campaign adviser Richard Allen, considered an asset by the far right, started out at the NSC. One of the founders of the conservative Georgetown University Center for Strategic and International Studies in Washington, D.C., Allen had served a short stint in the Nixon White House, where Kissinger reportedly regarded him as a member of the "sandbox right." From 1972 to 1974 Allen served as a foreign agent for the Overseas Companies of Portugal, trying to improve the image of Portuguese colonialism in Washington.[14] He resigned from the NSC under a cloud of suspicion over financial dealings in January 1982, becoming a Distinguished Fellow at the far-right Heritage Foundation in Washington. But he was present during the crucial first year, which set the tone of US hostility toward black Africa. Allen's Africa aide, Fred Wettering, who had served as CIA station chief in Mozambique in 1975–1977 and was a leading advocate of a hostile US approach to Marxist regimes, continued to hold the NSC Africa post until late 1984.

Allen was replaced at the NSC by William F. Clark, one of Reagan's California cronies, who admitted he had no knowledge of foreign policy before he was appointed as under secretary of state in 1981.[15] Clark shared the president's hardline instincts. Since he was a forceful advocate of increased military intervention in Central America and of a posture of increased "strength" toward the Soviet Union, Clark's high position reassured ideologues who feared the influence of "moderates" on the White House staff.

George Shultz's appointment as secretary of state in mid-1982 and Clark's replacement by Robert McFarlane at the NSC the following year established a somewhat more favorable climate for more pragmatic right-wing views, already established in the State Department's Africa Bureau.[16] Sharing the objectives of global counterrevolution, these practitioners of *Realpolitik* argued that a successful US policy had to take into account the limits posed by real conditions in southern Africa, using the carrot as well as the stick with left-wing regimes. Keeping an anxious watch over their right shoulders, the Africa Bureau pragmatists managed to win administration tolerance, if not always enthusiastic backing, for negotiations.

Crocker, the strategy's chief spokesman, had directed African Studies at Georgetown University's Center for Strategic and International Studies from 1976 to 1981. He had written prolifically about US foreign policy in Africa, offering what he billed as a hardheaded alternative to the "romantic illusion" of Carter's "regionalist" policies.[17] US policy, he argued, should take account of both the Soviet threat and local realities, and "raise the price of Soviet involvement in both regional and global terms."

Although he had supported the white-dominated internal settlement regime in Rhodesia and criticized the liberal realists in the US government who had persisted in negotiations, Crocker was willing to see hope for good US relations with the new government in Zimbabwe. Not only were the election victors committed to "moderation," but the dominant Zimbabwe African National Union (Zanu) had no debts to the Soviet Union, which had backed the rival Zimbabwe African People's Union (Zapu). Perhaps the West could take advantage of the new situation.

The British success in aiding Rhodesia's transition to independence, moreover, might provide a model for Namibia. Britain had played a dominant role as mediator, using its acknowledged bias against the guerrillas as leverage on both sides.[18] The British pressured Zanu and Zapu by threatening to accept a settlement excluding them and encouraged South African and Rhodesian whites to make concessions by supporting them on particular issues. A conservative US administration with a sufficiently active diplomacy might assume a similar role in defusing the continuing war on the Namibian-Angolan front. The United States could deliver an independent Namibia to Africa while reassuring South Africa that it could retain its regional influence. As a special bonus for both South Africa and the United States, Angola could be induced to send the Cubans home. Southern Africa could again become a "Soviet-free" zone.

The focus on getting the Cubans out of Angola is in part explained by Crocker's need to appease the ideological cold warriors. After all, Senator Jesse Helms held up Crocker's appointment until August 1981, bombarding him with questions testing his willingness to uphold the anticommunist cause. Protecting himself against Helms and keeping the support of the president required repeated reaffirmations of anticommunist shibboleths.

But the tilt to South Africa in the Crocker strategy was not merely an internal Washington ploy. It also expressed the instinctive sympathies and underlying strategic assumptions of the so-called moderates themselves. Although Crocker had a reputation as an Africanist scholar, one can search his writings in vain for either sympathy or detailed knowledge of any part of the continent save white South Africa.

Crocker shared the view—common to the right and far right—that the Cubans and the Soviets were the "destabilizing" factors in the subcontinent. The instability following the 1974 coup in Portugal had led to increased non-African involvement, he commented in a 1979 article, at the same time noting "a broad decline in European willingness to support African stability."[19] Western European involvement, including Portuguese

colonialism, apparently did not count as non-African involvement, which could only be Cuban or Soviet. Africans might see
gains in the end of the colonialist era, but Crocker, in contrast,
revealingly remarked in November 1982 that the major purpose
of "constructive engagement" was "to reverse the decline in
security and stability of southern Africa which has been under
way now since the early and mid-1970s."[20]

The slogan "constructive engagement" had already entered
the South African debate in reference to the role of foreign
investment. Merle Lipton, of Britain's establishment think tank
Chatham House, had argued in 1976 that industrialization was
improving the situation of South African blacks and that specific reforms by foreign companies could accelerate the process.
Crocker's version put the emphasis on political action, explicitly putting his faith in the *verligte* (enlightened) politicians.
US political scientist Samuel Huntington, infamous for his
diagnosis of an "excess of democracy" in Western societies, put
the thesis to the South African Political Science Association in
1981, citing South Africa's need for skillful and authoritarian
leadership to implement reform and avoid revolution. Effective
repression, he noted, might contribute to the "relatively happy
outcome" of a "quadri-racial polity" in which each ethnic group
had a share of power, without the drastic consequences of a
nonracial franchise.[21]

In South Africa, Crocker argued, the United States should
encourage "white-led change." The South African government,
controlled by Afrikaner reformers, deserved encouragement
and reassurance. It needed protection from the threat of violence and Soviet intervention, so it could make changes without fear of losing control. If the United States made clear that it
shared those goals, Crocker argued repeatedly, then South Africa's white oligarchy could be persuaded to make concessions
that would enhance the long-term stability of its position and
win greater international acceptability. The militarily inferior
Africans would just have to wait, be ready to make concessions

when necessary and recognize that the US diplomatic initiative was "the only game in town."

Crocker took the diplomatic task seriously, aided after April 1982 by Frank Wisner as his deputy who, unlike Crocker, won respect from African diplomats for his low-key professional stance.[22] But not even the most persistent diplomacy could counter the flawed assumption that stability could come from tilting to Pretoria. South Africa's position was fundamentally different from that of white Rhodesia.

The settlement in Rhodesia (Zimbabwe), the advocates of "constructive engagement" seemed to forget, came only after the Smith regime was decisively weakened by international sanctions and guerrilla warfare. Sanctions imposed to date on South Africa were far weaker than those inconsistently enforced against Rhodesia. And while guerrilla warfare was persistent to Namibia and beginning in South Africa, it was not yet a serious drain on South African resources. Without changes in these basic factors, no settlements were on the horizon.

The advocates of "constructive engagement" might urge moderation on South Africa's rulers. But their own strategic decision in favor of closer ties, together with the administatration's overall stance further to the right, sent a clear signal to South Africa that there would be no penalty for intransigence. Washington bolstered Pretoria's capacity to delay at home and intervene abroad, emboldening the hawks and postponing the day of reckoning.

TILTING TO PRETORIA

Only days after Reagan's inauguration, the South African regime launched its largest raid to date on Mozambique, killing 12 people in the capital city. The raid, following a speech by Secretary of State Haig condemning "rampant international terrorism," was justified by the South Africans as an attack on "terrorist bases" of the banned ANC. Throughout Africa the action was seen as a dramatic symbol of the new Washington team's support for the apartheid regime, an impression that was to be repeatedly confirmed.

"Let this be the new beginning of mutual trust and confidence between the United States and South Africa, old friends, like Minister Botha, who are getting together again." The specific reference, from Under Secretary of State Clark's toast to Foreign Minister Roelof "Pik" Botha in May 1981, was to Botha's experience as ambassador to Washington from 1975–1977. But the theme of mutual confidence pointed to the future. South Africa's leaders, Crocker had written in a "Scope Paper" for the May meetings in Washington, "are deeply suspicious of us, of our will, from the 1975–76 experience and the Carter period."[23]

In Crocker's view, the first step was to convince South Africa that the United States shared the same regional objectives. The "top US priority," Crocker had told the South Africans in April in Pretoria, "is to stop Soviet encroachment in Africa." According to the May "Scope Paper," the new relationship with South Africa "should be based upon our shared hopes for the future prosperity, security and stability of southern Africa, constructive internal change within South Africa and our shared perception of the role of the Soviet Union and its surrogates in thwarting those goals."

Crocker advised the secretary of state to tell the South Africans that "we cannot afford to give you a blank check regionally." Perhaps the check was not entirely blank. But Pretoria could count both on Washington's explicit desire to reestablish "confidence" and on the unspoken awareness that beyond Crocker, who was still not confirmed for office, were forces even more sympathetic to South Africa. This left room for quite a substantial overdraft. Small-print reminders that it would be nice to reach a settlement in Namibia could be postponed for later payment.

Pretoria's "total strategy" had, by early 1981, suffered setbacks at the regional level. The key to the strategy in 1978 and 1979 had been building a "constellation of states" under South African leadership, making it possible to rely primarily on economic and political influence rather than direct military power. But this depended on a favorable political outcome in Zimbabwe, an expectation punctured by Mugabe's landslide election victory announced on 4 March 1980. One month later, on 1 April, the official launching of the Southern African Development Coordination Conference (SADCC), a grouping of independent African states in the region, put an end to the idea of a formal Pretoria-centered constellation.

As the Botha regime intensified military intervention against its neighbors, the signals from Washington blinked bright green. The attack on Mozambique in January did not result in a rebuke from Washington; instead Pretoria watched as US-Mozambican relations deteriorated. In March the Mozambican government expelled several US diplomats, charging they had been part of a CIA intelligence network that had targetted the government, as well as South African exiles. Washington retaliated by cutting off food assistance.

Mozambique's action came only one day after President Reagan had strongly endorsed friendship with South Africa on nationwide television. In response to a question from broadcaster Walter Cronkite, the president rhetorically declaimed: "Can we abandon a country that has stood by us in every war we've ever fought, a country that is strategically essential to the free world?" Praising the remark, the South African Broadcasting Corporation noted that the US president had "disposed of the ambiguity and the veiled hostility which in recent years have characterized Washington's approach to this country."[24]

Two weeks later, five high-ranking military officers visited the United States at the invitation of a private far-right organization, the American Security Council, meeting with NSC and Defense Department officials, as well as with UN Ambassador

Kirkpatrick. The State Department was reportedly "taken by surprise."

Such incidents in early 1981 might be interpreted simply as signs of inchoate policy: Crocker was still unconfirmed, a policy review on southern Africa was begun but not completed, and the stance toward Angola was being contested from all sides. But South African actions soon provided a litmus test for the new administration.

In 1981, the pace of military action in the "operational zone" of southern Angola intensified, culminating in mid-August in the largest penetration of Angolan territory since 1976. Operation Protea, with a force of 11,000 men, went beyond the periodic raids of previous years to occupy much of Cunene province.

Official US reaction, billed as "evenhanded," echoed South Africa's justifications of its action. Deploring "escalation of violence in southern Africa regardless of its source," Secretary of State Haig reminded a press conference of the threat of Cuban forces, Soviet advisers and Soviet arms. These arms, he added, had "been used to refurbish Swapo elements that move back and forth freely across that frontier and inflict bloodshed and terrorism upon the innocent noncombatant inhabitants of Namibia."[25]

The following week the United States, breaking with its European allies, vetoed a UN Security Council resolution condemning the South African invasion, opposing even the verbal condemnation approved on a similar occasion in 1980. Crocker, in a major policy speech two days before the UN veto, said the United States "should sustain those who would resist the siren call of violence and the blandishments of Moscow and its clients."[26]

Implying that the South African action should be seen as defensive, he blamed the Warsaw Pact for supporting guerrillas in Namibia and South Africa and noted that South Africa "has clearly signalled its determination to resist guerrilla encroachments and strike at countries giving sanctuary."

Crocker regarded limited South African concessions as a rational strategy to insure greater stability. So advising Pretoria, US policy makers also sought to decrease the cost of making concessions by promising concomitant gains: closer US ties and the ouster of "Soviet surrogates." Closer ties were proffered in advance, however, and the prospect that the Soviet-supported Cuban presence in Angola could be removed by Washington's negotiating strategy was remote. Therefore the cost to South Africa of not making concessions and of escalating its military response was reduced. US pressure for "internal reform" receded into near invisibility. On the Namibian question, which dominated the diplomatic picture, the United States could not deliver a Cuban withdrawal and a Swapo sufficiently emasculated to cajole Pretoria into a settlement.

Most importantly, raising the costs for South African intransigence, by using pressures to make the continued stalemate or escalation less attractive, was ruled out in advance. This option was excluded not only on the premise that South Africa as the dominant regional power must be placated, but also because it might conflict with the priority goal of attacking the Cuban presence. Even if the State Department were willing to compromise, Reagan's ideological supporters would certainly object. Whatever South Africa's leaders did, they could be confident that Washington would not impose penalties.

Crocker might have thought he could convince the Angolan government to accept linking Cuban troop withdrawal to Namibian independence, promising as incentives peace and improved economic ties, while working on the language of an agreement acceptable to Angola. At a simple empirical level, "linkage" was obvious and accepted by all parties. Angola and Cuba had long taken the position that the troops would leave once the threat from South Africa was removed.

But the meaning of "linkage" depended entirely on context and timing. To accept a formal linkage between the two issues was to put Namibian independence—a cause with virtually universal international and legal legitimacy—on the same level with Angola's sovereign decisions on self-defense against South Africa. For African and most international opinion, the Cuban presence as defense against South Africa was at least as legitimate as that of US troops in Western Europe. The "sphere of influence" concepts of Washington or Pretoria, a "Monroe doctrine" for southern Africa, could not be conceded legitimacy.

Such issues might be finessed by diplomatic wording, but the United States repeatedly reinforced Angolan doubts on the central issue of security. If, in fact, Cuban troops were to be withdrawn, while South Africa still occupied Namibia and maintained its support for Unita guerrilla actions, what assurance could Angola have that its enemies would not try to move in for the kill? This question would remain even if direct South African attacks on Angola were suspended. Angolan acceptance, therefore, depended on building confidence that South Africa was ready to accept an independent Namibia not under its military influence or that the United States would compel South Africa to accept such an arrangement.

In June 1981, Under Secretary of State Clark pledged to the South Africans that the United States would ensure that Cuban troops left Angola, so that South Africa might feel secure enough to accept a Namibia settlement. Instead of pressuring South Africa to leave Namibia so the Cubans could leave Angola, the United States stressed the reverse sequence, giving South Africa a ready-made excuse for delay.

The United States also disqualified itself as a credible mediator by favoring Unita. Although this fell short of the full-scale support the far right demanded, it sufficed to raise suspicions in Luanda that Washington, as well as Pretoria, sought the downfall of the Angolan government.

Candidate Reagan had said he would provide Unita's forces with weapons, "to free themselves from the rule of an outside power, which is the Cubans and East Germans."[27] But in 1981, the administration failed to repeal the Clark amendment, in spite of a 66 to 29 repeal vote in the Senate. The measure was blocked by strong opposition within the Democratic-controlled House Foreign Affairs Committee and lobbying by US companies, as well as Africa-related groups in Washington.

One major reason for caution was the fact that US companies, including the giant Gulf Oil Corporation, had investments in Angola. These companies regarded the Angolan government as a trustworthy "businesslike" partner and were skeptical about efforts at destabilization. With good working relationships in Angola, they could hardly be expected to sacrifice profits to satisfy right-wing ideologues in the White House or Senate.

Even some voices close to the South African security establishment warned against going too far in Angola. Mike Hough, director of the Institute of Strategic Studies in Pretoria, noted that aid to Unita would increase Soviet and Cuban involvement. Support "massive" enough to bring Jonas Savimbi to power, he added, would mean the United States would "have to prop him up as they did the government in South Vietnam."[28]

Crocker's diplomatic strategy also imposed some caution. If US intervention grew too blatant, it could further antagonize African countries and upset European allies with investments in Angola. The Soviet Union might well match the new aid. And if Luanda felt Washington would stop short of nothing but its overthrow, negotiations would be beside the point. Still Crocker endorsed political support for Unita and tried to use the threat of escalation to pressure Luanda into accepting "linkage."

Savimbi arrived in Washington for a visit in December 1981. The same month Crocker met Angolan Foreign Minister Paulo Jorge in Paris, lecturing him on the need to brign Savimbi into the government and dismissing Angolan concerns about defense against South Africa.[29] Suspicions repeatedly surfaced that the United States was violating the spirit if not the letter of the Clark amendment, through CIA encouragement of Unita backers such as Israel, Morocco, Saudi Arabia and Zaire. In

January 1982 Savimbi told journalists in Morocco, "A great country like the United States has other channels. . . . The Clark Amendment means nothing."[30]

The Washington tilt to Pretoria was not only visible on the Namibian-Angolan front. Observers noted resumption of previous staffing levels for military attachés, attendance by two South African military officers at a US Coast Guard air and sea rescue mission, and visas issued for October visits for two South African Police (SAP) generals. These measures, commented a State Department official in November 1981, were altering the "intangible atmosphere" of bilateral relations with South Africa. The critics were wrong in seeing such moves as "tangible carrots," he added.[31]

More substantial "carrots" were on the way, however. First the sluice gate was opened wider for strategic exports, allowing small exceptions to flow through such as airport security equipment. Revised export regulations in 1982 lifted the ban on sale of nonmilitary items to the South African military and police. Licenses were issued for export of two powerful computers to the government's Council for Scientific and Industrial Research.

So lax were the controls that they were, ironically, used as cover for diversion of equipment to the Soviet Union. Two shipments of components for a Digital Vax 11/782 system were intercepted by US customs officials in Sweden and Federal Republic of Germany in November 1983. Routinely approved for export to South Africa, the computer became a "serious security concern" when discovered en route to the Soviet Union.[32]

In general, security-related trade with South Africa increased significantly. Trade in computers, for example, was running at more than twice the $78 million annual average of the three years after the Carter administration imposed its 1977 controls. Commerce Department license approvals for security-related exports totalled $547 million in 1981, almost as much as the

$577 million for the three previous years combined. In 1982, with all but the most sensitive items excluded from licensing requirements, approvals under license amounted to $585 million. Sales under separate munitions list regulations also rose sharply.[33] Restrictions on nuclear-related exports were also loosened, despite a continuing dispute over Pretoria's failure to agree to sign the Nuclear Non-Proliferation Treaty (NPT).

Equally welcome in Pretoria were US efforts to assuage South Africa's growing economic woes. Gold fell from an average price of some $613 per ounce in 1980 to $460 per ounce in 1981 and $350 per ounce in mid-1982. The balance of payments on current account dipped to a $4 billion deficit in 1981, forcing an accelerated turn to international capital markets. By mid-1982 financial analysts were speculating that Pretoria would again turn to special International Monetary Fund (IMF) credits. In November the IMF approved a $1.1 billion credit facility. The congressional Black Caucus had appealed to the Reagan administration to vote against the loan, but the United States enthusiastically endorsed the South African application, deciding the issue with its 20 percent share of the vote. The allocation was comparable to the increase in South Africa's military expenditures from 1980 to 1982.[34]

The IMF loan was accompanied by a sharp rise in US bank lending. In the 18 months from January 1981 through June 1982, US bank loans outstanding to South Africa increased by some 246 percent. The total reached $3.7 billion in 1982 and $4.6 billion in 1983. Over the same period, US direct investment declined slightly, from $2.6 billion to $2.3 billion, reflecting the generally difficult circumstances of the South African economy.[35] The inflow of loan capital, however, was a sign that South Africa could count on its Western economic backers in time of need.

Thus, midway through Reagan's first term, the primary effect of "constructive engagement" had been to encourage South Africa in its more aggressive regional policy. By 1983, however, it became harder to postpone counting the costs. In Pretoria's national security establishment some argued that it would be better to accept objectives more limited than the overthrow or constant destabilization of hostile regimes, to explore a *modus vivendi* that might cut war costs and win international credit for moderation.

In Washington there was increasing criticism of "constructive engagement" by Congress and others. Even among the policy's supporters there was recognition that the tilt might have gone too far, undercutting the spirit of compromise it was supposed to foster. Not least important, Western European governments were increasingly concerned at the damage done to their interests by the escalating warfare. The United States might be conceded the diplomatic initiative, but Europe had even more at stake in the region than Washington—not only in South Africa but also in the countries that were its targets.

THE HALTING DETENTE

In 1981 the tilt toward South Africa quickly became the dominant feature of Reagan administration policy. In the supposedly "evenhanded" approach, the "other hand" stretched out to Pretoria's opponents was, at best, hesitant. There was little effort at a serious dialogue with Angola or Mozambique, and a virtual boycott of contacts with the ANC and Swapo.

Washington initially tried to woo the newly independent Zimbabwe, approving Carter plans for boosting bilateral aid, but parlaying the Harare connection into an asset for Washington's regional strategy proved elusive. Regardless of its tensions with the Soviet Union, Harare was not to be recruited in a crusade against Cuban troops in Angola or other efforts to "reassure Pretoria." Meanwhile, South African attacks on Mozambique directly imperilled Zimbabwe. South Africa supplied arms to exploit discontent among former guerrillas of Joshua

Nkomo's Zapu in Matabeleland and delayed rail shipments to Harare. Such actions fell short of those against Angola, Mozambique or even Lesotho, but the threat of escalation was unmistakable. US development aid was hardly adequate compensation for an overall US policy that encouraged South African aggression.

Gradually, however, regional negotiations gained momentum. From 1982 and 1983 the balance in Washington shifted toward compromise, affected by more moderate oficials replacing hardliners in the administration. Professional diplomat Wisner joined the Crocker team in April 1982. Shultz took over from Haig as secretary of state in June. And National Security Adviser Clark, Reagan's far-right watchdog, was replaced by his "realist" deputy, McFarlane, in October 1983. Outside the administration, anti-apartheid groups and Africa sympathizers in the House of Representatives mounted a steady challenge to Reagan's South Africa tilt. The November 1982 election brought a larger Democratic majority and a more critical mood to the House of Representatives. Hearings exposed the loosening of export controls and questioned US complicity in South African destabilization of the Frontline states. The divestment movement continued a steady advance over the 1982–1984 period. With states and cities such as Michigan and Boston joining the drive public funds withdrawn from companies involved in South Africa approached the $1 billion mark.[36]

The 1982 IMF loan to South Africa led to an extended legislative battle over the US contribution to the fund's capital. A compromise resolution, passed in November 1983, mandated that the United States "actively oppose any facility involving use of Fund credit by any country which practices apartheid." In the same session, amendments to the Export Administration Act imposing penalties on South Africa first passed the House of Representatives. The measures had little chance of gaining Senate approval, but would be contended throughout 1984.

Pretoria, gauging reaction in the United States, increasingly had to weigh the prospect that Congress and the public might take action on their own. The administration remained apparently indifferent to criticism from the center and left, but its flexibility in granting new "carrots" to South Africa was hampered by the prospect of congressional reaction.

Another influence that Washington could not entirely ignore was the stance of its Western partners. Even with Margaret Thatcher's Conservative administration in London or the Helmut Kohl coalition that took over in Bonn in late 1982, Reagan's officials found little sympathy for hardline opposition to the Angolan and Mozambican governments. None of the other members of the UN "contact group" on Namibia—the Federal Republic of Germany, France, Britain and Canada—supported the Pretoria-Washington "linkage" concept. The European Economic Community (EEC) and the Commonwealth secretariat, as well as the Scandinavian countries, actively backed SADCC; they could see that their aid projects and economic opportunities were directly threatened by South Africa's destabilization campaign.

France, after the election of President François Mitterand in May 1981, was most outspoken in disagreeing with Washington on southern African poilcy. Paris broke with Washington to vote for a September 1981 UN Security Council resolution demanding withdrawal of South African troops from Angola and hosted Angolan President José Eduardo dos Santos later that year. An economic cooperation agreement was signed with Mozambique in December 1981. Two years later France officially withdrew from the "contact group" on Namibia.

Bonn, too, with its special interest in Namibia, encouraged contacts between Swapo and the German community there, and urged Washington to be more forthcoming in negotiations with Angola and with Swapo. Britian, for its part, had especially great economic stakes and other interests in Zimbabwe. British troops had stayed on as advisers and trainers with the postindependence Zimbabwe army. And yet Zimbabwe, as the land-locked hub of SADCC's plans for improved regional transportation, was vitally endangered by South Africa's campaign against Mozambique. The oil pipeline from Beira and rail connections to both Beira and Maputo were repeated targets. London was in no danger of being converted to sanctions against South Africa, which might endanger the enormous British business interests there, but the unrestrained ventures of Pretoria's hawks were also bad for business.

In June 1983 US Under Secretary of State Lawrence Eagleburger restated the themes of "constructive engagement" in a major speech. Some observers attached great importance to the stronger language he used to condemn apartheid, and to his avoidance of words such as "pro-Soviet" and "linkage."[37] It was not a red light for Pretoria, but the subtle shift at least indicated a yellow "caution" light.

By the time of Eagleburger's speech, moreover, Pretoria, as well as Washington, was having to ask some hard questions about the results of the destabilization policy. The far right in both capitals might want to pursue the maximum objectives of "rollback," or permanent destabilization of neighboring states, but there were also those concerned with the price tag.

In 1982 there was no sign of restraint. A new June attack on Angola came just as then US roving Ambassador Vernon Walters was in Luanda reassuring the Angolans that there would be no escalation. In December the South African Defense Force (SADF) launched an attack on Maseru, Lesotho, killing 42 people. Simultaneously, commandoes targetted the oil depot in Beira, Mozambique, where supplies vital to Zimbabwe were stored. In 1983, South African military pressure mounted, with a steady escalation of supplies to the Mozambique National Resistance (MNR) in Mozambique and continued occupation of southern Angola.

In August 1982 Mozambique's government put the country on a war footing and launched a diplomatic offensive to mobilize Western pressure on South Africa. Maputo aimed at convincing key leaders in the West that Mozambique was not, and indeed never had been, a Soviet satellite and that the blame for escalating conflict in the region, endangering Western investments as well as prospects for development, lay with South Africa.

Crocker had long argued that the United States and South Africa could live with the Mozambique Liberation Front (Frelimo), the ruling party, given the independent role the Maputo leadership had played in the Zimbabwe settlement and the low level of Soviet military presence. US diplomacy only began to reflect this view, however, after a meeting between Secretary of State Shultz and Mozambican Foreign Minister Joaquim Chissano in October 1982. A State Department statement in January 1983 acknowledging South African sponsorship of antigovernment bandits in Mozambique was another signal taken seriously in Maputo, leading to further talks between the two countries.

Mozambique also sought to influence Washington and Pretoria by appealing to Western Europe. On a European tour in October 1983 President Samora Machel won a sympathetic hearing from Thatcher and Mitterand, as well as from officials in Lisbon. South African Foreign Minister Pik Botha, visiting European capitals in the wake of the Machel trip, was told repeatedly that South African attacks were damaging Western interests in the area.

This added to the questioning among South Africa's leaders, who clearly had the military capacity to create ever-increasing chaos and destruction—but at what cost, and to what end?

The advocates of a "total strategy" first had to consider South Africa's increasing economic weakness. In the second half of 1982 the gold price recovered, rising from a low of $300 per ounce briefly to top $500 per ounce in January 1983. Still, the real gross domestic product (GDP) fell 1 percent in 1982. Then the gold price began another steep dive, plunging to almost $400 by the end of February and below the $400 mark by the end of the year. Real GDP declined 3 percent in 1983. Other economic indicators showed similarly disturbing trends. The rand exchange rate against the dollar, which had hit $1.35 in mid-1980, was down to $.85 by mid-1982. A brief recovery was then followed by a steady decline in 1983 and 1984 to under $.60 by mid-1984. With the added problems of drought, rising interest rates and inflation, South Africa faced its most serious economic crisis in 50 years.

Consequently the costs of war loomed larger. On the western front, in Namibia and Angola, military and other subsidies cost more than $1 billion a year. Still, the prospect of overthrowing Luanda was blocked. The Angolan army was reinforced in 1983 with new Soviet aid and strengthened by internal reorganization. The costs to Pretoria in December 1983 of its latest Angolan invasion were unexpectedly high, in men and material, as the Angolans effectively used new defense equipment including helicopter gunships and MiG fighters. The Soviet Union delivered an unprecedented direct and explicit warning to Pretoria that it would aid in countering any new South African escalation.

In the east, the cost was less direct expenditure than lost economic opportunities. Boycotting the port at Maputo bludgeoned the Mozambican government, but it also made transportation more expensive for South African business in the northern Transvaal Province. Chaos and bankruptcy in Mozambique removed a potential market. Sabotaged power lines meant South Africa had to do without electricity from Cahora Bassa in Mozambique.

Since 1982 Frelimo had improved its military capacity by reorganizing in smaller guerrilla-style units. But Pretoria was able to continue its escalation by increasing infiltration and supplies to their surrogates, the MNR; however, the MNR's character as a mercenary organization was a liability to the South Africans. Although it caused chaos and sapped confidence in the Mozambican government, it had no political program or credible leadership. Furthermore, its most vocal representatives abroad were former Portuguese settlers. In military terms, it perhaps could be installed in power, but then South Africa would have to provide support, and the military odds would change dramatically as South Africa's clients lost the advantage of the offensive.

By mid-1983 a balance sheet for the hardline military option showed a mixed picture. The toll of destruction was enormous, particularly in southern Angola and in Mozambique. Drought added to the devastation in Mozambique while the continuing MNR campaign targetted and largely crippled relief efforts. Both Angola and Mozambique had been forced virtually to suspend development plans while struggling for survival. Confidence in a socialist future, and even in the capacity of the governments to provide basic security and subsistence, was ebbing.

But without the capacity to install its clients in power, Pretoria's success in curbing Swapo or the ANC was problematic. Swapo camps in Angola were raided, but its low-level guerrilla warfare in Namibia seemed unimpaired. Politically, the movement continued to erode South Africa's efforts to build an "internal" political alternative in Windhoek. Pretoria was buying time to boost its protégés, but time could not substitute for political credibility. As for the ANC, its sabotage attacks were gaining visibility and expanding its support among blacks. The widespread geographic dispersion of targets—from the Koeberg nuclear plant in Cape Town to air force headquarters in Pretoria—refuted any suggestion of cross-border raids. Some guerrilla cadres were captured inside South Africa, others killed in attacks on Maputo and Maseru, but these dramatic incidents not only failed to stem ANC sabotage, they also helped to build the guerrillas' prestige among black South Africans. Most whites might be persuaded by the external threat hypothesis, but that propaganda backfired among blacks. Even some prominent white government supporters began to say that someday it would be necessary to talk to the ANC.

It was this context, more than US initiatives, that led to limited successes for US regional diplomacy. Taking advantage of the desire for respite from war in Luanda and Maputo, and of Pretoria's apparent willingness to limit its objectives, US diplomats helped to facilitate negotiations, taking the lead on the Angolan front and responding to the Mozambican initiative on the other side of the continent. To translate the appearance of detente into real restraints on Pretoria, however, would require penalties for South African violations; and that was still excluded from Washington's options. Washington, as well as Pretoria, would accept thankfully the restrictions placed on Swapo or the ANC, but neither would genuinely accept a bar to further counterrevolutionary intervention in Angola and Mozambique.

The first sign of limited detente came in February 1984; a US-brokered agreement for South African troop withdrawal and restrictions on Swapo guerrillas in southern Angola. In March, Mozambique and South Africa signed the Nkomati Accord, which bound the two states to forbid any violent acts against each other from their territories. Although Maputo pledged its continued "moral, political and diplomatic" support for the ANC, South African officials and the majority of international observers characterized the agreement as a sign of a "Pax Pretoriana." The term, however, was misleading not only because it exaggerated the imminence of peace, but also because it ignored the concessions South Africa would have made if it had implemented the security treaty and lifted its economic sanctions against Mozambique.

Given the military and economic odds they faced, even before the escalation of 1981–1983, the Mozambican leadership saw the Nkomati Accord as a victory. In spite of overwhelming material predominance, Pretoria had failed to install a political alternative and neither South Africa nor the United States had been able to impose a break in Mozambique's ties with the Soviet Union. In addition, Maputo would continue moral and diplomatic support to the ANC. Granted, limits would be imposed on possible ANC use of Mozambican territory to support guerrilla operations in South Africa, but, reasoned Frelimo, that would be a relatively minor tactical retreat for the ANC, with its strong base of support inside South Africa. Moreover, it would be reaffirming the long-held Mozambican position that it was simply not possible for adjacent states to offer the same kind of rear-base support to the ANC that the Mozambican and Zimbabwean movements had enjoyed.[38]

Mozambique, in implementing the treaty, restricted the ANC to a small diplomatic office in Maputo; several hundred ANC members left the country, but probably more significant for Pretoria was the widespread perception of the pact as a victory for South Africa. Most of the Frontline states, as well as the ANC, shared this view that Mozambique had conceded most; and Maputo found it hard to bridge the gap of understanding. This perception was more significant for Pretoria than the additional transit difficulties caused for guerrillas of the ANC. For Prime Minister P. W. Botha, Nkomati bought diplomatic credit and a European trip. South Africa basked in its image as a peacemaker while the Reagan administration cited the new trend as a victory for their policy of "constructive engagement."

The gains for both signatories were short-lived, however. In South Africa the focus shifted to the rising internal revolt, impossible to blame on guerrilla infiltration. And in Mozambique it soon became clear that the MNR was still receiving external support and that material assistance was coming through South Africa. The security situation improved in some areas of Mozambique, enabling new relief supplies to reach the drought- and war-battered countryside. But in other areas of the country, including Maputo province directly adjoining South Africa, attacks on civilians escalated.

Documents captured by Zimbabwean and Mozambican troops when they took the MNR central base at Gorongosa in August 1985 showed that South African military intelligence officers had actively violated the Nkomati Accord by continuing arms supplies, with the approval of their superiors. The evidence revealed disagreements among South Africa's leaders on implementing the agreement. But it was clear that the advocates of diplomacy were either unwilling or unable to stop the parallel military track targetting Maputo.

President Machel visited Washington in September 1985, carrying the proof of Pretoria's duplicity. The visit resulted in Reagan's reaffirmation of detente, countering the far-right critics who called for support of the MNR as anticommunist freedom fighters. But the United States, it seemed, was unwilling to mobilize more coercive pressures on South Africa to respect the treaty.

Across the continent, detente was even less effective. South Africa had taken more than a year to withdraw troops from southern Angola, originally scheduled for March 1984. Moves toward explicit US support to Unita had heartened the hawks in Pretoria and derailed talks with Luanda. Pretoria had released Swapo founder Toivo ja Toivo, but was not ready to end the long-practiced tactics of delay over Namibia. Since Washington was reluctant to compromise on its anti-Cuban and pro-Unita stand, South Africa could hardly expect condemnation for its failure to make similar concessions.

By 1985, accordingly, the regional situation had reached a new stalemate. Detente had halted far short of independence for Namibia. South African aggression had been reduced from its peak intensity, but that change was only in small part due to Washington's diplomacy. Moreover, this was a precarious and limited accomplishment. Inside South Africa, an unprecedented escalation of internal strife was making a mockery of the claim that "constructive engagement" was promoting reform. The temporary setback to guerrilla action imposed by slower infiltration through Mozambique proved secondary to the fact that the primary base of opposition to the South African regime lay within the country. Popular resistance, multifaceted and persistent, nonviolent and violent, aroused an extraordinary response from sympathizers overseas. It also showed signs of shaking the confidence of Western business and political leaders in the apartheid regime.

WHICH SIDE ARE YOU ON?

In November 1984, Randall Robinson of TransAfrica, Dr. Mary Berry of the US Civil Rights Commission and Delegate Walter Fantroy of the District of Columbia staged a sit-in at the South African embassy in Washington. Their arrest marked the beginning of daily demonstrations at the embassy by the Free South Africa Movement. The symbolic action, with arrests day after day for an entire year, sparked and sustained an upsurge of anti-apartheid demonstrations in dozens of cities and universities around the country. The black-led demonstrations symbolized the commitment of US black leadership to play a role in US policy toward South Africa. The racial and political diversity of the demonstrators symbolized a broad-based rejection of racial division and injustice, a call to the US public to reaffirm opposition to racial oppression whether at home or abroad. The "constructive engagement" policy of the recently reelected Reagan administration was pilloried as an unholy alliance with racism.

The popular anti-apartheid movement in the United States in 1985 was stimulated by resistance in South Africa, conveyed to the world by unprecedented media attention. Built on years of anti-apartheid work around the country, the movement was catalyzed by the blatant Reagan tilt toward the South African regime. It became a force that neither US business nor Congress nor even the Reagan administration could ignore. But its very strength held weaknesses as well.

Many of the anti-apartheid supporters in Congress were inclined to limit their backing to the most symbolic and least substantive sanctions against South Africa. Moreover, neither the media nor the demonstrations adequately portrayed the links between Pretoria's internal repression and its regional aggression. South Africa incurred little additional penalty for escalation of attacks against its neighbors. Mainstream commentators and politicians joined with the far right in portraying the Angolan conflict as only peripherally connected to South Africa, if at all. With that connection obscured, policy makers considering Angola were far more inclined to follow well-worn anticommunist impulses than to link the conflict to the novel and perhaps short-lived anti-apartheid clamor.

To understand US policy on southern Africa in Reagan's second term, one must pay attention to the unprecedented growth of anti-apartheid pressure, to the still well-entrenched opposition to substantive sanctions against Pretoria and to the continued ability of right-wing elements to exploit anticommunist sentiment in favor of a regional tilt to Pretoria.

The swell of the anti-apartheid movement overseas arose both from the failrue of "reform" in South Africa and the steady growth of South African liberation forces. Unlike the decade after Sharpeville, when repression had imposed a discouraging break in the momentum of liberation, resistance in the post-Soweto decade was too strong and multifaceted to repress successfully.

By 1981 Prime Minister Botha's reform agenda was taking shape in new legislation, with such steps as legalizing black union membership and granting 99-year leases on some homes in black townships. The *verkrampte* (far-right) wing of the National Party in South Africa conjured up visions of a slide from piecemeal reform to black domination. After P. W. Botha, under strong pressure from businessmen, expelled the *verkramptes* in early 1982, he presented constitutional proposals billed as the first step toward power sharing. The changes, however, were seen by blacks less as concessions than as part of a strategy to entrench their subordination.

The rising black trade union movement, for example, made use of the leeway provided by the new labor legislation, but it was also facing harassment leading to identification of the "state" as a central obstacle to real progress. Purported reform of the pass laws, which lessened restrictions for Africans with urban residence rights, was even more fatally flawed. Pass law arrests doubled between 1981 and 1983, and fines were raised for employers hiring illegal workers. But the culminating insult to rising African aspirations was the new constitution, approved by white voters in a November 1983 referendum. It provided for three separate parliamentary chambers, for whites, "coloureds" and Indians, with a white majority and a white veto on matters of "common interest," as well as a new executive presidency with increased powers. Most significantly, the arrangements excluded any national role for Africans.

The United Democratic Front (UDF), a broad coalition of hundreds of groups of all races, came together in 1983 to oppose the new constitution. This new body campaigned for a boycott of the Indian and "coloured" elections and for a nonracial vision of the future South Africa. Black consciousness groups and trade unions, while not all willing to join the new coalition, were equally vehement in rejecting the govrenment's plans.

Detaining many UDF leaders just before the vote, Pretoria claimed a mandate for the new system despite a turnout of less than 5 percent. On 14 September, P. W. Botha was sworn in as president, with Pretoria's Angolan protégé Jonas Savimbi the most prominent African leader in attendance.

As Botha took office, police were battling protesters in black townships, opening a new round of conflict that would rage unabated throughout the next two years. The rapid growth of the UDF was an indicator of an even broader proliferation of organizations embodying black confidence and militance. The growth of the black and nonracial trade unions established a potentially critical base of political as well as economic influence. The ANC gained increased legitimacy, and demonstrators chanted calls for the exiled leaders to bring them arms. The ANC, for its part, told its followers that the guerrilla cadres and arms infiltrated at high prices into the country could only do part of the job. The people themselves, the ANC 1985 New Year's message stressed, would have to "make South Africa ungovernable."

Over the next year, before Pretoria banned television cameras from the townships, the pictures of police and soldiers shooting African youths made a powerful impression throughout the world. Funerals attended by tens of thousands served as new occasions for confrontation with authority when police tried to disperse mourners. A mid-1985 state of emergency over much of the country, thousands of detentions, the removal by arrest or sometimes death of a whole stratum of black leadership—all failed to restore order.

The world's view of events was also affected by the powerful media presence of government critics. The UDF's Allan Boesak, who also served as head of the World Alliance of Reformed Churches, eloquently addressed overseas audiences in tones reminiscent of the US civil rights leader Martin Luther King, Jr. Winnie Mandela, wife of imprisoned ANC leader Nelson Mandela, openly defied her banning order, commanding international attention from press and politicians. Recently "unbanned" Beyers Naudé, who was head of the South African Council of Churches, spoke with dignity and urgency of his white compatriots' failure to understand the depth of the crisis, his credibility due, in part, to his own elite Afrikaner background. Naudé's predecessor, Bishop Desmond Tutu, was awarded the Nobel Peace Prize in October 1984, using the platform he gained to call incessantly for outside pressure to end apartheid.

The Free South Africa Movement demonstrations captured the attention of the media and the public, accelerating both the nationwide divestment movement and the congressional move to legislate sanctions. If the surge of public pressure emerged suddenly, however, it was not without deeper roots, particularly the burgeoning divestment movement. For over 15 years, sometimes more actively and sometimes less but never stopping altogether, a network of church people, students and other activists had demanded that US companies get out of South Africa. In the 1970s, after the Soweto upheaval, the movement focussed on university campuses, where students called for university funds to be removed from companies with subsidiaries in South Africa or from banks that had made loans to its public and private sectors. The US companies responded by arguing that they could stay in South Africa and promote reforms, adopting equal employment codes of conduct such as the Sullivan principles.

As the years passed this excuse wore thin while the divestment movement simultaneously broadened its appeal. From 1980 through 1983, states as diverse as Nebraska, Michigan, Maryland, Massachusetts and Connecticut passed divestment legislation. The city of Philadelphia pension fund sold off $90 million in stocks in 1981, and during 1982 cities and states withdrew more than $300 million from companies with South African ties. The Washington, D. C. City Council approved a divestment bill in 1983. In August 1984 New York City voted to divest pension funds from companies with South African subsidiaries, potentially affecting some $600 million in assets. Boston enacted a similar measure the same month.

Early in 1985 New York City passed an additional measure forbidding city deposits in banks that loan to the South African government. "We were talking big bucks here, and money speaks," remarked the city's assistant controller. One of the nation's largest banks, Citibank, immediately announced it would phase out such loans. Pittsburgh and New York City acted later in the year to restrict purchases from companies involved in South Africa, and divestment action was under consideration in more than half the US states. In March, the American Chamber of Commerce in South Africa, still fighting the demand for withdrawal, warned the South African government that failure to eliminate apartheid could produce disastrous economic results.

By the end of 1985, divestment actions by US state and local governments had mandated almost $4.5 billion to be withdrawn from companies involved in South Africa, including some $2.6 billion with the concurrence of the Democratic-controlled legislature and Republican governor of New Jersey. A wave of student demonstrations leading to hundreds of arrests increased the pressure on universities. Columbia University finally yielded to student demands in the fall, and almost 30 universities opted for divestment during that year. Free South Africa movement demonstrators around the United States targetted the sale of Kruger rands, substantially cutting into sales and forcing numerous dealers to stop importing the South African gold coin.[39]

The most substantive escalation in economic pressure came in August 1985 when international banks, led by Chase Manhattan and other US banks, refused to roll over short-term loans to the private sector in South Africa, representing almost two-thirds of South Africa's foreign debt of over $20 billion. As the exchange rate of the rand dropped precipitously, Pretoria declared a moratorium on debt repayment into 1986. Bankers denied that political considerations had caused the move, but it came shortly after a speech by P. W. Botha that failed to satisfy demands for change. Political reform also dominated the agenda as Swiss banker Fritz Leutwiler attempted to negotiate a settlement. The panic had started with banks in New York, where the city council had already prohibited city deposits in banks making loans to the South African government. Undoubtedly, fear of new domestic repercussions was a factor in the bankers' minds.

The price of gold levelled at a little over $300 per ounce by the end of 1984, but the general economic crisis in South

Africa was reflected in the continued low exchange rate for the rand, which even dipped below $.40 after the state of emergency was declared. South African economists argued that the economy had a solid base for recovery, but, more and more, renewed confidence was seen to depend on political reform as well.

Actions from Western governments, more openly political and less easily reversed than those by private bankers, were hotly contested. Scandinavian countries were seriously considering embargoes on all economic ties with South Africa. After the Botha government imposed a state of emergency in July 1985, France recalled its ambassador, announced a ban on new investment in South Africa and introduced a UN Security Council resolution calling for similar voluntary action by other countries. The resolution passed 13 to zero, with Britian and the United States abstaining. The member nations of the EEC, in spite of reluctance in Bonn and London, agreed in September to maintain bans on oil and arms exports, and to withdraw their military attachés from Pretoria.

When Commonwealth leaders met in October, Britain was again the principal obstacle to action as African states and India argued for comprehensive and mandatory sanctions. A compromise agreement finally included a ban on Krugerrand imports and an end to government loans or financing of trade missions to South Africa. The leaders of the 49-member group threatened stronger action if South Africa had not begun to dismantle apartheid within six months.

In the United States, the sustained controversy echoed in the halls of Congress as well as on the streets. In 1984 sanctions, including a ban on new investment in South Africa, had been attached to the Export Administration Act, and passed in the House. Leaders of the effort, including Congressman William Gray of the congressional Black Caucus, were infuriated when the House failed to stand up to administration and Senate pressure to gut the bill, which died as a result. During the primary election campaign the Reverend Jesse Jackson made southern Africa a prominent issue.

In 1985, congressional sanctions backers launched a major new effort. A bill introduced by Congressman Ronald Dellums of California mandated comprehensive sanctions. Congressmen Gray and Wolpe introduced the Anti-Apartheid Act of 1985, sponsored in the Senate by Senator Edward Kennedy and others. The draft bill barred new US investment in South Africa, loans and computer sales to the South African government and the import of Kruger rands.

In June the Gray-Wolpe bill won overwhelming approval in the House of Representatives, with one-third of the Republicans joining Democrats in the 295 to 127 vote. After compromising with the Republican-controlled Senate to defer the ban on new investment for possible action a year later, the House passed a revised version by 380 to 48. In September, in a final concession to head off Senate approval and a predicted congressional override of his veto, the president issued an executive order with his version of the compromise measures.[40]

The Reagan team that responded to the new situation in 1985 still comprised the same personnel in the essential State Department posts. At the UN the vocal Kirkpatrick had been replaced by the more discreet Vernon Walters, who was, however, said to share a similar hardline perspective. The most notable addition to the White House staff was Director of Communications Patrick Buchanan, a fanatic ideologue who opposed criticism of South Africa and deplored the lack of enthusiasm for the anticommunist crusade. In the debate over sanctions in September, National Security Adviser McFarlane reportedly prevailed over Buchanan's no-compromise position. In December, largely because of conflicts with White House chief of staff Donald Regan, McFarlane resigned.

Reagan's shift, imposing sanctions, however limited, was a dramatic measure of the impact of public anti-apartheid sentiment. As a signal to Pretoria, however, it was decidedly ambiguous. Although the executive order incorporated measures such as bans on the import of Krugerrands and on new loans to the South African government, it was subject to discretionary reversal by the president. And it omitted the threat of future sanctions in the case of South African intransigence.

Even the strongest version of the Anti-Apartheid Act fell far short of comprehensive measures actually intended to weaken the apartheid state. It was understood by its sponsors to be a first step, a signal that could have an impact only if seen as a portent of stronger sanctions to come. The president's action instead indicated to Pretoria that these measures marked the limits of US sanctions. In November 1985, the United States and Britain reinforced this message by vetoing mandatory UN sanctions against South Africa in response to its continued occupation of Namibia. The package of "mandatory selective sanctions," on which France abstained and all other Security Council members voted in favor, included an oil embargo, a ban on new investment and other trade restrictions.

Reagan's executive order, some argued, had effectively checked the momentum of sanctions. After a year of daily actions, the Free South Africa Movement demonstrations at the South African embassy had lost much of their publicity value and were cut back to occasional rallies.

But the check was temporary. For the first time, sanctions had become a serious issue in the political mainstream. As the escalation of crisis and repression in South Africa continued, the 1986 congressional session produced even more dramatic results than in 1985. In May, South African attacks on Botswana, Zambia and Zimbabwe put an abrupt end to the mediation efforts of the Commonwealth Eminent Persons Group (EPG). Sponsors of a new anti-apartheid act brought their proposal to the floor of the House of Representatives on the eve of the 10th anniversary of the Soweto uprisings, just as Pretoria was declaring a new state of emergency.

On 18 June, Congressman Dellums proposed his comprehensive sanctions bill as a substitute for the limited measures introduced by Congressmen Gray and Wolpe. To the astonishment of its supporters, the Dellums bill passed by an overwhelming voice vote. The House action, coming even as the United States and Britain were vetoing yet another Security Council sanctions resolution, put sanctions opponents in the administration and the Senate on the defensive.

The State Department announced a reexamination of policy and tried to defuse criticism by seeking a black ambassador for South Africa. Republican Senate leader Dole told journalists, "We need something, some positive thing to forestall action."[41] President Reagan defended his policy in a speech described as "nauseating" by Bishop Tutu, and as inadequate by Republican Senator Richard Lugar, chairman of the Senate Foreign Relations Committee. In August, the Senate voted 84 to 14 for a sanctions bill, including bans on new investments and loans, on landing rights for South African Airways and on imports of coal, steel, iron, uranium agricultural products and textiles. Although the House agreed to the Senate's more limited version of the bill, President Reagan vetoed it. But, on 2 October, Congress overrode the president's veto. For the first time, official US policy toward South Africa included sanctions that were substantive, albeit far short of comprehensive.

THE NINE LIVES OF
"DESTRUCTIVE ENGAGEMENT"

The sanctions victory was an impressive accomplishment for the anti-apartheid movement. The "constructive engagement" premise giving priority to conciliating Pretoria was surely ready for burial. In January 1987, the Advisory Committee to Secretary of State Shultz gave its own judgement that "the administration's policy of constructive engagement has failed to achieve its objectives" and called on the government to work for strong multilateral sanctions.[42] The same month Shultz himself met with President Oliver Tambo of the ANC, a significant symbolic shift.

Like apartheid, however, the "constructive engagement" policy seemed to survive repeated death sentences. Reviving congressional momentum toward stronger sanctions was difficult. The administration made no secret of its opposition even to those sanctions already enacted into law. Implementation was reluctant, and the search for bureaucratic loopholes sometimes produced blatant defiance of congressional intent. Public rancor was growing between Washington and Pretoria, but whatever his transgressions, P. W. Botha could still count on administration officials to lobby against increasing sanctions.

The Anti-Apartheid Act of 1986, for example, banned import of uranium or uranium oxide from South Africa or Namibia. A Treasury Department interpretation in March 1987 deemed this inapplicable to imports for reexport to third countries, the more significant portion of US uranium imports. Similarly, a ban on imports from South African parastatal corporations was vitiated by a State Department ruling excluding 10 "strategic minerals," including chromium, ferrochromium, manganese, titanium and even cobalt. The fact that many such minerals were available from other African states was even used as an additional reason not to boycott South Africa, since Zimbabwean chromium and Zambian and Zairean cobalt had to transit South Africa.

Perhaps the most telling contradiction to congressional intent was the US veto in February 1987 of a Security Council resolution containing a sanctions package roughly similar to the Anti-Apartheid Act. Section 401(e) of the act explicitly called for such action, as part of an active campaign for multilateral sanctions against South Africa. The policy would have made commercial as well as political sense. Making coal sanctions mandatory, for example, could have increased the pressure on South Africa significantly; holding European countries such as the Federal Republic of Germany to restrictions on computer exports similar to those legislated in the United States could hamper gains at the expense of US companies.

The US veto, nevertheless, as well as a subsequent veto of sanctions on the Namibian issue, was virtually unnoticed in the US political arena, except by the small core of Africa sympathizers in Congress who took note. The one-year anniversary of sanctions legislation offered the opportunity to push for new measures, but most legislators preferred to move on to other issues. The media blackout and relative quiescence in South Africa easily permitted the retreat of African issues to their customary low ranking on the Washington agenda.

Even more serious for southern Africa, however, was the fact that US condemnation of apartheid was matched by encouragement for Pretoria's regional wars, with signals from Congress as well as from the Reagan administration. Even as anti-apartheid legislation was making its tortuous way through Congress, support for South African military operations in Angola was rising. Aided in large part by ignorance of the regional context, but even more by a deliberate propaganda campaign to change the terms of debate, the far right launched an all-out crusade to support anticommunist "freedom fighters" in Angola and Mozambique. Democrats, as well as right-wing Republicans, joined in challenging the State Department's southern Africa policy as insufficiently anticommunist.

The crusade gained only limited momentum in the case of Mozambique, although restrictions were placed on aid. Unlike Angola, Mozambique had neither the legacy of direct US intervention nor the conspicuous presence of Cuban troops. And Mozambique's diplomatic offensive had convinced key US policy makers that the South African–backed MNR was not a credible alternative. When President Machel visited Washington in September 1985, far-right ideologues denounced Reagan for meeting with a "Marxist dictator," but legislation introduced to aid the MNR failed to win White House support.

On Angola, the far right found strong backing for their effort to present the conflict as a cold war battle unrelated to South Africa. Even in May 1985, when South African commandoes were surprised in the act of sabotaging oil storage tanks at Gulf Oil installations in Cabinda and were found carrying Unita leaflets claiming credit for the attack, neither the South African connection nor Unita's willingness to endanger US lives and property aroused outrage in Washington. Only days later President Reagan sent a message of support to a Unita-hosted international gathering of anticommunist rebels organized by New York Republican millionaire Lewis Lehrman.

Even more helpful to the hawks in Pretoria's State Security Council were subsequent events in Congress. The Angolan attack was downplayed in the debate on apartheid, and in June 1985 the Senate voted to repeal the Clark amendment, which had banned US intervention in Angola. The margin was 63 to 34, with 17 Democrats joining the Republican majority.

Both the President and the Senate were signalling support for South Africa's surrogate in Angola instead of moving toward stronger condemnation of South African regional aggression. The day after the Senate action, in a parallel tilt, the House caved in to Reagan's campaign for support to the contra insurgency in Nicaragua. In July, the House also repealed the Clark amendment by a vote of 236 to 185, on the same day the Senate passed its weaker version of the Anti-Apartheid Act.

These simultaneous actions could only confirm African impressions that US southern Africa policy, even when not consistently indifferent or hostile to African liberation, remained hopelessly confused. In Pretoria it made sense to conclude that, in actuality, the old cold war verities took priority over new anti-apartheid rhetoric.

In the last half of 1985, in addition to imposing an internal state of emergency, Pretoria again stepped up its attacks on neighboring countries. SADF chief General Constand Viljoen, justifying a raid on Botswana only days after the Senate's repeal of the Clark amendment, said the action was necessary to counter terrorist actions by the banned ANC. Moreover, he added, the possibility of an international outcry had been "very carefully debated and thought out."

The US government responded by withdrawing Ambassador Herman Nickel from Pretoria for consultations, a significant diplomatic move, but there was no sign that the Reagan administration would concede "punitive sanctions" in response to South African aggression. In three separate votes in June 1985, the UN Security Council condemned the Cabinda and Botswana attacks and denounced the unilateral South African installation of an interim government in Namibia. But Western pressure prevented the adoption of new UN sanctions.

In 1986 and 1987, the interventionist forces gained strength in both Washington and Pretoria. In February 1986, Jonas Savimbi visited Washington, the culmination of a more than $600,000 public relations campaign. He received a White House commitment to supply at least $15 million in covert aid, including Stinger missiles. Congressional proposals to grant openly far larger sums were held in abeyance, amidst skepticism from Democrats in the House and Senate intelligence committees. The Africa Bureau cautioned against going too far and totally upsetting the prospect for continued negotiations. But the opposition was too little and too late, crippled by the prevalent tendency to isolate the Angolan and South African issues.

Regional aggression, clearly, was unlikely to hurt Pretoria's standing in Washington and might even win favor, especially if Angola was the target. South African troops had secured Unita's headquarters aginst an Angolan government offensive in September 1985. Far from provoking additional sanctions pressures, the South Africans subsequently gained an open, albeit still officially "covert," alliance with Washington on that front. Even the mid-1986 raids on Botswana, Zimbabwe and Zambia had little direct effect on Washington opinion, their impact seen primarily as evidence of the failure of the Commonwealth mediation effort.

In September 1986, even as the sanctions bill was gaining momentum, an amendment to restrict aid to Unita presented by Lee Hamilton, chairman of the House Intelligence Committee, was defeated 229 to 186. Sixty-three Democrats joined Republicans in licensing the administration's covert aid. In April 1987 a similar amendment failed, by an eight to seven vote, to pass in Hamilton's own committee. Admissions by Savimbi that South African troops had joined in defending his headquarters in 1985 had little impact on US legislation. In the mainstream US political context, South Africa's regional war was virtually invisible and largely irrelevant.

Within the anti-apartheid movement there was a growing awareness of the regional dimension of apartheid. The Reverend Jesse Jackson's southern Africa trip in August 1986 drew some media attention, and SADCC's Beira corridor appeared in more and more news reports. The tragic and suspicious plane crash which killed President Machel and his companions shocked supporters of southern African liberation into a new sense of urgency. Key legislators launched new initiatives for increased aid to SADCC.

These efforts were clearly insufficient to overcome inertia and indifference, however, and were vulnerable to right-wing assault. The State Department pledged support to SADCC. Several of the most ardent right-wing advocates in the administration, such as CIA Director Casey and White House Communications Director Buchanan, left office. But Jackson's proposals for a summit meeting of Frontline presidents with President Reagan were brusquely rejected. (Reagan found time, however, to meet with KwaZulu Chief Gatsha Buthelezi in November.)

New South African raids on Zambia and Mozambique in 1987 received criticism from the State Department. Indeed, the administration sharply criticized the May 1987 raid on Maputo, which killed three Mozambicans. The US statements provoked an angry response from South African Foreign Minister Pik Botha. But the administration remained opposed to further sanctions, and its lobbying in Congress for aid to SADCC was on a low level. Even such nominal support for southern Africa was under intense attack from the far right.

In a series of votes in May 1987, senators targetted the Frontline states, calling for sanctions against Angola and restrictions on aid to other African countries. The measure were largely symbolic, but were significant because large numbers of moderate and liberal senators joined in the extreme right-wing campaign. Despite the Democratic majority in the Senate, the votes positioned Congress's upper chamber to the right of the Reagan administration itself on the issue of South Africa's war against Angola, Mozambique and other African states.

Two key votes came during the Senate debate on supplemental foreign aid funds for fiscal year 1987. An amendment by Democratic Senator Dennis DeConcini of Arizona condemned the "Soviet-Cuban build-up in Angola and the severe human rights violations of the Marxist regime in Angola." It also called on President Reagan to consider restrictions on US business dealings with Angola. The amendment passed 94 to zero, without debate.

The vote was a striking indication of the dominance of cold war perspectives on southern Africa. The amendment's language was extreme, accusing the Soviet Union of "aggression and subversion in southern Africa" and "the most blatant foreign intervention in post-colonial history of Africa." The MPLA, recognized as the legitimate government of Angola by every country except South Africa and the United States, was accused of having "illegally seized power" in 1975.

Passage of the amendment came as little surprise. Congress has consistently voted against Angola since the July 1985 repeal of the Clark amendment. Congressional observers, however, were shocked at the unanimity in the DeConcini vote. Not one senator recalled the Clark amendment. No one mentioned South African aggression against Angola, or challenged the premise that US interests lay in allying with South Africa rather than independent Africa.

An additional amendment by Republican Senator Larry Pressler of South Dakota barred aid to any country which did not condemn "necklacing" (a form of execution that occurred in violence against government collaborators in black townships) and expel "terrorists" who supported such "necklacing" in South Africa. This amendment met with some opposition. Senator Carl Levin of Michigan noted that aid to the Frontline states was "an integral part of the strategy to end apartheid." But many senators feared a negative vote would be interpreted as endorsement of "necklacing," and the amendment passed 77 to 15.

The Pressler and DeConcini amendments, attached to a supplemental appropriation bill given little chance of passage, were largely symbolic, but they foreboded more substantive measures. In May, Senate Republican leader Robert Dole, together with Democrats Lawton Chiles of Florida and Ernest Hollings of South Carolina, introduced a bill to increase US sanctions against Cuba and to impose an almost total trade embargo against Angola. Dole also joined Jesse Helms and 26 other senators in holding up the approval of a new ambassador to Mozambique, challenging the Reagan administration policy of cooperating with the government of Mozambique, rather than supporting the South African-backed MNR.

In late 1987 the prospect was continued incoherence in US southern African policy. In June, the divestment movement received a boost when the Reverend Leon Sullivan himself said his principles for US companies were not enough and called for corporate withdrawal and comprehensive sanctions. New legislative sanctions stood some chance of becoming an issue in the fall, but lobbyists working for aid to southern Africa were still handicapped by a lack of public awareness of the regional dimension of apartheid. In 1988 and 1989, if awareness does not increase, it seems likely that most US politicians will continue to feel free to condemn apartheid while simultaneously voting to victimize countries attacked by the apartheid regime.

ABBREVIATIONS

ANC	African National Congress (South Africa)
ARMSCOR	Armaments Corporation (South Africa)
BCP	Basutoland Congress Party
BDF	Botswana Defense Force
BDP	Bechuanaland Democratic Party (Botswana)
BLS	Botswana, Lesotho, Swaziland
BNP	Basutoland National Party
BOLESWA	Botswana, Lesotho, Swaziland
BOSS	Bureau of State Security (South Africa)
CAF	Central African Federation
CAZ	Conservative Alliance of Zimbabwe
CIA	Central Intelligence Agency (United States)
CIO	Central Intelligence Organization (Rhodesia)
CONSAS	Constellation of Southern African States
COREMO	Mozambique Revolutionary Council
COSATU	Council of South African Trade Unions
CPL	Communist Party of Lesotho
DGS	General Security Directorate (Portugal)
DTA	Democratic Turnhalle Alliance (Namibia)
EEC	European Economic Community
ESCOM	Electricity Supply Commission (South Africa)
FAPLA	People's Armed Forces for the Liberation of Angola
FLEC	Front for the Liberation of the Cabinda Enclave (Angola)
FNLA	National Front for the Liberation of Angola

FPLM	Mozambique People's Liberation Forces
FRELIMO	Mozambique Liberation Front
FRG	Federal Republic of Germany
FUMO	Mozambique United Front
GDP	Gross Domestic Product
GDR	Democratic Republic of Germany
GNP	Gross National Product
GRAE	Government of the Angolan Republic in Exile
IAEA	International Atomic Energy Agency
IMF	International Monetary Fund
JMC	Joint Management Centers
JMC	Joint Monitoring Commission (Angola/South Africa)
JSC	Joint Security Commission (Mozambique/South Africa)
LESOMA	League of Socialists of Malawi
LLA	Lesotho Liberation Army
MFA	Movement of the Armed Forces (Portugal)
MFP	Marema Tlou Freedom Party (Lesotho)
MID	Military Intelligence Directorate (Rhodesia, South Africa)
MNR	Mozambique National Resistance (see Renamo)
MPC	Multi-Party Conference (Namibia)
MPLA	People's Movement for the Liberation of Angola
MPR	Popular Movement of the Revolution (Zaire)
NATO	North Atlantic Treaty Organization
NIS	National Intelligence Service (South Africa)
NP	National Party (South Africa)
NPT	Non-Proliferation Treaty
NSC	National Security Council (United States)
OAU	Organization of African Unity
OECD	Organization for Economic Co-operation and Development
OPEC	Organization of Petroleum Exporting Countries
PAC	Pan-Africanist Congress
PAIGC	African Party for the Independence of Guinea-Bissau and Cape Verde
PF	Patriotic Front

PF-ZAPU	Patriotic Front–Zimbabwe African People's Union
PIDE	International Police for the Defense of the State (Portugal)
PTA	Preferential Trade Area
RENAMO	Mozambique National Resistance (see MNR)
RF	Rhodesian Front
SABC	South African Broadcasting Corporation
SACC	South African Council of Churches
SACU	Southern African Customs Union
SADCC	Southern African Development Coordination Conference
SADF	South African Defense Force
SAFTO	South African Foreign Trade Office
SAP	South African Police
SATCC	Southern African Transport and Communications Commission
SATS	South African Transport Services
SAS	Special Air Service
SB	Special Branch
SSC	State Security Council (South Africa)
SWA	Southwest Africa
SWANU	South West African National Union (Namibia)
SWAPO	South West Africa People's Organization (Namibia)
SWATF	South West Africa Territory Force
UANC	United African National Council (Zimbabwe)
UDENAMO	Mozambique National Democratic Union
UDF	United Democratic Front (South Africa)
UDI	Unilateral Declaration of Independence
UDP	United Democratic Party (Lesotho)
UN	United Nations
UNICEF	United Nations Children's Fund
UNITA	National Union for the Total Independence of Angola
UNTAG	United Nations Transitional Assistance Group (Namibia)
US	United States
USSR	Union of Soviet Socialist Republics
ZANLA	Zimbabwe African National Liberation Army

ZANU	Zimbabwe African National Union
ZANU-PF	Zimbabwe African National Union–Patriotic Front
ZAPU	Zimbabwe African People's Union
ZBC	Zimbabwe Broadcasting Corporation
ZIMOFA	Zimbabwe-Mozambique Friendship Association
ZRP	Zimbabwe Republic Police
ZPRA	Zimbabwe People's Revolutionary Army
ZNA	Zimbabwe National Army

APPENDIX 1

AGREEMENT ON NON-AGGRESSION AND
GOOD NEIGHBOURLINESS
between the Government of the People's Republic
of Mozambique and the Government of the
Republic of South Africa

The Government of the People's Republic of Mozambique and the Government of the Republic of South Africa, hereinafter referred to as the High Contracting Parties;

RECOGNISING the principles of strict respect for sovereignty and territorial integrity, sovereign equality, political independence and the inviolability of the borders of all states;

REAFFIRMING the principle of non-interference in the internal affairs of other states;

CONSIDERING the internationally recognised principle of the right of peoples to self-determination and independence and the principle of equal rights of all peoples;

CONSIDERING the obligation of all states to refrain, in their international relations, from the threat or use of force against the territorial integrity or political independence of any state;

CONSIDERING the obligation of states to settle conflicts by peaceful means, and thus safeguard international peace and security and justice;

RECOGNISING the responsibility of states not to allow their territory to be used for acts of war, aggression or violence against other states;

CONSCIOUS of the need to promote relations of good neighbourliness based on the principles of equality of rights and mutual advantage;

CONVINCED that relations of good neighbourliness between the High Contracting Parties will contribute to peace, security, stability and progress in Southern Africa, the Continent and the World;

Have solemnly agreed to the following:

ARTICLE ONE

The High Contracting Parties undertake to respect each other's sovereignty and independence and, in fulfilment of this fundamental obligation, to refrain from interfering in the internal affairs of the other.

ARTICLE TWO

1) The High Contracting Parties shall resolve differences and disputes that may arise between them and that may or are likely to endanger mutual peace and security or peace and security in the region, by means of negotiation, enquiry, mediation, conciliation, arbitration or other peaceful means, and undertake not to resort, individually or collectively, to the threat or use of force against each other's sovereignty, territorial integrity or political independence.

2) For the purposes of this article, the use of force shall include *inter alia*—

   a) attacks by land, air or sea forces;

   b) sabotage;

   c) unwarranted concentration of such forces at or near the international boundaries of the High Contracting Parties;

   d) violation of the international land, air or sea boundaries of either of the High Contracting Parties.

3) The High Contracting Parties shall not in any way assist the armed forces of any state or group of states deployed against the territorial sovereignty or political independence of the other.

ARTICLE THREE

1) The High Contracting Parties shall not allow their respective territories, territorial waters or air space to be used as a base, thoroughfare, or in any other way by another state, government, foreign military forces, organisations or individuals which plan or prepare to commit acts of violence, terrorism or aggression against the territorial integrity or political independence of the other or may threaten the security of its inhabitants.

2) The High Contracting Parties, in order to prevent or eliminate the acts or the preparation of acts mentioned in paragraph (1) of this article, undertake in particular to—

a) forbid and prevent in their respective territories the organisation of irregular forces or armed bands, including mercenaries, whose objective is to carry out the acts contemplated in paragraph (1) of this article;

b) eliminate from their respective territories bases, training centres, places of shelter, accommodation and transit for elements who intend to carry out acts contemplated in paragraph (1) of this article;

c) eliminate from their respective territories centres or depots containing armaments of whatever nature, destined to be used by the elements contemplated in paragraph (1) of this article;

d) eliminate from their respective territories command posts or other places for the command, direction and co-ordination of the elements contemplated in paragraph (1) of this article;

e) eliminate from their respective territories communication and telecommunication facilities between the command and the elements contemplated in paragraph (1) of this article;

f) eliminate and prohibit the installation in their respective territories of radio broadcasting stations, including unofficial or clandestine broadcasts, for the elements that carry out the acts contemplated in paragraph (1) of this article;

g) exercise strict control, in their respective territories, over elements which intend to carry out or plan the acts contemplated in paragraph (1) of this article;

h) prevent the transit of elements who intend to plan to commit the acts contemplated in paragraph (1) of this article, from a place in the territory of either to a place in the territory of the other or to a place in the territory of any third state which has a common boundary with the High Contracting Party against which such elements intend or plan to commit the said acts;

i) take appropriate steps in their respective territories to prevent the recruitment of elements of whatever nationality for the purpose of carrying out the acts contemplated in paragraph (1) of this article;

j) prevent the elements contemplated in paragraph (1) of this article from carrying out from their respective territories by any means acts of abduction or other acts, aimed at taking citizens of any nationality hostage in the territory of the other High Contracting Party; and

k) prohibit the provision on their respective territories of any logistic facilities for carrying out the acts contemplated in paragraph (1) of this article;

3) The High Contracting Parties will not use the territory of third states to carry out or support the acts contemplated in paragraphs (1) and (2) of this article;

ARTICLE FOUR

The High Contracting Parties shall take steps, individually and collectively, to ensure that the international boundary between their respective territories is effectively patrolled and that the border posts are efficiently administered to prevent illegal crossings from the territory of a High Contracting Party to the territory of the other, and in particular, by elements contemplated in Article Three of this Agreement.

ARTICLE FIVE

The High Contracting Parties shall prohibit within their territory acts of propaganda that incite a war of aggression against the other High Contracting Party and shall also prohibit acts of propaganda aimed at inciting acts of terrorism and civil war in the territory of the other High Contracting Party.

ARTICLE SIX

The High Contracting Parties declare that there is no conflict between their commitments in treaties and international obligations and the commitment undertaken in this Agreement.

ARTICLE SEVEN

The High Contracting Parties are committed to interpreting this Agreement in good faith and will maintain periodic contact to ensure the effective application of what has been agreed.

ARTICLE EIGHT

Nothing in this Agreement shall be construed as detracting from the High Contracting Parties' right to self-defence in the event of armed attacks, as provided for in the Charter of the United Nations.

ARTICLE NINE

1) Each of the High Contracting Parties shall appoint high-ranking representatives to serve on a Joint Security Commission with the aim of supervising and monitoring the application of this Agreement.

2) The Commission shall determine its own working procedure.

3) The Commission shall meet on a regular basis and may be specially convened whenever circumstances so require.

4) The Commission shall—
   a) Consider all allegations of infringements of the provisions of this Agreement;
   b) advise the High Contracting Parties of its conclusions; and
   c) make recommendations to the High Contracting Parties con-

cerning measures for the effective application of this Agreement and the settlement of disputes over infringements or alleged infringements.

5) The High Contracting Parties shall determine the mandate of their respective representatives in order to enable interim measures to be taken in cases of duly recognised emergency.

6) The High Contracting Parties shall make available all the facilities necessary for the effective functioning of the Commission and will jointly consider its conclusions and recommendations.

ARTICLE TEN

This Agreement will also be known as "The Accord of Nkomati".

ARTICLE ELEVEN

1) This agreement shall enter into force on the date of the signature thereof.

2) Any amendment to this Agreement agreed to by the High Contracting Parties shall be affected by the Exchange of Notes between them.

IN WITNESS WHEREOF, the signatories, in the name of their respective governments, have signed and sealed this Agreement, in quadruplicate in the Portuguese and English languages, both texts being equally authentic.

THUS DONE AND SIGNED AT the common border on the banks of the Nkomati River, on this the sixteenth day of March 1984.

SAMORA MOISÉS MACHEL
MARSHAL OF THE REPUBLIC
PRESIDENT OF THE PEOPLE'S
REPUBLIC OF MOZAMBIQUE
PRESIDENT OF THE COUNCIL OF MINISTERS
FOR THE GOVERNMENT OF THE
PEOPLE'S REPUBLIC OF
MOZAMBIQUE

PIETER WILLEM BOTHA
PRIME MINISTER OF THE
REPUBLIC OF SOUTH AFRICA
FOR THE GOVERNMENT OF THE
REPUBLIC OF SOUTH AFRICA

APPENDIX 2

MESSAGE FROM THE ANGOLAN HEAD OF STATE
to the United Nations Secretary-General
on the Problems of Southern Africa

Handed to United Nations Secretary-General Javier Perez de Cuellar in New York on Tuesday 20 November 1984 by Elisio de Figueiredo, Ambassador of the People's Republic of Angola to the United Nations

His Excellency Dr Javier Pérez de Cuellar, Secretary-General of the United Nations Organisation, New York

Mr Secretary-General:

I have the honour to address myself to Your Excellency to inform you of the steps taken by the Government of the People's Republic of Angola with the essential objective of guaranteeing the independence of Namibia, through the full implementation of United Nations Security Council resolution 435/78, achieving the withdrawal of South African forces from the south of Angola, securing international guarantees for Angola's security, independence and territorial integrity, and contributing to the establishment of lasting peace in Southern Africa.

As I stated publicly on 26 August 1983, on the occasion of your memorable visit to Luanda, the People's Republic of Angola has always shown its willingness to co-operate in the search for an adequate solution to the Namibian problem, thereby taking the first important step towards the establishment of the just and lasting peace we want for our peoples and the international community.

While ratifying the determination of the people and Government of Angola to continue to fight against the racist invaders, I reiterated our willingness to continue diplomatic action to seek a just solution, and I reaffirmed the following positions of our Party and Government:

1. The immediate and unconditional withdrawal of the South African forces occupying part of our territory;
2. The immediate implementation of Security Council resolution 435/78 leading to the true independence of Namibia;
3. The cessation of South African aggression against Angola;
4. The cessation of all logistical support for the Unita puppet bands.

On the basis of these positions, some of which had already been stated in the statement of the Foreign Ministers of the People's Republic of Angola and the Republic of Cuba of 4 February 1982, and are also contained in the joint statement of 19 March 1984 of both governments, we have held both direct and indirect talks with representatives of the governments of the United States and South Africa, with a view to achieving the above objectives.

These principled positions put forward by Angola are a categorical rejection of so-called 'linkage'—rejected by almost every government in the world and by world opinion—which seeks to make the implementation of resolution 435/78 contingent on the prior or parallel withdrawal of the Cuban military contingent legally present in the People's Republic of Angola at the request of its Government and in accordance with Article 51 of the United Nations Charter.

On the contrary, the implementation of resolution 435/78 and with it the independence of Namibia, is a fundamental factor which, together with the cessation of direct or indirect aggression and threats against Angola and help from abroad for the counter-revolutionary bands, will make it possible within an adequate period to ensure our security and the subsequent progressive withdrawal of Cuban internationalist troops from Angola, as stated very precisely in the above mentioned joint statements of Cuba and Angola of February 1982 and March 1984.

In the course of our talks with representatives of the United States held in Luanda on 6 and 7 September, we presented them with a platform for negotiations to be conveyed to the Government of South Africa, containing five points.

I here transcribe the full text of the said platform presented by the People's Republic of Angola:

1. The completion of the process of withdrawal of South African forces from the territory of the People's Republic of Angola and control by FAPLA of Angola's state borders.
2. A solemn statement by the Republic of South Africa in which it pledges to honour and to contribute to the implementation of United Nations resolution 435/78 on Namibian independence.
3. A ceasefire agreement between the Republic of South Africa and SWAPO.
4. A statement by the Government of the People's Republic of Angola reiterating its decision, in agreement with the Government of Cuba, to proceed with

the start of the withdrawal of the Cuban internationalist contingent, only when the implementation of resolution 435/78 is under way.

5. The signing, within the parameters of the UN Security Council, which would act as guarantor, of an international agreement between the governments of the People's Republic of Angola, the Republic of South Africa, the Republic of Cuba and a representative of SWAPO, in which would be defined the respective undertakings for achieving Namibia's independence, and the guarantees for the security and territorial integrity of the People's Republic of Angola and lasting peace in South-West Africa.

This agreement would consider:

1. United Nations troops having been established in Namibia, together with the UN authorities, within the prescribed period, the Republic of South Africa would completely withdraw its armed forces from Namibia, withdrawing first the air force and the units on the border with Angola, which would come under the immediate responsibility of the United Nations troops.

2. As soon as the air force had completely withdrawn from the territory of Namibia and there remained of the South African troops only one thousand five hundred infantrymen, Angola and Cuba would proceed with the withdrawal of five thousand Cuban internationalists from the troops grouped in the south, as a gesture of good will.

3. The Cuban troops would not carry out any kind of deployment of military units or any type of manoeuvre south of the 16th Parallel.

4. With regard to the remaining numbers of Cuban troops grouped in the south, they would be withdrawn to Cuba over a maximum period of three years.

5. If any act of aggression or threat of imminent aggression against Angola by South Africa were noted, the entire agreement would be suspended or annulled.

6. The Republic of South Africa would undertake from the very start to cease all support of the Unita bands, and the United Nations authorities would have to verify the dismantling of the Unita bases on Namibian territory.

7. The withdrawal of Cuban troops stationed in Cabinda Province and other regions in the north of the People's Republic of Angola, including the country's capital, would be programmed in accordance with a timetable to be established for this purpose by the People's Republic of Angola and Cuba.

As Your Excellency can confirm, the platform directly states the problems that must be resolved to secure the implementation of resolution 435/78 and, therefore, the independence of Namibia, as well as other steps to guarantee the disengagement of South African forces from our territory and the establishment of lasting peace in the region, which would create the requisite conditions to proceed with the disengagement of Cuban internationalist troops from southern Angola; all this, of course, within the framework of an international agreement subscribed to by all the parties concerned and guaranteed by the Security Council.

Subsequently, and as proof of the seriousness with which Angola is carrying out the negotiations, on 9 October this year we presented a text which complemented the platform and rigorously expressed our precise proposals with regard to the Cuban military personnel.

The full text of the document is as follows:

The People's Republic of Angola and the Republic of Cuba, in exercising their sovereign rights, and within the framework of Article 51 of the United Nations Charter, agree to proceed in the following manner in respect of the internationalist contingent of Cuban troops, so long as the points formulated in the platform of the People's Republic of Angola for an international agreement on independence, security and peace in South-West Africa (Angola and Namibia) are accepted, carried out and respected.

First, on the grouping of Cuban troops in the south of Angola (ATS):

1. Within 24 months of the entry of the UN troops contingent for the implementation of Security Council resolution 435/78, the 15,000 men of the present line defending the south of Angola—Namibe-Lubango-Matala-Jamba-Menongue—will be withdrawn in the following manner:
   — after the 16th week, within a four-month period, 5,000 men.
   — between the 12th and 16th month, another 5,000 men.
   — between the 20th and 24th month, a further 5,000 men.

   During this period, the Cuban troops would at no time cross the 16th Parallel, which is 160km from the Namibian border and 1,360km from the Orange River.

2. The remaining troops of the ATS, comprising approximately 5,000 men, deployed behind the said line, would be withdrawn between the 32nd and 36th month.

   During that third year, these troops would at no time cross the 13th Parallel, which is more than 500km from the land border with Namibia and 1,700km from the Orange River. That is, as from the 24th month, no ATS unit would cross the 13th Parallel.

   Thus, approximately 20,000 men of the total number of Cuban troops in Angola would withdraw in 36 months.

Second, on the remaining Cuban troops in Angola:

1. The remaining Cuban troops which have nothing to do with the defense of the south of the country, and no relationship to Namibia or South Africa, as pointed out in point 5-VII of the platform, would be withdrawn from Angola in accordance with an independent timetable to be agreed upon by the People's Republic of Angola and Cuba when the time comes.

   These remaining troops would also at no time cross the 13th Parallel.

   Angola and Cuba shall establish the dates indicated as the maximum limits for the ATS to stay in Angola, reserving the right to cut short those periods if security and territorial integrity so permit. In the same spirit, both governments, exercising their prerogatives of sovereignty, shall determine the moment and the appropriate timescale for the withdrawal of the remaining forces, once Angola's integrity and security are fully guaranteed.

2. Part of those troops are in Cabinda, which is 1,350km from the river border (the Cunene River) with Namibia and separated from the rest of the territory of the People's Republic of Angola by a strip of Zairean territory and by the Zaire River.

Cabinda is 2,550km from the Orange River.

Another part of this force would be in Luanda and the surrounding area (Bengo and Kwanza Norte), Luanda is Cabinda's rear, in view of the fact that it is only here that there can be the air and naval forces capable of going to the help of Cabinda in the event of aggression, as well as the ground forces which would be transported by air and ship.

Luanda is 945km from the river border (Cunene River) with Namibia and 2,145km from the Orange River.

Other units could be stationed in northern and eastern provinces and in strategic points north of the 13th Parallel which ensure communications and supplies to those provinces.

3. That is, the remaining forces would be very far from the southern border, and their mission, together with FAPLA, is to defend the territorial integrity of the People's Republic of Angola against aggression from the north and north-east, and more especially against Cabinda, as has already happened.

4. The People's Republic of Angola does not have the organised manpower resources with the required educational level, or the available material and financial resources to wage a war against the Unita bands and other puppet organisations, and simultaneously to replace the Cuban troops and armaments at strategic points in the south, centre and north of the country. Angola has to give priority to fighting the bandits who, supported, trained and equipped from abroad, have caused and are continuing to cause the country substantial human and economic losses.

At the same time, and if agreement is reached in the present negotiations, in only 36 months it will have to replace the strength in men and equipment of the grouping of Cuban troops in the south and assume responsibility for the installations and positions occupied by them.

For this reason, it is only after such replacement has been carried out and peace and internal order has been guaranteed, that Angola itself will be able to take on the tasks which, for the country's security and integrity, are performed by the remaining Cuban military personnel.

This will require time, substantial resources and a tremendous effort in the training of skilled and technical personnel. To demand more of our young State, after five centuries of colonialism, fourteen years of struggle for independence and almost ten years of fighting against foreign aggression and subversion organised from abroad, would reflect a lack of realism and a lack of consideration for our people.

Angola has given proof of its good will and seriousness in seeking peace. Angola cannot make concessions which would be suicidal to its national integrity and its political and social progress, forgetting the sacrifices made by tens of thousands of its finest sons and daughters.

Angola, Mr. Secretary-General, has given proof of its willingness and seriousness in seeking peace, but it cannot accept an arrangement which does not take into account the criteria outlined here or which does not fully respond in a satisfactory way to all the issues related to the rapid independence of Namibia, the disengagement of South African troops from our territory and the cessation of all external help for the Unita puppet bands.

In other words, and reaffirming what is stated at the end of the complementary text, it is not possible either to demand or to expect of Angola concessions which would be suicidal to its national integrity and the development of its political and social progress, and would mean forgetting the sacrifices made by tens of thousands of its finest sons and daughters.

Mr. Secretary-General, conscious of the fundamental role played by the United Nations in respect of the independence of Namibia and the implementation of resolution 435/78, we consider it indispensable not only that Your Excellency should be fully informed of how the negotiations are going, but also that, at an opportune moment in the not too distant future, that your representative should take part in them, so that you may also make your valuable and necessary contribution to our efforts.

Finally, I should like to say to you, Mr. Secretary-General, that Angola has carried out these negotiations in close co-ordination with Cuba and has its full support. At the same time, the leadership of SWAPO has also been informed about the evolution of the negotiations.

I should like to request of Your Excellency that this letter be circulated as an official document of the General Assembly and the Security Council.

Please accept, Mr. Secretary-General, the assurances of my highest consideration.

JOSE EDUARDO DOS SANTOS
President of the People's Republic of Angola

Issued by Information Department of the Central Committee of the MPLA-Workers' Party, Luanda, People's Republic of Angola.

The Times (United Kingdom) 24th November, 1984

APPENDIX 3

RESOLUTION 435 (1978)
*Adopted by the Security Council at its 2087th meeting
on 29 September 1978*

The Security Council,
Recalling its resolutions 385 (1976) and 431 (1978), and 432 (1978),
Having considered the report submitted by the Secretary-General pursuant to paragraph 2 of resolution in the Security Council on 29 September 1978 (S/12869),
Taking note of the relevant communications from the Government of South Africa addressed to the Secretary-General,
Taking note also of the letter dated 8 September 1978 from the President of the South West Africa People's Organization (SWAPO) addressed to the Secretary General (S/12841),
Reaffirming the legal responsibility of the United Nations over Namibia,
1. *Approves* the report of the Secretary-General (S/12827) for the implementation of the proposal for a settlement of the Namibian situation (S/12636) and his explanatory statement (S/12869);
2. *Reiterates* that its objective is the withdrawal of South Africa's illegal administration of Namibia and the transfer of

power to the people of Namibia with the assistance of the United Nations in accordance with resolution 385 (1976):

3. *Decides* to establish under its authority a United Nations Transition Assistance report of the Secretary-General for a period of up to 12 months in order to assist his Special Representative to carry out the mandate conferred upon him by paragraph 1 of Security Council resolution 431 (1978), namely, to ensure the early independence of Namibia through free and fair elections under the supervision and control of the United Nations;

4. *Welcomes* SWAPO's preparedness to co-operate in the implementation of the Secretary-General's report, including its expressed readiness to sign and observe the cease-fire provisions as manifested in the letter from the President of SWAPO dated 8 September 1978 (S/12841);

5. *Calls* on South Africa forthwith to co-operate with the Secretary-General in the implementation of this resolution;

6. *Declares* that all unilateral measures taken by the illegal administration in Namibia in relation to the electoral process, including unilateral registration of voters, or transfer of power, in contravention of Security Council resolutions 285 (1976), 431 (1978) and this resolution are null and void;

7. *Requests* the Secretary-General to report to the Security Council no later than 23 October 1978 on the implementation of this resolution.

APPENDIX 4

12 February 1982

His Majesty
King Sobhuza II of Swaziland
Mbzbane
SWAZILAND

Your Majesty

I have the honour to refer to various discussions and correspondence between the Foreign Ministers of the Kingdom of Swaziland and the Republic of South Africa which resulted in mutual agreement between our respective Governments to the effect that both Governments are aware of the fact that international terrorism, in all its manifestations, poses a real threat to international peace and security and that our respective Governments should take steps to protect our respective states and nationals against this threat.

Therefore, I now have the honour to inform you that the Government of the Republic of South Africa proposes the following Agreement between our respective Governments:

ARTICLE 1

The Contracting Parties undertake to combat terrorism, insurgency and subversion individually and collectively and shall call upon each other wherever possible for such assistance and steps as may be deemed necessary or expedient to eliminate this evil.

ARTICLE 2

In the conduct of their mutual relations the Contracting Parties shall furthermore respect each other's independence, sovereignty and territorial integrity and shall refrain from the unlawful threat or use of force and from any other act which is inconsistent with the purposes and principles of good neighbourliness.

ARTICLE 3

The Contracting Parties shall live in peace and further develop and maintain friendly relations with each other and shall therefore not allow any activities within their respective territories directed towards the commission of any act which involves a threat or use of force against each other's territorial integrity.

ARTICLE 4

The Contracting Parties shall not allow within their respective territories the installation or maintenance of foreign military bases or the presence of foreign military units except in accordance with their right of self-defence in the event of armed attacks as provided for in the Charter of the United Nations and only after due notification to the other. Should the Government of the Kingdom of Swaziland agree with the abovementioned provisions, this letter and your affirmative reply thereto shall constitute an Agreement between our two Governments.

Please accept, Your Majesty, the renewed assurance of my highest consideration.

P. W. BOTHA
Prime Minister of the Republic of South Africa

17th February, 1982

My Dear Prime Minister,

You are hereby authorise to sign on behalf of Swaziland the Letter of Understanding on Security Matters between the Kingdom of Swaziland and the Republic of South Africa in reply to the letter dated 12th February, 1982 from the Prime Minister of the Republic of South Africa.

SOBHUZA II
Ingwenyama, King of Swaziland

17th February, 1982

Honourable Prime Minister

I have the honour to refer to your letter of 12 February 1982 which reads as follows:

"I have the honour to refer to various discussions and correspondence between the Foreign Ministers of the Kingdom of Swaziland and the Republic of South Africa which resulted in mutual agreement between our respective Governments to the effect that both Governments are aware of the fact that international terrorism, in all its manifestations, poses a real threat to international peace and security and that our respective Governments should take steps to protect our respective states and nationals against this threat.

Therefore, I now have the honour to inform you that the Government of the Republic of South Africa proposes the following Agreement between our respective Governments:

ARTICLE 1

The Contracting Parties undertake to combat terrorism, insurgency and subversion individually and collectively and shall call upon each other wherever possible for such assistance and steps as may be deemed necessary or expedient to eliminate this evil.

ARTICLE 2

In the conduct of their mutual relations the Contracting Parties shall furthermore respect each other's independence, sovereignty and territorial integrity and shall refrain from the unlawful threat or use of force and from any other act which is inconsistent with the purposes and principles of good neighbourliness.

ARTICLE 3

The Contracting Parties shall live in peace and further develop and maintain friendly relations with each other and shall therefore not allow any activities within their respective territories directed towards the commission of any act which involves a threat or use of force against each other's territorial integrity.

ARTICLE 4

The Contracting Parties shall not allow within their respective territories the installation or maintenance of foreign military bases or the presence of foreign military units except in accordance with their right of self-defence in the event of armed attacks as provided for in the

> Charter of the United Nations and only after due notification to the other.

Should the Government of the Kingdom of Swaziland agree with the abovementioned provisions, this letter and your affirmative reply thereto shall constitute an Agreement between our two Governments.

Please accept, Your Majesty, the renewed assurance of my highest consideration."

Duly authorised by His Majesty King Sobhuza II, I have the honour to inform you, Mr Prime Minister, that the Government of the Kingdom of Swaziland agree to the abovementioned provisions and regard your letter and this reply as constituting an agreement between our two Governments.

Please accept, Mr Prime Minister, the assurance of my highest consideration.

MABANDLA FRED DLAMINI
Prime Minister of the Kingdom of Swaziland

THE HONOURABLE P. W. BOTHA
Prime Minister of the Republic of South Africa, Cape Town

EMBARGOED AND TO BE CHECKED AGAINST DELIVERY

AGREEMENT BETWEEN THE GOVERNMENT OF THE REPUBLIC OF SOUTH AFRICA AND THE GOVERNMENT OF THE KINGDOM OF SWAZILAND RELATING TO SECURITY MATTERS

JOINT STATEMENT BY THE HONOURABLE R F BOTHA, MINISTER OF FOREIGN AFFAIRS OF THE REPUBLIC OF SOUTH AFRICA, AND THE HONOURABLE R V DLAMINI, MINISTER OF FOREIGN AFFAIRS OF THE KINGDOM OF SWAZILAND: 31 MARCH 1984

During discussions between the Honourable R F Botha, Minister of Foreign Affairs of the Republic of South Africa, and the Honourable R V Dlamini, Minister of Foreign Affairs of the Kingdom of Swaziland, in Pretoria today, it was decided to make public, on behalf of their respective Governments, the existence and contents of an Agreement relating to Security Matters.

After having been granted full powers by the South African State President in Council and His Majesty the late King Sobhuza II of Swaziland, respectively the Honourable P W Botha, Prime Minister of the Republic of South Africa, and the Honourable M F Dlamini, former Prime Minister of the Kingdom of Swaziland, concluded the Agreement, which came into force on 17 February 1982, on behalf of the two Governments.

The introductory paragraph of the Agreement expresses the awareness of the two States that international terrorism, in all its manifestations, poses a real threat to international peace and security as well as their agreement that they should take steps to protect their respective States and nationals against this threat. The Agreement accordingly records the undertaking of the Parties to combat terrorism, insurgency and subversion individually and collectively as well as their right to call upon each other for such assistance and steps as may be deemed necessary or expedient to eliminate this evil.

The Parties are required to respect each other's independence, sovereignty and territorial integrity in the conduct of their mutual relations and to refrain from the threat or use of force as well as any other act which would be inconsistent with the purposes and principles of good neighbourliness.

In order to facilitate the maintenance and development of peace and friendly relations between the two States, they are required not to allow any activities within their respective territories which are directed towards the commission of any act which involves a threat or use of force against each other's territorial integrity.

The Parties are also required not to allow the installation or maintenance of foreign military bases or the presence of foreign military units within their respective territories except in accordance with their right of self-defence in the event of armed attacks and only after due notification to the other.

PRETORIA
31 MARCH 1984

APPENDIX 5

RESOLUTION 418 (1977)
of 4 November 1977

The Security Council,

Recalling its resolution 392 (1976) of 19 June 1976, strongly condemning the South African Government for its resort to massive violence against and killings of the African people, including schoolchildren and students and others opposing racial discrimination, and calling upon that Government urgently to end violence against the African people and to take steps to eliminate *apartheid* and racial discrimination,

Recognizing that the military build-up by South Africa and its persistent acts of aggression against the neighbouring States seriously disturb the security of those states,

Further recognizing that the existing arms embargo must be strengthened and universally applied, without any reservations or qualifications whatsoever, in order to prevent a further aggravation of the grave situation in South Africa,

Taking note of the Lagos Declaration for Action against *Apartheid,*

Gravely concerned that South Africa is at the threshold of producing nuclear weapons,

Condemning the South African Government for its acts of repression, its defiant continuance of the system of *apartheid* and its attacks against neighbouring independent States

Considering that the policies and acts of the South African

Government are fraught with danger to international peace and security,

Recalling its resolution 181 (1963) of 7 August 1963 and other resolutions concerning a voluntary arms embargo against South Africa,

Convinced that a mandatory arms embargo needs to be universally applied against South Africa in the first instance,

Acting therefore under Chapter VII of the Charter of the United Nations,

1. *Determines*, having regard to the policies and acts of the South African Government, that the acquisition by South Africa of arms and related materiél constitutes a threat to the maintenance of international peace and security;

2. *Decides* that all States shall cease forthwith any provision to South Africa of arms and related materiél of all types, including the sale or transfer of weapons and ammunition, military vehicles and equipment, paramilitary police equipment, and spare parts for the aforementioned, and shall cease as well the provision of all types of equipment and supplies and grants of licencing arrangements for the manufacture and development of nuclear weapons;

3. *Calls upon* all States to review, having regard to the objectives of the present resolution, all existing contractual arrangements with and licences granted to South Africa relating to the manufacture and maintenance of arms, ammunition of all types and military equipment and vehicles, with a view to terminating them.

4. *Further decides* that all States shall refrain from any co-operation with South Africa in the manufacture and development of nuclear weapons;

5. *Calls upon* all States, including States non-members of the United Nations, to act strictly in accordance with the provisions of the present resolution;

6. *Requests* the Secretary-General to report to the Security Council on the progress of the implementation of the present resolution, the first to be submitted not later than 1 May 1978;

7. *Decides* to keep this item on the agenda for further action, as appropriate in the light of developments.

                              Adopted unanimously at the 2046th meeting.

APPENDIX 6

RESOLUTION 558 (1984)
*Adopted by the Security Council at its 2564th meeting
on 13 December 1984*

The Security Council,

Recalling its resolution 418 (1977) of 4 November 1977, in which it decided upon a mandatory arms embargo against South Africa,

Recalling its resolution 421 (1977) of 9 December 1977, by which it entrusted a Committee consisting of all its members with the task of, among other things, studying ways and means by which the mandatory arms embargo could be made more effective against South Africa and to make recommendations to the Council,

Taking note of the Committee's report to the Security Council contained in document S/14179 of 19 September 1980,

Recognizing that South Africa's intensified efforts to build up its capacity to manufacture armaments undermines the effectiveness of the mandatory arms embargo against South Africa,

Considering that no State should contribute to South Africa's arms production capability by purchasing arms manufactured in South Africa,

1. *Reaffirms* its resolution 418 (1977) and stresses the continuing need for the strict application of all its provisions;

2. *Requests* all States to refrain from importing arms, ammunition of all types and military vehicles produced in South Africa;

3. *Requests* all States, including States non-members of the United

Nations to act strictly in accordance with the provisions of the present resolution;

4. *Requests* the Secretary-General to report to the Security Council Committee established by resolution 421 (1977) concerning the question of South Africa on the progress of the implementation of the present resolution before 31 December 1985.

NOTES

Introduction

1. Estimates by SADCC members and others.

2. *Children on the Front Line—The Impact of Apartheid, Destabilization and Warfare on Children in Southern Africa* (UNICEF, January 1987). This report uses official government figures of 100,000 military and civilian war deaths in Mozambique from 1980-85, and a further 100,000 deaths in southern Mozambique 1983-84 as a result of the disruption of food production and interference or prevention of food relief distribution. The report estimates at least another 100,000 deaths in Angola in this period from war-related famine and its effects. War-related deaths among infants and children are estimated at 380,000 in Mozambique and Angola 1980-85, through disruption of food production and destruction of health facilities. In 1986, these figures are given as 140,000 and a similar figure was anticipated for 1987. That totals 960,000 deaths to the end of 1987, excluding direct military and civilian fatalities in the latter two years. Thus the figure of one million dead in the two countries alone since 1980 is probably conservative.

3. Unicef, Maputo. Roy Stacey, Deputy Assistant Secretary for African Affairs in the US State Department at a UN-sponsored conference on the emergency appeal (Maputo, April 1988), described the situation in Mozambique as "one of the most brutal holocausts against ordinary human beings since World War Two."

4. On 25 April 1985, over a year after the signing of the Nkomati Accord, the South African foreign minister, R. F. "Pik" Botha, stated in parliament:

"There was of course a time when we helped to train Renamo and assisted it. . . . Renamo's requests for aid were acceded to. I wish to confirm today that in similar circumstances in southern Africa, we should do it again." (S A Hansard, 25 April 1985, col. 4214)

5. Chapter 1. After publication of the Gorongosa diaries, captured in 1985 at the main MNR base in central Mozambique, which revealed that the South Africans had repeatedly violated Mozambican sovereignty, broken the terms of Nkomati, and continued to fly in supplies, "Pik" Botha confirmed that the documents were genuine:

"One can go through all those entries in the diary . . . the information tallies with the flights undertaken by the air force. That is true. The times of our meetings [with MNR] in Pretoria are correct. The times that they indicated I had been present, are correct." (S A Hansard, 6 February 1986 , col. 353)

He later claimed the violations, such as building a clandestine air strip, were "technical."

6. Chapter 3. Letters between Savimbi and Ramires de Oliveira of the Portugese eastern military command in 1972, dealing with supply of arms, ammunition and medicine, and confirming the use of Unita members in other countries to gather information on MPLA for the Portuguese. Found in security files in Lisbon after the Portugese *coup d'état*, some of these letters were first published in *Jeune Afrique* in Paris and later in *The Times* of London. A padre involved as go-between has also confirmed to the editors the regular contacts between Unita and Portuguese military intelligence, maintained through timber merchants, Duarte and Oliveira.

7. For the best analysis of "total strategy" in its historical context and its application, see Robert Davies and Dan O'Meara, "Total Strategy in Southern Africa: An Analysis of South African Regional Policy since 1978," *Journal of Southern African Studies* 11, no. 2 (April 1985). See also John de St Jorre, "Destabilization and Dialogue: South Africa's Emergence as a Regional Superpower." *CSIS Africa Notes*, no. 26 (17 April 1984).

8. For further information on South Africa's nuclear capability, see Chapter 7; publications and testimony of the World Campaign against Nuclear and Military Collaboration with South Africa, Oslo; Robert S. Jaster, "Pretoria's Nuclear Diplomacy," *CSIS Africa Notes*, no. 81 (22 January 1988).

9. Edward Mortimer, *Financial Times*, London, 29 March 1988.

10. Commonwealth Eminent Persons Group on Southern Africa, *Mission to South Africa: The Commonwealth Report* (London: Penguin Books, 1986).

Chapter 1. MOZAMBIQUE: VICTIMS OF APARTHEID

1. *O Seculo Illustrado*, no. 1896, 4 May 1974. The photograph was taken by Eduardo Gageiro.

2. Ken Flower, interviews with authors. From his personal archives, Flower also supplied a copy of the photograph with the new caption written on it by his deputy, Ken Leaver. Over a three-year period from 14 November 1982, Flower was interviewed on a number of occasions, all in Harare. Some interviews were lengthy; others to check or clarify details were brief. Flower died in Harare in September 1987, three weeks before publication of his autobiography, *Serving Secretly* (London: John Murray; Harare: Quest, 1987). In the book he confirms the meeting with Major Silva Pais and many of the other details he told the authors.

3. For a full account of this period, see David Martin and Phyllis Johnson, *The Struggle for Zimbabwe: The Chimurenga War* (New York: Monthly Review Press, 1981).

4. Two CIO officers who asked not to be identified, interviews with authors, Harare, 25 November 1982, 8 February 1984, and 18 February 1985. At the time of the first two interviews, both men were still serving officers in the CIO. It may seem odd to the reader who is unaware of postindependence Zimbabwean realities that people who had served the rebel Rhodesian regime would wish—and be allowed—to continue working in Zimbabwe's main intelligence organization. In part, this arose from constraints imposed upon the Mugabe government by the Lancaster House agreement giving certain protections to Rhodesian civil servants. But, more importantly, it arose from Mugabe's policy of reconciliation and the need to retain professional skills while Zimbabweans were receiving special training.

5. Ibid.

6. The term "reeducation center" may have a sinister ring. But the Portuguese *centro de reeducação* could equally well be translated as "reform center" or "retraining center," terms that do not carry the same connotation.

7. The Mozambican government has refused to use the names MNR or Renamo, instead describing the group as *bandidos armados* which in English means "armed bandits." It is a phrase widely accepted, even by Western ambassadors in Maputo. The British ambassador John Stewart, interviewed in January 1984 on the external broadcast of Radio Mozambique just before relinquishing his post, said he fully agreed that the MNR was no morethan "armed bandits." His successor Eric Vines, in the Queen's birthday party speech on 13 June 1985, said, "Britain and Mozambique would go together in search of peace, dialogue, observance of the law, defeat of the armed bandits and the future prosperity of Mozambique." Another senior Western ambassador in Maputo described them as "a disparate group of gun-slingers, thugs, white Portuguese opportunists and other assorted anti-Frelimo types who lack any vision or programme for the future." The scale of atrocities the MNR has committed is massive and well documented. Their terrorization of the population has included acts such as cutting off ears, noses or lips, and hacking people to death with pickaxes.

8. Over a period of three years the authors interviewed, on a number of occasions, four of the seven CIO officers involved in the creation and operations of the MNR in its Rhodesian period. Flower spoke on the record about the CIO role in creating the MNR and includes details of this period in his autobiography. Of those directly involved, May was the only one of the CIO/MNR team to "defect" to the South Africans after Zimbabwe's independence. According to Flower, there was a "gentlemen's agreement" in the CIO that none of his officers would be recruited by the South Africans without his knowledge. May broke the agreement, taking a number of files with him to Pretoria. He is reputed to have become a brigadier in the MID before moving to Britain in late 1984. There he became "editor" of *Chief Executive* magazine owned by the Dutch shipping magnate Johan Deuss, who is heavily involved in supplying Middle East oil to South Africa in breach of sanctions.

9. Flower, interviews; CIO officers, interviews.

10. Evo Fernandes, interviews with authors; Lisbon, April and June 1984. Fernandes was removed as MNR Secretary-general in early 1987, during feuding within the leadership, and was made head of "research". He disappeared in Lisbon in mid-April 1988 and the Portuguese police announced a few days later that his body had been found outside the city with a bullet in the head.

11. Domingos Arouca, interviews with authors, Lisbon, April and June 1984. He spoke bitterly against the MNR and particularly against

Cristina and Fernandes who, he said, had blocked his attempts to obtain a rear base in Rhodesia for Fumo. Arouca announced his resignation from Fumo in late 1981 and his withdrawal from politics on the grounds of "ill health." This was "after talks with South Africa and after realizing South Africa was not interested in an independent Mozambique but only in putting pressure on Mozambique."

12. Frelimo, Statement, Dar es Salaam, 25 August 1964; Joaquim Chissano, interview with authors, Maputo, December 1985. Further details were supplied by Chissano, then minister of foreign affairs, who for many years during the liberation struggle was Frelimo's head of security. Milas is believed to have gone to Egypt and then Sudan after fleeing Dar es Salaam. The authors picked up his trail again in Ethiopia early in 1974, where he had been news editor of Radio Voice of the Gospel in Addis Ababa for some years, and traced him to Nairobi where he was involved in the Kenya Planned Parenthood Association. He worked for the UN agency Habitat and later became chief information officer for another UN agency in Nairobi, UNEP. Fernandes said that Milas was in Kenya as the MNR's deputy representative for Africa.

13. The MNR was so strongly identified with Matsangaiza that it was widely known as the "André movement" and its members as Matsangas or Machangas.

14. João Santa Rita, *Star*, Johannesburg, 18 March 1985. Following Cristina's death, the two brothers Adriano and Boaventura Bomba, both prominent in the MNR leadership, disappeared. A former Mozambican journalist, Santa Rita provided the first detailed report of Cristina's death. Quoting MNR sources, he said Boaventura had been behind the murder of Cristina and that subsequently both Bombas had been killed. "Boaventura accused Cristina, who was a white man, of being totally under South African control," wrote Santa Rita. "The row reached such a level that the MNR president, Mr. Afonso Dhlakama, wanted Boaventura to be executed for treason." The MNR alleged that Cristina had been killed by Frelimo "agents," but in the middle of an MNR training base in South Africa, this seems highly implausible. The much more probable explanation is that he was a victim of the internal feuding which had been a characteristic of the MNR since Dhlakama's takeover.

15. Flower, interviews; CIO officers, interviews. Flower was insistent that Vorster rejected his approach for support and that such support was only forthcoming after P. W. Botha took over as South African leader in late 1978. This assertion appears to be borne out by

the statements of CIO instructors stationed at Odzi that no South Africans or South African supplies appeared there until 1979.

16. CIO paymaster-administrator, interviews with authors. Details of these two phases of the transfer were given in these interviews.

17. CIO senior instructor, interview with authors, Harare, 16 January 1986.

18. Mozambique National Planning Commission, *Economic Report,* (Maputo, January 1984).

19. National Statistical Directorate, Mozambique National Planning Commission, Statistical information 1975–1984 (Maputo); Mozambique National Planning Commission, Export figures, 1985 and 1986 (Maputo).

20. National Railways of Zimbabwe. By early 1986, this trade was reduced to less than 10 percent, but it began to increase again later in the year and throughout 1987.

21. Eastwood to Mugabe, 26 June 1981, Report. Captain Eastwood's report, which white colleagues referred to as "The Bible," was prepared for a briefing for Mugabe on the MNR and the situation in Mozambique. Reading it again in early 1986, the authors are left with the distinct impression that it was intended to scare the new Zimbabwean government. If this is correct, then Eastwood's statistics for the MNR at that time may be too high. The report warns Mugabe against committing troops to Mozambique: "Should Zimbabwean troops become actively involved in the war in Mozambique it is axiomatic that each of the aforesaid links (to Beira and Maputo) will be forfeited as a reprisal." Later in the report, Eastwood says, "The strategic dangers of such involvement on our part have been pointed out on a number of occasions. Worse-case analysis means we will lose both links to the coast. Under such circumstances Zimbabwe may as well apply for Homeland status."

22. MNR documents found 5 December 1981 at Garagua, Mozambique (hereafter cited as Garagua documents), which included minutes of meetings in November 1980 at Zoabostad, the main MNR training camp in South Africa.

23. Ibid.

24. A report on this meeting was subsequently obtained by the Zimbabwean authorities from villagers crossing from Mozambique.

25. Garagua documents.

26. Senior Frelimo officials told us of the abundance of evidence to prove the Malawi-MNR connection, including highly compromising documentation found at Gorongosa in August 1985. US and British

officials are equally open about this connection, and late in 1985, the British government made formal representation to the Malawi government requesting the termination of support for the MNR.

27. *Herald,* Harare, 24 June 1982.

28. Paul Fauvet, "The SADCC Summit in Maputo," for the Mozambique News Agency (hereafter cited as AIM), July 1983.

29. *Observer,* London, 20 February 1983.

30. "Documentation about the Accord of Nkomati," AIM, May 1984. The first item in this dossier "The Nkomati Agreement: An Historical Perspective" contains details of the points Crocker made during his visit. Although this was a historical landmark in the process leading to Nkomati, the visit went badly, the abrasive Crocker clashing with Chissano, then foreign minister. Thereafter, Crocker's deputy Frank Wisner, an able career diplomat, handled contacts with the Mozambican government.

31. Lawrence Eagleburger, Address to National Conference of Editorial Writers, San Francisco, 23 June 1983.

32. AIM, "Documentation about the Accord of Nkomati."

33. Mozambican government officials, interviews with one of authors, Maputo, December 1985.

34. ANC Information Department, Statement, Lusaka, 16 March 1984.

35. *West Africa* (London), 2 April 1984.

36. Mozambique National Planning Commission, *Economic Report.*

37. Southern African Research & Documentation Centre (hereafter cited as SARDC), Report, Maputo; December 1986.

38. Ministry of Internal Trade, statistics supplied to authors, Maputo, December 1985. Other statistics in this section were supplied by the relevant ministries.

39. Mozambique National Planning Commission, *Economic Report.*

40. Mozambican government officials, briefings to authors, Maputo, December 1985.

41. The Portuguese connection may need some explanation here. In the wake of the Portuguese *coup d'état* in April 1974, before Mozambique's independence, Portuguese business interests were subject to a series of nationalizations by the soldiers who seized power in Lisbon. Jorge Jardim was one of those affected. Another was Manuel Bulhosa, a one-time business partner of Jardim and, until its nationalization, the owner of the Maputo oil refinery SONAREP. Bulhosa, reputedly Portu-

gal's richest businessman, employed Fernandes ostensibly at his Lisbon publishing house Livraria Bertrand. He also employed Jorge Correia, who replaced Fernandes as MNR representative in Europe when the latter became secretary general. These Portuguese MNR representatives came and went at will in Lisbon, which became MNR propaganda headquarters, notwithstanding Mozambique government protestations. It became clear early on that they had highly placed contacts among Portuguese civilian and military leaders who refused to accept Frelimo.

42. Bulhosa had denied to the Mozambican government that he was supporting the MNR, but proof of his links emerged in August 1985 in the Gorongosa documents.

43. Details of the agreement between Machel, Mugabe, and Nyerere are from briefings by officials of the three governments.

44. MNR documents found 28 August 1985 at Gorongosa, Mozambique (hereafter cited as Gorongosa documents). These documents included daily diaries kept by the MNR. One entry refers to a meeting in Pretoria on 23 February 1984, only three weeks before Mozambique and South Africa signed the Nkomati Accord, giving the objective of the meeting as: "Planning the war in the face of the situation taken up by South African republic." The South African team at that meeting was very high-powered indeed and included the head of the MID General Pieter van der Westhuizen and the commander of special forces General André Liebenberg, both since promoted. The contents of the documents were revealed at a news conference in Maputo on 30 September 1985 by Mozambique's minister of security Colonel Sergio Vieira and subsequently published in two volumes by the Mozambican Ministry of Information (Maputo, 1985).

45. From 1981 to March 1986, at least 34 foreign-contracted workers, known in Mozambique as *co-operantes*, were murdered, 66 kidnapped, and five wounded by the MNR. They included nationals of Brazil, Britain, Bulgaria, China, France, the German Democratic Republic, Ireland, Italy, Portugal, Romania, the Soviet Union, Sri Lanka, and Sweden. At least 12 priests and nuns were among those murdered and kidnapped. As a result of the South Africa–directed offensive against foreign-aid workers, most were withdrawn from the countryside bringing development projects to a standstill.

46. "Meanwhile, official South African sources have been leaking to journalists and Mozambican officials information implicating individuals in other nations, including Portugal, which is Mozambique's former colonial ruler, Oman, Saudi Arabia and the Comoros, in arms

shipments to the resistance movement" (*Washington Post*, 23 January 1985). Machel also did not appear to believe that these were the principal sources of supply to the MNR. In a speech in December 1984, he said, "South Africa is still the key to the problem."

47. MNR diary, 12 September 1984, Gorongosa documents. There has been some confusion as to whether Viljoen described Pik Botha as a "traitor" or "treacherous." This arises from a mistranslation of the documents. The entry in the diary uses the word *traiçoeiro*, correctly translated as "treacherous."

48. *Africa Research Bulletin* (ARB), hereafter cited as 22, no. 9 (15 October 1985); S A Hansard (6 February 1986).

49. ARB 22, No. 9 (15 October 1985).

50. *Financial Mail*, Joannesburg, 4 October 1985.

51. Mozambican government officials briefing to authors, Maputo, December 1985.

52. In one such attack at the Angonia state farm, 55 workers were killed. The wounded, who were evacuated to hospitals inside Malawi, found themselves sharing wards with MNR casualties from the same attack.

53. Dossiér of evidence of Malawi's involvement with MNR, September 1986. A copy of the dossier is in the possession of authors.

54. Mozambican government officials, briefings to authors; and Zimbabwean government officials, briefings to authors. Details of this period were given in briefings by government officials in Mozambique and Zimbabwe.

55. As well as personal briefings, a variety of sources are drawn upon for chronology and quotations including *ARB*, *Herald* (Harare), *Libération* (Paris), SABC, several South African newspapers, AIM, and its excellent published record of this period entitled *Samora—Why He Died*.

56. Carlos Cardoso, "Samora: A Possible Target?", AIM, 16 October 1986.

57. *Noticias de Beira*, 5 February 1988.

58. There were nine survivors. Among those who died with Machel were Luis Maria de Alcantara Santos, minister of transport; Jose Carlos Lobo, deputy minister of foreign affairs and former ambassador to the UN; Aquino da Bragança, director of the Center for African Studies at Eduardo Mondlane University; Fernando Honwana, personal assistant to the president; and most of the rest of Machel's personal staff, including his private secretary, press attaché, official photographer, interpreters, and other support staff.

59. The governments of Tanzania and Zimbabwe have large popular domestic support for their military commitments, and their citizens are active in civilian support for Mozambique. The Zimbabwe-Mozambique Friendship Association (ZIMOFA) has a large membership and is a dynamic mobilizer of funds, food and material support for "displaced people" in Mozambique. In Tanzania, 13 million shillings were raised within a few months of launching a solidarity fund drive for Mozambique. That amount (after a series of devaluations made necessary by actions of the IMF) equals some US $400,000. Yet Tanzania is one of the world's 25 poorest nations, and as most of the money came from the peasant sector, it represented a massive contribution of solidarity. Solidarity fund drives were also launched in Belgium, Holland, and Zimbabwe. As people in different countries became conscious of what was happening, the international mobilization for Mozambique took on dramatic new proportions.

60. The authors have in their possession five different photographs taken at the White House during the visit by an MNR delegation, which included Luis Serapião, a professor at Howard University and MNR representative in the United States; Jorge Correia, then chief MNR propagandist in Europe; and Arturo de Fonesca, MNR representative in the Federal Republic of Germany. See picture section.

61. Charles Redman, 13 July 1987. The MNR representative was again Serapião.

62. *Economist* (London), 11 July 1987.

63. *New York Times*, 23 May 1987.

64. Senate testimony by Chester Crocker on United States–Mozambique policy, 24 June 1987, released verbatim by the State Department.

65. Mark von Koevering, a 30-year-old Mennonite agronomist from Michigan working on a seed multiplication project in Homoine, said the invaders were dressed in new camouflage uniforms, were very well equipped, and were "shooting every person and building in sight."

66. *Guardian*, London, 25 July 1987.

67. Roland Hunter, who is still in prison, was an aid to the main MNR contact in South African military intelligence, Colonel Charles van Niekerk (later Brigadier). He handled large amounts of money on behalf of the military, making payments to MNR leaders. He witnessed new AK 47s being loaded into aircraft at South Africa's military headquarters destined for Mozambique, and was told by his superiors that this operation codenamed "Mila" was successful and cost-effective. Those released were Trish and Derek Hanekom.

68. Francisco Pelucio Silva (Unicef), Maputo.

69. Margaret L. Knox, *Washington Post*, 5 January 1988.

70. Ibid.

71. Ibid.

72. SARDC, Report; and Reginald H. Green et al., *Children on the Front Line—The Impact of Apartheid, Destabilization and Warfare on Children in Southern Africa*, prepared for Unicef, January 1987.

73. Mozambique government and United Nations Development Program (UNDP), "The Emergency Situation in Mozambique: Priority Requirements for the Period 1988–89" (Maputo: UNDP, March 1988).

74. Green et al., *Children on the Front Line.*

75. President Joaquim Chissano, Press conference, 4 December 1986.

Chapter 2: Zimbabwe: Apartheid's Dilemma

1. The names the various parties used in the 1980 elections are confusing. In the April 1979 "internal settlement" election, in which Mugabe's and Nkomo's parties did not participate, the Reverend Ndabaningi Sithole had registered and used the name Zanu despite having been deposed as its leader four years earlier. This forced Mugabe's party to run under the name Zanu-PF in 1980. Nkomo had hoped that his and Mugabe's parties would run under the name Patriotic Front. But this would not have resolved who would be the leader, and Mugabe's party chose to run on its own. In the event, Zanu-PF took 63 percent of the votes cast, Nkomo's Patriotic Front 24 percent, and the UANC only 8 percent. In the "internal settlement" election 10 months earlier, the Rhodesians had claimed that Muzorewa's party had taken 67 percent of votes cast.

2. Eschel Rhoodie, *The Real Information Scandal* (Johannesburg: Orbis SA (Pty), 1983). Rhoodie was secretary for information of the South African government and was one of the casualties of the "Muldergate" information scandal which also brought down the then prime minister B. J. Vorster. According to Rhoodie, one of South Africa's many secret projects was code-named Operation Chicken. This involved funding some Zimbabwean nationalist leaders, and he specifically mentions Muzorewa, Sithole, and James Chikerema as beneficiaries of South African largesse. Approximately US $1 million were committed to the 1979 Muzorewa campaign and, in 1980, some four hundred vehicles costing about US $2.5 million. Muzorewa's three seats cost Pretoria US $750,000 each.

3. British Parliamentary Human Rights Group, *Free and Fair! The 1979 Rhodesian Election* (London: 1979). This report was prepared by observers on behalf of the British Parliamentary Human Rights Group.

4. For the background on Sithole's removal, see Martin and Johnson, *The Struggle for Zimbabwe*.

5. Ministry of Information, Harare, 4 March 1980.

6. From information obtained, the Zimbabwean authorities are certain that the killers were former Rhodesian soldiers who had gone south in 1980 and joined the SADF. At a press conference in Stockholm on 25 September 1981, Mugabe said the assassination had been carried out by former Selous Scouts (*Herald*, Harare, 26 September 1981).

7. Zimbabwe Ministerial Statement to House of Assembly, 10 February 1983, *Hansard Parliamentary Debates*, vol. 6, no. 28. Among the many incidents Evans and Hartlebury admitted to was gaining entry to the house of the authors (disguised, we believe, as electricians) to try to photograph the manuscript of a previous book, *The Struggle for Zimbabwe*. They failed in that mission because the book was still at the research stage and writing had not yet begun.

8. *Herald*, Harare, 13 September 1981. The minister of state (security) Emmerson Munangagwa is reported to have said that the blasts were recorded by seismographic stations as far away as Malawi where they registered between 1.8 and 2.7 on the Richter scale.

9. Gericke was originally arrested on suspicion of spying for South Africa. It was during questioning that police began to focus on his possible role in the Inkomo sabotage.

10. Varkevisser's role in Gericke's escape continues to raise questions. He was accompanied to the Central Police Station in Harare by another man who has never been identified. It is thought that Varkevisser's role in the "hot extraction" may have been "involuntary." According to former colleagues, his wife Marisa and two children, aged nine and five, along with some of his property, had been "removed" from his home prior to his role in Gericke's escape. His colleagues believe they may have been taken hostage to ensure his cooperation and that the unidentified third man went with him to the police station to ensure that he did what he had been told. One point which may lend credence to this interpretation is that whereas others involved in operations for South Africa in Zimbabwe were given jobs in the SADF, MID and so on, Varkevisser was not. When last heard of, he was a salesman in Cape Town.

11. The extent of the damage at Thornhill has been widely misreported. A SADCC document, "Estimates of the Cost of South African

Destabilization," to the OAU summit in 1985 says that 13 planes were destroyed. This is incorrect. In all, 10 planes were damaged, five of which were write-offs. According to Zimbabwean air force documents, five Hunters were damaged. Three were totally destroyed, and the other two repaired in Zimbabwe. Four Hawk fighters that had just arrived from Britain were damaged. One was a write-off, two were repaired in Britain and one locally. In addition, a Cessna 337 was completely destroyed.

12. *Times*, London, 28 August 1982.

13. On 27 April 1980, there were 5,267 guerrillas at Assembly Point Papa. The contents of the seven truck loads the government found included 15 BIO recoilless rifles, 27 82 mm mortars, 34 ZGU-1s, five 12.7 anti-aircraft guns, six SAM-7 missiles, 14 assorted missiles ranging from rifle grenades to 122 mm rockets, seven 57 mm field guns, 13 GRAD-P 122 mm rockets, one 60 mm mortar, and two 75 mm recoilless rifles. The discovery of the cache, the authorities presumed, prevented more armaments from being brought in on that route.

14. The Zimbabwean government obtained copies of the railways manifests showing the arms that had been unloaded at Dett. In that period, the instruction to unload would have had to come from a white officer in charge.

15. Senior members of PF-Zapu subsequently conducted an internal enquiry into the property purchases to ascertain where the money had come from and who had authorized the expenditures. This report has not been made public. But a document in the authors' possession lists 52 properties purchased by Nkomo in his individual capacity, by PF-Zapu as a party, and by PF-Zapu–owned companies. The report shows Nkomo as director of Walmer Ranching Company, and as owner of Walmer Farm (5,139 hectares) and Makwe Farm (2,570 hectares). PF-Zapu as a party is shown as owning 20 properties. These include 10 farms, two slaughterhouses, two hotels, a manufacturing company, a building, a hauling firm, a garage, a supermarket, and a store. At the time, the other properties were owned through PF-Zapu companies such as NITRAM, of which Nkomo was a director. Many of these companies were seized by the government after the discovery of the arms caches on the premises of some of them. Allegations that the caching was part of a plot was "a straightforward lie," Nkomo said.

16. ZRP records.

17. Dube and Nzima were brought before Harare Magistrates' Court on 4 January 1983. The prosecutor said they would be charged with murder and attempted murder. On 10 August 1983, they were

found guilty in the High Court of murder and sentenced to death. Both men denied the charges, claiming they had been abducted and forced to accompany the bandits. The judge Mr. Justice Waddington dismissed their claim as "inherently improbable" and ruled that their original statements to the police were made freely and voluntarily and were admissable as evidence. Appeals against sentence and conviction were dismissed by the Supreme Court on 4 April 1984. Thereafter, the two men appealed for clemency. The appeal was rejected, and they were executed in Harare on 7 April 1986.

18. ZRP records. The details were supplied to the South Africans as part of Zimbabwe's case proving Pretoria's involvement in resupplying bandits.

19. Benson Dube, Statement during his trial in the High Court, Harare, August 1983.

20. Judia Ncube, Statement to ZRP.

21. Hillary Vincent Ndhlovu, Statement to ZRP.

22. *Herald*, Harare, 4 February 1984.

23. Zimbabwean government officials, briefing to authors, Harare, January 1986.

24. ZRP records.

25. Radio Truth, transcript, 30 November 1983.

26. Zimbabwean government estimate.

27. John Sprack, *Rhodesia: South Africa's Sixth Province* (London: International Defence and Aid Fund, 1974).

28. Anthony Wilkinson, "The Impact of War," *Journal of Commonwealth and Comparative Politics* (1980).

29. R. Riddell, "Zimbabwe's Manufactured Exports and the Ending of the Trade Agreement with South Africa" (Confederation of Zimbabwe Industries, December 1981, Mimeographed).

30. *New York Times*, 19 April 1981.

31. *New York Times*, 1 February 1981.

32. This occurred immediately prior to the resumption of pumping. The cost of repairs was US $11 million.

33. *ARB* 23, no. 5 (15 June 1986): 8079.

34. Ibid.

35. *Mission to South Africa: The Commonwealth Report: Findings of the Commonwealth Eminent Persons Group on Southern Africa* (Harmondsworth: Penguin Books, 1986).

36. A State Department official told the authors about the meeting with Sithole. Details of his approach to the South African embassy were made public by the Zimbabwean authorities.

37. *Daily Telegraph*, London, 23 January 1987.
38. *Financial Times*, London, 30 October 1986.
39. ZRP records.

Chapter 3. ANGOLA: THE STRUGGLE CONTINUES

1. For a full list of those tried, see John Marcum, *The Angolan Revolution* (Cambridge, Mass.: MIT Press, 1969), 1:34. Apart from four officials of the UPNA (former name of UPA/FNLA) who were tried in absentia, it is overwhelmingly a list of well-known MPLA members, many of whom spent years in prison.

2. The author, closely associated with the MPLA since the mid-1960s and working as President Neto's information secretary after independence, bases this statement on the testimony of many of those former prisoners.

3. *Observer*, London, 7 May 1961.

4. For a well-documented account of this period, see Robert Davezies, *Les Angolais* (Paris: Editions de Minuit, 1965), 23–30. A French priest, he describes the links between the capital and the villages, the people who went back and forth, and the leaflets brought from Luanda to the countryside. Ciel, a young man then in a rural area, is quoted: "The people were fed up. They wanted to rise up . . . and they wanted to know how to do it." After the 4 February 1961 events in Luanda, he said, armed settlers arrived in jeeps "to tell the people not to do what the others had done in Luanda," because if they did "they would finish them all off." The local population, Ciel said, got wind of a secret settler plan to massacre them on 20 March. The people rose up on 15 March, with whatever crude weapons and implements they could muster, preempting the massacre by five days. The commander who mobilized his group, Ciel said, had taken part in the 4 February events in Luanda.

5. Ibid., 35. Interviewed by Davezies, a former FNLA chief of staff who went over to the MPLA, José Kalundongo, said that there were never more than three thousand men trained at the FNLA's Kinkuzu camp in Zaire and that they remained there for months because Roberto "wanted them at the base at the disposal of photographers, mainly Americans." Referring to the fact that training was given by Americans, he went on to say: "Anyway, one wonders why Mr Holden Roberto, after having refused Algerian volunteers, accepted the ser-

vices of the American officer Bernard Meinherz, a Vietnam veteran engaged to direct the FNLA's military wing" (Ibid., 212).

6. Citing "four official sources," the New York Times of 25 September 1975 said that the CIA started to send arms and funds to Roberto in 1962. In an article printed in the Congressional Record of 16 December 1975, a former White House aide was cited as saying that during Lyndon Johnson's administration, Washington's policy was "to play both ends against the middle," adding that the CIA "had the habit of picking out single individuals and making them our guys" (Ernest Harsch and Tony Thomas, Angola: The Hidden History of Washington's War [New York: Pathfinder Press, 1976], 21).

7. Marcelo Caetano, Depoimento (Rio de Janeiro and São Paulo: Distribuidora Record, 1975), 180–181.

8. An assimilado from Bié province, Savimbi was in Lausanne, Switzerland in 1962, the year after the start of the armed struggle, studying political science after dropping out of medical school in Portugal. He joined the MPLA; but later, at a conference at Makerere University in Uganda, he met Tom Mboya, the Kenyan politician known for his strong American ties, who is said to have prevailed upon him to leave the MPLA for the FNLA. A subsequent visit by a US State Department official bearing a checkbook appears to have convinced him to take that course. A similar offer made at the time to an MPLA official now working with the Angolan government was refused. Savimbi soon became "foreign minister" in GRAE, whose overseas mentors doubtless hoped that this would bestow a national image on the FNLA, then headed by elements associated with the royal family of the old Kongo Kingdom. However, in July 1964, at the All-African Meeting of Heads of State in Cairo, Savimbi resigned from the FNLA in characteristically flamboyant style, publicly accusing Roberto of tribalism and of having been a "United States creation" since 1961. He denounced the US advisers working with the FNLA and the army's lack of activity. The way was open to him to rejoin the MPLA. He travelled to Brazzaville, where he met Agostinho Neto and other leaders, and he stated that his condition for rejoining was to be made vice-president with responsibility for foreign affairs. The answer to this arrogant demand was simply that no appointments could be made without democratic collective decisions. Savimbi did not wait. He returned to Europe, and nothing more was heard of him for the next two years, apart from the fleeting creation in Switzerland of something called Amangola, "Manifesto of the Friends of Angola."

9. On 5 May 1972, for example, the Tanzanian newspaper the

Standard announced that Unita had donated two thousand kilograms of surplus maize from its cooperative farms to Zambia to help that country overcome shortages aggravated by the Portuguese blockade of Zambian goods in the port of Beira. On 12 May, under the headline "Maize gift 'a Joke'," the *Standard* published the MPLA spokesman's refutation. Referring to Unita's "imaginary people's co-operatives," the spokesman said: "If they had surplus maize to give away, why not give it to the people of Angola, some of whom are starving in the liberated areas because of Portuguese bombing and destruction of their crops with herbicides?"

10. Costa Gomes, interview with editors, Lisbon, April 1984.

11. *Times*, London, 23 August 1982.

12. J. Sotto-Maior, *A história de uma traição* (Luanda: Edições Alvorada, 1985), 15–30. This recent book quotes extensively from the documents related to Savimbi's collaboration with the Portuguese military and contains photocopies of many of them.

13. Ibid., 31–33. Sotto-Maior quotes a letter published in the Portuguese weekly *Expresso* from a former soldier in the colonial army in Angola: "In early 1969, I cannot remember the precise date at the moment, I was a member of a military force which passed through Gago Coutinho, headquarters of the battalion, in transit. We received orders to proceed in vehicles to a place between Gago Coutinho and Cangumbe. . . . We stopped about twenty or thirty kilometres away and mounted security in the area. MPLA operations were becoming increasingly intensive and effective in the east. Two coloured people, I think, went off into the bush. They came back accompanied by local people in a visible state of deprivation and by a number of young guerrillas, ragged and armed, and I even remember one of them was quite debonair. It was a Unita detachment which had long had relations with the PIDE [Portuguese security police] in Gago Coutinho and had given itself up in order to fight the MPLA which, as I said, was already showing itself to be the best organised force throughout the east. . . . They got into our vehicles and we arrived at Gago Coutinho at night. We were met by a major in charge of operations in the zone, the local head of the PIDE, Martins, and an African aged about 40, bearded, wearing glasses and with a gold chain on his chest, who I learned was negotiating this strange collaboration on the Unita side. It was he who received his colleagues, put them in a semi-circle and made them sing what I learned to be the Unita anthem. We were then ordered to withdraw." Commenting on the letter, the Portuguese newspaper *Expresso* said that from many similar eyewitness accounts and

documents in their possession, it appeared that the then PIDE director in Angola Aníbal de São José Lopes had contacts with Savimbi since before 1969, although it was not known if they had ever met.

14. MPLA, Statement, Lusaka, 25 March 1970.

15. MPLA, Statement, October 1973. The statement announced the thwarting of the Chipenda plot, saying: "Hand in glove with world reaction, the colonialists were preparing for the final attack. Their aim was the physical elimination of the most illustrious leaders of the genuine liberation movements in the Portuguese colonies. To this end they formed alliances with reactionary forces within the respective liberation movements, in the MPLA's case using the mindlessness of a former leader who, through personal ambition, became a turncoat, giving a Judas kiss while betraying his comrades. Playing the enemy's game of divide and rule, he used tribalism, seeking to drag some members of his tribe along with him in his inordinate ambition. But the colonialists and traitors failed. They had overlooked the fact that the new generation had been moulded by the valiant MPLA and that the youth know what they want and why they are fighting."

16. Frelimo, the Mozambican liberation movement, also suffered the effects of agents infiltrated into it. But it was fortunate in that the Tanzanian authorities took action against these agents. This was true in the case of Lazaro Nkavandame, who tried to split Frelimo along tribal lines, and of Frelimo vice-president Uria Simango, who tried to oust the other leaders after the assassination of President Mondlane and who was deported from Tanzania.

17. *To the Point,* 1 June 1974. This South African magazine reported that on a visit to Mozambique soon after the *coup d'état,* Costa Gomes said on several occasions that he was sure the people of the "overseas territories" would chose between the "extremes" of the status quo and independence.

18. *Notícias,* Luanda, 22 June 1974.

19. Communiqué, Lisbon, Junta of National Salvation, 8 August 1974.

20. The proclamation stated: "At this time when the people are called upon to assume their historic responsibilities in an independent Angola, concealed interests are busying themselves, seeking to distort the meaning of what you have been fighting for for thirteen years." It called upon the people and the guerrillas to carry on the struggle "for a democratic, popular and progressive regime, for one indivisible nation, for territorial integrity and for independent and sovereign participation in the free concert of nations."

21. Another secessionist scheme was denounced at a press conference in Luanda by Lúcio Lara on 5 December 1974. He said that an individual had presented himself to the MPLA asking to do propaganda work in the Lunda region in northeast Angola. On closer examination, it was found that he was born in Zaire and had held responsible posts in the Zairean political party MPR, and that in addition to Zairean citizenship and MPR membership cards, he had an MPLA/Chipenda card. This person, described by Lúcio Lara as a "good family man" with three wives and a great number of children, also had on him a plan for the establishment of something called the "State of Moxico," to include Lunda, Moxico, and Kuando Kubango, Angola's eastern provinces.

22. *Times*, London, 7 January 1976. "Sources in Washington now say that the CIA first decided that steps must be taken to help the anti-communists among the Angolan nationalists in January 1975. The 40 Committee, which supervises the CIA, then approved sending $300 000 to the FNLA."

23. *Guardian*, London, 30 May 1974.

24. This was reported to the US secretary of state Dr. Henry Kissinger by his consul general in Luanda Tom Killoran, after a meeting with Neto. Killoran, who opposed US involvement in Angola, was removed from his post by Kissinger and refused promotion, thus destroying his diplomatic career.

25. John Stockwell, *In Search of Enemies* (New York: W. W. Norton & Co. Inc.; London: Andre Deutsch, 1978) 86–87, 161–162. Stockwell resigned from the CIA in 1976.

26. *Argus*, Cape Town, 25 August 1984.

27. Stockwell, *In Search of Enemies*, 187. "To the CIA, the South Africans were the ideal solution for central Angola. . . . Especially in the field, CIA officers liked the South Africans, who tended to be bluff, aggressive men without guile. . . . Quietly South African planes and trucks turned up throughout Angola with just the gasoline or ammunition needed for an impending operation. On October 20, after a flurry of cables between headquarters and Kinshasa, two South African C-130 airplanes, similar to those used by the Israelis in their raid on Entebbe, feathered into Ndjili Airport [Kinshasa] at night to meet a CIA C-141 flight and whisk its load of arms down to Silva Porto [Kuito]. CIA officers and BOSS representatives met the planes at Ndjili and jointly supervised the transloading. At the same time, St. Martin requested and received headquarters' permission to meet BOSS representatives on a regular basis in Kinshasa. Other CIA officers cla-

moured for permission to visit South African bases in South-West Africa. On two occasions the BOSS director visited Washington and held secret meetings with Jim Potts. On another, he met with the CIA station chief in Paris. The COS, Pretoria, was ordered to brief BOSS about IAFEATURE [code name for the CIA's Angola operation], and nearly all CIA intelligence reports on the subject were relayed to Pretoria so his briefings would be accurate and up to date."

28. John Vorster, Interview *Newsweek*, May 1976. "Q: Would it be accurate to say that the US solicited South Africa's help to turn the tide against the Russians and Cubans in Angola last fall? *A*. I do not want to comment on that. The US government can speak for itself. I am sure you will appreciate that I cannot violate the confidentiality of government-to-government communications. But if you are making the statement, I won't call you a liar. Q. Would it also be accurate to say you received a green light from Kissinger for a military operation in Angola? *A*. If you say that of your own accord, I will not call you a liar."

The *Washington Post*, 24 December 1975, suggested that "the United States, in its anti-Communist idiocy, seems hellbent on making another of the colossal blunders that brought us Vietnam. The reference, obviously, is to Angola. . . . Incidentally, the United States might have a larger reservoir of Angolan goodwill to draw upon if we had given some small measure of support to the Angolans in their struggle to overthrow the Portuguese colonizers. Instead, we chose to maintain our alliance with Portugal. And now the Portuguese are gone, we are throwing in with the South Africans."

29. Stockwell, *In Search of Enemies*, 164.

30. *Granma Weekly Review* (Havana), 14 February 1982. An article in this issue, "The Angola Campaign," gives a very detailed Cuban military history of the events of 1975–76.

31. Ibid.

32. Ibid. See also Joint Angolan-Cuban Statement, 4 February 1982: "With a view to achieving its plans to liquidate the Angolan revolutionary movement, on 14 October 1975 the Government of the United States of America sent the South African army against Angola, taking advantage of the fact of the racist South Africans' illegal occupation of Namibia, which still persists to this day. In less than 20 days South African troops advanced more than 700km inside Angolan territory. Meanwhile, from the north, foreign regular and mercenary forces were moving threateningly close to the capital. *It was at that moment that*

President Agostinho Neto requested Cuban military cooperation" (emphasis added). The author, in Angola at the time, was told at the highest level of the importance of staving off the invading armies until independence on 11 November, before which date the Cuban combat troop contingents could not arrive in the country.

33. Stockwell, *In Search of Enemies*, 67–68.

34. *Daily Telegraph*, London, February 1976. "More than £10m[illion], mainly from the American CIA, is to be spent on the employment of British mercenaries in Angola."

35. Stockwell, *In Search of Enemies*, 234–235.

36. Angolan government, *White Paper on Acts of Aggression by the Racist South African Regime against the People's Republic of Angola, 1975–1982* (N.p., n.d.), 12. "The damage caused to the People's Republic of Angola by the big South African invasion of 1975–76 amounted to an extremely high sum, representing a heavy burden for a young country freed from colonialism which was starting on a new life of independence. In a report submitted to the United Nations at the time, this damage was estimated to be US $6.7 billion."

37. Stockwell, *In Search of Enemies*, 204.

38. *Diário de Luanda*, 5 January 1976.

39. Stockwell, *In Search of Enemies*, 204–205.

40. Ibid., 193.

41. Joint Angolan-Cuban Statement, 4 February 1982. "The Governments of Angola and Cuba, merely one month after the expulsion of the racist South African troops, on 22 April 1976, agreed on a programme for the progressive reduction of those forces. In less than a year, the Cuban military contingent was reduced by more than one-third, a process which was halted because of fresh external threats to Angola. . . . In mid-1979, the Governments of Angola and Cuba again agreed to start to carry out another programme for the gradual reduction of Cuban forces. Almost immediately afterwards, in September that year, the South Africans carried out repeated large-scale acts of aggression against Cunene and Huila provinces."

42. Angolan government, *White Paper*, 16–17.

43. Ibid., 24–25.

44. *International Herald Tribune*, Paris, 14 February 1981.

45. *Sunday Telegraph*, London, 29 March 1981.

46. "Texas Guns Were for Angola Rebels," *Observer*, London, 17 May 1981.

47. *US State Department Documents on Southern Africa Leaked to*

American Press, May–June 1981 (Swapo Western Europe, N.p., n.d., booklet of photocopies).

48. *Africa News*, 10 March 1986. The US biweekly quotes Dr. Steve Weissman, staff director of the House Foreign Affairs subcommittee on Africa: "I think it is unlikely the South Africans will agree to a timetable for Cuban withdrawal that Angola can accept. They want the Cubans there so [South Africa] can be seen to be working alongside the US against the Soviets."

49. Registered South African military operations against Angola up to August 1981 were 1,617 reconnaissance flights, one hundred bombing raids, 50 strafing incidents, 26 ground reconnaissance operations, 67 troop build-ups, four paratroop landings, 34 ground attacks, seven shelling operations, and nine mine-laying and other operations.

50. The partial sabotage of the oil refinery cost US $12,550,000 to repair and a further US $24 million in oil not exported between December 1981 and January 1982, when the refinery was again fully operational.

51. When Savimbi visited the United States in January 1986, a Madison Avenue publicity firm was hired at a cost of $600,000 to project him to an American audience and tell him how to dress.

52. *Windhoek Observer*, 20 November 1982. "Dr. Jonas Savimbi, the Unita leader, who had become a God-like legendary figure in the eyes of the white South Africans, but who lives at the mercy of South Africa's armed forces, having a very comfortable bungalow complex virtually on the border, from where he can direct his vast business operations with certain South African interests and involving Angolan teak, ivory and other valuables."

53. Human losses as a result of South African aggression in 1981 were assessed as 206 soldiers killed, 389 soldiers wounded and 1,086 missing, 158 civilians killed and 265 wounded, and 160,000 homeless people, inhabitants of Cunene province who fled north to seek refuge from the bombing, fighting, and occupation and were taken care of by the Angolan authorities.

54. In the central highland town of Huambo, in March 1983, the author had occasion to speak to a prisoner, a former Unita political commissar named Teodoro Silva Gideão, who spoke of a Unita congress held in the border area in July 1982. Some members, he said, had been expelled at the congress. It was said they wanted to organize a *coup d'état* against Savimbi because they were fed up with fighting a war they could not win. Among those expelled, he said, were Jorge Sangumba and Samuel Chiwale.

55. *Africa News*, 3 December 1984. "Escalating tensions within the anti-government Unita movement erupted into open fighting earlier this year, with the Ovimbundu [Umbundu] leadership of the rebel group openly executing its opponents. In interviews with recent deserters from Unita in Lubango and in the central city of Huambo, *Africa News* has learned that the South African–backed dissident group, while certainly not on the verge of collapse, is experiencing serious internal difficulties. . . . In an attempt to capitalize on these problems, the Angolan government has given a great deal of publicity to recent defections by Unita members and has widely publicized its long-standing amnesty for Unita soldiers and civilians who voluntarily turn themselves in. The biggest defection occurred in early November when 46 soldiers and 285 civilians who had been living with the rebel movement for over seven years surrendered to authorities in the southern province of Cunene. . . . [A farmer], who is of Kwanyama ancestry, charged that Unita members from Angola's largest ethnic group, the Ovimbundu, had been systematically isolating and killing members of other ethnic groups, such as the Kwanyama, the Gangela and the Chokwe."

56. *Daily Telegraph*, 28 December 1983. "S. Africa may have to quit Angola. . . . South African forces faced the prospect last night of being forced to make a strategic withdrawal from southern Angola. They have encountered stiff opposition from Angolan and Cuban units. . . . [There were no Cuban units in the area.] General Constand Viljoen, chief of the SADF, returned to Pretoria on Monday night after spending four days in the operational area with his troops and personally taking over command of a deteriorating situation. . . . General Viljoen said Swapo was . . . ducking under the protection of Angolan government Fapla and Cuban forces when faced by the South Africans."

57. *Financial Mail*, Johannesburg, 13 January 1984.

58. *Sunday Times*, Johannesburg, 25 November 1984. "Pretoria is reportedly furious with a decision by Angolan President dos Santos to send a memorandum to the UN Secretary-General, Dr. Pérez de Cuéllar, setting out Luanda's position on the thorny issue of Cuban withdrawal. . . . The leaks contradict the solemn assurances given by all the parties to the Cape Verdean talks that the negotiations would be conducted with maximum secrecy."

59. *Sunday Express*, Johannesburg, 25 November 1984.

60. *Observer*, London, 11 November 1984.

61. "The Selling of Jonas Savimbi: Public Relations Firm Paved Guerrilla's Way," *Washington Post*, 9 February 1986.

62. *Financial Mail*, Johannesburg, 18 October 1985.

63. Ibid. "SA denied having sent troops to help Unita, but intelligence sources allege that the anti-Swapo drive was merely a smokescreen for the troops sent to Mavinga. These sources also confirm MPLA allegations that the mechanised Fapla columns advancing on Mavinga were attacked by SAAF bombers, and that SA's 32 Battalion (Buffalo) fought with Unita till the end."

64. *Sunday Times*, Johannesburg, 22 September 1985. "Calling for help from the United States, he said the alleged Soviet involvement in the fighting introduced a new element to the civil war."

65. "Pretoria Seeks US Help to Rescue Unita from Defeat in Angola," *Times*, London, 24 September 1985; *Daily Telegraph*, London, 28 September 1985. "An urgent diplomatic effort is being made by South Africa to win American help for Dr. Jonas Savimbi's pro-western Unita movement in Angola now under pressure from a major offensive by Marxist government forces (*Daily Telegraph*).

66. Stockwell, *In Search of Enemies*, 193.

67. *Washington Post*, 30 and 31 March 1986.

68. *Citizen*, Johannesburg, 31 March 1986.

69. *Sunday Star*, Johannesburg, 14 September 1986.

70. *Cape Times*, Cape Town, 9 January 1987.

71. *Daily Dispatch*, East London, 5 June 1987. This report quotes Professor Mike Hough, Director of the Institute of Strategic Studies of the University of Pretoria.

72. *Guardian*, London, 14 May 1987.

73. "SA's Aid to Unita Over, Says Official," *Star*, Johannesburg, 29 May 1987. The article points out that this claim by Washington-based Chitunda "conflicts with the statements of Unita leader Dr. Jonas Savimbi that South Africa does provide military supplies."

74. *Southscan*, London, 10 June 1987; *International Herald Tribune*, Paris, 8 June 1987; *Star*, Johannesburg, 8 June 1987. The *Star* quoted Savimbi as having "urged South Africa not to withdraw from the responsibilities it exercised as a regional power in Southern Africa."

75. *Independent*, London, 9 December 1986, 9 February and 23 March 1987; *New York Times*, 2 February 1987.

76. *New York Times*, 2 February 1987.

77. *West Africa* (London), 30 March 1987.

78. *Jane's Defence Weekly* (London), 18 April 1987.

79. *Washington Post*, 30 April 1987.

Chapter 4. NAMIBIA: PREPARATIONS FOR DESTABILIZATION

1. Festus Thomas, interview with editors, Windhoek, 26 June 1978. Thomas was interviewed at the Swapo office by a number of journalists. Appearing in many publications around the world, his story, corroborated by evidence from doctors, nurses and lawyers, was not denied by the South Africans.

2. H. Hunke and J. Ellis, comps. *Torture—A Cancer in Our Society* (Windhoek: H. Hunke and J. Ellis, n.d.); D. Soggot, *Namibia: The Violent Heritage* (London: Rex Collings, 1986).

3. Randolph Vigne, *A Dwelling Place of Our Own* (London: International Defence and Aid Fund [hereafter cited as IDAF], 1973).

4. Ibid.

5. J. Dugard, *The South West Africa/Namibia Dispute* (Geneva: International Commission of Jurists [ICJ], n.d.).

6. UN General Assembly Resolution 2145 (1966).

7. A. T. Moleah, *Namibia: The Struggle for Liberation* (Wilmington, Del.: Disa Press, 1983).

8. Ibid.

9. Dugard, *South West Africa/Namibia Dispute*.

10. Moleah, *Namibia: The Struggle for Liberation*.

11. Pik Botha to UN Secretary General Kurt Waldheim, Foreign Minister Letter, S/12836, 6 September 1978.

12. This announcement was made by South Africa's prime minister Vorster, who announced his own resignation in the same speech.

13. President Ronald Reagan, interview with Walter Cronkite, "CBS News," 3 March 1981.

14. US State Department documents leaked to the US press and later published by the Swapo office in London.

15. Ibid.

16. Paul Hare to Chester Crocker, 13 May 1981, ibid.

17. *New York Times*, various dates in June 1981. US State Department and South African officials have both since confirmed that "linkage" was an American invention.

18. UN Security Council Resolution 539 (1983).

19. Pretoria continues to claim that Swanu is part of the MPC. However, as reported in the *Rand Daily Mail*, 3 September 1985, the old Swanu leadership was ousted that month and replaced. The new

leaders promptly withdrew Swanu from the MPC. Moses Katjiuongua, one of the ousted leaders, continued to lead a delegation to the MPC which he claimed represented Swanu. Probably 90 percent of Swanu's members now regard themselves as allied to Swapo and opposed to the MPC.

20. *Windhoek Advertiser,* January 1984.

21. Ibid.

22. Swapo senior officials, briefing. Details of the meetings in this phase involving Kaunda were given to the editors in a briefing by Swapo senior officials who had participated in them.

23. John de St. Jorre, "Destabilization and Dialogue: South Africa's Emergence as a Regional Superpower," *CSIS Africa Notes,* no. 26 (17 April 1984).

24. *Paratus,* January 1979; and *Focus,* no. 3 (March 1976). *Paratus* is the journal of the SADF.

25. Apart from formal control, the officers commanding the SWATF and other senior ranks are simply transferred between the SWATF and the SADF. For further details, see IDAF, *Apartheid's Army in Namibia,* (London: IDAF, 1982).

26. See Committee of South African War Resisters (COSAWR), "The South African Military Occupation of Namibia," articles reproduced from *Register* between September 1983 and March 1984 (Paper 11, International Conference on Namibia, London, 10–13, September 1984).

27. For further details about Namibia's political economy, see *Namibia: Toward National Reconstruction and Development* (London: Hutchinson, 1985); the chapters on Namibia in *African Contemporary Record* (hereafter cited as *ACR*), Colin Legum ed. (New York and London: Africana, 1983–85); *South West Africa: Statistical and Economic Review,* 1983–84; and Reginald H. Green, K. Kiljunen, and M. L. Kiljunen, *Namibia: The Last Colony* (London: Longman, 1981).

28. R. Moorsom, *Agriculture: Transforming a Wasted Land* (London: Catholic Institute for International Relations [hereafter cited as CIIR], 1982).

29. *ACR,* 1983–85.

30. This position could be altered if the Kudu gas field off the southern Namibian coast is proven to be large and exploitable.

31. *Namibia: Toward National Reconstruction.*

32. See *ACR,* 1983–84; and C. Allison and R. H. Green, "Political Economy and Structural Change: The Case of Namibia" (Discussion paper at the Institute of Development Studies [IDS], University of Sussex, UK, 1985–86).

33. *ACR,* 1983–84; and *ACR* (New York and London: Africana, 1986).

34. See *ACR,* 1983–84; and W. Thomas, "Namibia 1985: A New Start? Challenge of a Namibian Nationhood Strategy" (Manuscript of speech, n.p., 3 June 1985). This is a continuation of Thomas's attack on South Africa's fiscal policy as irresponsible and on its claim of inherent Namibian bankruptcy as equally so. These attacks are notable in that they come from the most able economic analyst promoting a "neocolonial" or "moderate" political economic transition.

35. *Namibia: Toward National Reconstruction.* R. Moorsom, *Walvis Bay: Namibia's Port* (London: IDAF, 1984).

36. Denis Herbstein, "Secret Pretoria Fear for Namibia Troops," *Observer,* London, 9 September 1984.

37. *New Unions in Namibia* (London: Namibia Support Committee, 1987).

Chapter 5. BOTSWANA, LESOTHO, SWAZILAND: CAPTIVE STATES

1. *Guardian,* London, 15 January 1986.

2. *Eastern Province Herald,* 28 December 1983.

3. South Africa denies responsibility for this raid, but their denial is so inherently improbable that few people give any credence to Pretoria's claim.

4. For a detailed discussion of the origins of political parties in Lesotho, see Khakhetla, *Lesotho 1970* (N.p., n.d.).

5. For a discussion at length of the extent of South Africa's domination, see Khakhetla, ibid.

6. Ibid.

7. Lesotho Interim Assembly, *Assembly Debates* (30 April 1973).

8. For further discussion of Chief Jonathan's about-face, see D. Hirschman, "Changes in Lesotho Policy towards South Africa," *African Affairs* (1978).

9. Department of Information, Statement, Maseru, July 1976.

10. For detailed discussion of the split within the exiled BCP and the background to the formation of the LLA, see "Interview with Chakela," *Vanguard* (National University of Lesotho, December 1980).

11. *Vanguard* (National University of Lesotho, January–March 1981).

12. "Lesotho Non-Elections: An Analysis of the Background to and Implications of the Cancellation of the Proposed General Election," *Southern Africa Dossier* (Centre of African Studies, Maputo, 1985).

13. Details of the background to the formation of the BDA were revealed to the local paper at the time by a certain T. J. Mokotso, a participant in the initial meeting with Pik Botha.

14. "Lesotho Non-Elections."

15. *Rand Daily Mail*, Johannesburg, 27 September 1984.

16. *Business Day*, Johannesburg, 23 March 1987.

17. *South African Digest* (hereafter cited as *SAD*), (Pretoria: Bureau of Information, 8 May 1987).

18. *ARB*, 22, no. 6 (n.d.):7668–7669.

19. Michael D. Appleby, "A Profile of Victims of the South African Raid on Gaborone, Botswana" (23 June 1985, Mimeographed).

20. *Sunday Star*, Johannesburg, 16 June 1985. The remark was reported to have been made by a Crocker aide.

21. Thomas M. Callaghy, ed., *South Africa in Southern Africa: The Intensifying Vortex of Violence* (New York: Praeger Publishers, 1983).

22. *ARB*, 16, no. 6 (n.d.):5154–5155.

23. *ARB*, 17, no. 3 (n.d.):5458–5459.

24. *African Economic Digest* (hereafter cited as *AED*), 31 July 1987 and Economist Intelligence Unit (hereafter cited as EIU), *Country Report for Namibia, Botswana, Lesotho and Swaziland*, no. 3 (1987).

25. South African Minister of Agriculture Hendrik Schoeman, in 1980.

26. *AED* and EIU, *Country Report*.

27. *New York Times*, 13 April 1982.

28. *Herald*, 1 January 1985.

29. *Financial Mail*, Johannesburg, Festus Moagae, interview, 12 July 1985. Moagae is permanent secretary to President Masire and head of the Botswana civil service.

30. *Rand Daily Mail*, 9 October 1985. This report cited Pik Botha. In March 1985, the South Africans had claimed that 48 sabotage missions had been launched and/or planned by the ANC in Botswana. See the *Rand Daily Mail*, 15 March 1985.

31. *Herald*, 14 September 1986.

32. Patrick Laurence, "Security Drive with Lesotho and Botswana Speeds Up," *Rand Daily Mail*, 11 May 1984.

33. *Financial Mail*, Johannesburg, 28 June 1985. Williamson had some years earlier infiltrated the International University Exchange Fund (hereafter cited as IUEF) in Europe which provided scholarships

to, among others, refugees from South Africa. Over a period of years, he provided Pretoria with invaluable information through his anti-apartheid contacts. Recently, it was claimed that he had resigned from the security police and set up his own security company in South Africa, a claim treated with considerable skepticism.

34. Joint Swazi–South African Statement, Pretoria, 31 March 1984.

35. P. W. Botha's letter and King Sobhuza's note authorizing his prime minister to sign are for the first time published here.

36. Pik Botha said that the matter of the land transfer "was very close to [Sobhuza's] heart. . . . The King made it clear to me that he very much wanted all his children together" (*Rand Daily Mail*, 29 June 1984).

37. In early March 1986, Enos Mabuza, representing the Inyandza National Movement, had three days of talks with the ANC in Lusaka. Mabuza was received by the Tanzanian high commissioner and representatives of Botswana and Angola, and had a private meeting with President Kaunda of Zambia (*Financial Mail*, Johannesburg, 7 March 1986).

38. For an analysis of Swaziland's dependence, see the *Times*, London, 5 September 1985. For statistical details on this dependence, see SADCC, *Macro-Economic Survey 1986* (Gaborone: SADCC, 1986). For economic information on the new Mpaka to Mananga rail link, see *Business in Swaziland*, June 1983.

39. *Rand Daily Mail*, 17 January 1985; and *AED*, 15 March 1985.

40. *Africa*, February 1982; and *Rand Daily Mail*, 9 December 1981.

41. *Moto*, Harare, September 1984.

42. For campus unrest and expulsion of white radicals, see *AfricaAsia* (Paris, April and June 1985). For other reports on these events, see the *Rand Daily Mail*, 22 December 1984, and 4 and 5 January 1985.

43. EIU, *Country Report*.

44. *Herald*, 27 January 1986.

Chapter 6. SOUTH AFRICA'S MILITARY BUILD-UP: THE REGION AT WAR

1. The Freedom Charter contains the philosophy of the ANC.

2. For further details, see Abdul S. Minty, *South Africa's Defence Strategy* (London: Anti-Apartheid Movement, 1969).

3. *Rand Daily Mail,* Johannesburg, 29 September 1983.

4. *Business Day,* Johannesburg, 11 December 1985.

5. *Rand Daily Mail,* 12 April 1984.

6. *Times,* London, 19 September 1980.

7. *Times,* London, 3 December 1983; and *Financial Mail,* Johannesburg, 6 August 1982.

8. *Times,* London, 2 August 1984; *Star,* Johannesburg, 17 September 1984.

9. Kenneth W. Grundy, *The Rise of the South African Security Establishment—An Essay on the Changing Locus of State Power* (N.p.: South African Institute of International Affairs, August 1983). See also Deon Geldenhuys, Kenneth W. Grundy, and John Seiler, "South Africa's Evolving State Security System" (Paper presented to the Study Group on Armed Forces and Society of the International Political Science Association, West Berlin, 15 September 1984); various press reports, including *Financial Mail,* Johannesburg, 8 October 1982; *Star,* Johannesburg, 24 and 26 September 1983; *Guardian,* London, 14 September 1983; especially Nicholas Ashford, *Times,* London, 1 September 1980; *Africa News,* 10 October 1983; and *Press Trust of South Africa,* 24 August 1983.

10. *Financial Mail,* Johannesburg, 15 January 1982.

11. *Sash,* Johannesburg, May 1987.

12. *Cape Times,* Cape Town, 10 September 1964.

13. *International Defence Review* (hereafter cited as *IDR*) (Geneva, October 1984).

14. Abdul S. Minty, Statement to UN Security Council Committee, 9 April 1984 (Oslo: World Campaign against Military and Nuclear Collaboration with South Africa, 1984).

15. Abdul S. Minty, Statement to UN Special Committee against Apartheid (12 December 1977), 22 December 1977, Document A/AC. 115/L.485.

16. Report of the UN Security Council Committee Established by Resolution 421 (1977), 19 September 1980, Document S/14179.

17. For details of specific cases, see Abdul S. Minty, Statements to the UN Security Council Committee Established by Resolution 421 (1977), 23 September 1983 and 9 April 1984.

18. Anti-Apartheid Movement, *How Britain Arms Apartheid* (London: Anti-Apartheid Movement, 1985).

19. Minty, Statement to UN Security Council Committee, 23 September 1983.

20. Report of the UN Security Council Committee Established by Resolution 421 (1977), 31 December 1979, Document S/13721.

21. The 421 Committee reported that "more clarity was needed with regard to (i) the provision to the South African authorities of certain items of strategic importance under the contention that such items did not form part of a weapons system and were, therefore, not covered by the embargo; (ii) the continued provision, directly to the South African military establishment, of certain items intended for and known in advance to be destined for their use, under the contention that such items were 'non-military' in nature, and therefore, not part of the embargo; (iii) the provision to various companies or civilian customers in South Africa of certain items of strategic and military importance, which later found their way, inexplicably, into the hands of the South African military authorities, and which, either directly or indirectly, helped to strengthen the South African military or police forces" (Report of UN Security Council Committee, 19 September 1980).

22. NARMIC/American Friends Service Committee, *Automating Apartheid* (Washington: NARMIC/American Friends Service Committee, 1982).

23. Anti-Apartheid Movement, *Plessey Arms Apartheid* (London: World Campaign and Anti-Apartheid Movement, 21 May 1981).

24. *Guardian*, London, 6, 9 and 10 December 1975.

25. *Background Note on Marconi Radar to Be Exported to South Africa by Britain* (Oslo: World Campaign, 20 May 1983). Representations made to Britain by the heads of delegations of all the African states, as well as the Group of Nonaligned Countries, attending an international conference on Namibia in Paris on 29 April 1983, failed to prevent the equipment from being exported to South Africa.

26. For details about what the embargo does not cover, see Minty, Statement to UN Special Committee against Apartheid (12 December 1977).

27. *Financial Times*, London, 14 September 1982.

28. *SAD* (Pretoria: Bureau of Information, 17 September 1982).

29. *Cape Times*, Cape Town, 10 June 1983.

30. *Newsweek*, 29 November 1982.

31. *Sunday Express*, Johannesburg, 17 October 1982.

32. For example, see *Jane's Defence Review* 4, nos. 1, 4, 6, and 7 (1983); and *IDR* (Geneva) 16, no. 3 (1983).

33. See *Sunday Express*, Johannesburg, 12 September 1982.

34. *SAD* (Pretoria: Bureau of Information, 9 March 1984).

35. *Rand Daily Mail*, 8 December 1983.

36. *Jane's Defence Weekly* (London) 23 November 1985.

37. *Star*, Johannesburg, 12 April 1969.

38. *SAD* (Pretoria: Bureau of Information, 16 March 1973).

39. *Sunday Times*, Johannesburg, 21 October 1973.

40. See *NATO Review* (Brussels) no. 4 (1973).

41. *Hansard Parliamentary Debates* (London: 6 November 1974), col. 1042.

42. For detailed information about this and the role of the Advokaat system, see Abdul S. Minty, *Apartheid, a Threat to Peace* (London: Anti-Apartheid Movement, 1976).

43. *Times*, London, 6 November 1975.

44. *Guardian*, London, 19, 20, and 21 November 1980.

45. British Government to Anti-Apartheid Movement, Letter, 1 December 1980, London.

46. *Mail on Sunday*, London, 20 November 1983; and *Sunday Times*, London, 20 November 1983.

47. Republic of South Africa, House of Assembly *Debates* (Cape Town: 24 September 1981), cols 4677–4678.

Chapter 8. RISING COST OF APARTHEID: THE ECONOMIC CRISIS

1. The term "capital" employed in the text refers generically to that social class that predominantly owns the major means of production—the capital assets of the economy—and is the main employer of labor. This does not necessarily imply a uniformity or unity among the different grouping or "fractions" of capital. What is suggested is that in relation to the cheap labor system of apartheid, there exists a wide range of common interests within the class of capital operating in South Africa.

2. Pallister, Stewart, and Lepper, *South Africa, Inc.* (London: Simon and Schuster, 1987).

3. For an extensive analysis of the historical roots and development of the colonialist base in South Africa, see H. J. Simons and R. E. Simons, *Class and Colour in South Africa 1850–1950* (London: Penguin, 1969).

4. These estimates were made by Michael Savage of the University of Cape Town.

5. In Lewis Carroll's *Through the Looking Glass* (1872), the Red Queen takes Alice by the hand, and they run very fast for some time only to find they have not left the tree where they started.

6. For a comprehensive contemporary analysis of the South African gold-mining industry, see Vella Pillay, *Apartheid Gold* (New York: UN Centre against Apartheid and British Anti-Apartheid Movement, 1981).

7. Jeremy Keenan, *South African Review*, no. 2 (1984).

8. Reuters, 19 September 1987.

9. Keenan, *South African Review*. The Carnegie enquiry derives from the Carnegie Commission which held a conference in South Africa in 1985 at which academics and others presented papers on the social and economic situation in the country. The commission was sponsored by the US-based Carnegie Endowment for International Peace.

10. Fatima Meer, "Indentured Labour and Group Formations in Apartheid Society," *Race and Class* (Spring 1985).

11. R. Horwitz, *The Political Economy of South Africa* (London: Weidenfeld & Nicolson, 1967); W. H. Hutt, *The Economics of the Colour Bar*, (London: Deutsch, 1964); and M. C. O'Dowd, in *South Africa: Economic Growth and Political Change*, ed. Leftwich (London: Allison & Busby, 1974).

12. *Guardian*, London, 7 October 1985.

13. Herbert Blumer, in *Industrialization and Race Relations*, ed. Guy Hunter (Oxford: Oxford University Press, 1965).

14. Merle Lipton, *Capitalism and Apartheid: South Africa 1910–84* (London: Temple Smith/Gower, 1985).

15. *Guardian*, 7 October 1985.

Chapter 9. POLITICAL ECONOMIES IN CONFLICT: SADCC, SOUTH AFRICA AND SANCTIONS

1. See three studies by South Africa's would-be Henry Kissinger, Deon Geldenhuys: "Some Strategic Implications of Regional Economic Relations for the Republic of South Africa," *ISSUP Review* (Institute of Strategic Studies, University of Pretoria), (January 1981): a government study that played a seminal role in the evolution of economic destabilization and selective sabotage tactics; "Destabilization Controversy in Southern Africa," *South African Forum* (September 1982): a position

paper that further promotes those destabilization tactics; and *The Diplomacy of Isolation: South African Foreign Policy Making* (Johannesburg: Macmillan, 1984): an extremely thorough and authoritative study of all aspects of South African foreign affairs.

2. See E. L. McFarland, "Benefits to the RSA of Her Exports to the BLS Countries" in *Botswana's Economy since Independence*, ed. M. A. Oommen (New Delhi: Tata–McGraw-Hill, 1983).

3. See Economic Sanctions against South Africa Series (Geneva: International University Exchange Fund, 1980), especially: M. Bailey, *Oil*, no. 5; R. Riddell, *Agriculture*, no. 10; M. Fransman, *Manufacturing*, no. 11; and R. Murray, *Mining*, no. 12.

4. This point is emphasized in the founding declaration of the SADCC, *Southern Africa: Toward Economic Liberation*, ed. A. Nsekela (Gaborone: SADCC, 1980; London: Rex Collings, 1981).

5. For a detailed exposition including transport, energy, agriculture, mining, and private enterprise, see Geldenhuys, *Diplomacy of Isolation*, 121–166. The role of the railways built up by the former general manager J. G. H. Loubser has been especially important. See Geldenhuys, *Diplomacy of Isolation*, 153–155; J. G. B. Loubser, "The Function of Transport as a Line of Communication between States in Southern Africa" (Speech, South African Railways and Harbours, 1980), and "Transport Diplomacy" (Lecture at the Institute of Strategic Studies, University of Pretoria, 26 September 1979); and G. H. Pirie, "Aspects of the Political Economy of Railways of Southern Africa" (Occasional Paper 24, Environmental Studies, Department of Geography, University of the Witwatersrand, Johannesburg, 1982).

6. See sectoral papers to annual consultative conferences: SADCC, *Transport and Communications* (Gaborone: SADCC, 1981–87); and SATCC, *Transport and Communications* (Maputo: SATCC, 1981–87). See also SADCC, *Southern Africa: Toward Economic Liberation*, especially chapter on transport.

7. Lusaka SADCC Declaration; Geldenhuys, *Diplomacy of Isolation*; and Loubser, "Transport Diplomacy."

8. Geldenhuys, "Some Strategic Implications."

9. Every SADCC annual conference except the first has had a "calling card" in the form of a sabotage raid against a SADCC project. The blockade of Lesotho just prior to the January 1986 annual conference was a sharp retort to SADCC's prosanctions position and the 1987 interference with Botswana's rail routes through South Africa a reminder of the region's dependence on SATS. Geldenhuys, in *The Diplomacy of Isolation*, clearly shows that Pretoria's perceived regional

interests, including transport, are much more threatened by a body committed to economic liberation than by a trade promotion body. PTA comprises 15 states in eastern and southern Africa, such as Kenya, Uganda, Ethiopia, Djibouti. Three SADCC states (Angola, Botswana, Mozambique) are *not* members of PTA.

10. For a detailed discussion, see C. Legum, ed., *ACR* (London: Africana, 1979–80); and Geldenhuys, *Diplomacy of Isolation*, 107–158. Geldenhuys clearly views "constellation" proposals as overambitious, and he deprecates "communist bogey" thinking as inaccurate and misleading for analysts and politicians.

11. For a standard description of SACU, see D. Hudson, "Botswana's Membership in the SACU," in *Papers on the Economy of Botswana*, C. Harvey, ed. (London: Heinemann, 1981). But cf. sources in note 14 as at the time Hudson still believed membership to benefit Botswana.

12. J. Stephens, "Rate Cutting and the Presentation of Dependence: South Africa's Response to Transport Initiatives in SADCC" (Forthcoming).

13. Ibid. However, if the rand continues to recover, further rand cuts will be needed to preserve this advantage.

14. P. Selwyn and Reginald H. Green, "Swaziland 1966–1976" (Manuscript study); and P. Selwyn, "Botswana 1966–1976" (Manuscript study). A Botswana study prepared for a 1981 SACU meeting, "Estimate of Duty Content of Botswana's Imports," arrives at a no gain–no loss estimate. Another study shows a tax gain, but at the cost of an 8.5 percent higher average import cost, so that world sourcing and constant tax revenue would still allow lower user prices (J. S. Gray and S. G. Houhlo, "The Direct Duty Content of Lesotho's Imports" [Rome: Ford Research Project Paper no. 1, 1978]).

15. See Loubser, "Transport Diplomacy" and Stephens, "Rate Cuttings."

16. See SADCC, *Overview* (Gaborone: SADCC, 1981–1987). See also Reginald H. Green, chapters on southern African economic cooperation, ed. C. Legum, in *ACR* (London: Africana, 1981–82 and 1984–85).

17. Enterprise, transport, and government officials, personal communications to authors.

18. See Reginald H. Green, "Constellation, Association, Liberation: The Struggle for Southern Africa Development Coordination," in *ACR*, ed. C. Legum (1979–80).

19. SAFTO, interview with Diana Cammack, N.p., August 1984; and *Financial Mail*, Johannesburg, 12 April 1985.

20. See Stephens, "Rate Cutting."

21. Mozambique has since struck back. New special contract rates are being negotiated with Zimbabwean exporters. These are effectively to be payable in US currency, but with a set rand-dollar conversion rate so as to remove the risk of currency fluctuation for the exporter. As of January 1986, this counterattack appeared to be regaining ground lost as far back as 1983.

22. See Stephens, "Rate Cutting"; SADCC, *Macro-Economic Survey 1986*; A. Rusinga, "SA Firms 'Thwarting Freighting in SADCC'," *Business Herald*, 30 January 1986, and related editorial, 31 January 1986.

23. Stephens, "Rate Cutting;" SADCC, *Macro-Economic Survey 1986*; Rusinga, "Thwarting Freighting in SADCC."

24. For trade and transport data, see Zambia Central Statistical Office, *Monthly Digest of Statistics* (Lusaka, n.d.). See also Stephens, "Rate Cutting." For a South African account of the background to Zambia's reversion to using SATS routes and ports, see also Geldenhuys, *Diplomacy of Isolation*, 271–272.

25. For example, the Zambian Mineworkers' Union chairman Timothy Walamba defended imports from South Africa, indeed called for more purchases, saying: "Much as we have to help our brothers and sisters still under racist regimes, this should not be at the expense of our own people" (*Daily Mail*, 29 December 1983). This is a grimly ironic tribute to South Africa's public relations since its consumer goods are in general more expensive in Lusaka than local or Zimbabwean products.

26. Loubser, "Function of Transport" and "Transport Diplomacy"; Geldenhuys, *Diplomacy of Isolation*.

27. Stephens, "Rate Cutting." Port Elizabeth in particular would be moribund without copper and other metals and concentrates from Zambia, Zaire, and to a lesser extent, Zimbabwe.

28. Loubser, "Function of Transport" and "Transport Diplomacy."

29. See Lipton, *Capitalism and Apartheid*. Lipton may well overstate the degree of conflict between big business and apartheid, but her case as to the weakness of high capitalism's political influence is compelling.

30. Carol B. Thompson, Chapter 4, in *Challenge to Imperialism: The Frontline States in the Liberation of Zimbabwe* (Harare: Zimbabwe Publishing House; Boulder: Westview Press, 1985).

31. *AIM Bulletin*, no. 97 (July 1984): 12.

32. For a fuller account of procedures, see Reginald H. Green,

"Building Economic Regionalism in Sub-Saharan Africa," *Development and South-South Cooperation* 11, no.2 (June 1986).

33. Among many other sources that document colonialism in southern Africa, see Barry Munslow, *Mozambique: The Revolution and Its Origins* (London: Longman, 1983); and Gerald Bender, *Angola under the Portuguese* (Los Angeles: University of California Press, 1978).

34. Ann Seidman et al., "Transnational Corporations and the Sugar Trade: The Zimbabwe Case" (Mimeographed, Economics Department, University of Zimbabwe, November 1982), 4.

35. Robin Palmer, *Land and Racial Domination in Rhodesia* (Berkeley: University of California Press, 1977); R. Riddell, *From Rhodesia to Zimbabwe: The Land Question* (London: CIIR, 1978); and *Herald* Harare, 1 December 1984.

36. Ann Seidman, "A Development Strategy for Zimbabwe" (Mimeographed, Economics Department, University of Zimbabwe, 1982), 1.

37. Michael Sefali, Speech at SADCC conference, Harare, 30 January 1986.

38. SADCC, *Overview* (Harare: SADCC, 30-31 January 1986), 12; and SADCC, *Programme of Action: Annual Report 1985-86* (Gaborone: SADCC, n.d.).

39. SADCC, *Programme of Action: Annual Report 1985-86.* and Sectoral paper . . . SADCC, *Transport and Communication* (February 1987); *Development of Infrastructure and Enterprise* (Arusha: SADCC, 28-29 January 1988), 6.

40. SADCC, *Food, Agriculture and Natural Resources* (Arusha: SADCC, 28-29 January 1988), 157-174. Lesotho, Malawi, and Zimbabwe each coordinate a different sector of agriculture (see chap. 9, n. 43).

41. Reginald H. Green, "Economic Liberation and Economic Survival, SADCC 1980-84" (Mimeograph, N.p., n.d.), 8.

42. SADCC, *Food and Agriculture* (Mbabane: SADCC, January-February 1985), 38.

43. Each country is assigned a sector or sectors as follows:
Angola—energy
Botswana—agricultural research, livestock
Lesotho—soil and water conservation, tourism
Malawi—fisheries, forestry, wildlife
Mozambique—transportation, communication
Swaziland—manpower training
Tanzania—industry

Zambia—mining, Southern Africa Development Fund

Zimbabwe—agriculture, food security

44. SADCC, *Industry* (Mbabane: SADCC, 31 January–1 February 1985).

45. Ibid., 20–21, 33.

46. *Herald*, Harare, 28 November 1983.

47. Barry Munslow et al., "Effects of World Recession and Crisis on SADCC" (Mimeographed Review, African Political Economy Conference, University of Keele, September 1984), 16.

48. SADCC official, interview with authors, SADCC Conference, Lusaka, January 1984.

49. D. G. Clarke, "Economic Linkages in Southern Africa" (Mimeographed, Geneva, April 1982), 25.

50. SADCC, *Overview* (Mbabane: SADCC, 31 January–1 February 1985), 4.

51. *African Business*, London, January 1985.

52. *Herald*, Harare, 5 October 1984.

53. UN Food and Agricultural Organization, *SADCC Agriculture toward 2000* (Rome, 1984), 7–8.

54. SADCC officials, interviews with authors, Swaziland and Mozambique, March 1984.

55. Pedro Figueiredo (SATCC Technical Unit), interview with authors, Maputo, 28 March 1984.

56. SADCC, *Programme of Action: Annual Report 1984–85* (Gaborone: SADCC, n.d.), 6.

57. SADCC, *Industry*, 42.

58. Julius Nyerere, speech at Gaborone SADCC summit, 6 July 1984, quoted in *Africa Research Bulletin (ARB)—Economic, Financial, Technical* 21, no. 6 (31 July 1984): 7327.

59. SADCC agricultural ministers, "Response to Policies in Agriculture and Rural Development, Prepared by the Nordic Countries, February 1984" (Maseru, September 1984).

60. Thandika Mkandawire, "SADCC: Problems and Prospects" (Paper presented at the Conference on Regional Development in Canada and Southern Africa, University of Zimbabwe, 16 February 1984).

61. For more information about the SADCC Annual Consultative Conference, Gaborone, see *Africa Economic Digest*, February 1987.

62. For a fuller discussion of these issues, see Reginald H. Green, "Economic Liberation and Economic Survival."

63. For goods from PTA to be considered, the basic value-added requirement is 45 percent ("Protocol on the Rules of Origin for Pro-

ducts to Be Traded between the Member States of the PTA," *CZI Industrial Review* [Harare] [October 1984]: 19–21).

64. Duncan Innes, *Anglo American and the Rise of Modern South Africa* (London: Heinemann Educational Books; New York: Monthly Review Press, 1984).

65. Peter Mmusi, Opening address at SADCC Council of Ministers, Mbabane, 31 January–1 February 1985.

66. SADCC, Annex B, *Overview* (Gaborone: SADCC, 1986).

67. See R. H. Green, M. Mauras, D. Asrat, R. Morgan. *Children on the Front Line* (UNICEF: January 1987), especially Annex B to "Children in Southern Africa"; Mozambique statistics from D. Martin and P. Johnson, with R. H. Green, a study "To Identify and Quantify the Economic and Social Cost of South African Destabilization and Sanctions Against Mozambique" (1986, unpublished).

68. United Nations High Commission for Refugees (UNHCR) and Government of Angola (Luanda: April 1988): internally displaced, 533,000; fled to neighbouring countries, 400,000; experiencing severe food shortages, at least one million, not including large numbers in non-accessible areas. United Nations Development Program (UNDP) and Government of Mozambique, "The Emergency Situation in Mozambique: Priority Requirements for the Period 1988–89" (Maputo: March 1988): internally displaced, 1.1 million; severe food shortage, 2.2 million rural and 2.6 million urban. UNHCR (April 1988), Mozambicans displaced in neighboring countries: 700,000.

69. Marta Mauras, Unicef representative in Mozambique.

70. Sanctions against South Africa were specifically endorsed by SADCC Chairman Peter Mmusi in his opening statement to the SADCC annual conference, Harare, 30 January 1986.

71. See Economic Sanctions against South Africa Series; CIIR, *Sanctions against South Africa* (London: CIIR, 1985); Reginald H. Green, "Economic Sanctions against South Africa: Some Notes on Problematics and Potentialities" (UNA/Anti-Apartheid Conference on the Frontline States and South Africa's Policies of Aggression and Destabilization, 29 February 1984, available from CIIR).

72. In the meantime, the improved current account balance and halted debt service have raised the rand, leading Reserve Bank governor Gerhard De Kock to quip, "Prepare to meet thy boom." But with both unemployment and inflation at record levels, there is little prospect of significant recovery. See also McFarland, "Benefits to the RSA." Furthermore, the unilateral rescheduling virtually guarantees that in-

terest and repayments will exceed new loans for the forseeable future unless South Africa defaults.

73. See sources cited in n. 71, especially Economic Sanctions Against South Africa Series: Reginald H. Green, *South Africa: The Impact of Sanctions on Southern African Economies*, no. 3; and R. J. Davies, *Trade Sanctions and Regional Impact in Southern Africa*, no. 9.

74. See press reports such as "Human Flotsam at Botha's Mercy," *Sunday Times*, London, 4 August 1985; and "Unemployment in SA Strengthens Dismissal Threats," *Zambia Daily Mail*, Lusaka, 6 June 1985.

75. SADCC, *Record* (Gaborone: SADCC, 1986).

76. See chairman's opening statement, SADCC annual conference communiqué (Harare: SADCC, 30–31 January 1986).

77. These effects were amply demonstrated in South Africa's January 1986 blockade.

78. For comparable earlier estimates, see Reginald H. Green, "Sanctions and the SADCC Economies," in *Third World Affairs 1987* (London: Third World Foundation, 1986).

Chapter 10: DESTRUCTIVE ENGAGEMENT: THE UNITED STATES AND SOUTH AFRICA IN THE REAGAN ERA

1. James A. Michener, *The Covenant* (New York: Fawcett Crest, 1980), 1,227.

2. For more detail on the period 1960–80, see chapters 5 through 8 in William Minter, *King Solomon's Mines Revisited* (New York: Basic Books, 1986). A useful brief summary focussed on South Africa is Thomas Karis, "United States Policy toward South Africa," in *Southern Africa: The Continuing Crisis*, Gwendolen Carter and Patrick O'Meara, eds. (Bloomington: Indiana University Press, 1982).

3. See the text of the memorandum in Mohamed El-Khawas and Barry Cohen, eds., *The Kissinger Study of Southern Africa* (Westport, Ct.: Lawrence Hill, 1976).

4. 19 October 1964, G. Mennen Williams papers, National Archives, Washington, D. C.

5. Study Commission on U.S. Policy toward Southern Africa, *Time Running Out* (Berkeley: University of California Press, 1981), xxii.

6. William J. Foltz, *Elite Opinion on U.S. Policy toward Africa*

(New York: Council on Foreign Relations, 1979), 20–21; see also *Africa News*, 25 May 1979.

7. Laurence I. Barrett, *Gambling with History: Reagan in the White House* (Harmondsworth: Penguin, 1984), 61.

8. Kevin Danaher, "The Political Economy of U.S. Policy toward South Africa" (Ph.D. diss., University of California, Santa Cruz, 1982), 5.

9. Donald de Kieffer, whose law firm had received as much as $2.5 million for lobbying for South Africa from 1974 to 1979, became special counsel in the office of the President's Trade Representative after the election, where he played a role in loosening restrictions on South African trade. De Kieffer's firm was replaced as the major lobbyist for South Africa by former Reagan campaign manager John Sears's law firm at a rate of $500,000 a year. Another former Reagan campaign manager, Stuart Spencer, picked up a $12,500 a month contract to lobby for the South Africans on Namibian issues. Marion Smoak and Carl Shipley, who from 1980 ran the U.S.-SWA Trade and Cultural Council, were also prominent in Republican party circles.

By 1985, the panoply of South African agents, which also included the Democrat-connected law firm of Smathers, Hickey and Riley and right-wing black lobbyist William Keyes, had an annual budget of well over $2 million. In addition, Christopher Lehman, brother of the secretary of the navy, left his post at the National Security Council to handle a $600,000 Unita account for Black, Manafort, Stone and Kelly, whose partner Paul Manafort had served as national political director for Reagan's 1984 campaign. See *Africa News*, 16 December 1985 and 24 February 1986.

10. The article is reprinted in Jeane J. Kirkpatrick, *Dictatorships and Double Standards* (New York: Simon and Schuster, 1982). On Kirkpatrick, see also the article by Seymour Finger, *Foreign Affairs* (Winter, 1983–84).

The neoconservatives, who claimed a liberal heritage, were led by Norman Podhoretz, editor of *Commentary* magazine and author of the anticommunist manifesto *The Present Danger*. Kirkpatrick's UN mission was populated by ideological soul mates, such as Kenneth Adelman, who set out his right-wing views in a 1980 book, *African Realities*, and Carl Gershman, head of the militantly anticommunist Social Democrats–USA and a longtime prominent backer of Jonas Savimbi in Angola. At the State Department, Kirkpatrick could count on allies such as Norman Podhoretz's son-in-law Elliot Abrams, who started out as assistant secretary for international organization in 1981 and later moved to the State Department human rights post. Kirkpatrick and her colleagues at the mission showed little respect for UN majority views on African issues and, indeed, hardly disguised their antagonism toward the institution as such.

11. On William J. Casey, see Philip Taubman, "Casey and His C.I.A. on the Rebound," *New York Times Magazine*, 16 January 1983; and Louis Wolf, "The Cyclone' Moves in at Langley," *Covert Action Information Bulletin* (April 1981). See also Bob Woodward, *Veil: The Secret Ways of the CIA 1981–1987* (New York: Simon and Schuster, 1987).

12. On Alexander Haig, see Roger Morris, *Haig: The General's Progress* (New York: Playboy Press, 1982); Alexander M. Haig, Jr., *Caveat* (New York: Macmillan, 1984); and for the comment by Norman Podhoretz, see the *New York Times*, 23 December 1980.

13. The significance of the mineral resources of southern Africa and the area's strategic importance were favorite propaganda themes of South Africa and the US far right. See the analysis by Larry W. Bowman, "The Strategic Significance of South Africa to the United States: An Appraisal and Policy Analysis," *African Affairs*, no. 81 (1982); and the author's review of several publications on the subject in *Africa News*, 13 October 1980. The topic is to a large extent a red herring, however, since whatever the strategic importance of the region, the question remains whether US interests are best served by alliance with the South African regime.

14. Seymour M. Hersh, *The Price of Power: Kissinger in the Nixon White House* (New York: Summit Books, 1983), 38–39. As spokesman for the Overseas Companies of Portugal, Richard Allen denied the reports of the Wiriyamu massacres in Mozambique in 1972, which he termed a Czech disinformation scheme. See *Mother Jones*, November 1980; and the syndicated Jack Anderson column of December 17, 1981.

15. On William P. Clark, see Steven R. Weisman, "The Influence of William Clark," *New York Times Magazine*, 14 August 1983.

16. Neither George P. Shultz nor Robert McFarlane were innocent of "hardline" views, as exemplified by those they held on the Middle East and Central America. But on Africa policy, the two were generally seen as more realistic and open to negotiations than their predecessors. Haig's downfall, when it came, was not precipitated by policy differences so much as his imperious manner and personal conflicts with others in the administration. Nevertheless, his replacement in June 1982 by Shultz was generally taken as a gain for "moderate" establishment views. President of the far-flung multinational Bechtel Corporation and former secretary of the treasury, Shultz was a man

with a conciliatory manner who was comfortable with "pragmatic" solutions when necessary. The ideologues might balk at doing business or negotiating with communists and revolutionaries while fighting them; but Shultz was a more sophisticated conservative, open to using a variety of tactics and even to compromise when it seemed the most advantageous thing to do. When Clark resigned in October 1983 to take over the Department of the Interior, he was replaced by his deputy Robert McFarlane. McFarlane, a former Marine Corps officer, had a reputation as an effective administrator. In a *New York Times* profile of October 1982, he was described as a "hardliner," but "also a realist." The far right was reportedly not happy with his appointment. On Shultz, see B. Gwertzman, "The Shultz Method," *New York Times Magazine*, 2 January 1983. On McFarlane, see Leslie H. Gelb, "Taking Charge: The Rising Power of National Security Adviser McFarlane," *New York Times Magazine*, 26 May 1985.

17. See Chester A. Crocker and William H. Lewis, "Missing Opportunities in Africa," *Foreign Policy* (Summer 1979). Other typical statements of Crocker's point of view include Chester A. Crocker et al., "Southern Africa: A U.S. Policy for the '80s," *Freedom at Issue* November–December 1980); Chester A. Crocker, "South Africa: Strategy for Change," *Foreign Affairs* (Winter 1980); and Chester A. Crocker, "African Policy in the 1980s," *Washington Quarterly* (Summer 1980). For Crocker's early views on Rhodesia, see Chester A. Crocker, *From Rhodesia to Zimbabwe: The Fine Art of Transition* (Washington, D.C.: CSIS Monograph, 1977).

18. For an extended analysis of the negotiations along these lines from the point of view of a State Department observer, see Jeffrey Davidow, *A Peace in Southern Africa* (Boulder: Westview, 1984).

19. Crocker and Lewis, "Missing Opportunities in Africa," 146–147.

20. Chester A. Crocker et al., "United States Policy Towards Africa," *Issue* (Fall–Winter 1982).

21. Merle Lipton, "British Investment in South Africa: Is Constructive Engagement Possible?" *South African Labour Bulletin* (October 1976); and Samuel P. Huntington, "Reform and Stability in a Modernizing, Multi-Ethnic Society," *Politikon* (December 1981).

22. Frank Wisner had served as a key aide to both Henry Kissinger and Cyrus Vance in southern African negotiations and was appointed by President Carter as ambassador to Zambia in 1979. He also derived some status in Washington from prominent family connections. His father, Allen Dulles's right-hand man in CIA covert operations, had coordinated the program to bring former Nazis to the United States

after World War II. The senior Wisner's last post had been CIA station chief in London (1959–62) before his retirement and suicide in 1965. Wisner's stepfather was the experienced Washington columnist Clayton Frichey, whose son-in-law, *Fortune* editor Herman Nickel, was appointed US ambassador to South Africa in February 1982.

23. See documents in *TransAfrica News Report* (August 1981).

24. SABC, 5 March 1981.

25. Secretary of State Alexander Haig, Press conference, 28 August 1981.

26. Chester A. Crocker, "Regional Strategy for Southern Africa," (Address to the American Legion, Honolulu, 29 August 1981).

27. *Wall Street Journal*, 6 May 1980.

28. *Guardian*, London, 26 March 1981.

29. *AfriqueAsie*, Paris, 1 February 1982.

30. *Washington Post*, 23 January 1982.

31. *Africa News*, 7 December 1981.

32. *Africa News*, 22 October 1984.

33. Ibid. On nuclear ties, see *Washington Notes on Africa* (Washington Office on Africa), (Summer 1982 and Winter 1983); and *Africa News*, 27 September 1982, 26 September 1983, and 8 April 1985.

34. *Africa News*, 6 December 1982 and 13 June 1983.

35. *Africa News*, 9 May 1983 and 22 October 1984.

36. See *Africa News*, 8 April 1985 and 20 May 1985.

37. Helen Kitchen, "The Eagleburger Contribution," *CSIS Africa Notes* (30 July 1983).

38. For example, see William Minter, "Major Themes in Mozambican Foreign Relations, 1975–1977," *Issue* (Spring 1978); and William Minter, "Setting the Terms for Pretoria," *Africa News*, 17 March 1980.

39. See summary statistics maintained and updated by the American Committee of Africa (ACOA) and *ACOA Action News* issues during 1985.

40. See *Washington Notes on Africa* (Washington Office on Africa, 1985); and other reports by the Washington Office on Africa during 1985.

41. *New York Times*, 22 July 1986.

42. Secretary of State's Advisory Committee on South Africa, *Report*, 29 January 1987, 1, 22.

AUTHORS

ROK AJULU is currently a research student at the Institute of Development Studies (IDS), University of Sussex, in Britain. Born in Kenya, he lived and worked in Lesotho for over seven years. During that period he was a part-time lecturer in the Departments of History, Politics, and the Institute of Labour Studies at the National University of Lesotho for four years. He is also a freelance journalist who has covered Lesotho and southern Africa for many years.

DIANA CAMMACK has been research co-ordinator for this three-year study of *Frontline Southern Africa*. She did her doctoral thesis at the University of California in 1983 on early twentieth century labor and political history in South Africa, entitled "Class, Politics and War." More recently she has been studying contemporary regional politics and is currently engaged in research on Mozambique's "displaced persons."

REGINALD HERBOLD GREEN is Professorial Fellow at the Institute of Development Studies (IDS), University of Sussex. He has been active in teaching and research consultancy in Africa since 1960, and is an advisor to SWAPO, UNICEF, World Council of Churches, Catholic Institute for International Relations and the International Centre for Law in Development. He

511

is a member of SADCC's Liaison Committee and an advisor to SADCC, as well as to several of its member states.

MARGA HOLNESS has worked with the People's Movement for the Liberation of Angola (MPLA) since the 1960s and on the staff of both Angolan presidents. She headed the Angola Information Office in London and is now working with ANGOP, the Angolan news agency. She is the author of numerous articles and translator of several books.

PHYLLIS JOHNSON is a long-time student of southern African affairs. As correspondent of the Canadian Broadcasting Corporation (CBC) from 1973 to 1980, she travelled widely in eastern and southern Africa. She has since written many articles, produced a televison documentary and co-authored two books, *The Struggle for Zimbabwe: The Chimurenga War* and *The Chitepo Assassination.* She is a director of the Southern African Research and Documentation Centre (SARDC).

PETER MANNING was a full-time functionary of the South West Africa People's Organization (SWAPO) in Namibia between 1976 and 1978. Since 1978 he has been based in the London office of SWAPO as Information Officer.

DAVID MARTIN has written about southern Africa for over 20 years, as Africa correspondent for the London Sunday newspaper, *The Observer*, as correspondent for several other organizations including *The Guardian* and the BBC, and as assistant editor of the *Daily News*, Tanzania. He has written several books including *General Amin, The Struggle for Zimbabwe: The Chimurenga War*, and *The Chitepo Assassination.* He is a director of the Southern African Research and Documentation Centre (SARDC).

WILLIAM MINTER is a writer and contributing editor of *Africa News.* He has taught in Tanzania and Mozambique, and now lives in Washington DC. He has just completed a book on Western policies toward southern Africa, *King Solomon's Mines Revisited: Western Interests, Images and Policies in Southern Africa.* He has written numerous papers and articles, two monographs and an earlier book, *Portuguese Africa and the West.*

ABDUL SAMAD MINTY is a South African who went to Britain in 1958 and, together with others, founded the Anti-Apartheid Movement (AAM) of which he has been Honorary Secretary for over 20 years. He has been active in international anti-apartheid campaigns, participated in numerous UN and other conferences, lobbied governments and organizations on behalf of the AAM and addressed the UN Security Council. Since 1979 he has been involved in the World Campaign against Military and Nuclear Collaboration with South Africa, which was initiated by the AAM at the suggestion of the UN Special Commission against Apartheid and whose founder patrons include the leaders of the Frontline States.

VELLA PILLAY is an international economist. He is economic adviser to a major international bank, director of the Greater London Enterprise Board, and vice-chairman of the British Anti-Apartheid Movement. He is the author of *Apartheid Gold* (United Nations) as well as numerous papers and studies on international economic and monetary relations, and on the South African economy.

CAROL B. THOMPSON is Associate Professor of Political Science at the University of Southern California and editor of the *African Studies Review.* She worked in Tanzania from 1977 to 1979 and in Zimbabwe from 1984 to 1986. Her writing includes many articles on the Southern African Development Coordination Conference (SADCC) as well as the books, *Challenge to Imperialism: The Frontline States in the Libera-*

tion of *Zimbabwe* and *Harvest Under Fire: Southern African Regional Food Security.*

The views expressed in this book are those of the authors and not of governments, organizations or institutions which some of them represent.

INDEX

515